W9-BBX-515

WHY I LEFT JIHAD

THE ROOT OF TERRORISM AND THE RISE OF ISLAM

BY EX-MUSLIM TERRORIST WALID SHOEBAT

TO ALL WHO SEEK ISRAEL'S
DESTRUCTION, I SAY
"THINK AGAIN"

Born in Bethlehem of Judea in 1960, Walid Shoebat has won international acclaim as an advocate for Jewish rights, for the state of Israel and for telling the true story of the Mideast conflict. He is in demand at churches, synagogues, colleges, and major organizations such as Aish Hatorah, and has addressed Muslim, Christian and Jewish audiences throughout the world.

Mr. Shoebat was the keynote speaker, along with Israeli Tourist Minister Benny Elon, at the National Radio Broadcasters conference in Charlotte, North Carolina. He has met with members of the United States Congress.

London — Mr. Shoebat was the first non-Jew to speak at the Jewish Outreach Encounter Conference in London, one of the largest in the world, with 2500 attendees. He was a keynote speaker, along with the Chief Rabbi of Great Britain, Jonathan Sachs, and the former Chief Rabbi Lau of Israel.

South America — On his first official visit to Chile, he addressed the Jewish community in Santiago, which is also home to the largest South American Palestinian community in that country. Mr. Shoebat also met with members of the Chilean government.

Ireland — he appeared on national television, met with editors of major newspapers and leading members of the Ministry of Foreign Affairs.

He recently spoke in Birmingham, Alabama at The Cathedral of the Cross Church to an audience of 3000, and his growing number of Christian supporters is helping Mr. Shoebat reach his goal to address millions of Christians on Sunday mornings.

He is the author of several online books including "Dear Muslim, Let Me Tell You Why I Believed" and "Israel, And the World's Mock Trial," in which he exposes anti-Semitism and the hatred of Jews in both the Islamic, Christian and secular worlds.

Editor: June S. Neal

ISBN 0-9771021-1-4

Published in the United States of America
By
Top Executive Media

**"Love is the only force capable of
transforming an enemy
into friend"**

Dr. Martin Luther King, Jr.
1929–1968

*I would like to dedicate this book to the
two Jewish men who saved the lives of my father
and also my cousin, Abrahim Awad Allah*

– Walid Shoebat

Published by

top executive media

"Walid Shoebat is the real deal...his story should be a best seller."

Michael Medved, noted film critic, best-selling author and nationally syndicated radio talk show host.

"In the 25 years I have been in Washington I have never heard anything so extraordinary and the truth so eloquently told by someone like this [Walid Shoebat]."

Frank Gaffney, President, Center for Security Policy, Washington, D.C.

"Walid Shoebat is a very remarkable and very courageous human being. This is a sick world...and you are one of the lights."

Dennis Prager, noted columnist and radio talk show host.

"So far, Fouad Ajami, Salman Rushdie, Ali Salem, "Newsweek" columnist Fareed Zakaria, Walid Shoebat, Irshad Manji are some of the vocal moderates from that part of the world who do not view everything through a veil of Islamic and xenophobic hatred."

The Jay Blog, the Falseness of Anti-Americanism, September 9, 2003.

"Shoebat's talk was "a revelation, even for someone like myself...an unequivocal and enthusiastic supporter of Israel and the democratic principles it practices. All those on the left and in America and Europe who turn a blind eye to the blatant and vicious anti-Semitism pervasive in the Middle East should be required to attend one of [his] lectures."

Central Connecticut State University Professor Jay Bergman, President of the Connecticut Chapter of the National Association of Scholars.

Why I Left Jihad

Table of Contents

Introduction

This book was a work of love. After living with hate for so many years, I now dedicate my life to bringing truth and love to all who will hear me.

I have seen what hate produces: suffering beyond the telling. Only truth can dispel the hate. Only truth can offer hope for peace.

This was not an easy journey. I have lost my homeland, my family of origin, and my land. I went from one culture to another one so different it was as though I had been transported to another planet.

Yet I gained so much. My deep Christian faith is my driving force. I love America. I love the Jewish people, who have suffered so much and who are trying to hold onto this tiny spot of land called Israel as a homeland after thousands of years of persecution. And I love my fellow Christians to whom I bring the truth as I have witnessed it.

Much has happened since I wrote the first draft of this book.

America was attacked by Islamist terrorists who murdered nearly 3,000 innocent children, women and men.

President George Bush declared war on Osama bin Laden, Al-Qaeda, the Taliban in Afghanistan and Iraq's murderous dictator, Saddam Hussein.

Pro-Chechnya Muslim barbarians attacked a school in Breslan, Russia, murdering and injuring scores of innocent children and their families on what was supposed to be the first day of school.

Spain mourned the deaths of innocents after terrorists struck a train and sent fear through the country just before its national election.

Yasser Arafat died after refusing all peace offers, stealing millions from the Palestinian people and leaving them in ruins.

Yet the world will not confront the truth, will not call out, "These Islamists are terrorists. These monsters act against every notion held dear by civilized societies. They recognize no ethics or moral code outside their own twisted social structure. They are a threat to the entire world and the world should end this epidemic of barbarism." Instead, most of the world cowers.

Words are important. Everything decent in the universe calls out for us to speak the truth. However, the West bends its collective head, searching for words to disguise and soften the atrocities, like chickens searching for specks of grain in the sand.

Dr. Daniel Pipes, the respected scholar and author, said it best: *"It is bad enough that only one of five articles discussing the Beslan atrocity mentions its Islamist origins; worse is the miasma of words that insulates the public from the evil of terrorism."* [Dr. Daniel Pipes "They're Terrorists, not 'Activists' or 'Militants,' September 1, 2004, Militant Islam Monitor.org]

Had the conspiracy of silence been broken, had there been no "miasma of words" to perpetrate the fraud, had the world spoken, I would not have to.

Shalom,
Walid Shoebat

Chapter One
CONFESSIONS OF A TERRORIST

CONFESSION IS THE BEGINNING OF HEALING

Hatred develops like a drug addiction. First, you throw a stone. Then you throw a Molotov cocktail. Then you toss a bomb on top of a bank. I know. I was born and raised in Beit Sahour, Bethlehem, in the West Bank. Hatred of Jews was my education, what I was taught each day by teachers and parents and the entire community. I knew nothing else, so I believed it was a righteous thing to grow up and kill Jews.

That's what I would have done with my life except that events brought me to the United States and to my study of Christianity and Judaism. My life was turned upside down when I discovered that everything I had been taught about the Jews was a lie. The shock, like an earthquake under my feet, was followed by a powerful drive, urging me to tell the world the truth. Tell what it is really like in the Middle East and what the Jews in Israel truly face. People filled with hate accuse the Jews of stealing land, of usurping a "Palestinian state," of mistreating the Palestinians who lived under Arafat's control until his death.

None of it is true. Israel has tried many times to negotiate. Negotiate! The Barak agreement gave the Palestinians everything they asked for. Yasser Arafat smiled for the cameras at Camp David, left the United States, came back and started killing Jews again. He wanted nothing to do with the agreement and said so on American national television.

The truth is that the Israelis face an enemy with whom they cannot negotiate, because the enemy's primary goal isn't the land. That's secondary. The enemy wants all Jews dead and Israel eliminated from the face of the earth.

As for stealing the land, I will show that the land now called Israel was either owned by Jews who had started purchasing it from Arabs in the 1800's, or was government-owned and given to them under the British mandate or retained after the Arab attacks.

The condition of the Palestinian people has nothing to do with Israel. Israel stands guard only to prevent more suicide bombers and guerrilla attacks from killing innocent Israeli civilians. The Palestinians could be living quite well with the millions of dollars that were sent to them from America and many other governments. Instead, they live like paupers because Yasser Arafat stole their money.

My goal is to show the world the truth about Islamism and the Biblical right—no—*God's promise*, for the Jews to live in Israel as their home.

# # #

An American friend asked me how the terrorists can behead people and do so in front of a video camera for the world to see. She cannot believe that anyone can do something so barbaric.

She, and all of you in the western world who read this book, may finally understand why Muslim fanatics can behead people on TV. It is no different from the Nazis throwing human beings into ovens. We are witnessing the rise of terror, all over the world, no different from what happened in Nazi Germany. Nationality is no protection. Even German citizens who failed to become good party members were exterminated. No one was safe then; no one is safe now.

Nazism, like Islamism, was a cult that brainwashed an entire society to believe that members of the "Aryan race" were more valuable than other human beings. It was dressed up as "national pride."

With Islamism, only those who adhere to militant, radical fundamentalism are safe; the rest of the world are infidels who must be converted or destroyed. We have watched in horror as they carry body parts through the Palestinian capital of Ramallah, praising Allah, for the whole world to see.

These are not an "isolated few extremists." When the body parts were paraded, the entire city of Ramallah openly cheered, just as the Palestinians and much of the Arab world cheered at the death of almost 3,000 Americans murdered by a suicide mission on 9/11. In the Middle East, no one dares object, other than a few designated public officials who play to the media; the others would be branded as traitors and lynched.

The photographs of these public lynchings are never relayed by the western media. If such atrocities took place in Israel, they would make front pages and prime time news. The World Court would be called into session. The United Nations would vote to condemn. But not when the atrocities are directed against Jews. And the incidents of anti-Semitism are taking place in Holland, France, Argentina, everywhere.

The Jews are not their only target. If every Jew in the world were dead, it would not end. The rest of you are infidels, too: Koreans, Japanese, Britons, anyone—even other Muslims who don't adhere to this cult of violence. The motto is "Islam to the world." The earth, they claim, belongs to *"Allah and His prophet."*

I WAS A TERRORIST

I was initiated into Yasser Arafat's Fatah terror group and recruited by a well-known bomb maker named Mahmoud Al-Mughrabi from Jerusalem. I met up with him on Bab-El-Wad Street at the Judo-Star marshal arts club run by his father near the Temple Mount in Jerusalem. Mahmoud gave me a very sophisticated explosive device he had assembled. I was supposed to use the bomb—an explosive charge hidden in a loaf of bread—to blow up the Bank Leumi branch in Bethlehem. He helped me smuggle it with the aid of the Muslim Wakf religious police on the Temple Mount so I could enter one of the world's most holy places.

From the Temple Mount, I walked on the platform with explosives and a timer in my hand. We walked to the walls and avoided the checkpoints. I went to the bus station and took a bus to Bethlehem, fully ready to give my life if I had to. My hand was ready to pitch the bomb forward when I saw some Palestinian children walking near the bank. Instead, I threw the bomb on the bank's rooftop.

I ran. The bomb exploded as I reached the Church of the Nativity on my way home. I was so scared and so depressed I couldn't sleep. I was only 16 years old. I wondered if anyone were killed. That was the first time I came to grips with what it would be like having blood on my hands. I felt both terrified and depressed. I didn't enjoy what I had done, but I felt compelled to do it because it was my duty. I felt I had to be a martyr, to kill Jews in order to go to heaven and meet the 72 virgins.

I posed with a grim face for the school picture, as if I knew that my turn to have my obituary as a martyr in the newspaper would be next.

During school riots against what we called the Israeli occupation, I would prepare speeches and slogans and write anti-Israeli graffiti in an effort to provoke students to throw rocks at the armed Israeli soldiers. We shouted, "No peace or negotiations with the enemy! Our blood and our souls we sacrifice to Arafat! Our blood and our souls we sacrifice to Palestine! Death to the Zionists!" I vowed to fight my Jewish enemy, believing that I was doing God's will on earth. I remained true to my word and tried to inflict harm by any means I could devise. I would participate in any riot: in schools, the streets, and even in the holiest place, the Temple Mount in Jerusalem, called by Arabs "Al-Masjid Al-Aqsa." All through high school I would be one of the first to provoke a riot. We used terror tactics, bombs and armed assaults against Jews in an attempt to force them to leave Israel. But we never succeeded.

Like drug pushers, hate pushers have neither sight nor insight. Sheikh Umar Abdulrahman was blind when he instigated the first bombing of the Twin Towers in New York. Blind men, like Abdul-Hamid Kishk from Egypt who gave me my weekly dose of the hate drug through tapes recorded in Egypt, calling for America's destruction.

When I was only 16, I joined in with other Palestinian youngsters throwing rocks at an Israeli truck driver who had accidentally struck a Palestinian girl. We broke the glass of the truck to kill him, yet he was still calling for help for the girl. Finally, he started up the truck to get out with his life. So we went back to school. A man who had been blind since birth at Dar-Jaser High School in Bethlehem, and who was part of the student association, gave a fiery speech, shouting that the accident was intentional. Allah Akbar! Death to all Jews! It now seems unbelievable to me, but 1,000 students believed him then. He almost sparked an intifada, and the riot police came. Recalling the scene 20 years later, I thought, why did an entire school follow a blind man who obviously could not see what happened?

The intifada did start from a similar incident. It was an accident in Gaza when an Israeli Jeep accidentally struck a boy and killed him. Hatred is like a hydrogen-filled balloon, awaiting any spark, and the rest is tragedy. Now, some of these same, trigger-happy governments are pushing for rights to build not hydrogen balloons but nuclear bombs.

I remember my first attempt to lynch a Jew. Stones were flying everywhere like swarms of locusts. We set fire to a row of tires to use as a blockade. One Jewish soldier tried to catch the kid who hit him with a stone. Instead, we caught the Jew. I had a club and pounded him in the head with it until it broke. Another teenager had a stick with a nail sticking out and he kept whacking his skull with it. We nearly killed him. Incredibly, (perhaps the adrenaline that's stored up for facing wild animals kicked in) he lunged across the fire to the other side.

The irony was that while terrorizing others, I terrorized myself with my beliefs that required me to gain enough merit and good deeds to go to heaven. But I never was sure if my good deeds would outweigh the bad when Allah judged me. Of course, to die fighting the Jews would ease Allah's anger toward my sins and I would be assured of a good spot in heaven with beautiful wide-eyed women to fulfill my most intimate desires. Either way I won, as long as I terrorized my enemies.

I remember one time in Bethlehem when the entire audience in a packed theater clapped their hands with joy watching the movie, "21 Days in Munich," the story of how 8 members of the PLO faction, Black September, murdered the entire Israeli wrestling team that had come to Munich to compete in the Olympic games. The moment we saw the Palestinians throwing grenades into the helicopter, killing the Israeli athletes, hundreds of viewers yelled, "Allahu Akbar!" (Allah is the greatest). This is the slogan of joy used by Muslims for victorious events.

What Muslims should do is show by *example* how Allah is great, not by committing acts of violence and cheering for death and mayhem.

But that is who Islamists are. And the world doesn't know—or doesn't want to know. The West today is focused on creating a Palestinian state, but, fair warning, that state will not be a mini-America, but a mini-Iran. The Palestinian charter calls for an Arab state with no Jews and with Islam as the official state religion. No cultural diversity here, folks.

Is this the new nation the West envisions? One that won't allow Jews? One with an official state religion that calls for the murder of all infidels? Why would any Christian support such a state, knowing that Islamism will not accept Christians? Whether secular or Islamic fundamentalist, much of the Arab world is still calling for the destruction of the Jewish state. In "Palestine," the only difference between organizations like Hamas and the Palestinian Authority is the size of the dose of Islamofascism. No matter what percentage of the power struggle goes to Hamas or Shari'a law or the new Palestinian government, Islamic jihad will fuel it.

The western world has been duped to believe that secular Arabs or "moderate" Islam will make a difference. They won't even be players. Islamism will gather in as many other non-Arab nations as it can to join its cause for the destruction of the Jewish state, a cause that has a long history, one that began long before Israel was declared a state.

Do not think that because Arafat is dead his brand of Fascism died with him.

In December 1920, long before Arafat, Musa Kazem el-Husseini, of the Haj Amin Al-Husseni clan, demanded restoration of Islamic theocracy in Palestine in a letter to British High Commissioner Herbert Samuel.[1]

The PA Constitution, moreover, formally adopted rigid, anti-democratic Islamic Shari'a law. Lest there be any doubt about its meaning, Islamic law carefully spells out the institutional inferiority that has been forced on non-Muslims by majority Muslim societies since the time of Muhammad. As Sheik Muhammad Ibrahim al-Mahdi explained on official Palestinian Authority TV in 2001, "Muslims of Palestine want to meet Allah and we are the soldiers of the Caliphate that was announced by the Prophet. Therefore, the Caliphate will be in accordance with the prophecy, in Al-Aqsa, in Jerusalem, and in its surroundings…we welcome the Jews to live as Dhimmis, but the rule in this land and in all the Muslim countries must be the rule of Allah… Those from amongst the Jews and from amongst those who are not Jews who came to this land as plunderers, must return humiliated and disrespected to their countries."[2] (Dhimmis are residents of a country that allows them few, if any, rights.)

THE HEART DOES CHANGE

I am no longer a terrorist. I am a Christian. I am a man who is dedicated to peace and truth. What gave birth to my profound change of heart and mind? How did I shed the mantle of the terrorist? How did I escape from the prison of thought that had held me for so long? The drug of hate that is so addictive? The answer is through a self-detoxification program. It started in America, with a question my wife asked me in the process of my attempting to *convert her* to Islam. She would not accept my hatred of the Jews. "Show me in the Bible the bad things the Jews did," she demanded.

By accepting her challenge, I walked into a new world. For the first time, I studied *factual* history, the Christian Bible, the Jewish Bible, Jewish history and Jewish songs and art, but I couldn't find anything about the murderous, terrible Jews that had been in my mind for so long. In fact, I could not find the words "kill" or "war" in Jewish songs! When I finally found one Jewish song with the word *Milchama*, one of the few Hebrew words I knew that meant *war*, I said, "Ha! There it is!" But I was stunned when the translation from Isaiah 2:4 was: "And man will not learn war any more…"

The Jews sing "Lo Yisa Goy"

And every man 'neath his vine and fig tree

shall live in peace and unafraid.

And every man 'neath his vine and fig tree

shall live in peace and unafraid.

And into plowshares beat their swords,

nations shall learn war no more.

And into plowshares beat their swords,

nations shall learn war no more.

Compare this to the songs I learned as a child:

"Sharpen my bones into swords, for I am a bomb,

I shall eat the flesh of my [Israeli] occupier,

O killers, your blood is 'Halal' for us," (meaning

"kosher" or "all right" for us to spill).

My lullabies and many of the poems we memorized were about flying body parts and rolling heads.

But in this new world, the United States, I was studying the Christian and Jewish Bibles and Jewish history, art, culture and music. And I discovered that Jews did not start wars, did not take over other nations, did not commit genocide. There were no calls for mutilation or degradation. On the contrary, it was all about following God's Commandments, sticking to the laws of living provided by the Torah, and maintaining Jewish ethics such as tzedakah (charity), tikun olam (repair of the world) and mitzvot (good deeds). They also had a remarkable way of atoning for any wrongdoing. They did not just ask God to be forgiven; they were required to go out and make right what was wrong. If you hurt someone, go to him or her and apologize or repair the damage you caused. If he or she is no longer around, then perhaps do something for that person's family. If not that, then do something for the community. For Jews, to be a good person means doing, not just talking. I wondered, how did they live like this when they were always in self-defense mode throughout Biblical history, and as they are, unfortunately, today? From the attacks by the Babylonians, Assyrians, Amorites, Philistines, Edomites—always in self-defense mode.

Who *are* these people?

Little did I know that someday I would find out the answer to that question. At home in the West Bank, I was taught that when the Jews come back to the land, that we would kill them, and the *"Trees and*

I said earlier that hatred is like drug addiction; its desire for more hate becomes insatiable. But hatred is also a like a cancer that spreads. I know that some estimate that Islamism is only 15% of the Muslim world, but a cancer starts small. And this is a cancer, and it's spreading. We are not winning fanatics into the fold, but losing secular Muslims to the fanatics. We need to fight. Extracting cancer, physical or metaphorical, is painful. I know, I felt the pain. But, in return, my eyes were opened as I read and studied, read and studied and put what I discovered into this book you are now reading.

# # #

It's a myth that the Palestinians are the underdogs in this conflict. It's not an Israeli-Palestinian war, but an Arab-Islamofascist war. The issue is not land or a Palestinian state. It is the destruction of Israel, and for one reason—we simply hated Jews.

Today, I see so many Westerners who, on the far left side of politics, demonize Israel and exonerate Islamic-Arab terror. And Americans love to psychoanalyze everything, trying to understand evil. You cannot psychoanalyze evil. Why do these people think the way they do? I have told you. They are steeped in hate. Finally, we must acknowledge the reality of Satan, of evil in this world.

To ignore or deny such evil is deadly. And too many are in denial.

For example, people who believe there can be peace in the Middle East if only the two parties can get together, share their toys, and "play nice." Such expectations assume a moral equivalency.

There is none. The Jews and the Islamists live on two different moral planets. The Jews want peace more than the world knows, having suffered for so long. But they will never compromise their Jewish ethics and basic sense of decency to wipe out their enemy. The Palestinians want only the death of the Jews. Further, Christians, as well as the American and the Israeli Jewish communities, have allowed the Muslims to put a wedge between them called "Palestine." Many who support a separate Palestinian state, Jews and Christians, do so not because they believe the Palestinians are right, but because they simply want to stop the bloodshed. As one Israeli girl put it, "Blood is more precious than land."

If people truly believe there can be a peaceful Palestinian state, they should at least call for a *democratic* Palestine. Arabs now live in Israel with the same rights as Jews. But any Jew who stepped foot into Ramallah would be killed on the spot. If Israel has no right to Hebron, Ramallah, and Bethlehem, then by what right are Palestinians in Tel Aviv? Without answering these questions, the liberals claim that negotiations can succeed. They had the same faith in Oslo. I did not. They criticized me for predicting that Oslo would bring more dead Jews. This was in 1993. Oslo failed. There were many more dead Jews.

Israel defends herself, as any country would and does. However, her Western critics condemn her every act of self-defense, whether she is engaged in outright battle or destroying a bomb factory. Condemning her turns logic on its head, but we are not dealing with logic here. From some, the condemnation stems from anger, from too many, pure hate. Who denies America's right to strike back at Osama Bin Laden? Israelis face terrorists every hour. We go shopping and hope to get home without facing a traffic jam. Israelis go shopping and hope to get home.

The hypocrisy is striking. Where are the accusations when it comes to true aggression? The world is basically silent when more than a million Sudanese are dead from starvation and mass execution. Silent when Christians die in Indonesia. Silent when Turks kill Cypriots.

The West is blind to the unprovoked stoning of the minority Jews by Palestinians in Hebron or, more recently, the slaughter of nearly an entire Jewish family—a pregnant mother and her four children, out on a shopping trip. I cannot imagine what that father has gone through. But there was no worldwide outcry for this family. The world simply concludes that the Jews must have done something to deserve this, a kind of "it takes two to tango" mentality.

So what did the Jews do to "tango" in Nazi Germany? I asked my interviewers on the Jeremy Bowen show, Radio-5, on the BBC in London. "Did it take two to tango in Nazi Germany?" One blurted out immediately "yes." Another panelist quickly concluded the interview, grumbling, "Fundamentalists are all the same." He was shocked when I looked straight into his eyes and said, "Yes indeed, but with a slight difference: Christian fundamentalists can give people a headache, since they love to proselytize, but a Muslim fundamentalist will take your head right off your shoulders." He was silent. I was thanked for stopping by at the BBC.

THERE IS NO MORAL EQUIVALENCY BETWEEN THE PALESTINIANS AND THE JEWS

The Islamists and the Jews simply don't live on the same moral plane. Let's look at two issues to show what Israel really faces across the table:

1. FEMICIDE AND THE DEGRADATION OF WOMEN

Why does the West remain silent about the horrific abuse and murder of women in Muslim countries? These are euphemistically called "honor" killings, when a male in a family murders a female for dishonoring him through some alleged sexual offense, including being the victim of rape. Although statistics for most countries other than Jordan are difficult to obtain, most assessments reveal that honor killings constitute a large percentage of murders in Muslim nations: Pakistan, Lebanon, Afghanistan, Jordan, Yemen, Iraq, Egypt, Syria, the Gaza strip and the West Bank, and among Israeli Arabs.

In "For Shame—Arab Honor's Price: A Woman's Blood," published in the June 20, 1999 edition of the New York Times on the web, Douglas Jehl said:

> Except in Jordan, government officials tend to treat the issue as taboo, at least in response to queries from foreign journalists. But the statistics show that honor killings regularly claim 25 lives a year in Jordan alone, *about one in four homicides in a country* of just four million people, according to Jordanian officials.
>
> In Egypt, which last reported crime statistics in 1995, a Government report counted 52 honor killings out of 819 slayings. In Yemen, with a population of 16 million, Muhammad Ba Obaid, who heads the department of Women's Studies in Sanaa University, said his

surveys found that more than 400 women were killed for reasons of honor in 1997, the last year for which research is complete. The experts say it would be safe to estimate that the number of Arab women killed for reasons of honor amounts to hundreds each year.

In the Nov 4, 2003 issue of *About* online, Nikki Katz in "What you Need to Know About Honor Killings," reported:

"The United Nations Population Fund estimates as many as 5000 females being killed each year." She notes that although honor killings occur in countries such as India, Uganda and Italy…they…tend to be prevalent in countries with a majority Muslim population."

Remember, the numbers are much lower than the actual incidents, since many of these crimes go unreported and many of the murderers never face a courtroom.

Never will you see a Jewish community performing such a barbaric act.

THE HEBRON MASSACRE

Way before the existence of the state of Israel, the Jews of Hebron were exterminated. The Muslims cut off the Jewish men's testicles, raped the women and chopped off their breasts, and slashed the babies to death. The massacre was ordered by the Grand Mufti, Haj Amin Al-Husseni, who instigated the riots and called on the masses to "kill them where ever you find them and rape their women." Al-Husseni collaborated with Adolf Hitler to rid the Muslim world of Jews and even organized an SS Hanjar ("dagger") Muslim division for the service of Hitler that was literally Islamo-Nazi.

You will never hear of Jews carrying out such atrocities.

The two cultures are different in that they share no universal language of ethics or morality to allow for any true détente.

There is no moral equivalency in the Palestinian-Israeli conflict.

The West not only refuses to see this, it makes the murderers sympathetic characters. We never hear about the Hebron massacre, but everyone talks of Jenin, accusing Israel of being an aggressor and forgetting that many Israeli soldiers were killed in their attempt to dismantle bomb factories created in former houses. They do not understand that they are looking at wolves in sheep's clothing. But even some wolves can be transformed into sheep. Nothing is impossible in my view. After all, I myself was once a wolf.

# # #

The world condemns Israel for taking over the "Palestinian nation." However, there is not and never was a nation called Palestine. Prior to 1967, we in the West Bank were *Jordanians* and we lived under Jordanian rule, acknowledging King Abdullah, then King Hussein, as our country's leaders.

Until the Jews returned to Jerusalem. Then suddenly, we were "Palestinians!" The Arab leaders removed the star from the Jordanian flag and instantly, we had a Palestinian flag!

The same is true of Gaza which was part of Egypt and whose people accepted Nasser, and then Anwar Sadat, as their leader. Until the Jews formed the state of Israel. Magically, the people were no longer Egyptians, but Palestinians! The Palestinian Charter never included Judea, which was in Jordan, as part of Palestine.

The "Palestinian nation" is a fiction of the Islamists.

We never wanted a Palestinian state. Yet Arafat made it his battle cry and it became a successful political strategy. So now, while the territorial tug-of-war distracts Western attention, the real issue, the destruction of the Jews, is what consumes the fanatics. It's a religious holy war, not a political one. It's in the culture, the tradition, the religion, the music, and in every other aspect of the Arab life. Destroy the Jews. This was Arafat's game plan, and he was a chip off the same block as Saddam Hussein, Osama bin Laden, and Ahmed Yassin—different names, same goals.

The nations of the world are weakening Israel, the country that deserves and needs our support, by pressuring it to create this Palestinian state. Why? If the nations of the world want to stop the bloodshed, why grow a state from a community that produced some of the world's most notorious thugs—Haj Amin Al-Husseni, Mustafa Azzam, Sheikh Yassin, and Yasser Arafat?

After all, it was Mustafa Azzam, a Palestinian from Jenin, who was Osama bin Laden's mentor and the inspiration for Al-Qaeda (The Base.) I rarely find any Westerner who knows that. I remember my interview with Peter Graph for Reuters in England. He stated that Hamas and Al-Qaeda were different. Hamas, he said, has a legitimate reason to fight for Palestinian rights, while Al-Qaeda simply wants to kill everyone and anyone. I asked him if he knew the name of the man who inspired Al-Qaeda. He responded like most, "Osama bin Laden."

We all live in some state of ignorance.

In the West Bank, we lived the media lies. After we lost the Six Day War, my father in Jericho felt as though the walls of ancient Jericho had tumbled down on him. During the war, he listened constantly to the Jordanian and Egyptian radio stations. He believed them when they claimed that the Arabs were winning the war. But he was listening to the wrong stations.

My father chose to trust the Arabs who claimed that the Israelis were promoting "propaganda lies" when they announced their daily victories against us. We discovered the truth when we opened the door of our home and saw the Israeli tanks parading the streets of Jericho with the Star of David flags flying on them. Now *there's* proof.

Al-Jazeera TV, the mouthpiece of the Arab world, spews out hype to appease Arab ears. When we watched CNN cover the Gulf War, we didn't believe anything that came from its reporters. We were told that Saddam Hussein could withstand an American attack. We discovered differently. Unfortunately, my people will find out much more—when it's too late.

I ended up in the Muscovite Prison in Jerusalem because of my violent activities. In another room, my neighbor, the son-in-law of the Muezzin Ramadan in our village, had his legs broken. We heard his cries as the Israelis clubbed him. Why did they do this? Because they were racing against the clock to find out where he had hidden the explosives before his colleagues could re-locate them to a new hiding place. They were desperately trying to save countless lives. This treatment was rare in Israel and was used only when lives were at stake. However, Israeli law today prohibits any form of torture for any reason. There is no such law in Palestine.

I don't claim that the Palestinians have not suffered. I suffered, as did others I knew. However, was I in jail because of the Jews trying to steal my land? No, it was because I had tried to kill them. Ironically, an Israeli jailer gave me a kind of "father to son" talk and urged me to consider why I was throwing my life away.

But I returned to violence straight away, bombing that Israeli bank in Bethlehem.

THE TERRORISTS ARE RIGHT HERE

I was introduced to Western society and education at Loop College in Chicago where I became president of the Palestinian Students' Association, raising funds for the PLO and recruiting volunteers to fight in Lebanon. I worked with others to organize events, and to smuggle a shipment of United States military outfits to Lebanon. We were all activists. Very few were really doing any studying. It was just a ruse to allow us to stay here and do our real work. Most of us worked on obtaining green cards from American girls who were unaware that they were simply pawns for a greater cause. If anyone of us fell in love, the others would chastise him, reminding him that we could marry only a "homegrown" Muslim.

Other women served the cause, too. I recall luring a girl who was an activist, serving on a board for the defense of Ziad Abu Eain, a terrorist seeking asylum in the U.S. and who was wanted for extradition to Israel for a 1979 Palestine Liberation Organization (PLO) bombing. Having a relationship with an American girl for the "cause" was justified—as long as the girl did her part to help our colleague, Ziad.

Chicago was notorious for its influx of Arab students. The Loop College cafeteria looked like an Arab coffee shop (Qahwah); Islamists, PLO, PFLP (Popular Front to Liberate Palestine), DFLP (Democratic Front to Liberate Palestine), were all competing against each other. Jordanians hated the Palestinians for Black September; the Lebanese had not forgotten the massacres committed by the PLO in Damur. No one got along with the other. But when it came to hating Israel, they were united.

Now began what I thought would be a return to Islam. Sheikh Jamal Sa'id was connected with Mustafa Azzam, Osama bin Laden's mentor.

I joined some Islamic fundamentalists, recruited by Sheikh Jamal Sa'id, who worked with a network of scholars from Jordan and elsewhere to recruit students in the United States to train for jihad, "holy war" operations against America and Israel.

This was the boot camp from hell. The training was underground. I lived in a basement infested with rats the size of a cat. No music was allowed. I had broken off with my girlfriend. We had to wake up in the middle of the night with Sheikh Sa'id for vigorous training, martial arts, and chanting of slogans hate and indoctrination.

If this frightens you, it should. We must find ways to stop the influx of terrorists. Tougher screening of people entering the country will solve part of the problem. But it is not difficult for extremists already here to explain Islam in a completely untruthful fashion to the unquestioning moderates and win them over by the droves. It's a kind of mental indoctrination button that can turn moderates into extremist robots, ready to carry out instructions.

They are on your children's college campuses. There are "Peace Weekends," sponsored by the Palestinian Solidarity Movement, whose agendas look like a day at Bible school. Then comes the party line. At campus events, they will speak of peace in English and talk about infiltration in Arabic. The idea is to galvanize the Muslims and to win over naïve, idealistic students who believe their David and Goliath stories, only with the wrong Goliath.

They collect enormous sums of money. And they have far-reaching access to the Western world through the Internet.

Why didn't I realize this was all about Jew-hatred? Even living in America, a civilized society, and years after I had left these groups— I still had not changed my mind about Israel and the Jews, because of the intense indoctrination I received in the school of hate back home.

LET ME TAKE YOU BACK HOME

My father and uncles were teachers. So why did they sit there smirking when I asked, "Why did you never tell us about Rachel's Tomb, why not a single field trip to this holy place? You were teachers and I went to Dar-Jaser school, right smack next to Rachel's Tomb.

Why didn't you tell us who Rachel was?" They all replied, "Rachel is a whore, a prostitute." Why such hatred? "You deserve to be spat at," my uncle Salameh Shoebat replied, and my cousin asked me to leave his house.

Though they called themselves teachers, they knew nothing about history; all they knew was the same propaganda that I had been taught. Yet when I asked them, "Which life style do you prefer, living under Arafat or under the occupation?" they all answered, "The occupation was the "good old days." "Then why not speak up?" I asked. "We will never accept Jewish rule, we will always hate Jews, it's in our blood." And so it seems.

My American-born mother and grandmother were the only relatives to stand by me, yet even my mother didn't suspect my change of heart and mind and it was much too dangerous to talk to her about it. She still lived in the West Bank and was effectively held prisoner by my father for 35 years. Every time she would try to escape back to America, we were too eager to drag her back to the "house of obedience" where a woman belongs in that part of the world. I was never told that she was a Christian. Yet I had my suspicions. I remember that once, my mother tried to escape with me and my brother and sister, but the neighbors, always looking out from their balconies, reported her leaving with her children and their suitcases. When we arrived in Jerusalem, my Muslim relatives were waiting at the gate of the United States Consulate to force us to go back home.

Years later, when I re-united with my mother in America, I found out for sure she was a Christian. I discovered she had been influenced by an American missionary couple who she secretly asked to baptize her to bring her back to her true faith. When she refused to be submerged in a pond full of green algae, the missionary, Edmond Davis from Texas, had to plead with the people at the YMCA in Jerusalem to clear their pool of men, and my mother was baptized. Years later, I searched for Mr. Davis in Texas and he told me her story. No one from our family knew.

I recall when my mother would take me on trips to museums in Israel and I fell in love with archeology. I was fascinated with it. In my many arguments with her, I would bluntly say that the Jews and

Christians had corrupted the Bible. She responded by taking me to the Israel Scroll Museum in Jerusalem and showing me the scroll of Isaiah, still intact. She often answered my questions with silence.

The Islamist culture can even cause a child to turn on his mother. I remember when I tormented my mother by calling her an "infidel." I had doubted her profession of faith to Islam and viewed her as an American imperialist. I'd show her the pictures in the newspaper of all the teenagers supposedly martyred because of violence, demanding that she respond to me. At times, we all hated her and the family would ask my father to divorce her and marry a "good Muslim woman."

My father cracked my mother's skull with a hammer. Fed up with my father's ignoring her and spending most of his time with friends, she barged in on a game of Shesh-Besh backgammon and, in front of the men, she threw the game to the floor. "I am an American and I am not used to this life," she cried out. The crack of the hammer was her sympathy. I finally rescued my mother in 1995, thank God, since today, Bethlehem has become so dangerous that no one is safe.

I lived in Israel during the Six Day War, the PLO resistance, the Jordanian Black September civil war, the bloody wars in Lebanon, and the Yom Kippur war. With no real chance to destroy Israel and with defeat after defeat, we still dreamed of that single victory, since we believed that was all it would take to destroy the Jews.

Today, I know something of what it feels like to be a Jew, to stand alone, to say, "I object, I cannot stand by and remain silent." If I went back to my village of Beit Sahour-Bethlehem I would probably have five minutes to live. Today, I run into people who call me names, hate me, try to discredit me. I know something of what it feels like to be a Jew.

I remember students used to ask our teacher, Na'eem Ayyad, during our Islamic studies in Bethlehem High School, if it were permitted for Muslims to rape the Jewish women after we defeated them. His response was, "The women captured in battle have no choice in this matter, they are concubines and they need to obey their masters, having sex with slave captives is not a matter of choice for slaves." He said that sexual intercourse with Jewish captives does not have to be consensual. Surah: The Women (al-Nisa, verse 20) in fact, documented

Allah's decree: "Forbidden to you also are married women, except those who are in your hand as slaves, this is the law of Allah for you."

And Surah: Confederates (al-Ahzab verse 50):

"O prophet; we allowed thee thy wives to whom thou hast paid their dowries, and the slaves whom thy right hand possesseth out of the booty which Allah hath granted thee, and the daughters of thy uncle, and of thy maternal aunt, who fled with thee to Medina, and any believing woman who hath given herself up to the prophet, if the prophet desired to wed her, a privilege to thee above the rest of the faithful."

We had no problem with Muhammad taking advantage of this privilege. He married many wives and took several slave girls from the booty he collected from his victorious battles. We never knew how many wives he had and that question was always a debatable issue for us. One of these wives was taken from his own adopted son, Zaid, as Allah declared that she was given to the prophet. Others were Jewish captives forced into slavery after Muhammad beheaded their husbands and families.

I also remember my first visit to the Jerusalem Zoo. My uncle Salameh, the school teacher, threw a cigarette butt in the gorilla's cage, and the gorilla started smoking it instantly. Everyone laughed. I was wondering how the gorilla learned such a habit. He said that this monkey was a descendant of the Jews, "sons of the detestable apes." This was my first lesson in the Quran. In September 1996, the Hamas monthly, *Falastin Al-Muslima*, ran this from an article by Ibrahim Al-'Ali:

"And ye know of those of you who broke the Sabbath, how We said unto them: Be ye apes, despised and hated!" (Quran, the Cow, v65) and "Allah did not mete out the punishment of transformation on any nation except the Jews. The significance of it is actual change in the appearance of the Jew and perfect transformation from human to bestial condition...from human appearance to the form of genuine apes, pigs, mice, and lizards..."

Nazism is not dead.

The Israelis, in an attempt at reconciliation, once took students from our school for a week to a Jewish camp on the coast of Eshdod so we could mingle with Jewish kids. It didn't work. Any teacher who spoke to a Jew was mocked and accused of all sorts of things from sedition to betrayal. I remained a good Muslim and full of hate.

# # #

On the other side of the world, in America. Here I began my journey in "self-detoxification," when I started reading the Christian and Jewish Bibles, when I no longer was a good Muslim, when I didn't say my five daily prayers, when I fasted on Ramadan only, and when I failed to keep many of the observances. Yet a Muslim is a Muslim and I was still true to my beliefs.

I bought my first Bible for $10 in order to teach my wife about the terrible Jews. At that point, I had asked the God of Abraham, Isaac and Jacob to reveal to me whether the Bible was indeed corrupted as I was taught. After a long, thorough parallel study of the Bible and the Quran, I came to a crossroad of logic: Why did Yahweh love Jews so much, and Allah despise them? Either the Jews had indeed altered the Scripture to say that—because how could God be on the side of an evil people—or the Quran had something to hide, in which case I was the evil one and not the Jews. I decided to weigh each side. I began to understand the spiritual link between the Jewish people and their land. Why were the Jews always in self-defense mode in all these battles? Why are their enemies attacking Israel?

Slowly a change came over my Jihadist ideology. After reading the Hebrew Bible, and learning about all the attacks on Israel from Biblical times until the present, it dawned on me: how could it be that Allah was on our side if the Six-Day-War in 1967 resulted in the greatest victory for the Jews since Joshua's encirclement of Jericho? Further, Israel's victory—unlike Muslim conquests full of rape, pillage and massacre—brought freedom for all of Israel's various peoples and religions. All my fellow Arabs living in Jericho at the time witnessed it.

We got our answer from Sheikh Qaradawi who said it was because we [the Muslims] were not *good enough*," our Islam needed "purification," and that when Allah is truly on our side, the Jewish weapons will cease to fire. This will allow the stones and trees to *"Cry out, here is a Jew, come and kill him."* I realized that our eyes are not the windows to pass truth to our hearts; this was an issue of a dysfunctional spirit. A corrupt spirit, no matter what, cannot see the truth.

I woke up my wife and said "Maria, I think I was wrong to try to convert you to Islam."

# # #

I set out on a path of reconciliation, experiencing agonizing regret for my past actions as well as anger toward the "drug pushers" who indoctrinated me to carry out their acts of hatred. This pathology needs to be exposed for what it is: Nazi-style mind control and the corruption of children's souls.

I set out on foot, going from synagogue to synagogue, Jewish organization to Jewish organization, knocking on doors, saying, "Please listen to me." And I am saying, "Listen to me" again in this book.

From all Jews I beg forgiveness. Please understand that I underwent an "occupation of the mind." We were taught hate since we were children and I did not know any better. I vowed, as a way of repentance, to fight the hate-drug pushers as long as I live.

Today, in response to what has become a mantra since September 11,—that "true Islam is a religion of peace," I say no. I grew up there. I was there at the mosques, the Friday Madrassa, listening to sermons by Ikrima Sabri, tapes by Abdul Hamid Kishk. They taught only the destruction of the Jews and hatred of the West. To kill, to maim, to hate, these were all the same as getting an "A" on your report card.

What the West does not understand about Islamism is that jihad has stages. If Muslims have the upper hand, then jihad is waged by force. If Muslims do not have the upper hand, then jihad is waged through financial and political means. Since Muslims do not have the upper hand in America or Europe, they talk about peace in front of you while supporting Hamas and Hezbollah in the back room. The whole idea of Islam being a peaceful religion emanates from that silent stage of jihad. As Sheikh Qaradawi taught Muslims in Chicago, when Salahu-Deen Al-Ayubi (Saladin) was asked to concede to peace with the verse, Quran 8:61, "And if they incline to peace, then incline to it and trust in Allah." However, from Quran 47:35, he replied, "And be not slack so as to cry for peace and you have the upper hand."

In Islam, conceding to peace means that the Islamic Umma, nation, is weak. So as soon as Islam becomes the dominating force, it switches into war gear.

It is a fallacy that *jihad* represents an inner struggle; jihad means the kind of genocidal slaughter of infidels that Osama bin Laden calls for. Inner struggle? Despite over one hundred quotes by Muhammad referring to jihad by the sword, by killing, by taking no prisoners, by forced conversion, or by enslavement—with only one quote referring to an internal struggle—called for by Muhammad after the complete conquest and occupation of Arabia? Public claims of pacifism are typical of the Islamic leadership, and the West eagerly devours them, refusing to believe that a major world religion poses such a danger to humanity.

Of course, there are Muslims who reject many of the classical sources and truly focus on the peaceful verses of the Quran, seeking to re-interpret the verses because they truly do not want to engage in violence. These "liberal" Muslims seem to "re-write" Islam rather then correctly interpret it. They are peaceful *despite* Islam, not because of it.

In one dialogue, Professor Khaleel Muhammad, Assistant Professor at the Department of Religious Studies at San Diego state University, quoted Abu Hamid al-Ghazali, 12th century jurist and theologian, ignoring that when Ghazali was asked a question regarding living in foreign non-Muslim countries, Ghazali responded:

"Muslims could live under non-Muslim rule as long as they do not forget that they are Allah's missionaries and, if needed, His soldiers."[3] I suppose that Muhammad might have another meaning of "soldiers."

He also pointed to Khalid Abou el Fadl whose argument is that "only fringe elements among Muslims consider that [jihad is] war" and that "the Quran refers to jihad only in terms of intellectual effort to apply divine revelation in promoting peace through justice." Abou el Fadl also was quoted saying, "There is no such thing as Islamic terrorism, but there have always been Muslim terrorists."[4]

I have heard Hamza Yusuf, Tariq Ramadan, Fazlur Rahman, and Amina Wadud who say the same, yet on the other hand, their advocacy consists of "extreme" denial of the facts regarding the meaning of jihad according to Islam.

You cannot fight Islamic terrorism by denying what the Quran or Islam actually say or by twisting and re-interpreting verses, but by combating their principles of violence.

Christians should take the lead. Do they wish to see the West converted to Islam? Do they want the doors of Saudi Arabia, Afghanistan, Iran, and all other Muslim states to remain closed to Christian missionaries?

Abou el Fadl, whom Muhammad quoted, gave the following definition of jihad:

"...struggle for the sake of God, whether for self-discipline and self-purification or against oppression and justice." [5]

Is this a *reformation* or a *re-interpretation* of jihad? Islamic scholars have written volumes about the Quran's "abrogation of peace" agreements between the faithful and the infidels, a concept affirmed by the most highly regarded interpreters: *Kitab Al-Nasekh Wal-Mansookh*, by Al-Neesaburi, Al-Hafeth Ibnu Katheer Ibin Abas, *Al-Tasheel Lulum Al-Tanzeel*, Al-Husain Ibn Fadl, Abu Abdullah Muhammad Ibn Hazm, Al-Muhaqiq Abu Al-Qasim Hibatullah Ibn Salameh, Al-Sudy Wa-Al-Dahak, Muhammad Abdulsalam Faraj.

The classical Muslim jurist, al-Mawardi, (a Shafi'ite jurist, d. 1058) from Baghdad was a seminal, prolific scholar who lived during the so-called Islamic "Golden Age" of the Abbasid-Baghdadian Caliphate. He wrote the following, based on widely accepted interpretations of the Quran and Sunna regarding infidel prisoners of jihad campaigns:

"As for the captives, the emir [ruler] has the choice of taking the most beneficial action of four possibilities: the first to put them to death by cutting their necks; the second, to enslave them and apply the laws of slavery regarding their sale and manumission; the third, to ransom them in exchange for goods or prisoners; and fourth, to show favor to them and pardon them." [6]

Such odious "rules" are iterated by all four classical schools of Islamic jurisprudence across the vast Muslim empire. According to Shafi'i Maliki, Hanbali, and Hanafi, *all Muslims* are bound by these four choices. And there is no debate that the definition of jihad (besides the personal jihad apologists speak about) is to fight and kill non-Muslims (the Kuffar):

Hanafi Fiqh: "to call the unbelievers towards the true religion of Islam [and] to fight against them, if they are unwilling to accept this true religion." [7]

The Christian Reformation started when followers went to the text and to the founders of the faith, who clearly prohibited genocide and murder.

As we see in Luke 6:27-28: "But I tell you who hear me: Love your enemies, do good to those who hate you, bless those who curse you, pray for those who mistreat you. If one strikes you on one cheek, turn to him the other also."

Yet Muslims cannot do the same. Not a single verse exists in the Quran with *"love your enemies,"* since the founders themselves, Muhammad, the prophet of Islam; the Sahaba; and the Caliphs all participated in jihad by killing infidels and anyone who opposed the Islamic system. Now compare Romans 8:27-35:

"Who is afraid of dying? Who is afraid of a threat from any quarter? Who shall separate us from the love of Christ? Shall trouble or persecution...or danger of sword? As it is written: 'For your sake we face death all day long; we are considered as sheep to be slaughtered. No, in all these things we are more than conquerors through Him who loved us.'"

REPLACEMENT THEOLOGY

When it comes to Islam, the talk of reformation can never be about "re-interpretation" but true reformation and confession. The question is, are they ready to do that? I am, one from a handful out of millions.

Christian Arabs are not immune to the effects of Islamism. In Israel, they get their education from their leaders and the local Church. They pretty much adhere to Replacement Theology, the idea that God replaced Israel with the Church. They have also come up with a new Liberation Theology, co-opted by the Palestinian movement. Many organizations call for peace, yet in reality they support the utter destruction of the state of Israel. I have dealt with them face to face. Emil Salayta, who heads the Latin Patriarchate schools in Jerusalem, once spoke on "peace" at the Presbyterian Church in Walnut Creek, California. I attended and challenged him. "Could peace be achieved by bombing Israeli buses?" I asked. I have his answer on tape. "Israel must be eliminated, by whatever means," he replied. No one else seemed concerned.

I care about peace. Therefore, I say without ambiguity, these people back terrorism: Michael Sabbah, Niam Ateek, Elias Chacour (a candidate for a Noble Prize), Riah Abu el-Assal and Emil Salayta.

# # #

Family values? This is what Islam does to a family member who changes his faith. When my family learned I had converted to Christianity:

My brother made his last call to me—through my wife. "I know what your husband is doing against Islam; I also know where you live."

My father's threats came at odd hours of the night—"You will die by shooting."

Blood may be thicker then water, but for those who leave Islam, blood is spilled as easily as water.

I had written to a Christian lawyer in Jerusalem, Jonathan Kuttab, and I got this reply: *"If you ever come back not only will you lose property, but your son will be taken as well."*

Islam allows no rights whatever to born Muslims who leave the faith—formally, *murtadd fitri*—including the right to life. So I was warned. Yet, even Jonathan Kuttab says nothing about this in all his human rights activist writings. He simply points a finger at Israel as guilty of everything under the sun. Terrorism in the name of Allah and the decay of legal rights for Christians in the Holy Land finds no space in the writings of these activists. For him, I also write this book.

I lost my family, my friends, my community, my culture, my money and my land. How ironic. The Jews did not take these things from me, my own family did. I am branded as a traitor by Arab Christians, by my own family, and by the Muslims in my community.

This treatment by my fellow Arabs, be they Christian, Muslim, or atheist, is indicative of Islam's fatal flaw. If Islam truly were a peaceful religion, then my family might consider me a disappointment, but my own brother would not threaten to kill me, my family would not have confiscated my land and demanded I come back to Bethlehem and declare, "There is no god but Allah and Muhammad is his prophet." If I do not believe in Islam anymore, why should I lie and declare such a thing? The answer is because Muhammad clearly demanded that one who changes his faith must be killed. What part of "kill' does the West not understand? Is it any wonder why I have to stay in hiding and be so careful even though I live in a free society here in America?

LET ME SAY AS MUCH AS I CAN BEFORE THEY COME TO GET ME

I choose to speak out because I know what is wrong. And what is wrong has nothing to do with Israel's "occupation of the land;" it is Islam's occupation of the mind. There are other victims, just like me, millions of them, and like Hitler's *Jugend*—they are all kids. They are taught the same songs about killing Jews as I was. When will we get rid of the education propaganda promoting both destruction and self-destruction? Will it take a generation? Ten? Until then, there will be no peace, no matter what kind of land settlement the world tries to enforce. Not when Muslim children undergo this occupation of the mind. *There is no solution unless we liberate the children from an evil and growing menace and stop the cycle.*

# # #

ISRAEL AND THE LAND: WHO IS THE RIGHTFUL HEIR?

Israel must never relinquish the land.

Yet the West pushes Israel to do just that, especially Christians who threaten divestment from companies who do business with Israel. Many American Jews accept a two-state solution. It seems like a simple solution. The danger is that once the Palestinians' state is in place, they will continue killing Jews. Israel needs to wake up and smell the hummus. We must return to the status quo—what detractors call "the occupation." Before Arafat, we had jobs; people went to work and supported their families. Terrorists were exiled or imprisoned, as is true in any modern country. Israel must stand strong and fight—dismantle Hamas and take away all the weapons, the way it used to be. The introduction of weapons into Palestinian society by Israel under the Oslo agreement, when Israel gave assault rifles to Arafat's "police force," has been a disaster. Those weapons must be confiscated.

Some people believe that moderate Islam can flourish as a peaceful force, a catalyst for change that allows Islam and Western society to coexist successfully.

The problem with this idea is that Islam is not simply a religion. Islam is a system of government. How do you untangle the two? How do you take away Khilafa and jihad and still call it Islam? This is why I call jihadists "Nazis with a religious twist."

Can Islam be reformed?

Reform was successful in the Christian church, but the success came as a result of *adhering* to the Biblical text and not doing away with it, and of challenging the institutions that abused their authority.

The opposite is true when it comes to Islam. Adhering to the text means acting out violence and hate. Peace starts when we make it illegal to follow the text and ultimately de-fang Islamism and jihad and their government, just as we did to the Islamic Ottoman Empire, which the Islamists are trying right now to revive.

We can find nothing in the tenets of the Christianity or Judaism that comes even close to Islam's form of government. Of course, the Jewish and Christian faiths have nothing to do with government.

Also, the Bible clearly states that the faithful need to "obey the laws of the land," making it clear that the Biblical God is not enforcing a theocracy on earth by the sword of any mortal being, be it vicar or king.

We simply cannot compare the reforms in the Judeo-Christian culture with reforms in Islam. I have heard the term "Islamic democracy." It's an oxymoron, like "capitalistic communism."

Islam is many things: a moral code, Khilafa, civil law, and a global government. Learning Arabic is crucial for all Muslims in order to worship, since Muhammad the prophet clearly taught "La-Yuta'abbadu Illa Be-Tilawateh"—one cannot worship Allah unless he recites the Quranic verses in Arabic. Arabic would unite the Islamic world. There are groups such as the Free Muslim Coalition Against Terrorism that are working toward change. The question is, to change what? Any change of the text would be a corruption. Are these groups speaking of "reformation," "re-writing," "re-interpretation," or creation of a new kind of Islam?" True reformation must come within, if we can even apply this term to Islam.

Islamic reformation is not the business of the West. The 55 Muslim states need to deal with each other, on their own turf. Then, they cannot accuse the West of interfering in their business. If we stay out of it, there can be no liberal accusations of imperialism and no conservative cries about working with the enemy.

CONFESSION—OUR NAZI EDUCATION

My grandfather Daud was the Mukhtar (chieftain) of the Shoebat clan in the village of Beit Sahour of the district of Bethlehem. He had owned much land in his village and as a landowner and Mukhtar, he entertained Arab leaders with feasts and songs, hiring special cooks for the preparation of lamb and delicate dishes for men of great stature. Men like Abdul Qader Al-Husseni, leader of the Palestinian Revolution and Haj Amin Al-Husseni, the religious Grand Mufti of Jerusalem, who was a staunch friend of Adolf Hitler.

Few people seem to know the close connection that Islam had with the Nazis. The Grand Mufti of Jerusalem was with Adolph Hitler on the eve of the "Final Solution" to the world's "Jewish Problem" on November 21, 1941.

Top: The Grand Mufti of Jerusalem, head of the Islamic Supreme Council, with Adolph Hitler on the Eve of the Final Solution.

Bottom: A picture taken in 1943 of the Grand Mufti of Jerusalem, Haj Amin Al-Husseni, reviewing Bosnian-Muslim troops—a unit of the Hanjar (Saber) Division of the Waffen SS that he personally recruited for Hitler.

One of the Grand Mufti's "accomplishments" was a letter written to Hungary's Minister of Foreign Affairs asking him to stop the immigration of a half million Hungarian Jews. They honored his request and every one of those Jews was put to death in the extermination camps.

That my grandfather was a friend to such a man is a shame I cannot change; the only thing I can do is to teach my children to love Jews like any other people and to tell the truth to all who will listen.

Of course, "friendship" in that place did not have the same meaning as it does in the West. My grandfather survived a trial by Al-Husseni's henchman for selling land to Jews. The facts are, many Arabs were selling land to Jews for high profits, but the Revolution officially forbid it. Selling land to immigrant Jews was treason, although it was all right for someone like Haj Amin Al-Husseni to sell his soul to Satan by collaborating with Hitler and helping to kill and pillage Jewish immigrants. Once again, the innocent were butchered while the guilty were set free.

My grandfather liked everyone, and he had no problem selling land to Jewish or Christian immigrants. The village had much land with only a handful of families that immigrated in the last decade prior to the 1948 war. Many Arabs sold land, since they were getting high prices from the Jews and they were not using it anyway. Yet my grandfather was not free to do with his land whatever he wished. Al-Husseni kidnapped him and took him to the village of Al-Khader.

The execution rope was hanging. Someone summoned my great grandfather, Abdullah Ali, known for his great physical strength, bravery and courage. He walked in and saw the rope and my grandfather standing ready for his execution. Abdullah Ali pleaded for his son-in-law's life. My grandfather was given his last warning, and set free. Many were not so lucky. Between 1936 and 1938 Husseni's men murdered Sheikh Daoud Ansari (Imam of Al Aqsa Mosque), Sheikh Ali Nur el Khattib (Al Aqsa Mosque), Sheikh Nusbi Abdal Rahim (Council of Muslim Religious Court), Sheikh Abdul el Badoui (Acre, Palestine), Sheikh El Namouri (Hebron), and Nasr El Din Nassr (Mayor of Hebron). Between Feb. 1937 and Nov. 1938, eleven Mukhtars (community leaders) and their entire families were slain by Amin Al-Husseni's men.[8]

When the film, "The Passion of the Christ," came out, some Jews feared it would stir anti-Jewish feelings because the film falsely accused Jews of complicity in the death of Christ. It is a lie that has been perpetuated for centuries. Christ was a Jew. His family were all Jews. Christianity grew out of Judaism. Jews stood at the cross weeping while others mocked. Yet the Jews earned the title "Christ killers" when the Bible clearly states that we "all" killed Christ, each and every sinner, for He came to die for our sins.

I used to hate words like *Yerushalayim, Shalom, Yesrael.* I considered them foreign invaders in my land. To me, Israel was an occupier, an oppressor, a thief in the night who sneaked in to rob me of my home, my heritage, and my land.

I hated the Jews in Israel and I was bent on destroying them through rioting and terrorism. Israel must be eliminated by any means. Years later, I put myself in the shoes of a Jew when I started studying the Bible. I realized that the Jew was always on trial, and one Jew in particular.

His name was Yeshua ben Yosef, known to gentiles as Jesus of Nazareth. I concluded that the only way to reach peace in this turbulent world is for us to remove ourselves for a while, see through the eyes of this Jewish Messiah, see how He sees, feel the way He feels, and understand how and why things are the way they are.

My eyes were opening. Having lived in the Holy Land, with all those trips to Jerusalem, I failed to see why the Jews were restricted to only the Wailing Wall, their holiest place, for prayer. Why couldn't Jews worship on the Temple Mount or rebuild it? If the Muslim world has Mecca, and the Catholic world has the Vatican, and Christian pilgrims may visit all the holy sites, why is the Jew barred from his Temple, the Temple that was originally his? Can you imagine the uproar if someone other than Muslims were to take over Mecca?

The Crusades were fought, in part, so Christian pilgrims could visit their holy sites in Jerusalem. Yet, here we have Jews in Israel who are more powerful than their enemy, yet they have not waged war to recapture their most holy site from the Muslims.

A terrible, terrible wrong is committed here. Sheik Ikrimeh Sabri, Jerusalem's Grand Mufti, preached daily sermons from Israel's foremost holy site, calling for the destruction of the very people to whom it belongs! The Jews are forced to listen to this through the loud speakers, while they worship outside in any weather, in the bottom Western side designated for them. They must listen to cries that the Wailing Wall area is in reality an Islamic site called *Al-Buraq*, and it too belongs to the Muslims: *"The 'Al-Buraq' Wall [the Western Wall] is a part of the Al-Aqsa Mosque. The Jews have no relation to it, whether or not a decision to expropriate it was made."*

TURNING THE TABLES

As Mecca is the only place required for Muslims in the Quran, Jerusalem is an inseparable part of Judaism, according to the Bible. Jews alone are mandated by Biblical law to celebrate their religion in Jerusalem. Muslims refer to a tradition of Lesser Pilgrimage (Al-Umra) to visit Jerusalem, yet this practice has never been followed from time immemorial. *Jerusalem gained importance for Muslims only when the Jews laid claim to it.* Just as "Palestine" was cobbled overnight when the state of Israel was born.

How is it that the Jew, under all circumstances, must remain silent? Why is it that much of the world is in denial when we have archeological and historical evidence that the Temple Mount sits atop the first and second Temples built on that site by Jews and for Jews and which are holy to them to this day? Does a Muslim mosque staked out on top the Temple Mount make null and void all those years of Jewish worship?

The lies and hate are broadcast all around this holy place. Palestinian prominent historian Jarid Al-Kidwa announced from the Palestinian TV that:

"The stories of the Torah and the Bible did not take place in the Land of Israel—they occurred in the Arabian Peninsula, primarily in Yemen. The identity of our father Ibrahim [Abraham] who is mentioned in the Quran is clear. From the Koran's description of him it arises that he lived in the southern Hejaz [Saudi Arabia], near Mecca." [9]

Mr. Al-Kidwa also announced that the Arab, in reality, has the true Jewish blood while the Jew is from a Khazarian race. [10]

THE UNLIKELY SCENARIO

Try this. Turn Mr. Al-Kidwa's fictional history around and assume that Mecca was built for the Jews by their father, Abraham. So they attack the Arabs and take over Saudi Arabia, put their Kohanim Ha-Gadol (High Priest) in charge, destroy everything Arabic, have Hebrew calligraphy written all over the Kaaba's wall, and make it an abomination for any Muslim to set foot on its ground.

Would the Mullahs of Islam stand silently and allow this sacrilege to continue? What do you think the Arab and Muslim masses would do to these Jews? Yet, the Jew, who has never taken over Mecca or any Arab nation, suffers insults and humiliation at his holy places, and lives with it all in an attempt to make peace.

Jews don't escape the wrath of their Muslim enemies even in death. The Muslims dug a tunnel through the Jews' holiest city where there is a 2,500-year-old Jewish cemetery on the Mount of Olives. They used the Jewish tombstones for a pathway to the Arab Legion army latrine. Yet the Jew has not avenged; he remains silent. This silence in front of a world of false accusers is nothing short of amazing.

The Bible taught me that to be a good Christian is also to be a "spiritual" Jew. Christianity is not a new religion; it is simply an offshoot sect of the Jewish faith that followed Yeshua (Jesus) as Messiah. I realized that the way to true and everlasting peace is to see how God in the Bible is able to reconcile Jew and Gentile. I saw that God is indeed a God of peace and that the God of Islam is bent on destroying the Jew. The Bible does not have a single verse calling on Christians to destroy Jews, although the *tyrants* of Christendom said it loud and clear. How can Christians claim to follow God's commandments, yet fail to have peace with the Jew?

Fortunately, many traditional Christian movements have existed throughout history; these "spiritual" Jews followed the Bible, and not only were they successful in making peace with the Jews, but they also helped them to obtain freedom. True Christianity will always reconcile Jew and Gentile.

It was after I removed the scales from my eyes, and healed my prejudiced heart, that I decided to become a Christian. It's a long testimony, and I am amazed that I became quite the opposite of everything I was. And I learned that whatever the Popes declared or whatever Martin Luther wrote against the Jews were the works of their own hearts and had nothing to do with our Lord.

Today, I love the Jews and Israel, and I am ready to fight for her right to exist as long as there is still a breath left in me.

Defenders of Jews in Nazi Germany were viewed by their neighbors as traitors, but after the evil ended, these "traitors" were recognized as righteous gentiles. So why did the same neighbors choose to live through a nightmare instead of stopping it? The Middle East and the Islamic world in general are bent on destroying Israel; why not stop the repetition of history and save so much human suffering?

There is no freedom of speech, thought, or religion in any Arab or Muslim nation. These nations, once fully taken over by Islam, would be no different from Communism or Nazism. And like Communism and Nazism, Islamism has the same inclination to export its ideas. Islamism does not respect national borders, and the end justifies the means. As we read in 2 Peter 2:19:

"While they promise them liberty, they themselves are the servants of corruption..."

One day, I jumped in on an Internet debate, and gave my views to a group of Muslims and Arabs. Out of the whole group, everyone, except one woman, agreed that I should be killed because of my "apostate" opinions.

The Middle East cannot seem to get rid of its tyrants. One is gone, another more evil rises up. The truth is, people have no right to complain, since the tyrants they get are the representation of their own hearts; they condemn others, so they themselves are condemned. Corruption only begets more corruption, evil only begets more evil; none will end until we have a change of heart.

Our convictions have nothing to do with facts; the truth is, we are driven by culture and upbringing. Tradition plants attitudes and prejudice and we will bend or eliminate facts to stay within our comfort zones.

No one is immune. We are all capable of bigotry. In Nazi Germany, a majority of once-normal Germans supported Hitler. And the Arab masses stood behind Hitler's great friend, the Mufti Haj Amin Al-Husseni, President of the Supreme Muslim Council, who called for the death of every Jew, civilian or soldier. Why is academia so silent on this segment of history, the Nazi-Islamic connection? Why does no Palestinian on the streets of the West Bank discuss it? In many Christian communities, where people are supposed to be truth seekers, Christian Arabs support a Palestinian state, defying all the Scripture supporting Israel. It cannot be that both the pro-Israel and anti-Israel camps are right. Does God have two different and opposite opinions? Scripture tells us He does not.

Hate is a condition of the heart. To destroy the hate, we must look at Scripture, which was written to be understood by ordinary people. God's Word requires no attorney, high priest, enlightened spiritualist, Vatican, or seminary graduate to interpret what He has made abundantly clear. God has set down His declarations and promises. He is the only one that can fulfill them, and in His own way.

In the meantime, God has warned us to be as wise as serpents and innocent as doves.

CONFESSION—LIKE THE NAZIS, WE TWISTED HISTORY

A Palestinian's opinion:

"We the Arabs had nothing to do with the Holocaust. We don't hate Jews. We only kill Zionists who moved into our land."

"The Arab hate towards the Jews wasn't what forced the Jews into moving to Palestine, it was after the Jews entered Palestine forcefully in 1948, after the Jews started killing our people."

"Arabs are Semites, they cannot possibly be anti-Semitic."

"Before the promises to create or before the existence of the state of Israel, did we do anything against you [The Jews]? Please, ask the good Jews who lived in Morocco, Tunisia, Egypt, Iraq, Iran, Palestine,

Syria and Lebanon. Arab Muslims welcomed you always; they did not fight with you for at least the last 1000 years." [11]

Response:

This is historic manipulation. Even Christian writers assist Islamism in this agenda. The Reverend Colin Chapman, a Christian minister who wrote <u>Whose Promised Land?</u> ignored the persecution by the Arabs and Muslims in the Mideast and included only the persecution of Jews in Europe, leaving the Arabs and Muslims with clean hands.

In fact, he closes his book stating: "...the Arabs were being made to suffer for the crimes of Europe. Is one view right and the other wrong?" [12]

Arabs are suffering for the crimes of Europe? All the centuries of persecution culminated with the *Arabs forcing the Jews to flee* between 1918 and 1948. I will discuss the persecution of the Jews by the Arabs prior to 1948 later in this book.

The supposed "Golden Age" for Jews living under Islamic and Arab rule was in reality like Nazism, plagued with death, torture, expulsion, rape, slavery, annihilation, and extradition of mass proportions. To blame the immigration of Jews to Israel for today's conflict is a blatant distortion of history and truth.

The assertion "...*Arabs are Semites and cannot be accused of anti-Semitism*" is a semantic pretzel that ignores the reality of Arab discrimination and hostility toward Jews. Arabs, like any other people, can indeed be anti-Semitic. The term "anti-Semite" was coined in Germany in 1879 by Wilhelm Marrih to refer to the anti-Jewish manifestations of the period and to give Jew hatred a more scientific sounding name. [13]

Jews were no strangers to persecution and humiliation among the Arabs in Muslim nations, as Princeton University historian Bernard Lewis wrote:

"The Golden Age of equal rights was a myth, and belief in it was a result, more than a cause, of Jewish sympathy for Islam." [14]

CONFESSION — VIOLENCE IN ISLAM

In the wake of September 11, President George Bush, in an attempt to soothe anger and restore order, said, *"Islam is a peaceful religion."* So did Tony Blair, Ian Duncan-Smith, and an endless string of journalists, members of the clergy and other politicians. People fear to say anything critical about Islam.

However, Islam, like any other religion, cannot be vaccinated from critical scrutiny. The Bible had to endure archeological, historic, and scientific reviews from the academic circles, as well as accusations of corruption by people in the highest levels of Islamic jurisprudence. Muslims freely deny the crucifixion and the integrity of the Bible. A Judeo-Christian culture respects and fights for the rights of all to express their views. Yet in the Islamic world, the measuring stick is very different when examining the Quran and Hadith. Indeed, if freedom of religion is what Muslims fight for, then where does the freedom to disagree with Islam exist in 55 Muslim states? Look at Surah 5:32 in context:

"...whoever kills a soul, not in retaliation for a soul or corruption in the land, is like one who has killed the whole of mankind; and whoever saves a life is like one who saves the lives of all mankind. Our messengers came to them with the clear proof; but afterwards many of them continued to commit excesses in the land."

The catch, seldom quoted, is *"corruption in the land."* Although Muslims in general are angered when the Quran is *misquoted*, no one objects to the *corruption* of the text by politicians as long as it serves certain goals. The next verse, Q5:34, continues:

"Indeed, the punishment of those who fight Allah and His Messenger and go around *corrupting the land is to be killed, crucified, have their hands and feet cut off on opposite sides, or to be banished from the land.* That is a disgrace for them in this life, and in the life to come theirs will be a terrible punishment."

The tribe of Ukl faced such a fate for simply changing their minds and denouncing Islam. Sahih Al-Bukhari, Vol. 8, put it graphically:

Narrated Anas: Some people from the tribe of 'Ukl came to the Prophet and embraced Islam. The climate of

Medina did not suit them, so the Prophet ordered them to go to the (herd of milch) camels of charity and to drink, their milk and urine (as a medicine). They did so, and after they had recovered from their ailment (became healthy) they turned renegades (reverted from Islam) and killed the shepherd of the camels and took the camels away. The Prophet sent (some people) in their pursuit and so they were (caught and) brought, and the Prophets ordered that their hands and legs should be cut off and that their eyes should be branded with heated pieces of iron, and that their cut hands and legs should not be cauterized, till they die.

The Quran teaches its followers to respect the sanctity of life of other Muslims, except those who *"fight Allah and his Messenger"* and are guilty of *"corruption in the land."* These people must be killed, mutilated, or banished.

In Q2:216: "Warfare is ordained for you, though it is hateful unto you; but it may happen that you hate a thing which is good for you and it may happen that you love a thing which is bad for you."

"Believers, do not make friends with any but your own people. They [i.e., non-Muslims] *will not fail to corrupt you.* They long for your ruin. Hatred has already shown itself out of their mouths, but more grievous is what their breasts conceal." In this context of Q3:118, non-Muslims seek to "corrupt" Muslims.

Despite references in the Quran that call for tolerance, Surah 9 verse 73, according to Islamic highest jurisprudence, abrogates (cancels) them all. In Surah Al-Tawbah (repentance), the most famous verse on jihad is the Verse of the Sword. This verse abrogates over one hundred other verses in the Quran. It made null and void most of the Quranic verses calling for tolerance, forgiveness and peace towards non-believers. The Law of Abrogation (Al-Nasekh Wal-Mansookh) was given by Allah in the Quran.

Verses from the Quran were abrogated (Mansookh) by newer ones (Nasekh) many times. From Al-Tawbah 9:5, the verse of the Sword says the following:

"When the sacred months are passed, kill those who join other gods with Allah wherever Ye shall find them, besiege them, and lay wait for them with every kind of ambush."

And in 9:29, "Make war upon such of those whom the Scriptures have been given as they believe not in Allah, or the last day, and forbid not that which Allah and His Apostle have forbidden..."

In his book, How to Perfect the Science of the Quran (Al-Itqan), Al-Syoti, in volume 2 page 37, writes:

"The Verse of the Sword has abrogated (annulled) one hundred and twenty four Quranic verses, and all that came in the Quran on matters of forgiving and ignoring unbelievers, have been replaced (Mansookh), by the verse of the sword."

For further examples, refer to the following: Kitab Al-Nasekh Wal-Mansookh by Al-Neesaburi, Al-Hafeth Ibnu Katheer Ibin Abas, Al-Tasheel Lulum Al-Tanzeel, Al-Husain Ibn Fadl, Abu Abdullah Muhammad Ibn Hazm, Al-Muhaqiq Abu Al-Qasim Hibatullah Ibn Salameh, Al-Sudy Wa-Al-Dahak, Muhammad Abdulsalam Faraj.

The evidence of the abrogation of the verses that call for tolerance and patience cannot be refuted. People in the West must not ignore what is taught in the East, that is, *"Islam to the West."* The banners held high at Islamic rallies and demonstrations go beyond even this — *"Islam to the World."*

Other places in the Quran, such as the thoroughly reasonable Surah 10:99, ask Muslims:

"Had your Lord willed, everyone on earth would have believed. Will you then compel people to become believers?"

However, just a few pages before, Q9:123, the same Islamic Word of God exhorts the faithful to "make war on the infidels who dwell around you and let them see how harsh you can be." The problem is that the infernal passages in the Quran by far outnumber the ecumenical.

Allah revealed His will to the angels in Q8:12-13, saying: "I shall be with you. Give courage to the believers. I shall cast terror into the hearts of the infidels. *Strike off their heads,* strike off the very tips of their fingers!" That was because they defied Allah and His apostle.

"He that defies Allah and his apostle shall be sternly punished by Allah."

Q8:55: "Lo, the worst of beasts in Allah's sight are the ungrateful who will not believe."

Q8:60: "Muster against them [i.e., non-Muslims] all the men and cavalry at your command, so that you may strike terror into the enemy of Allah and your enemy, and others besides them who are unknown to you but known to Allah. All that you give in the cause of Allah shall be repaid to you. You shall not be wronged."

Q9:28: "Believers, know that the idolaters are unclean."

Q48:29: "Muhammad is Allah's apostle. Those who follow him are ruthless to the unbelievers but merciful to one another."

Allah is described repeatedly in the Quran as a *"schemer"* (Al-Maqer) 8:30. "They schemed, but Allah also schemed. Allah is most profound in his machinations." And Surah 4:101 suggests his people should follow his example: "Be patient with unbelievers until you have strength…"

Be patient? A much smaller dose of political correctness would be more helpful so that real history could speak for itself. For example, most Muslims know that what they describe as *"righteous killing"* regarding the annihilation of the Banu Quraiza was in fact a literal massacre committed by the founder of Islam himself: Muhammad.

Soon after the Battle of the Trench was over, Muhammad claimed that the Archangel Gabriel had visited him "asking that he should unsheathe his sword and head for the habitation of the seditious Banu Quraiza and fight them. Gabriel noted that he with a procession of angels would go ahead to shake their forts and cast fear in their hearts." [15]

Huyai, Ibn Akhtab, the chief of the Bani Nadeer and Safiyah's father was captured in this siege and brought to the Prophet with his hands tied to his neck with a rope. In an audacious defiance, he rejected Muhammad and preferred to be beheaded rather than submit to his Religion by force. He was ordered to sit down and was beheaded on the spot.

The youngsters were examined and if they had grown any pubic hair, it was enough to behead them:

> "I was among the captives of Banu Qurayzah. They (the Companions) examined us, and those who had begun to grow hair (pubes) were killed, and those who had not were not killed. I was among those who had not grown hair." [16]

Banu Al-Mustaliq had a similar fate, especially since Muhammad's army lusted after their women and raped them:

> "We were lusting after women and chastity had become too hard for us, but we wanted to get the ransom money for our prisoners. Therefore, we wanted to use the "Azl" (Coitus Interruptus where the man withdraws before ejaculating)...We asked the Prophet about it and he said: "You are not under any obligation to stop yourselves from doing it like that..." Later on the women and children were given for ransom to their envoys. They all went away to their country and not One wanted to stay although they had the choice..." [17]

Abu Sa'id al-Khudri said:

The Apostle of Allah sent a military expedition to Awtas at the battle of Hunain. They met their enemy and fought with them. They defeated them and took them captives. Some of the Companions of the Apostle of Allah were reluctant to have intercourse with the female captives in the presence of their husbands who were unbelievers. Therefore, Allah, the Exalted, sent down the Quranic verse: *"And all married women (are forbidden) unto you save those (captives) whom your right hand possesses."* [18]

The very same Quran and Sunna that served as the rules of conduct in the seventh century remain the basis for Islamic law today.

> A slave is the property of his/her master. He/She is subject to the master's power, insomuch that if a master should kill his slave he is not liable to retaliation. With female slaves a master has the 'mulk-i-moot' at, or right of enjoyment, and his children by them, when acknowledged, have the same rights and privileges as his chil-

dren by his wives. A slave is incompetent to anything that implies the exercise of authority over others. Hence a slave cannot be a witness, a judge, or an executor or guardian to any but his master and his children. A slave cannot inherit from anyone, and a bequest to him is a bequest to his master.[19]

The attitude of the Muslims toward the Christians and the Jews, according to Islam's founder, is that of a master towards slaves, whom they treat with a certain lordly tolerance so long as they keep their place. Any sign of pretension to equality is promptly repressed.[20]

In Surah 9:

...Fight against such of those who have been given the Scriptures [Jews & Christians] as believe not in Allah nor the last day, and forbid not that which Allah has forbidden by his Messenger and follow not the religion of truth [Islam], until they "pay tribute" (taxes paid by Jews & Christians who do not want to renounce their religion), being brought low...

Then we have the private killings

Abu Musa said, "I came to the *Prophet along with two men of Ash'ariyin, one on my right and the other on my left*, while Allah's Apostle was brushing his teeth, and both men asked him for some employment. The Prophet said, 'O Abu Musa (O 'Abdullah bin Qais!). I said, 'By Him Who sent you with the Truth, these two men did not tell me what was in their hearts and I did not feel (realize) that they were seeking employment.' As if I were looking now at his Siwak (tooth brush) being drawn to a corner under his lips, and he said, 'We never appoint for our affairs anyone who seeks to be employed. But O Abu Musa, go to Yemen.' The Prophet then sent Mu'adh bin Jabal after him and when Mu'adh reached him, he spread out a cushion for him and requested him to get down (and sit on the cushion). Behold: There was a fettered man beside Abu Musa. Mu'adh asked, "Who is this (man)?" Abu Musa said, "He was a Jew and became a Muslim and then reverted back to Judaism." Then Abu Musa requested Mu'adh to sit down but Mu'adh said, "I will not sit down till he has been killed." This is the judgment of Allah and His Apostle [for such cases] and he repeated it three times. Then Abu Musa ordered that the man be killed, and he was killed. Abu Musa added, "Then we discussed the night prayers and one of us said, 'I pray and sleep, and I hope that Allah will reward me for my sleep as well as for my prayers.' [21]

The jihad against the Jews stems from the prophet of Islam himself:

"I have been ordered to fight the people till they say: 'None has the right to be worshiped but Allah,' 'and if they say no, pray our prayers face our Qibla and slaughter as we slaughter, their blood and property will be sacred to us.'" [22]

Throughout the centuries and to this day, the Jews suffered because of the founders of the Islamic faith. The infamous Omar Charter declared:

The necks of Dhimmis (Jews and Christians with no rights in the land) are to be sealed when collecting the Jezzieh (tax imposed on Jews and Christians). The method of sealing is to bind the necks of the person with a collar, in it is a piece of lead, stamped on it the amount of his payment, the collar is not to be broken until the payment is completed. This is in accordance to the Quranic verse 'Until they pay the Jezzieh by an upper hand, may they be subjugated (humiliated)'...And if the person was a Jew, he must wear on his shoulder a red or yellow banner, so he is recognized as a Jew. And if the person is a Christian, he needs to wear harsh clothes, with a large pocket in the chest area like women. As for Christian women, they must wear shoes with different colors, one black and the other white. And if a Jew or a Christian goes into a public bath, he must wear an iron, copper, or lead made collar around his neck so he can be identified from Muslims. Never a Jew or a Christian can build houses higher than a Muslim. They are not to crowd public roads but need to use narrow alley ways, and small streets. They are not to be saluted, nor their graves can be extended beyond the surface of the ground.[23]

Much of Islam's success and prosperity must be credited to the Eastern Jews. It was the oppressed Persian Jews who helped the Muslims to subdue and conquer the Persians. The relationship between the Jews and the Muslims was constantly changing. At the time of Al-Mutawakil, in the beginning of the eighth century, he was very hard on the Jews and Christians alike. The Muslim Caliph Al-Mamun (813-832), and the rest of the Muslim rulers knew how much could be learned from the Jews in their midst. They sought out Jewish physicians, teachers, and merchants. Fleets of trading vessels commanded by Jewish captains were sailing in the Mediterranean. In the beginning of the Ninth Century, the Jews, called the Gaonim, contributed many scholars and schools, and the Bible was translated for the first time into Arabic by a Jew, Saadia ben Joseph (892-942).[24]

Rabbi Menachim ben Saruk compiled and completed the first Bible dictionary. The Gaonim schools flourished until 997 A.D. Hai was the last of the Gaonim; when the Caliph got jealous of the wealth of the Gaonim, he made up some false charges, imprisoned Hai, and his father, and confiscated their wealth. Hai escaped, and a little later, the last attempt made to reconstruct the Gaonim schools failed by Hezekiah. The last Gaonim was executed (1036) by the order of the Caliph. All Jewish schools were closed, and the scholars were scattered. Palestine and the whole of the Byzantine Empire became almost deserted by Jews.[25]

The well-known Orientalist, G.E. von Grunebaum, wrote:

"It would not be difficult to put together the names of a very sizeable number of Jewish subjects or citizens of the Islamic area who have attained to high rank, to power, to great financial influence, to significant and recognized intellectual attainment; and the same could be done for Christians. But it would again not be difficult to compile a lengthy list of persecutions, arbitrary confiscations, attempted forced conversions, or pogroms." [26]

Yet, despite this history, Muslims argue that the Islamic treatment of non-Muslims in general has been good, compared to other religions, even to the point of denying that Islam had anything to do with any Holocaust. The Grand Muslim leader, the Mufti of Jerusalem Ikrima Sabri, stated:

"[the Holocaust] is not my problem. Muslims didn't do anything on this issue. It's the doing of Hitler who hated the Jews." [27]

That, despite that the thriving relationship between the Arab/Muslim world and Nazi Germany was well documented. Sabri's very own predecessor, the Grand Mufti of Jerusalem, Haj Amin Al-Husseni, recruited Hitler's Bosnian-Muslim troops—a unit of the Hanjar (dagger) Division of the Waffen SS, one of eight Nazi divisions. Haj Muhammad Effendi Amin Al-Husseni oversaw the extermination of Orthodox Serbs in Bosnia and in Kosovo. Husseni never stood trial for the genocide of thousands of Orthodox Serbs.[28] And way before Haj Amin, Umar bin Al-Khattab, the Apostle of Muhammad, the founder of Islam, the second Caliph of Islam, and one of the ten promised by the Prophet of Islam to enter paradise, was not the only Muslim leader who instituted harsh measures towards the "heathen" Jews. In many Arab and Islamic countries, Jews had to obey Umar's rule and wear distinctive clothing and even a yellow badge of shame on their shoulders.

In the ninth century, for example, Baghdad's Caliph Al-Mutawakkil designated a yellow badge for Jews, setting a precedent that would be repeated centuries later in Nazi Germany. Harun al-Rashid in 807, Al-Hakim the Fatimid Caliph in 1005, and Emir Ismael Abu-Al-Walid in Granada, from 1315-1326, all enforced this decree ordering Jews to wear yellow markers.

It is amazing that during today's demonstrations, Islamists and the liberal left wave the slogan *Zionism = Nazism,* yet a comparison between Nazi law toward Jews, and Dhimmi Law (Jews and other citizens with no rights) in the Omar Charter will reveal a true commonality:

Nazism: Jews need to wear a mark on their clothing to identify them as Jews. The Star of David for identification with the word (Jude) (must be) on the chest. A yellow banner is to be fixed around the shoulder or arm, as to be recognized as a Jew. They must live in the Jewish Ghettos.

Islam: Dhimmis (Jews & Christians) must wear identifiable clothing and live in a clearly marked house. For Jews, a yellow banner is to be fixed around the shoulder or arm, as to be recognized as a Jew.

Nazism: Jews are not permitted to serve in the army or navy. They are not allowed to bear arms.

Islam: He must not ride a horse or bear arms. He must yield the right-of-way to Muslims.

Nazism: Jews cannot hold public offices, whether national, state, or municipal, salaried or honorary, (they) are closed to Jews. Jews cannot be Judges in criminal and disciplinary cases. Jews cannot serve on juries.

Islam: Dhimmis (Jews & Christians) cannot be a witness in a legal court except in matters relating to other "Dhimmis" (Jews & Christians) or be a judge in a Muslim court.

Nazism: As compensation for the protection that Jews enjoy as aliens, they must pay double the taxes the Germans pay.

Islam: As compensation for the protection that Dhimmis (Jews & Christians) enjoy, they must pay "Jizzieh," a special tax to be imposed on Dhimmis (Jews & Christians) only.

Nazism: Marriage to Jews is prohibited. Adoption of Jews and by Jews is prohibited.

Islam: A Jew cannot be the guardian of a Muslim child, or the owner of a Muslim slave.

Nazism: Jews must live in Ghettos.

Islam: They may not build their houses in the neighborhood of Muslims.[29]

I can hear the argument: the Omar Pact was not part of the Quran or Muhammad (the Sunna). True, Omar was not the author; he derived his covenant from the highest of Islamic sources:

1. The killing of converts (after their three-day warning), came from Muhammad, the prophet of Islam:

"Whoever changes his Islamic religion, kill him."[30]

2. The Quran, 9:29, orders that non-Muslims must be fought until they believe in Islam or pay Al-Jizyah Tax.

"Fight against such of those who have been given the Scripture as believe not in Allah nor the Last Day, and forbid not that which Allah hath forbidden by His messenger, and follow not the Religion of Truth, until they pay the tribute readily, being brought low."

3. Muhammad ordered:

"Allah's Apostle said, 'I have been ordered to fight with the people till they say,' 'None has the right to be worshiped but Allah,' and whoever says, 'None has the right to be worshiped but Allah,' his life and property will be saved by me except for Islamic law, and his accounts will be with Allah, (either to punish him or to forgive him.)'"[31]

4. Muhammad ordered that in a Muslim society, if a Muslim kills a non-Muslim, the Muslim is not put to death:

"No Muslim should be killed for killing a Kafir (infidel)."[32]

5. While a Muslim who kills a Muslim, and a non-Muslim who kills a Muslim, are both to be killed, Q 2:178:

"O ye who believe! the law of equality is prescribed to you in cases of murder: the free for the free, the slave for the slave, the woman for the woman. But if any remission is made by the brother of the slain, then grant any reasonable demand, and compensate him with handsome gratitude, this is a concession and a Mercy from your Lord. After this whoever exceeds the limits shall be in grave penalty."

"Yahya related to me from Malik that he heard that Umar ibn Abd al-Aziz gave a decision that when a Jew or Christian was killed, his blood-money was half the blood-money of a free Muslim."[33]

6. Muhammad practiced and ordered ethnic cleansing by removing all Jews, Christians and pagans from the Arabian Peninsula. In fact, just before his death, he stated:

"While we were in the Mosque, the Prophet came out and said, 'Let us go to the Jews.' We went out till we reached Bait-ul-Midras. He said to them, 'If you embrace Islam, you will be safe. You should know that the earth belongs to Allah and His Apostle, and I want to expel you from this land. So, if anyone amongst you owns some property, he is permitted to sell it, otherwise you should know that the Earth belongs to Allah and His Apostle'"[34]

7. Muslims are ordered to push the non-Muslims to the narrowest part of the road when meeting them:

"Do not initiate the greeting of salaam to a Jew or Christian, and if you meet them in the street, push them to the narrowest part of the road."

In summary from the highest levels of authority in Islam—the Quran, Muhammad, and His apostles— Christians and Jews:

a. Cannot build any new houses of worship in their neighborhoods, and can't repair the ones that fall into ruin

b. Cannot evangelize, and yet they cannot forbid their kin from becoming Muslims

c. Cannot wear clothes that could make them look like Muslims, and they must wear distinguishing clothes

d. Cannot engrave Arabic inscription on their seals

e. Cannot do anything pertaining to their religion publicly (show their crosses or stars, be heard worshipping, etc.)

f. Cannot take slaves who have been allotted to Muslims (the reverse is possible)

g. Cannot build houses overtopping the houses of the Muslims

Hatred has a long history. The Mufti of Jerusalem, Haj Amin Al-Husseni, the good friend of Adolf Hitler, was not original when he publicly stated:

"I declare a holy war, my Muslim brothers! Murder the Jews! Murder them all!"[35]

Neither was he simply a hijacker of the faith. Neither did he see much difference between Islamist goals and Nazi goals. He was always in close contact with the Nazi Party. He had communications with Heinrich Himmler, a good friend of Adolf Hitler, with whom he coordinated the *final solution* for the Jews on November 21, 1941.

It was pure hate, fed from the religious leaders to the schools and through the Arab media. Even the prominent Egyptian writer, Anis Mansour, who is respected by almost every Arab, wrote:

"People all over the world come to realize that Hitler was right, since Jews are bloodsuckers...interested in destroying the whole world which has...expelled them and despised them for centuries...and burnt them in Hitler's crematoria...one million...six million. Would that he had finished it!" [36]

The Führer's puppet, the Grand Mufti who fled Palestine after agitating against the British during the Arab Revolt of 1936-39, found refuge in Iraq after instigating the Iraqi coup of 1941, orchestrated by Hitler. When Britain crushed the rebellion, the Mufti escaped to Berlin. In Berlin, he was enthusiastically received by the "Islamische Zentralinstitut" which welcomed him as the "Führer of the Arabic world." In an introductory speech, he called the Jews the "most fierce enemies of the Muslims" and an "ever corruptive element" in the world.

Husseni soon became an honored guest of the Nazi leadership. He personally lobbied the Führer against the plan to let Jews leave Hungary, fearing they would immigrate to Palestine. He intervened when Adolf Eichman tried to cut a deal with the British government to exchange German POWs for 5000 Jewish children who also could have fled to Palestine. The Mufti's protests with the SS were successful, and the children were instead sent to death camps in Poland. One German officer noted in his journals that the Mufti would like to have seen the Jews "preferably all killed." On a visit to Auschwitz, he reportedly admonished the guards running the gas chambers to work more diligently. Throughout the war, he appeared regularly on German radio broadcasts to the Middle East, preaching his pro-Nazi, anti-Semitic message to the Arab masses back home.

To show gratitude towards his hosts, in 1943 the Mufti traveled several times to Bosnia, where his specially recruited Bosnian troopers slaughtered 90% of Bosnia's Jews and burned countless Serbian churches and villages. These Bosnian Muslim recruits rapidly found favor with Himmler, who established a special Mullah Military school in Dresden. The only condition the Mufti set for his help was that after Hitler won the war, the entire Jewish population in Palestine should be liquidated.[37]

After the war, Husseni fled to Switzerland and from there escaped via France to Cairo, where he was warmly received. The Mufti used funds received earlier from the Hitler regime to finance the Nazi-inspired Arab Liberation Army that terrorized Jews in Palestine. The American-Christian Palestine Committee wrote,

"Of the long list of hundreds of Arab agents on the German payroll, only a few are mentioned. Of the numerous cases of sabotage, only a few are recorded. Of the thousands of available documents, fewer then a dozen are published here."[38]

"The Arab riots of 1936 in Palestine were carried out by the Mufti with funds supplied by the Nazis…"[39]

Even the captured files of the German High Command in Flensburg, Germany, indicated that:

"Only through funds available by Germany to the Grand Mufti of Jerusalem was it possible to carry out the revolt in Palestine."

The Mufti demanded that Hitler; Joachim von Ribbentrop, Hitler's Foreign Minister; and the Bulgarian, Hungarian, and Rumanian governments, keep their promise of the destruction of the so-called Jewish National Home:

"I asked you, Reichsfuhrer, to take all measures to prevent the Jews from going…"

In an October 3, 1994 letter to Himmler, the Mufti offered the Arab Legion for use against the Allies.[40]

The Nazi-Arab connection did not end with Hitler's defeat. Hundreds of former Nazis were allowed to take up residence in Egypt and given positions in the government. The head of the Polish

Gestapo, Leopold Gleim (who had been sentenced to death in absentia), controlled the Egyptian secret police.

Syria's Nazi connection sheltered Alois Brunner, one of the most notorious Nazi war criminals. Brunner was a chief aide to Adolf Eichmann who served as an adviser to the Assad regime.[41]

Today, among the Palestinians, *Hitler is one of the heroes of Palestinian youth*, reveal researchers from the University of Hamburg, conducting an international study on the perceptions of democracy among young people around the world. Booksellers in the territories report that Hitler's book *Mein Kampf* is one of the most popular there. The book is distributed by Al-Shurouq, a Ramallah-based company, to East Jerusalem and the territories controlled by the Palestinian Authority.

According to Agence France Presse, the book, previously banned by Israel, was allowed by the Palestinian Authority. Bisan publishers in Lebanon first published this edition in 1963 and again in 1995. The book costs about $10. The cover shows a picture of Hitler, a swastika, and the title in both German and Arabic.

The translator of Mein Kampf, Luis Al-Haj, wrote the next four paragraphs as part of his introduction:

"Hitler the soldier left behind not only a legend stained by tragedy itself; the tragedy of a state whose dreams were shattered, a regime whose pillars were torn down, and a political party that was crushed. Hitler was a man of ideology who bequeathed an ideological heritage whose decay is inconceivable. This ideological heritage includes politics, society, science, culture, and war as science and culture."

"The National Socialism that Hitler preached for and whose characteristics were presented in his book My Struggle, and whose principles he explained in his speeches before he took power, as well as during the 13 years he spent at the head of the German nation—this National Socialism did not die with the death of its herald. Rather, its seeds multiplied under each star."

"We cannot really understand the efforts of this man without examining the principles enclosed in his book My Struggle that the Nazis turned into the "Gospel of National Socialism.""

"This translation of the book My Struggle has never been presented to Arab speakers. It is taken from the original text of the author, Adolf Hitler. The text was untouched by the censor. We made a point to deliver Hitler's opinions and theories on nationalism, regimes, and ethnicity without any changes because they are not yet outmoded and because we, in the Arab world, still proceed haphazardly in all three fields." [42]

Palestinian journalists are in the habit of comparing Israel's actions in the territories with those of the Nazis. Alongside the anti-Semitic publications, Israeli leaders are portrayed as oppressors. Binyamin Netanyahu, while serving as prime minister, was portrayed as a Nazi and described as *"a Zionist terrorist who is worse than Hitler."* Then Ehud Barak, in Arafat's eyes, was worse than Netanyahu. The Holocaust has become a tool for despicably undermining the Jews in the hands of Palestinian Holocaust deniers:

"It was a good day for the Jews, when the Nazi Hitler began his campaign of persecution against them," writes Sif Ali Algeruan in Al-Hayat Al-Jedida, a Palestinian newspaper:

"They began to disseminate, in a terrifying manner, pictures of mass shootings directed at them, and to invent the shocking story about the gas ovens in which, according to them, Hitler used to burn them. The newspapers are filled with pictures of Jews who were mowed down by Hitler's machine guns, and of Jews being led to the gas ovens. In these pictures they concentrated on women, babies and old people, and they took advantage of it, in order to elicit sympathy towards them, when they demand financial reparations, contributions and grants from all over the world. The truth is that the persecution of the Jews is a myth, that the Jews dubbed 'the tragedy of the Holocaust' and took advantage of, in order to elicit sympathy towards them..."

Even the crossword puzzles that appeared in the newspapers contain definitions such as *"a Jewish center for commemorating the Holocaust and the lie,"* as a clue for Yad Vashem.

"Some of them go hand in glove with the Holocaust deniers," says Esti Vebman, researcher of anti-Semitism. "It is true that there have been of late intellectual circles that are willing to agree that such a historical incident, like the Holocaust, did indeed happen, but from the deniers' point of view there were no gas chambers and no six million who died."

"Clearly, it was the Arab Nazi-like bursts of brutality, and mass extradition of the Jews from all the Arab lands, which forced the Jews to immigrate to Israel. In fact, the irony is that it was the Nazi and Arab hatred of the Jews that caused the creation of Israel. Out of more than 850,000 Jews in Arab lands, fewer than 29,000 remained, forced to leave to Israel." [43]

Sadly, Nazism, now in religious garb, was again awaiting them. The difference this time was that the Jews had control over this tiny spot of land, while a hostile world surrounded them.

CONFESSION—THE MYTH OF A GOLDEN AGE

Argument:

"Jews and other Christian minorities lived a decent life in the Arab Muslim world. The Golden Age of Islam is coined after an era of enlightenment."

Response:

It is true that there were times in the past when Muslim societies reached higher levels of civilization and culture than they did at other times. Yet what Islam's apologists claim is a stretch of the imagination. Islam has never produced a democratic or prosperous society, or social and cultural forms admired by the world community. Indeed, we have nothing in Islamic societies to compare to American freedom. Even in the supposed past Golden Days, in Baghdad under Harun al-Rashid

> ...the whole Gaza region up to Caesarea was sacked and devastated in the campaign of 634. Four thousand Jewish, Christian, and Samaritan peasants who defended their land were massacred. The villages of the Negev were pillaged...Towns such as Jerusalem, Gaza, Jaffa,

Caesarea, Nablus, and Beth Shean were isolated and closed their gates. In his sermon on Christmas day 634, the patriarch of Jerusalem, Sophronius, lamented...that the Christians were being forcibly kept in Jerusalem: '...chained and nailed by fear of the Saracens,' whose 'savage, barbarous and bloody sword' kept them locked up in the town...Sophronius, in his sermon on the Day of the Epiphany 636, bewailed the destruction of the churches and monasteries, the sacked towns, the fields laid waste, the villages burned down by the nomads who were overrunning the country. In a letter the same year to Sergius, the patriarch of Constantinople, he mentions the ravages wrought by the Arabs. Thousands of people perished in 639, victims of the famine and plague that resulted from these destructions.[44]

Both Harun al-Rashid (786-809) and al-Mutawwakil (847-861) have not practiced democracy or freedom of any kind. The respected author, Bat Ye'or, summarizes the oppression of the *Dhimmis* throughout the Abbasid Empire under al-Mutawwakil as

"...a wave of religious persecution, forced conversions, and the elimination of churches and synagogues..."[45]

Harun al-Rashid's persecution and killing of Christians is well documented. The isolated episodes against Muslims in Spain in Cordova are endlessly invoked by Islam's Western apologists, and hardly stand against the volumes of historic persecution of Christians.

The Abbasids absorbed the Syrian and Persian cultures and government by which they transmitted Greek, Hindu, and other pre-Islamic fruits of knowledge to Westerners. Yet, even these were not all Muslim; Moses Maimonides was a Jew who documented Islamic persecution. Constantine "the African," was a Christian and a native of *Carthage.*

This so-called "Golden-Age" has come from non-Muslim sources. Al-Kindi, al-Farabi, and Avicenna were all Persian and greatly influenced by Baghdad's Greek heritage. Al-Farabi was considered a heretic by the Islamists of his time since he questioned the authority of the Quran. There was much persecution and killing of philosophers whose beliefs did not conform to the Quran.

The problem with turning this list of intellectual achievements into a convincing 'Islamic Golden Age' is that whatever flourished did so not because of Islam, but in spite of it.

"Muslims overran societies (Persian, Greek, Egyptian, Byzantine, Syrian, Jewish) that possessed intellectual sophistication in their own right and failed to destroy their cultures. To give Islam the credit for what the remnants of these cultures achieved is like crediting the Red Army for the survival of Chopin in Warsaw in 1970. Islam per se never encouraged science, in the sense of disinterested inquiry, because the only knowledge it accepts is religious belief." [46]

Furthermore, the intellectual achievements of Islam's 'Golden Age' were of limited value. There was a lot of speculation and very little application, be it in technology or politics. To the present day, for almost a thousand years, even the speculation has stopped, and the bounds of what is considered orthodox Islam have frozen, except when they contracted, as in the case of Wahabism. Those who try to push the fundamentals of Muslim thought any further into the light of modernity frequently pay for it with their lives. The fundamentalists who ruled Afghanistan until recently and still rule in Iran hold up the their supposed Golden Age as a model for their people and as a justification for their tyranny. Westerners should know better. [47]

The classical Muslim jurist al-Mawardi (a Shafi'ite jurist, d. 1058) from Baghdad was a seminal, prolific scholar who lived during the so-called Islamic "Golden Age" of the Abbasid-Baghdadian Caliphate. He wrote the following, based on widely accepted interpretations of the Quran and Sunna (i.e., the recorded words and deeds of Muhammad), regarding infidel prisoners of jihad campaigns:

As for the captives, the emir [ruler] has the choice of taking the most beneficial action of four possibilities: the first to put them to death by cutting their necks; the second, to enslave them and apply the laws of slavery regarding their sale and manumission; the third, to ransom them in exchange for goods or prisoners; and fourth, to show favor to them and pardon them. Indeed such odious "rules" were iterated by all four classical schools of Islamic jurisprudence, across the vast Muslim empire.

CONFESSION—WE HATED THE JEWS LONG BEFORE THE STATE OF ISRAEL WAS CREATED

Argument:

"There was no hatred of Jews in the Arab-Muslim world. It's only after the occupation and the creation of the state of Israel."

Response:

The following histories from the "Jews in Arab countries: Before and after 1948," Historical Society of Jews From Egypt online, presents the facts about Jewish persecution centuries before the modern state of Israel was created.

THE PERSECUTION OF JEWS IN ARABIA PRIOR TO 1948

The rise of Islamism, with whose power the Arabian Jews came in contact when it was yet in its infancy, marks the beginning of a new period in Jewish history. Several centuries before Muhammad's birth (C.570), the Jews had effected important settlements in Arabia, and in the course of time, they had acquired a considerable influence upon the heathen population. In fact, in Yemen, an Arab-Jewish kingdom existed. The Arabian Jews were numerous and powerful, in the Hedjaz, north of Yemen. To win the Israelites to his cause, the "Prophet" made various concessions to their religion and adopted some of their customs. As this was useless, and as the Jews were a constant menace to his cause, he resolved to get rid of their tribes one after another. He first put an end to the Jews near Medina, and next (628) subjected those of the district of Khaibar and of Wadi al-Kura.

The Jewish community in Arabia was totally destroyed or extradited from Saudi Arabia in barbaric fashion by Muhammad, the originator of Islam. Banu Qurayza were all killed and the women and children became loot, and much of the other tribes like Banu Qaynuqa, and Al-Natheer were either killed, sold to slavery, or extradited. The Jews in Saudi Arabia were accused of treason, and in a few days, trenches were dug in the market-place in Medina, and the men of Qurayza were brought out in groups and their necks were struck. Estimates of those killed vary from 400 to 900:

Abu 'Ubayda told me on the authority of Abu 'Amr, the Medinan, when the apostle got the better of the Banu (tribe of) Qurayza he seized about four hundred men from the Jews who had been allies of Aus against Khazraj, and ordered that they should be beheaded. Accordingly Khazraj began to cut off their heads with great satisfaction. The apostle saw that the faces of Khazraj showed their pleasure, but there was no such indication on the part of Aus, and he suspected that that was because of the alliance that had existed between them and the B. Qurayza. When there were only twelve of them left he gave them over to Aus, assigning one Jew to every two of Aus, saying, 'Let so-and-so strike him and so-and-so finish him off.' One of those who was so handed over to them was Ka'b b. Yahudha, who was an important man among them. He gave him to Muhayyisa and Abu Burda b. Niyar (it was Abu Burda to whom the apostle had given permission to sacrifice a young goat on the feast of Adha). He said, 'Let Muhayyisa strike him and Abu Burda finish him off.' So Muhayyisa fetched him a blow, which did not cut in properly, and Abu Burda dispatched him and gave him the finishing stroke. Huwayyisa, who was still an unbeliever, said to his brother, Muhayyisa, 'Did you kill Ka'b b. Yahudha?', and when he said he did, he said, 'By God, much of the flesh on your belly comes from his wealth; you are a miserable fellow, Muhayyisa.' He replied, 'If the one who ordered me to kill him had ordered me to kill you, I would have done so.' He was amazed at this remark and went away astounded. They say that he used to wake up in the night astonished at his brother's words, until in the morning he said, 'By God, this is indeed a religion.' Then he came to the prophet and accepted Islam. Muhayyisa then spoke the lines which we have written above.[48]

[The writings of Al-Kindy (circa 830 A.D.) give us a picture of Muhammad's killings of Jews:]

Abu Afek was also a Jew. This last was an aged man, decrepit and helpless, whom Ibn Omeir perfidiously stabbed to death while asleep at night upon his bed, because he had spoken despitefully of thy Master. Tell me, now, I pray thee, whether thou hast anywhere heard or read of so unjustifiable an act. Hath any revelation ever sanctioned it; and what kind of ordinance is this, to slay a man simply for speaking of blame? Had this aged man done anything worthy at all of death, much less of being assassinated unawares? If he spake the truth, should he have been slain for the same? And if he lied, still even for that, one is not to be put to death, but rather chastised that he may in time to come refrain therefrom. My friend, thou well knowest (the Lord be gracious unto thee!) how that it is unlawful to disturb a bird resting in its little nest by night; how much more to slay a man, sleeping securely in his bed, and that for only speaking words of blame! Is this aught but murder? I find not that such an act is justified either by the law of God, of reason, or of nature. Nay, by my life! It is but the old work of Satan towards Adam and his race ever since he wrought his fall. And how consisteth all this with the saying of thine (the Lord guide thee aright, my friend!) that thy Master 'was sent a Blessing and a Mercy to all mankind.' [49]

The killing of the men went on day and night; one by one was beheaded and thrown into a ditch. The women were split among the Muslims; Muhammad the prophet of Islam had (Zaynab), the wife of the tribe's leader, after he killed her husband and her brother, he took his "God given" trophy on the same night.

Like Christendom in Europe under the banner of Christianity, Muhammad destroyed the Jews under the banner of religion. Muslims simply write off these atrocities with the same excuses used by everyone who hated the Jews; they used mock trials and accused them of treason. The excuses presented by the Hadith is the typical one, a Jew was chosen "Sa'd b. Mu'adh" to pass judgment, and the death penalty was given, so the Jew was blamed.

Then and as it is now, Holocaust deniers and Muslim apologists blame the Jews for "inventing" the story: "His contemporary, the early jurist, Malik, called him [Ibn Ishaq] unequivocally 'a liar' and 'an impostor'...who transmits his stories from the Jews." [50]

THE ARMENIAN HOLOCAUST

During 1894-1923, the Ottoman Empire conducted a policy of genocide of the Christian population living within its extensive territory. The Sultan, Abdul Hamid, began the program in 1894. When WWI broke out, the Ottoman Empire was ruled by the "Young Turk" dictatorship that allied itself with Germany. The Turkish government decided to eliminate the whole of the Christian population of Greeks, Armenians, Syrians and Nestorians.

In 1915, Talaiat Basha, the Minister of Interior in the Ottoman government sent an order to the Governor of the city of Halab Nuri Bek:

Despite a previous decision concerning the elimination of the Armenian Race, as the necessities of time did not allow the fulfillment of this holy intent, and now, after we eliminated all obstacles, and seeing that the time has come to redeem our nation from the dangerous race, we have entrusted you, and we insist, that you do not surrender yourselves to the feelings of pity, as you face their miserable situation. For the cause of putting an end to their existence, you need to work with all your strength, to completely destroy the Armenian name in Turkey, once and for all.[51]

Following this order, one and a half million Armenians were butchered in an effort to destroy Christianity in an Islamic Ottomon Empire. If anything, Christians who are looking for the "*blood of the Martyrs of Jesus*" in the 20th century should look no further. Islam by far has killed more Christians in our era then the world killed in the last two millennia combined. It is estimated that over 10,000,000 people were killed by Jihad-style genocide from 1915-2003.

THE PERSECUTION OF THE JEWS IN PALESTINE PRIOR TO 1948

Arab terrorism in the Holy Land originated centuries before the recent "tool" of the Palestinian cause was invented. Towns where Jews lived for hundreds of years [saw their people] periodically robbed, raped, and massacred. The survivors were obliged to abandon their possessions and run. At the beginning of this century, the presence of Jews was recorded in nearly every town that today is considered to have been "purely Arab." Jewish refugees were forced to flee from their homes within Palestine to other areas. David Landes in Palestine Before the Zionists writes:

"Jews had to pass Muslims on their left side, because that was the side of Satan. They had to yield the right of way, step off the pavement to let the Arab go by, above all make sure not to touch him in passing, because this could provoke a violent response. In the same way, anything that reminded the Muslims of the presence of alternative religions, any demonstration of alternative forms of worship, had to be avoided, so synagogues were in humble, hidden places, and the sounds of Jewish prayers carefully muted."

Historian Frank DeHass writes: "Murad III decreed that all Jews throughout his empire be executed," this decree was prevented by Solomon Ashkenazi, Murad's confidential agent. In 1576 Sultan Murad III enacted legislation to uproot and deport 1000 of the 15,000 Safed's Jews to Cyprus.

In the 16th century in Jerusalem, the Jews were taxed to the point of extortion and most of Jerusalem's Jews ran to Hebron, Gaza, and Tiberius to become refugees. Bedouin raiders, general anarchy, tax corruption, and an additional tax burden were aimed solely at the Jews, yet they held steadfast in Judah-cum-Palestine. The Jerusalem Jews were bitterly and mercilessly persecuted during the 17th century reign of an Arab ruler, Ibn Barouk, who bought the rule from Murad IV. In 1660, Arabs massacred the entire Jewish community leaving a single survivor.

DeHass tells us, "we don't know for sure how Ahmad Basha El-Jazzar [The Butcher] got his name, but it isn't hard to figure out. His sadistic, wanton exploits became a legend during the 1800s, and he was known to travel accompanied by an executioner. When The Butcher encountered a subject who was judged to be misbehaving, 'The criminal bowed his neck, the executioner struck, and the head fell.'"

Hayim Farhi, the only Jew who had risen to power in the area, was imprisoned by The Butcher, [who cut off] his nose, ear, and [and gouged] out his eye. The Jews had to pay to pray at the Wailing Wall, to pay protection money to safeguard against the destruction and vandalism of the Jewish burial grounds, and to prevent molestation of Jewish travelers.

In the 1830s, there was havoc during the Egyptian reign of Palestine, and the Jews were brutally persecuted throughout the country. In 1834, the inhabitants of Eastern Palestine crossed the Jordan River to join natives of Nablus, Hebron, and Bethlehem; 40,000 of them rushed on Jerusalem and looted the city for five days where the Jews had their homes sacked and their women raped.[52]

The Jewish story in Palestine was like the story of a rape victim, blamed for being there at the time. In the following few decades (1848-1878) scores of incidents involving anti-Jewish violence, persecution, and extortions filled page after page of documented reports from the British Consulate in Jerusalem too overwhelming to show in these pages.]

Throughout the 19th century, Jews were victims of mass hunger and of Arab attacks. The 1929 Arab riots resulted in the rape and massacre of most of Hebron's Jewish community.

Later Muftism, by Haj Amin Al-Husseni, who initiated fatwas (religious decrees) against all the Jews as a response to the Zionist movement. His collaboration with Hitler on the eve of The Final Solution left an everlasting mark on the history of Muftism in The Holy Land. Letters of collaboration with Heinrich Himmler and the Hungarian Prime Minister resulted in the death of 400,000 Jews when he succeeded in stopping them from emigrating to the Holy Land. Until now, no apology, hearing, or condemnation has ever been made by any Arab government or religious official.

THE PERSECUTION OF JEWS IN MOROCCO PRIOR TO 1948

The Jewish community of present-day Morocco dates back more than 2,000 years. There were Jewish colonies in the country before it became a Roman province. In 1032 AD, 6,000 Jews were murdered. In fact, the greatest persecution by the Arabs towards the Jews was in Fez, Morocco: the slaughter of 120,000 Jews in 1146 and 1160. Maimonides, the great Jewish physician and thinker, in his Epistle concerning apostasy, writes his fellow Jews:

"Now we are asked to render the active homage to heathenism but only to recite an empty formula which the Muslims themselves knew we utter insincerely in order to circumvent the bigot...indeed, any Jew who, after uttering the Muslim formula, wishes to observe the whole 613 precepts in the privacy of his home, may do so without hindrance. Nevertheless, if, even under circumstances, a Jew surrenders his life for the sanctification of the name of God before men, he has done nobly and his reward is great before the Lord. But if a man asked me, 'shall I be slain or utter the formula of Islam?' I answer, 'utter the formula and live...'"[53]

In 1391, a wave of Jewish refugees expelled from Spain brought new life to the community, as did new arrivals from Spain and Portugal in 1492 and 1497. From 1438, the Jews of Fez were forced to live in special quarters called mellahs, a name derived from the Arabic word for salt, because the Jews in Morocco were forced to carry out the job of salting the heads of executed prisoners prior to their public display.

In 1465, Arab mobs in Fez slaughtered thousands of Jews, leaving only eleven alive, after a Jewish deputy vizier was accused of treating a Muslim woman in *"an offensive manner."* The killings touched off a wave of similar massacres throughout Morocco.

Andrè Chouraqui, noted political, religious, and literary figure, summed up the Jewish plight in general when he wrote: "such restriction and humiliation as to exceed anything in Europe."

In 1883, Charles de Foucauld, who was not generally sympathetic to Jews, said of them: "They are the most unfortunate of men, every Jew belongs body and soul to his seigneur, the sid [Arab master]."

THE PERSECUTION OF JEWS IN MOROCCO AFTER 1948

Centuries later, Morocco was still killing Jews. In June 1948, bloody riots in Oujda and Djerada killed 44 Jews and wounded scores more. That same year, an unofficial economic boycott was instigated against Moroccan Jews.

Morocco declared its independence in 1956, and Jewish emigration to Israel was suspended. In 1963, emigration resumed, allowing more than 100,000 Moroccan Jews to reach Israel.

In 1965, Moroccan writer Said Ghallab described the attitude of his fellow Muslims toward their Jewish neighbors:

"The worst insult that a Moroccan could possibly offer was to treat someone as a Jew...My childhood friends have remained anti-Jewish. They hide their virulent anti-Semitism by contending that the state of Israel was the creature of Western imperialism. A whole Hitlerite myth is being cultivated among the populace. The massacres of the Jews by Hitler are exalted ecstatically. It is even credited that Hitler is not dead, but alive and well, and his arrival is awaited to deliver the Arabs from Israel." [54]

THE PERSECUTION OF JEWS IN YEMEN PRIOR TO 1948

In Yemen, from the seventh century on, the Jewish population suffered the severest possible interpretation of the Charter of Omar. For about four centuries, the Jews suffered under the fierce fanatical edict of the most intolerant Islamic sects. In the Yemen Epistle by Rambam (Maimonides), he commiserated with Yemen's Jewry and besought them to keep the faith, but in 1724 fanatical rulers ordered synagogues destroyed, and Jewish public prayers forbidden. The Jews were exiled, many died from starvation and the survivors were ordered to settle in Mausa, but later, this order was annulled by a decree in 1781 only because of the need of their skilled craftsmen. Jacob Sappir, a Jerusalem writer describes Yemeni Jews in 1886:

"The Arab natives have always considered the Jew unclean, but his blood for them was not considered unclean. They lay claims to all his belongings, and if he is unwilling, they employ force...The Jews live outside the town in dark dwellings like prison cells or caves out of fear for the least offense, he is sentenced to outrageous fines, which he is quite unable to pay. In case of non-payment, he is put in chains and cruelly beaten every day. Before the punishment is inflicted, the Cadi [judge] addresses him in gentle tones and urges him to change his faith and obtain a share of all the glory of this world and of the world beyond. His refusal is again regarded as penal obstinacy. On the other hand, it is not open to the Jew to prosecute a Muslim, as the Muslim by right of law can dispose of the life and the property of the Jew, and it is only to be regarded as an act of magnanimity if the Jews are allowed to live. The Jew is not admissible as a witness, nor has his oath any validity."[55]

Danish-German explorer Garsten Neibuhr visited Yemen in 1762 and described Jewish life in Yemen:

"By day they work in their shops in San'a, but by night they must withdraw to their isolated dwellings, shortly before my arrival, 12 of the 14 synagogues of the Jews were torn down, and all their beautiful houses wrecked."[56]

The Jews' lives did not improve until the establishment of the French Protectorate in 1912, when they were granted equality and religious autonomy. However, during World War II, when the anti-Semitic Vichy government ruled France, King Muhammad V prevented the deportation of Jews from Morocco.

In A History of Israel, Howard Sachar tells us that in 1922, the government of Yemen reintroduced an ancient Islamic law that decreed that Jewish orphans under age 12 were to be forcibly converted to Islam. In 1947, after the partition vote, Muslim rioters, joined by the local police force, engaged in a bloody pogrom in Aden that killed 82 Jews and destroyed hundreds of Jewish homes. Aden's Jewish community was economically paralyzed, as most of the Jewish stores and businesses were destroyed. Early in 1948, looting occurred after six Jews were falsely accused of the ritual murder of two Arab girls.

By 1948, there were some 270,000 Jews in Morocco. In an atmosphere of uncertainty and grinding poverty, many Jews elected to leave for Israel, France, the United States, and Canada.

Finally, nearly 50,000 traditionally religious Yemeni Jews, who had never seen a plane, were airlifted to Israel in 1949 and 1950 in Operation "Magic Carpet." As the Book of Isaiah promised, "They shall mount up with wings, as eagles." The Jewish community boarded *The Eagles* contentedly; to the pilots consternation some of them lit a bon fire aboard to cook their food.

THE PERSECUTION OF THE JEWS IN TUNISIA PRIOR TO 1948

The first documented evidence of Jews in this area dates back to 200 A.D. and demonstrates the existence of a community in Latin Carthage under Roman rule. Latin Carthage contained a significant Jewish presence, and several sages mentioned in the Talmud lived in this area from the second to the 4th centuries.

During the Byzantine period, the condition of the community took a turn for the worse. An edict issued by Justinian in 535 excluded Jews from public office, prohibited Jewish practice, and resulted in the transformation of synagogues into churches. Many fled to the Berber communities in the mountains and in the desert.

After the Arab conquest of Tunisia in the 7th century, Jews lived under satisfactory conditions, despite discriminatory measures such as a poll tax. From the seventh century Arab conquest down through the Almahdiyeen atrocities, Tunisia fared little better than its neighbors. The complete expulsion of Jews from Kairouan near Tunis occurred after years of hardship in the 13th century when Kairouan was anointed as a holy city of Islam.

In the 16th century, the "hated and despised" Jews of Tunis were periodically attacked by violence and they were subjected to "vehement anti-Jewish policy" during the various political struggles of the period. In 1869, Muslims butchered many Jews in the defenseless ghetto.

Conditions worsened during the Spanish invasions of 1535-1574, resulting in the flight of Jews from the coastal areas. The situation of the community improved once more under Ottoman rule.

During this period, the community split due to strong cultural differences between the Touransa (native Tunisians) and the Grana (those adhering to Spanish or Italian customs). Improvements in the condition of the community occurred during the reign of Ahmed Bey, which began in 1837. He and his successors implemented liberal legislation, and a large number of Jews rose to positions of political power during this reign.

Under French rule, Jews were gradually emancipated. However, beginning in November 1940, when the Vichy authorities ruled the country, Jews were subjected to harsh anti-Semitic laws. From November 1942 until May 1943, German forces occupied the country. During that time, the condition of the Jews deteriorated, and many were deported to labor camps and had their property seized.

Jews suffered once more in 1956, after Israel achieved independence. The rabbinical tribunal was abolished in 1957, and a year later, Jewish community councils were dissolved. In addition, the Jewish quarter of Tunis was destroyed by the government. Anti-Jewish rioting followed the outbreak of the Six-Day War; Muslims burned down the Great Synagogue of Tunis. While the community was compensated for the damage, these events increased the steady stream of emigration.

THE PERSECUTION OF JEWS IN LIBYA PRIOR TO 1948

The Jewish community of Libya traces its origin back to the 3rd century B.C. Under Roman rule, Jews prospered. In 73 A.D., a zealot from Israel, Jonathan the Weaver, incited the poor of the community in Cyrene to revolt. The Romans reacted with swift vengeance, murdering him and his followers and executing other wealthy Jews in the community. This revolt foreshadowed that of 115 A.D., which broke out not only in Cyrene, but in Egypt and Cyprus as well.

In 1785, Ali Burzi Pasha murdered hundreds of Jews.

With the Italian occupation of Libya in 1911, the situation remained good and the Jews made great strides in education. At that time, there were about 21,000 Jews in the country, the majority in Tripoli. In the late 1930s, Fascist anti-Jewish laws were gradually enforced, and Jews were subjected to terrible repression. Still, by 1941, the Jews accounted for a quarter of the population of Tripoli and maintained 44 synagogues. In 1942, the Germans occupied the Jewish quarter of Benghazi, plundered shops, and deported more than 2,000 Jews across the desert, where more than one-fifth of them perished. Many Jews from Tripoli were sent to forced labor camps.

Conditions did not improve much following the liberation. During the British occupation, there was a series of pogroms, the worst of which, in 1945, resulted in the deaths of more than 100 Jews in Tripoli and other towns and the destruction of five synagogues.

The establishment of the state of Israel encouraged many Jews to leave the country.

Sachar notes that a savage pogrom in Tripoli on November 5, 1945 left 140 Jews massacred and almost every synagogue looted.

In June 1948, rioters murdered another 12 Jews and destroyed 280 Jewish homes. Thousands of Jews fled the country after Libya was granted independence and membership in the Arab League in 1951.[57]

After the Six-Day War, the Jewish population of 7,000 was again subjected to pogroms in which 18 were killed, and many more injured, sparking a near-total exodus that left fewer than 100 Jews in Libya. When Col. Qaddafi came to power in 1969, all Jewish property was confiscated and all debts to Jews cancelled. It is believed that no Jews live in Libya today.

THE PERSECUTION OF JEWS IN ALGERIA PRIOR TO 1948

Jewish settlement in present-day Algeria can be traced back to the first centuries of the Common Era. In the 14th century, with the deterioration of conditions in Spain, many Spanish Jews moved to Algeria. Among them were a number of outstanding scholars, including those known as the Ribash and the Rashbatz. After the French occupation of the country in 1830, Jews gradually adopted French culture and were granted French citizenship.

On the eve of the civil war that gripped the country in the late 1950s, there were some 130,000 Jews in Algeria, approximately 30,000 of whom lived in the capital. Nearly all Algerian Jews fled the country shortly after it gained independence from France in 1962. Most of the remaining Jews live in Algiers, but there are individual Jews in Oran and Blida. A single synagogue functions in Algiers, although there is no resident rabbi. All other synagogues were taken over for use as mosques.

In 1934, a Nazi-incited pogrom in Constantine left 25 Jews dead and scores injured. After being granted independence in 1962, the Algerian government harassed the Jewish community and deprived

Jews of their principle economic rights. As a result, almost 130,000 Algerian Jews immigrated to France. Since 1948, 25,681 Algerian Jews have immigrated to Israel.

THE PERSECUTION OF JEWS IN SYRIA PRIOR TO 1948

The last Jews who wanted to leave Syria departed with the chief rabbi in October 1994. Prior to 1947, there were some 30,000 Jews made up of three distinct communities, each with its own traditions: the Kurdish-speaking Jews of Kamishli, the Jews of Aleppo with roots in Spain, and the original eastern Jews of Damascus, called Must'arab. Today only a tiny remnant of these communities remains.

The Jewish presence in Syria dates back to Biblical times and is intertwined with the history of Jews in neighboring Eretz Israel. With the advent of Christianity, restrictions were imposed on the community. The Arab conquest in 636 A.D., however, greatly improved the lot of the Jews. Unrest in neighboring Iraq in the 10th century resulted in Jewish migration to Syria and brought about a boom in commerce, banking, and crafts. During the reign of the Fatimids, the Jew Menashe Ibrahim El-Kazzaz ran the Syrian administration, and he granted Jews positions in the government.

Syrian Jewry supported the aspirations of the Arab nationalists and Zionism, and Syrian Jews believed that the two parties could be reconciled and that the conflict in Palestine could be resolved. However, following Syrian independence from France in 1946, attacks against Jews and their property increased, culminating in the pogroms of 1947, which left all shops and synagogues in Aleppo in ruins. Thousands of Jews fled the country, and their homes and property were taken over by the local Muslims.

For the next decades, Syrian Jews were, in effect, hostages of a hostile regime. They could leave Syria only on the condition that they leave members of their family behind. Thus, the community lived under siege, constantly under fearful surveillance of the secret police. Due to an international effort to secure the human rights of the Jews, the changing world order, and the Syrian need for Western support. the conditions of the Jews improved somewhat.

THE PERSECUTION OF THE JEWS IN EGYPT PRIOR TO 1948

Jews have lived in Egypt since Biblical times, and the conditions of the community have constantly fluctuated with the political situation of the land. Israelite tribes first moved to the Land of Goshen (the northeastern edge of the Nile Delta) during the reign of the Egyptian pharaoh Amenhotep IV (1375-1358 B.C.).

During the reign of Ramses II (1298-1232 B.C.), they were enslaved for the Pharaoh's building projects. His successor, Merneptah, continued the same anti-Jewish policies, and around the year 1220 B.C., the Jews revolted and escaped across the Sinai to Canaan.

This is the great Biblical Exodus commemorated by Jews on the holiday of Passover. Over the years, many Jews in Eretz Israel who were not deported to Babylon sought shelter in Egypt, among them the prophet Jeremiah. By 1897, there were more than 25,000 Jews in Egypt, concentrated in Cairo and Alexandria. In 1937, the population reached a peak of 63,500.

Pulitzer Prize winning commentator Thomas Friedman wrote in The Myth of Arab Tolerance,

"One Caliph, Al-Hakem of the Fatimids devised particularly insidious humiliations for the Jews in his attempt to perform what he deemed his roll as "Redeemer of mankind," first the Jews were forced to wear miniature golden calf images around their necks, as though they still worshiped the golden calf, but the Jews refused to convert. Next, they wore bells, and after that six pound wooden blocks were hung around their necks. In fury at his failure, the Caliph had the Cairo Jewish quarter destroyed, along with its Jewish residents."

In 1945, with the rise of Egyptian nationalism and the cultivation of anti-Western and anti-Jewish sentiment, riots erupted. In the violence, 10 Jews were killed, 350 injured, and a synagogue, a Jewish hospital, and an old-age home were burned down. The establishment of the state of Israel led to further anti-Jewish hostility: Between June and November 1948, bombs set off in the Jewish Quarter killed more than 70 Jews and wounded nearly 200. Two thousand Jews were arrested and many had their property confiscated. Rioting over the next few months resulted in many more Jewish deaths. Between June and

November 1948, bombs set off in the Jewish Quarter killed more than 70 Jews and wounded nearly 200.

In 1956, the Egyptian government used the Sinai Campaign as a pretext for expelling almost 25,000 Egyptian Jews and confiscating their property. Approximately 1,000 more Jews were sent to prisons and detention camps. On November 23, 1956, a proclamation signed by the Minister of Religious Affairs, and read aloud in mosques throughout Egypt, declared, "...all Jews are Zionists and enemies of the state," and promised that they would be soon expelled.

Thousands of Jews were ordered to leave the country. They were allowed to take only one suitcase and a small sum of cash, and forced to sign declarations "donating" their property to the Egyptian government. Foreign observers reported that members of Jewish families were taken hostage, apparently to insure that those forced to leave did not speak out against the Egyptian government.[58]

By 1957, the Jewish population had fallen to 15,000. In 1967, after the Six-Day War, there was a renewed wave of persecution, and the community dropped to 2,500. By the 1970s, after the remaining Jews were given permission to leave the country, the community dwindled to a few families. Jewish rights were finally restored in 1979 after President Anwar Sadat signed the Camp David Accords with Israel. Only then was the community allowed to establish ties with Israel and with world Jewry. In 1979, the Egyptian Jewish community became the first in the Arab world to establish official contact with Israel. The majority of Jews reside in Cairo, but there is still a handful in Alexandria. In addition, there are about 15 Karaites in the community. Nearly all the Jews are elderly, and the community is on the verge of extinction.

In 1979, the Egyptian Jewish community became the first in the Arab world to establish official contact with Israel.

THE PERSECUTION OF JEWS IN IRAN/PERSIA PRIOR TO 1948

The Jewish community of Persia, modern-day Iran, is one of the oldest in the Diaspora, and its historical roots reach back to the 6th century BC, the time of the First Temple. Their history in the pre-

Islamic period is intertwined with that of the Jews of neighboring Babylon.

Cyrus, the first Achaemid emperor, conquered Babylon in 539 BC, and permitted by special decree the return of the Jewish exiles to the Land of Israel; this ended the First Exile. The Jewish colonies were scattered from centers in Babylon to Persian provinces and cities such as Hamadan and Susa.

The books of Esther, Ezra, Nehemiah, and Daniel give a favorable description of the relationship of the Jews to the court of the Achaemids at Susa.

Under the Sassanid dynasty (226-642 A.D.), the Jewish population in Persia grew considerably and spread throughout the region, yet Jews nevertheless suffered intermittent oppression and persecution. The invasion by Arab Muslims in 642 A.D. terminated the independence of Persia, installed Islam as the state religion, and made a deep impact on the Jews by changing their sociopolitical status.

Throughout the 19th century, Jews were persecuted and discriminated against. Sometimes whole communities were forced to convert. There was considerable emigration to the Land of Israel, and the Zionist movement spread throughout the community.

In 1925, under the Pahlevi Dynasty, the country was secularized and oriented towards the West. This greatly benefited the Jews who were emancipated and who then played an important role in the economy and in cultural life. On the eve of the Islamic Revolution in 1979, there were 80,000 Jews in Iran, concentrated in Teheran (60,000), Shiraz (8,000), Kermanshah (4,000), Isfahan (3,000), and in the cities of Kuzistahn. In the wake of the upheaval, tens of thousands of Jews, especially the wealthy, left the country, leaving behind vast amounts of property.

THE PERSECUTION OF JEWS IN IRAQ PRIOR TO 1948

The Iraqi Jews took pride in their distinguished Jewish community, with its history of scholarship and achievement. Jews had prospered in what was then Babylonia for 1200 years before the Muslim conquest in 634 A.D.; it was not until the 9th century that Dhimmi laws such as the yellow patch, heavy per head tax, and residence restrictions were enforced. Capricious and extreme oppression under some Arab caliphs and Momlukes brought taxation amounting to expropriation in 1000 A.D., and in 1333, the persecution culminated in pillage and destruction of the Baghdad Sanctuary. In 1776, there was a slaughter of Jews at Bozrah, and bitterness with anti-Jewish measures taken by Turkish Muslim rulers in the 18th century caused many Jews to flee.

The Iraqi Jewish community is one of the oldest in the world and has a great history of learning. Abraham, the father of the Jewish people, was born in Ur of the Chaldees, in southern Iraq, around 2,000 B.C. The community traces its history back to 6th century AD, when Nebuchadnezzar conquered Judea and sent most of the population into exile in Babylonia.

The community also maintained strong ties with the Land of Israel and, with the aid of rabbis from Israel, succeeded in establishing many prominent rabbinical academies. By the 3rd century, Babylonia became the center of Jewish scholarship, as is attested to by the community's most influential creation, the Babylonian Talmud.

Under Muslim rule, beginning in the 7th century, the situation of the community fluctuated. Many Jews held high positions in government or prospered in commerce and trade. At the same time, Jews were subjected to special taxes, restrictions on their professional activity, and anti-Jewish incitement among the masses.

Under British rule, which began in 1917, Jews fared well economically, and many were elected to government posts. This traditionally observant community was also allowed to found Zionist organizations and to pursue Hebrew studies. All of this progress ended when Iraq gained independence in 1932.

In June 1941, the Mufti-inspired, pro-Nazi coup of Rashid Ali sparked rioting and a pogrom in Baghdad. Armed Iraqi mobs, with the complicity of the police and the army, murdered 180 Jews and wounded almost 1,000.

Additional outbreaks of anti-Jewish rioting occurred from 1946-49. After the establishment of Israel in 1948, Zionism became a capital crime.

THE PERSECUTION OF JEWS IN IRAQ AFTER 1948

Although emigration was prohibited, many Jews made their way to Israel in the early forties, with the aid of an underground movement. In 1950, the Iraqi parliament finally legalized emigration to Israel and between May 1950 and August 1951, the Jewish Agency and the Israeli government succeeded in airlifting approximately 110,000 Jews to Israel in Operations Ezra and Nehemiah. This figure includes 18,000 Kurdish Jews, who have many distinct traditions. Thus a community that had reached a peak of 150,000 in 1947 dwindled to a mere 6,000 after 1951.

In 1950, Iraqi Jews were permitted to leave the country within a year, provided they forfeited their citizenship. A year later, however, the property of Jews who emigrated was frozen and economic restrictions were placed on Jews who chose to remain in the country. From 1949 to 1951, 104,000 Jews were evacuated from Iraq in Operations Ezra and Nehemiah; another 20,000 were smuggled out through Iran. In 1952, Iraq's government barred Jews from emigrating and publicly hanged two Jews after falsely charging them with hurling a bomb at the Baghdad office of the U.S. Information Agency.

With the rise of competing Ba'ath factions in 1963, additional restrictions were placed on the remaining Iraqi Jews. The sale of property was forbidden and all Jews were forced to carry yellow identity cards. After the Six-Day War, more repressive measures were imposed: Jewish property was expropriated; Jewish bank accounts were frozen; Jews were dismissed from public posts; businesses were shut; trading permits were cancelled; and telephones were disconnected. Jews were placed under house arrest for long periods or restricted to the cities.

Persecution was at its worst at the end of 1968. Scores were jailed when a local "spy ring" composed of Jewish businessmen was discovered. Fourteen men, eleven of them Jews, were sentenced to death in staged trials and hanged in the public squares of Baghdad; others died of torture. On January 27, 1969, Baghdad Radio called upon Iraqis to "come and enjoy the feast." Some 500,000 men, women and children paraded and danced past the scaffolds where the bodies of the hanged Jews swung; the mob rhythmically chanted *"Death to Israel"* and

"Death to all traitors." This display brought a worldwide public out-cry that Radio Baghdad dismissed by declaring: "We hanged spies, but the Jews crucified Christ."[59]

Jews remained under constant surveillance by the Iraqi government. Max Sawadayee, in <u>All Waiting to be Hanged,</u> writes a testimony of an Iraqi Jew who later escaped:

"The dehumanization of the Jewish personality resulting from con-tinuous humiliation and torment...have dragged us down to the lowest level of our physical and mental faculties, and deprived us of the power to recover."

In response to international pressure, the Baghdad government qui-etly allowed most of the remaining Jews to emigrate in the early 1970s, even while leaving other restrictions in force. Most of Iraq's remaining Jews are now too old to leave. They have been pressured by the government to turn over title, without compensation, to more than $200 million worth of Jewish community property.[60]

Only one synagogue continues to function in Iraq, "a crumbling buff-colored building tucked away in an alleyway" in Baghdad. According to the synagogue's administrator, "there are few children to be bar-mitzvahed, or couples to be married. Jews can practice their religion but are not allowed to hold jobs in state enterprises or join the army."[61]

In 1991, prior to the Gulf War, the state Department said "there is no recent evidence of overt persecution of Jews, but the regime restricts travel, (particularly to Israel) and contacts with Jewish groups abroad."

The Jews were persecuted throughout the centuries in all the Arabic speaking countries. At one time, Baghdad was one-fifth Jewish and other Jewish communities had first been established 2,500 years ago. Today, approximately 61 Jews are left in Baghdad and another 200 or so are in Kurdish areas in the north. Only one synagogue remains in Bataween—once Baghdad's main Jewish neighborhood. The rabbi died in 1996 and none of the remaining Jews can perform the liturgy and only a few know Hebrew.[37]

THE PERSECUTION OF JEWS IN SPAIN BY THE MUSLIMS

In Spain, the Caliphs had great interest in their scholarly Jews; Caliph Abderahman III had a Jewish minister, Hasdai ben Isaac, whom he greatly valued; the entire Jewish nation was historically judged by an individual here or there, which, in this case, influenced the Caliph in his general policy towards the Jews.

Another Jew came to enjoy great powers and privileges, and held the title of Nagid, or Prince, of the Jewish community in Spain. Just like Daniel in Babylon and Joseph in Egypt, God appoints a Jew to preserve His chosen people. He was one of the most famous of the Jewish notables of Muslim Spain. Beginning life as a shopkeeper, Samuel HaLevi ultimately became the chief minister at the court of Granada. By virtue of this office he became the political head of the Jews in Granada and probably thus received the title Nagid ("Prince"), and so his name becoming Samuel HaNagid. He served his community as rabbi and did a great deal to further Jewish learning throughout the world. Samuel was a fine linguist, a scholar, a diplomat, and a distinguished soldier. His reputation in the middle Ages was based on his excellent poetry, some of which was written on the battlefield.

The following account of his life is taken from Sefer Seder ha-Kabbalah (The Line of Tradition), a Hebrew historical work written by Abraham ibn Daud of Toledo in 1161:

"One of the great disciples of Rabbi Enoch [d. 1014], was Rabbi Samuel HaLevi, the Prince, the son of Joseph, who was known as Ibn Nagrela, of the community of Cordova. He was an unusually fine Talmudic scholar and was also well versed in Arabic literature and language. He was the type who could occupy a high position in the royal palace. Samuel was a merchant, supporting himself with great difficulty until the devastating days in Spain, which followed the fall of the Amirid kingdom when the Berbers secured the power." [The civil war, which began in Spain in 1009, reached its climax in 1012 in the sack of Cordova by the Berbers.]

It was then that the land of Cordova began to decline and its inhabitants fled. Some of them ran away to Saragossa, where their descendants are even now; some fled to Toledo and their descendants are known there even to this day.

This Rabbi, Samuel HaLevi, fled to Malaga. There he had a shop and was a petty merchant. His shop happened to be near the palace of Ibn al Arif, the vizier of King Habbus [1019-1038], the son of Maksan, the King of the Berbers, in Granada. At the request of a maidservant of the vizier, Samuel used to write letters for her to her master the vizier, Abul Kasim ibn al Arif, who saw Samuel's letters and was amazed at his wisdom.

Some time later, Ibn al Arif got permission from his king, Habbus, to return to his home in Malaga. There he asked the people of his house, "Who used to write those letters that came to me from you?" "A certain Jew," they answered, "who comes from the community of Cordova and lives near your palace. He used to write them for us." Immediately the secretary issued a command and they rushed Rabbi Samuel HaLevi to him. "It is unbecoming for you to sit in a shop," he said to him. "Stay here with me." He did so and became his secretary and adviser.

The vizier used to counsel the King according to the advice given by Rabbi Samuel HaLevi. All his advice was as though it came from God, and King Habbus prospered by it very much. After some time, Ibn al Arif became mortally ill, and King Habbus, who came to visit him, said to him, "What shall I do? Who will advise me in the wars which encompass me?" "I have never advised you," he answered him, "out of my own mind, but at the suggestion of this Jew, my secretary. Take care of him, and he will be as a father and a minister to you. Do whatever he advises you, and God will help you." So after the death of the vizier, King Habbus took Rabbi Samuel HaLevi and brought him to his palace and he became his vizier and counselor.

In 1020, HaLevi was in the palace of King Habbus. [Samuel was already an important official before 1020.] The king had two sons: the name of the elder was Badis, and the younger, Bulukkin. All the Berber princes favored Bulukkin, the younger son, as the successor, but all the rest of the people favored Badis, including the Jews. Among them, Rabbi Joseph ibn Migas, Rabbi Isaac ben Leon, and Rabbi Nehemiah, (who was called Escafa), all three of them Granada notables, favored Bulukkin, but Rabbi Samuel HaLevi favored Badis.

On the day that King Habbus died, the Berber princes and their distinguished men rose in the morning to crown his son Bulukkin. Bulukkin, however, immediately went and kissed the hand of his elder brother Badis. Thus Badis was crowned in 1027 and the face of his enemies turned black like the bottom of a pot; and against their will they had to crown Badis. [Badis was really crowned in 1038 and died in 1073.]

After this Bulukkin regretted that he had made his brother king and kept on getting the upper hand over his brother Badis, with the result that King Badis was unable to do a thing, big or small, without his brother's interference. But after this, his brother Bulukkin became sick, and the King gave orders to the physician not to cure him. The physician obeyed, and Bulukkin died. Thus was the kingdom established in the hands of Badis. These three distinguished Jews of the city, whom we have mentioned, fled to the land of Seville [then hostile to Granada].

Rabbi Samuel HaLevi was appointed Prince in the year 4787 [1027], and he conferred great benefits on Israel in Spain, in northeastern and north central Africa, in the land of Egypt, in Sicily, as far as the Babylonian academy, and the Holy City, Jerusalem. All the students who lived in those lands benefited by his generosity, for he bought numerous copies of the Holy Scriptures, the Mishnah, and the Talmud holy writings. [Ibn Daud here refutes the Karaites who denied the authority of the Mishnah and the Talmud.]

To every one in all the land of Spain and in all the lands that have been mentioned, who wanted to make the study of the Torah his profession, he would give of his money. He had scribes who used to copy Mishnahs and Talmuds, and he would give them as a gift to students in the academies of Spain or in the lands we have mentioned, who were not able to buy them with their own means. (Printing was not yet invented. Manuscripts were very expensive.) Besides this, he furnished olive oil every year for the lamps of the synagogues in Jerusalem. He spread the knowledge of the Torah [Jewish learning] very widely and died an old man, at a ripe age, after having acquired the four crowns: the crown of the Torah, the crown of high station, the crown of Levitical descent, and what is more than all these, the crown of a good name merited by good deeds. He died in the year 1055 and his son, Rabbi Joseph HaLevi, the Prince, succeeded him. (It is more probable that Samuel died in 1056 or later when Joseph (b. 1035), succeeded him as vizier.)

Of all the good traits of his father, Joseph lacked but one. He was not humble like his father because he grew up in riches, and he never had to bear the yoke (of poverty and discipline) in his youth. He was proud to his own hurt, and the Berber princes were jealous of him with the result that on the Sabbath, on the 9th of Tebet in the year 4827 [Saturday, December 30, 1066], he and the Community of Granada were murdered. (About 150 families were killed. This is the first known massacre of Jews in Spain by Muslims.)

"All those who had come from distant lands to see his learning and his greatness mourned for him, and the lament for him spread to all lands and to all cities. Since the days of the ancient rabbis of blessed memory who wrote the Scroll of Fasts and decreed that the 9th of Tebet should be a fast, the reason for the decree was never known. However, from this incident we know that they were directed by the Holy Spirit to fix this day. After his death, his books and treasures were scattered and dispersed throughout the world. So, too, were the disciples whom he had raised up. After his death they became the rabbis of Spain and the leaders of the generation." [Sassoon, D. S., "Diwan of the Vizier Samuel Hannaghid," The Jewish Chronicle, (London), March 28, 1924]

Another Jew, Samuel HaLevi ibin-Nagrela, or Samuel Ha-Nagid, as he was called, was a first-rate theologian, a poet and the minister for the Caliph. Nonetheless, the talents of the Jews did not make them valuable to the rules of the land. Later the Jews were falsely accused of converting their neighbors and 1,500 families were persecuted and in 1066 they were forced to leave Granada for other cities.

The Almohade Dynasty (Al-Mahdeyeen), which created fanatic warriors, Abdel-Mumen, gave two choices to both Jews and Christians: Islam or exile. Many Jews and Christians secretly preferred exile to conversion.

Many other notable Jewish men contributed to the Islamic world. Solomon Ibn Gabirol (1021-1070) in poetry and philosophy, Maimonides (1135-1204) and many others. When Jews were perceived as having achieved too comfortable a position in Islamic society, anti-Semitism would surface, often with devastating results. On December 30, 1066, Joseph HaNagid, the Jewish vizier of Granada, Spain, was crucified by an Arab mob that proceeded to raze the Jewish quarter of the city and slaughter its 5,000 inhabitants. Muslim preachers who had angrily objected to what they saw as inordinate Jewish political power incited the riot.

Chapter Two
CONFESSION—OUR NAZI EDUCATION

JIHAD IS NOT A STRUGGLE WITHIN

Despite the efforts of the media and academia at political correctness, Islam means "*submission*," not "*peace*." Submission to the complete will of Allah (Islamic god) and the duties laid out in the Quran for his followers, and this includes jihad. The Hans Wehr Dictionary of Modern Written Arabic defines "*Islam*" as "*submission, resignation*."

Quran 49.15 states: "The believers are only those who believe in Allah and His Apostle, then they doubt not and struggle hard with their wealth and their lives in the way of Allah; they are the truthful ones."

Jihad is not just a struggle with the temptations in life, but the struggle to wage war against the infidels, to protect the nation of Islam from the heathens and to convert them to Islam. This is Islam's definition of peace.

Muhammad explained in one of the Hadiths:

"Allah's apostle was asked, 'What is the best deed?' He replied, 'To believe in Allah and his Apostle.' The questioner then asked, 'What is the next?' He replied, 'To participate in Jihad (war) in Allah's cause.'" [1]

The definition of jihad, according to scholars such as Ibn Qudamah Al-Maqdisi, Ibn Taymiyyah and Ibn Aabideen, is:

"Exhausting the utmost effort fighting for the sake of Allah, directly by your body or by assisting by money or by your saying or by recruiting Mujahideen (Islamic fighters) or by any other means to help fighting,"

According to Maliki Fiqh Imam Ibn Arafa, Jihad is "a Muslim to fight the infidel without a treaty, for the sake of Allah to make his name the highest through his presence." [2]

Shaafi: Jihad is "to fight the (Infidels) for the sake of Allah by your body or money or tongue or by recruiting the people." [3]

Sa'id to Hanbali: Jihad means "to start to fight the (Infidels) whether as a Fard Kifayah (acquired knowledge) or Fard Ayn (revealed knowledge) i.e., both are mandatory one for the community of Muslims and one for the individual Muslim, protecting the believers from the Infidels or guarding the border or frontier and to fight in the front line is the pillar." [4]

All four major Islamic schools of thought agree that jihad is not merely a personal struggle, but a call to wage war on the infidels by all means possible: giving money and recruiting and training people are also means of jihad.

The highest authority is the prophet of Islam:

Surah 47.4: "When you meet the unbelievers in jihad, chop off their heads. And when you have brought them low, bind your prisoners rigorously. Then set them free or take ransom from them until the war is ended."

Surah 48.29: "Muhammad is Allah's apostle. Those who follow him are ruthless to the unbelievers but merciful to one another."

Surah 5.33-34: "Those that make war against Allah and His apostle and spread disorder in the land shall be slain or crucified or have their hands and feet cut off on alternate sides, or be banished from the land. They shall be held up to shame in this world and sternly punished in the hereafter."

Surah 8.12-13: "Allah revealed His will to the angels, saying: 'I shall be with you. Give courage to the believers. I shall cast terror into the hearts of the infidels. Strike off their heads, strike off the very tips of their fingers!' That was because they defied Allah and His apostle. He that defies Allah and his apostle shall be sternly punished by Allah."

Surah 8.37: "In order that Allah may separate the pure from the impure, put all the impure ones [i.e., non-Muslims] one on top of another in a heap and cast them into hell. They will have been the ones to have lost."

Surah 8.60: "Muster against them [i.e., non-Muslims] all the men and cavalry at your command, so that you may strike terror into the enemy of Allah and your enemy, and others besides them who are unknown to you but known to Allah."

Surah 9.73: "Prophet, make war on the unbelievers and the hypocrites, and deal harshly with them. Hell shall be their home: an evil fate."

Surah 17.16-17: "When We resolve to raze a city, We first give warning to those of its people who live in comfort. If they persist in sin, judgment is irrevocably passed, and We destroy it utterly."

Surah 21.11-15: "We have destroyed many a sinful nation and replaced them by other men. And when they felt Our Might they took to their heels and fled. They were told: 'Do not run away. Return to your comforts and to your dwellings. You shall be questioned all.' 'Woe betide us, we have done wrong' was their reply. And this they kept repeating until We mowed them down and put out their light."

OUR SCHOOLS ARE TERROR FACTORIES

As it was with the Nazis, the Palestinian schools are terror factories, where children are robbed of any true education. A textbook teaches:

"...This noble [Quranic] Surah [Surat Muhammad]... deals with questions of which the most important are as follows: 'Encouraging the faithful to perform jihad in God's cause, to behead the infidels, take them prisoner, break their power, and make their souls humble— all that in a style which contains the highest examples of urging to fight.' You see that in His words: 'When you meet the unbelievers in the battlefield strike off their heads and, when you have laid them low, bind your captives firmly. Then grant them their freedom or take a ransom from them, until war shall lay down its burdens.'" [5]

"...When you meet them in order to fight [them], do not be seized by compassion [towards them] but strike the [the] necks powerfully.... Striking the neck means fighting, because killing a person is often done by striking off his head. Thus, it has become an expression for killing even if the fighter strikes him elsewhere. This expression contains a harshness and emphasis that are not found in the word 'kill,' because it describes killing in the ugliest manner, i.e., cutting the neck and making the organ—the head of the body—fly off (the body)." [6]

Although chilling to our modern sensibilities, particularly when being taught to children, these are merely classical interpretations of the rules for jihad war, based on over a millennium of Muslim theology and jurisprudence. And the context of these teachings is unambiguous, as the translator makes clear:[7]

"... (the) concept of jihad is interpreted in the Egyptian school curriculum almost exclusively as a military endeavor...it is war against God's enemies, i.e., the infidels...it is war against the homeland's enemies and a means to strengthening the Muslim states in the world. In both cases, jihad is encouraged, and those who refrain from participating in it are denounced."[8]

Teaching Egyptian school children anti-infidel jihad hatred is a long-lived and ignoble tradition. As the scholar E. W. Lane reported after several years of residence in both Cairo and Luxor, initially in 1825-1828, then in 1833-1835:

"I am credibly informed that children in Egypt are often taught at school, a regular set of curses to denounce upon the persons and property of Christians, Jews, and all other unbelievers in the religion of Mohammad."[9]

Lane translated the prayer below from a contemporary 19th century Arabic text, containing a typical curse on non-Muslims, recited daily by Muslim schoolchildren:

I seek refuge with God from Satan the accursed. In the name of God, the Compassionate, the Merciful. O God, aid El-Islam, and exalt the word of truth, and the faith, by the preservation of thy servant and the son of thy servant, the Sultan of the two continents (Europe and Asia), and the Khakan (Emperor or monarch) of the two seas [the Mediterranean and Black Seas], the Sultan, son of the Sultan (Mahmood) Khan (the reigning Sultan when this prayer was composed). O God, assist him, and assist his armies, and all the forces of the Muslims: O Lord of the beings of the whole world. O God, destroy the infidels and polytheists, thine enemies, the enemies of the religion. O God, make their children orphans, and defile their abodes, and cause their feet to slip, and give them and their families, and their households and their women and their children and their relations by marriage and their brothers and their friends and their possessions and their race and their wealth and their lands as booty to the Muslims: O Lord of the beings of the whole world.

In 1949, the seminal modern scholar of Islamic civilization, S.D. Goitein, speaking of the Arab world generally and in particular Egypt, warned:

"Islamic fanaticism is now openly encouraged ...writers whose altogether Western style (was mentioned earlier) have been vying with each other for some time in compiling books on the heroes and virtues of Islam...What has now become possible in educated circles may be gathered from the following quotation from an issue of the 'New East', an Arab monthly periodical describing itself as the 'organ of the academic youth of the East.'

"Let us fight fanatically for our religion; let us love a man—because he is a Muslim; let us honor a man—because he is a Muslim; let us prefer him to anyone else—because he is a Muslim; and never let us make friends with unbelievers, because they have nothing but evil for us."[10]

And a decade later, in 1958, Lebanese law professor Antoine Fattal, perhaps the greatest scholar of the legal condition of non-Muslims living under the Shari'a lamented,

"No social relationship, no fellowship is possible between Muslims and Dhimmis. Even today, the study of the jihad is part of the curriculum of all the Islamic institutes. In the universities of Al-Azhar, Nagaf, and Zaitoune, students are still taught that the holy war is a binding prescriptive decree, pronounced against the Infidels, which will only be revoked with the end of the world..."[11]

"Sadly, almost fifty years after Fattal made his observations, Jihad hatred is still part of the formal education of Muslim youth in Egypt, the most populous Arab country, and throughout the Arab Muslim, and larger, non-Arab Muslim world. We in the West must press our political and religious leaders to demand that such belli-cose, hate-mongering 'educational' practices be abol-ished in Islamic nations, under threat of severe, broad ranging economic sanctions."[12]

WE ARE TAUGHT THE LIES FROM INFANCY

Argument:

"Islamic fanaticism and anti-Semitism are only taught within small groups. These are but a small fraction of the Muslim world."

Response:

Beginning with our lullabies, Jew-hatred is an integral part of daily life for all Palestinian children and for Muslim children in many countries around the world.

When I was a child, my hungry young cousin picked up a piece of bread off the ground outside of the house. My grandmother caught her just before she could put it in her mouth. Grandma reprimanded, *"Don't you know the Jews are putting bread in front of Arab houses that is tainted with poison?"* I never knew that grandma's suspicions would turn to a national accusation. In school, we were sometimes warned that the Jews would put chemicals in the school water to cause sterility.

Today's reality is much worse than my grandmother's fairy tale. The volumes of accusations against Israel include arson attempts on the Temple Mount area, destruction and the digging of tunnels, creation of artificial earthquakes and the spread of arms in the new Palestinian state. Absurdly, they even accuse them of terrorist attacks on Jewish civilians. They are said to have spread spoiled corn oil in the West Bank, sold English Cadbury chocolate tainted with the Mad Cow disease, used a chemical agent in attempted assassinations, sold sexually stimulating gum, spread cancer agents, and even injected Palestinian infants with the HIV virus causing AIDS. As with the Nazi-controlled media, the news organizations throughout the Middle East have been co-opted by Islamism. Regarding weapons in the hands of Arab terrorists, Arafat said,

"These weapons could be obtained only from high authorities with great influence on the Israeli side." [13]

"An unholy conspiracy of Israeli 'fanatics,' who are members of a shadowy group of ex-IDF [Israel Defense Force] people called 'OAS,' and Muslim extremists were behind [the Feb. 1996] suicide bombings, Palestinian Authority President Yasser Arafat told foreign diplomats...Arafat is known to have said last year, before [Ehud Barak became [Israel's] foreign minister, that 'Barak is one of the big bosses of the OAS...'" [14]

> PLO chairman Yasser Arafat, in interviews published yesterday, accused IDF troops of aiding the spread of arms in the territories in a plot to create chaos in Palestinian self-rule areas...'This weapons trade is being carried out under the auspices of some Israeli officers in the West Bank and Gaza. This is part of a wicked plan.' [16]

"Israel has been using chemical weapons against Palestinians in the territories for 27 months with the support of the U.S. It's not tear gas, it's chemical weapons." [17]

> Referring to the Arab terrorist attack in Beit Lid, in which 22 Israelis were killed, and other attacks in 1995, Arafat said, "I have evidences that these terrorist activities have been done through coordination between these fanatic Islamic groups and some elements on the Israeli side."[15]

OUR LIBELOUS ACCUSATIONS

As in Nazi Germany, the media throughout the Middle East is plagued with myth:

> Maher al-Dasuki, head of the Palestinian Consumer Protection Council, said that spoiled corn oil is being distributed in the West Bank. According to al-Dasuki, the oil is marketed after having been smuggled in from Israel, where the plastic bottle is refilled a second time inside the settlements and then distributed with the help of collaborators...Al-Dasuki emphasized that residents

must be on guard regarding chocolate produced in England, and especially that of Cadbury, which is widely available on Palestinian markets, since they make use of milk tainted with the 'Mad Cow' disease. Al-Dasuki said that the sale of such chocolate is forbidden in Britain, but Israeli merchants have smuggled it into the **Palestinian** areas and they entice people to buy it via the teacups distributed for free along with the purchase of each pack.[18]

Abd Al-Fatah Hamid, the Head of the Control and Inspection Department in the PA Ministry of Supplies, said that a committee will work...against spoiled goods and food supplies, which are one of Israel's means in its war against Palestinian society. Hamid said that the source of most of the spoiled food was the settlements, and pointed to the fact that the Ministry puts much effort in tracking the settlements and those smuggling spoiled food.[19]

In order to establish the Temple in place of the Al-Aqsa mosque, Israel employed different methods starting with arson attempts, destruction, and the digging of tunnels... and ending with the creation of artificial earthquakes that can be triggered from afar which will undermine its foundations and will destroy it—and then Israel will not permit its renovation...but will use the opportunity to complete its destruction and to establish the [Jewish] Temple in its place...[20]

The failed attempt to assassinate Khaled Mish'al in Aman raises many questions...In light of the use of a chemical agent in the attempted assassination and in light of repeated reports in the Israeli press itself about medical experiments conducted on Palestinian prisoners, the human rights organizations are being called upon today...to re-examine the cases of unexplained deaths in Israeli jails and the cases of prisoners who died of unknown diseases.[21]

"There is an Israeli mafia which is distributing spoiled food products under the aegis of Israeli generals in the territories of the Palestinian Authority…they are distributors of death."[22]

> Israel is distributing food containing material that causes cancer and hormones that harm male virility and other spoiled food products in the Palestinian Authority's territories in order to poison and harm the Palestinian population. We absolutely feel that it is an organized plan and conspiracy which is under the auspices of the Israel Defense Forces…this is a planned and initiated war against the Palestinian people.[23]

"Laboratory tests made on seven brands of Israeli gum smuggled into the West Bank and Gaza showed they contain a sexually-stimulating adrenaline substance."[24]

"They brought Russian Jewish girls with AIDS to spread the disease among Palestinian youth."[25]

"Since the very beginning of the Arab-Israeli conflict, Israeli governments were anxious to apply the most dangerous ethnic cleansing theory against the Palestinian people. According to their racist ideology, the Israeli policy makers were dedicated to capturing a land without a people for a people without a land."[26]

"Israeli authorities…infected by injection 300 Palestinian children with the HIV virus during the years of the intifada."[27]

THE JEWS ARE ILLEGITIMATE

> The archeology of Jerusalem is diverse—excavations in the Old City and the areas surrounding it revealed Umayyad Islamic palaces, Roman ruins, Armenian ruins and others, but nothing Jewish. Outside of what is mentioned written in the Old and New Testaments, there is no tangible evidence of any Jewish traces remains in the old city of Jerusalem and its immediate vicinity.[28]

"Why do the Jews from all over the world gather together to establish their false state on the Land of Palestine when the true owners of the land are prevented from establishing their state on it?"[29]

There is no people or land named Israel. Israel is our patriarch Yaaqoub, peace be upon him, and the children of Israel are the sons of Yaaqoub...We are the children of Israel...These people are the children of the Zionist entity, they are the children of the colonialist entity, they are nothing more than thieves. They came and took land which does not belong to them. Therefore, the normalization of relations with them is impossible...even if Palestine remains occupied for hundreds of years... These Zionists are not fit to establish a nation or to have their own language or even their own religion. They are nothing more than a hodgepodge.[30]

"The words 'State of Israel' should be replaced with 'Zionist entity' in the Palestinian lexicon."[31]

High-ranking officials in Israel's Religious Affairs Ministry and Antiquities Office recently stole a stone from the Umayyad Palaces located in the vicinity of Al-Haram Al-Kudsi [The Al-Aqsa and Dome of the Rock Mosques in Jerusalem]...This stone was sent to Germany for special laboratory tests...in order to prove the claim that the stone belonged to their alleged temple...Hamad Yusef, head of The Institution for the Rejuvenation of the Palestinian Heritage, said that the aim in analyzing the stone was to prove the false historical claim of the Jews in the holy city, a claim which they were unable to prove in all of the excavations conducted by foreign groups for the past hundred years, as well as in the Israeli excavations being carried out under the foundations of Al-Haram Al-Kudsi for the past thirty years. Hamad accused the Israelis of unprecedented historical forgeries, emphasizing the Palestinian, the Arab and the Islamic nature of the holy city for the past 6000 years. Israel fails in her attempt to find a historical connection to Jerusalem.[32]

THE JEWS ARE THE DEVIL

It is important to conduct the conflict according to the foundations which both are leaning on...particularly the Jews...such as the Torah, the Talmud and the Protocols [of the elders of Zion]...All signs unequivocally prove that the conflict between the Jews and the Muslims is an eternal and on-going conflict, even if it stops for short intervals...This conflict resembles the conflict between man and Satan...This is the fate of the Muslim nation, and beyond that the fate of all of the nations of the world, to be tormented by this nation [the Jews]. The fate of the Palestinian people is to struggle against the Jews on behalf of the Arab peoples, the Islamic peoples and the peoples of the entire world.[33]

THE JEWS ARE RACIST

There are many indications that the American initiative, in case it is proposed, will reflect a strong bias toward the Zionist-racist solution to the Palestine problem...It will adopt the idea of giving the name 'Palestinian state' to lands crowded with Palestinian population and construction in the West Bank and Gaza...Hard conditions will be forced on this state which will be demilitarized and limited [in authority] enabling the Zionist entity to control its affairs in such a way that will make this state look like a series of 'enclaves' within the Zionist-racist entity called 'Israel.'[34]

Zionist thought gave birth to political Zionism...this blind military power and extreme racism. For one hundred years the Zionist movement has been spreading the poison of Zionist ideology...What is happening these days, expresses this ideology which their children suckle with their mother's milk...When the UN General Assembly defined Zionism as a form of racism, it expressed this as a fact, a fact which is backed up by Israeli operations which the human conscience cannot bear. Zionism remains...another face of racism, despite all the pressure the US has put in order to change the UN decision or to cancel it...Accordingly, we are facing a Zionist ideology which belongs to a dynasty of dinosaurs. And if human history has swallowed all the dynasties of dinosauran ideologies from Hulagu [the Mongolian conqueror] to Hitler, in addition to the racist ideology in South Africa, the survival of Zionist ideology on this piece of our planet, is a deviant phenomenon and a historical lie...[35]

"The Israeli colonialist occupation of Palestine is turning into aggression against all Islam and Christian holy sites. Zionist racism reaches its peak with this Talmudic offensive, which tears the pages of the Koran, and which offends the Master of Prophets, Muhammad, Allah's blessing be with him, and the Blessed Virgin, mother of Christ, may they rest in peace."[36]

THE JEWS SPILL BLOOD

"Jews Spread Death and Spill Blood:" an article in Al-Hayat Al-Jadeeda, which condemned

"...those who spread death and murder and spill blood, and who are said to be our cousins and, like us, 'the children of Abraham,' despite the fact that Abraham did not immigrate to Poland, did not visit New York and New Jersey, and did not live in Russia."[37]

THE JEWS ARE LEACHES

...A doctor currently dealing with the national dialogue says:...in my experience Israeli blood is AB minus—which takes from everyone and doesn't give to anyone except those of his own [blood] type—while Palestinian blood is O minus—which gives to everyone and takes only from his own type..." Generosity is an Arab custom and stinginess is a Jewish custom. Therefore, it is only natural that we give and they take. We are killed and they incarcerate! We build and they destroy! We agree and they refuse! We make commitments and they close us off![38]

"We believe that the Israelis are not adventuresome because the Jewish brain is cowardly and does not tend toward adventure, but rather exchanges it for plotting..."[39] "These things have to be said as a description of the situation, and as a description of the baseness of this reactionary and cruel American Jewish world."[40]

THE JEWS ARE SHYLOCKS

"Whoever comes in contact with the banks discovers that they act in Shylock's way...We do not want Shylock-style banks that empty our pockets, but national banks; we have had enough of the Shylock of the lands and settlements."[41]

"We are fighting and struggling with an enemy who is Shylock. We must know that he is Shylock."[42]

> The portrait of the usurious Jew painted by Shakespeare in his well-known masterpiece, "The Merchant of Venice" did not ignite a Jewish attack accusing him of anti-Semitism, since it fit the general view held by Europeans at that time, when the European continent...vomited the Jews to the periphery...The Israelis wish to contain Christian pilgrims in the year 2000...put them next to the settlers who have their sights set on large financial compensation and immediate profit out of land ownership which has been confiscated by a mayor backed by fanatical religious and nationalistic trends and by a millionaire usurer who comes from across the ocean...At this moment the portrait of the Shakespearean hero reappears...and all signs point to the fact that this merchant of Venice will become a new Dracula.[43]

> ...It is impossible to rely on international or Arab national circles as long as Netanyahu's claws of hatred dive into our Palestinian blood in search of oxygen-rich blood cells...our movement found in Netanyahu something it could not ignore which is the dismemberment of the agreement by the fangs of hatred and the chewing of the peace by the teeth of the Talmud...We must recog-

nize that this stubborn enemy, locks itself in the Talmud's cocoon…[44]

"The [Palestinian] Authority cannot do a thing, except protect its people and itself from an enemy which bares its Jewish fangs from the four corners of the earth…"[45]

Shylock, Shakespeare's famous character in the Merchant of Venice, has long been elevated to the archetypal Jew, especially by those who seek to confirm their prejudices. However, Shylock has his finest hour when, speaking from the pain and anger provoked by his tormentors, he poignantly affirms that he is a man like any other:

> "…I am a Jew.
>
> Hath not a Jew eyes? Hath not a Jew hands, organs,
>
> dimensions, senses, affections, passions; fed with
>
> the same food, hurt with the same weapons, subject
>
> to the same diseases, heal'd by the same means,
>
> warm'd and cool'd by the same winter and summer
>
> as a Christian is? If you prick us, do we not bleed?
>
> If you tickle us, do we not laugh? If you
>
> poison us, shall we not die?" (III, I, 58-66)

WE WERE TAUGHT HISTORIC LIES

Yasser Arafat the "Nobel Peace Prize" winner stated:

"Abraham was neither Jewish nor a Hebrew, but was simply an Iraqi. The Jews have no right to claim part of the Tomb of the Patriarchs in Hebron, Abraham's resting place, as a synagogue. Rather, the whole building should be a mosque."[46]

"The Palestinian Authority is now claiming that Rachel's Tomb in Bethlehem is the traditional tomb of the Cushite servant of Muhammad."[47]

"That is not the Western Wall at all, but a Muslim shrine."[48]

"The people of Israel realize perfectly well that they have no temples or ruins near Al Aqsa Mosque. According to the Koran, the people of Israel lived somewhere to the west of Bethlehem...they were living in Bethlehem and not in Jerusalem." [49]

Arafat once "convened a conference of the international press to claim that an imprint of an ancient Judean coin on the Israeli 10-agorot coin was Israel's imperialistic expansion map. This coin, he said, shows that Israel plans to conquer Jordan, Syria, Lebanon and parts of Egypt and Saudi Arabia." [50]

"...'Netanyahu's Plan' completely matches the foundations of the greater Zionist plan which is organized according to specific stages that were determined when the Protocols of the Elders of Zion were composed and when Herzl along with Weizmann traveled around the world in order to determine the appropriate location for the implementation of this conspiracy.[51]

OUR PALESTINIAN SCHOOLS TEACH HATE

Palestinian Arab schools promote hate, not peace. Arafat's orders: schools must teach that Israel's existence is a "catastrophe."

> The Palestinian Education Ministry has decided that the topic [Balfour Declaration] will now be introduced into the Palestinian educational curriculum...every year, on November 2, teachers will devote a lesson to studying the Balfour Declaration and its 'catastrophic' ramifications on the Palestinian people. Likewise, the Palestinian news media, including the radio and television, will dedicate special programs to the topic...Teachers and educators were asked to explain to students that the anniversary is a 'painful' memorial and a 'disaster' for the Palestinian people.[52]

Palestinian Arab denunciations of the Balfour Declaration are a rejection of the idea that a Jewish state of any size has a right to exist.

The Israeli daily *Ha'aretz* described the first of the PA's new school textbooks, History of the Arabs and the World, which "compares Zionism with Nazism and describes the Talmud as a book of hatred toward gentiles...is to be used in most of the Palestinian Authority's schools...also claims Zionism advocated the liquidation [of the Palestinian Arabs]..."the racist and aggressive nature of the Zionist movement...the basic similarity between Nazism, Fascism, and Zionism." [53]

THE TRUTH ABOUT OUR MUSLIM CLERGY IN JERUSALEM

It seems that nothing has changed since Haj Amin Al-Husseni's Nazi propaganda. Ikrima Sabri is a carbon copy of the original Muftis:

"Oh, Allah, destroy America for it is controlled by Zionist Jews...Allah will avenge, in the name of his Prophet, the colonialist settlers who are the descendants of monkeys and pigs...forgive us, oh Muhammad, for the acts of these monkeys and pigs who wished to profane your holiness." [54]

When comparing Sabri with his predecessors, it is understood that they have much in common, since Islamic fundamentalism is what fuels their speeches and rhetoric.

"Jerusalem is a symbol for every Muslim in the world. The claim of the Jews to the right over it is false, and we recognize nothing but an entirely Islamic Jerusalem under Islamic supervision..." [55]

"The Zionist entity exists on seized land. The Jews remain enemies because they expropriate lands, build settlements and pay high sums to buy properties. They are the greatest enemies of us Muslims." [56]

"The existing state of Israel is not worthy of ruling since they know no religion and no God." [57]

"...the Jews always set a trap for the community of Muslims...The Koran repeatedly warns against the traps and plots of the 'people of the book.' They relentlessly scheme in all times and places and this is what they do today and tomorrow against the Muslim camp..." [58]

THE PALESTINIAN MEDIA

"Egypt declared its absolute refusal to grant a prize to Israel—the convening of the Doha summit—and displayed its indifference to American pressure-tactics employed by the Judaized Congress." [59]

"There is a need to formulate a clear information plan... In order for us to oppose the Zionist media, which dominates more than half of the media in the world—newspapers, radio and television..." [60]

"Israeli society started feeling ashamed of Netanyahu's rise to the highest position of power...when all of his qualities amount to his outdated Talmudic arrogance and his absolute belief that he is the spoiled child of Brooklyn's nymphs." [61]

"We did not take into account the way of thinking of the other side which is a Jewish mentality based on the love of controlling everything, and which does not easily grant others their rights..." [62]

US Ambassador-Designate to Israel Edward Walker "underwent extensive hearings in the Congress or, that is, in the 'Council of the Elders of Zion,' in order to win his post." [63]

"This is a pitiful show that expresses nothing other than the Talmudic quarrel-mongering mentality that rules Netanyahu and the members of his group who govern Tel Aviv...But we know that Netanyahu did not change and will not change because [not even] lipstick could make his blood-sucking lips beautiful..." [64]

"The White House is a hostage of 'the two prisons' or the two Houses, the Senate and the House of Representatives, which are more extreme than the 'elders of Zion.'" [65]

"...We exude the scent of jasmine...throughout the world, and they release the darkness and hatred of the mobs with the long beards over the land. We declare life...while they have shut themselves up behind death and have been entrenching themselves in its excavations for the last fifty years, which is also their age, the age of evil..." [66]

"The soldiers of the Talmudic offensive do not hesitate to call openly for revenge against Christianity for having persecuted European Jewry...we know that Jesus was a victim of the roots of Talmudic extremism, which is currently waving a national flag, wearing a helmet of a national army and employing state-run terrorism by means of armed settlers and an army." [67]

"Announcer: The occupation is shooting at children, women and infants... The latest reports reaching us from Hebron prove that the occupation forces have opened fire on children, women and infants..." Voice of a Hebron resident: "...our enemies have no mercy and no heart...this shows that they have no conscience. Their hearts are like stone. They are not human beings. One cannot compare them to people. They are like animals, they are like animals." [68]

"O our beautiful land imprisoned in a cage and surrounded by wolves, My shaded garden, the tormentors have destroyed you, and the dogs have settled in you, O Jerusalem, O my city, With my notebook and pencil and the fire of my rifle I will shatter the cage, I will kill the wolves and plant the flag. The dogs will not bark in the heroic cities." [69]

"We must not lay aside the blade of the Palestinian struggle which we grasp with Arab and international support, a blade with which we must struggle to shatter the two elements in the Likud's ideology: the racist-Torah part and the nationalist-fascist part. This is our fate." [70]

"The occupation forces have imposed a siege on the camp of Al-Aroub...whose children set new records in their opposition to the acts of the occupation with the little stones they throw from behind the wire fences dozens of meters in height which...show the world the Nazism of the occupation at the end of the 20th century, in an era known as 'the era of peace'...Al-Aroub residents tell the story of one of the crimes of 'Nazism in a period of peace...'" [71]

"We must act on the international level in the framework of a detailed information plan which will expose the Zionist-Colonialist plot and its goals, which destroy not only our people but the entire world." [72]

NAZIS ACCUSE JEWS OF NAZISM

The appearance of the Zionist movement prompted the emergence of terrorist, racist ideologies, such as the Nazi ideology. There is great similarity between the two ideologies: the Zionists believe that they are "God's Chosen People," and that other nations were created to be used and ridiculed...the Zionist Jews claim that they hate the nations since they persecute them out of jealousy of their wisdom, their success and their being God's chosen. Similarly, the Nazis claim that the Aryans are the chosen and the pure and that anti-Semitism is the punishment of the Jewish Germans who betrayed their country...Of course the similarity between the two racist ideologies—the Zionist and the Nazi—is obvious and the despicable racial content of each of them is clear. The Zionist movement, as well as Nazism, believes that it represents the absolute truth that must be maintained; otherwise it will lose its value...The Nazi ideology pushed the world into the hell of the Second World War...and during the war applied all forms of terrorism, exactly as the Zionists are doing now. After the passing of one hundred years since the establishment of Zionism, here comes Benyamin Netanyahu, the Prime Minister of the Zionist enemy, and presents a Nazi formula when he says that "peace between Israel and the Arabs must be based on the principle of Israeli strength." Since its establishment, the racist Zionist entity has been implementing various forms of terrorism on a daily basis which are a repetition of the Nazi terror. This proves the shared roots of Nazi and Zionist thought. This also explains the cooperation between the Jews and the Nazis during World War II, through which were revealed the forged claims of the Zionists regarding alleged acts of slaughter perpetrated against the Jews during the same period...There is no difference between Hitler and Ben-Gurion, and if there was a difference at all, it was one of quantity and not one of substance. Anyone who investigates the crimes of the Zionists...discovers explicitly the complementary traits between Zionism, which is a racist terrorist movement, and the Nazi movement.

...The rumor about the 'superior Jew' versus the 'stupid' others which are not worthy of anything but of serving as subjects, is spread around the world. The Jews put their best efforts into creating it. Every genius has to be of Jewish descent; if he is not of Jewish descent he is forced to make one up for himself. Additionally, any talented military commander, either his mother is Jewish if his name is reminiscent of anything Jewish, or, if his mother is not Jewish—then he ends up being a Jewish agent. The Jews succeeded, during their history, to turn the massacres they were subjected to into a 'weapon of mass destruction' against their adversaries and used the weapon of anti-Semitism in an impressive way...In order to establish their "superiority" they provided proof and claimed that the founder of modern psychology, Sigmund Freud, is a Jew in origin and blood; that the father of the Theory of Relativity, who changed the face of science, Albert Einstein, is a Jew inside and out, and that Isaac Newton, who discovered Gravity, is wholeheartedly a Jew. The best proof of the Jewish political ability is the Communist Karl Marx, who is also a Jew from birth. Regarding the millionaires...from Rothschild through Montefiore to Moskowitz: aren't they sufficient proof of Jewish 'superiority?'[73]

"Netanyahu was blinded by the tyranny of power and is interested in total Palestinian and Arab surrender to his unlimited desires...perhaps in the European style of the German armies so that he will be able to impose greater Israel and establish the superiority of the Hebrew race..."[74]

"While the Israeli government is speaking about the atrocities committed against the Jews at Auschwitz, Birkenau and Dachau concentration camps... it is directly involved these days in weaving plots and causing two major catastrophes to their neighbors...Our homeland was transformed into a big concentration camp..."[75] Cruelly, the portrayal of Israel as both Nazi and Fascist permeates Palestinian newspapers, schools, mosques, and even the walls:

Jerusalemites and any other Muslim who is able to reach the gates of the Al-Aqsa mosque for Friday prayers must report to the Israeli police at the gates to hand in his ID to be checked and on many occasions is prevented from entry or even arrested. This of course should remind the Europeans of Nazi occupation by Nazi soldiers surrounding churches and places of worship during the Second World War. Israeli practices in many aspects are equal with, if not more brutal than, those practiced by occupying Nazi soldiers dealing with French-Dutch citizens during the Second World War.[76]

"...the Arab sees with his own eyes an Israeli occupation in Palestine, the Golan and Lebanon, which can not be compared to any occupation in this century except the Nazi occupation..."[77]

MILITARY OFFICIALS

What 'Israel' is trying to do...by way of its control over a number of institutions in the US, such as the Congress and its allies...reveals the nakedness of those people and their blind submission to world Zionism...The peace equation was somewhat violated, since the Zionists were able to demonstrate their power in the US...that is the power which was clearly revealed in the Zionist American Congress which led to the terrorizing of the American president and the administration, through threats of sex and morals scandals which are disseminated by the obedient media in the US...[78]

MINISTRY OF JUSTICE

"Five Zionist Jews are running the policy of the United States in the Middle East: Madeleine Albright, William Cohen, Dennis Ross, Miller and Martin Indyk. It is not possible that the American nation, which consists of 250 million people, can not find anyone other than five Zionist Jews to conduct the peace process with the Palestinians."[79]

Just as Hitler's Mein Kampf was a warning sign for his future political path which brought disaster on Germany and the world, so Netanyahu's A Place Among the Nations explains all of the author's initiatives since he took power in Israel...The racist curses against the enemy and the legendary praises of himself make a noticeable point of similarity between Hitler's and Netanyahu's books...Netanyahu tries to calm Jewish fears about the demographic superiority and the natu-

115

ral Arab birth rates in Palestine…He does not refer to the means he will employ to achieve the goal of a reduction of the Arab birth rate… In this point we are reminded of Hitler's statements about the sterilization of undesired segments of the population.[80]

THE CIVIL AUTHORITY

"This reminds me of Goebbels (Hitler's propaganda minister) who said 'tell lies and lies, and in the end they will believe you.' The same is true of the Jews. It is a disgrace that they are issuing an arrest warrant against me. Apparently they have learned Goebbels' methods."[81]

WE DENIED THE HOLOCAUST

Our first black and white TV was purchased in the 70s. Joyful, my father allowed us to watch until the channel completed its broadcast for the day. That week was a special one. Israel was showing footage of the Holocaust for several days, non-stop. We watched for hours, feasting on popcorn and laughing and mocking. It is said that "a picture is worth a thousand words" yet to us, a whole documentary with millions of pictures was worth nothing. We simply refused to believe it. Even after watching the footage, we still denied the Holocaust as a Jewish fabrication. As I've said, the state of the heart is what governs people, not facts, for not many are concerned about facts.

Mahmoud Abbas (Abu Mazen), Arafat's number two man and author of the book The Other Side, accused the Jews of having a secret relationship between Nazism and the Zionist movement and said less than one million Jews were killed:

"…the Zionist movement was a partner in the slaughter of the Jews."[82]

In a letter to UN Secretary General Kofi Annan, the United Nations Ambassador from Israel, Yehuda Lancry, protested:

"…an alarming campaign of anti-Israel and anti-Jewish incitement emanating from the Arab world…This campaign of propaganda knows no bounds, demonization of the Israeli enemy, the most abhorrent anti-Semitism and the denial of the Holocaust have emerged in *full force."* He also noted that the campaign of rhetoric against Israel has increased as efforts to promote negotiations are intensified.

General Kofi Annan, currently the embattled head of the United Nations, told the American Jewish Committee he supports permanent status privileges for Israel in the UN. Annan acknowledged the misguided efforts to isolate Israel and the *"regrettable impression of bias and one-sidedness"* at the UN. Annan did note some progress, as anti-Semitism finally was listed as a form of racism by the General Assembly. However, he also said that the body again had just passed some anti-Israeli resolutions that *"might prejudice the outcome of delicate [peace] negotiations."*

In the U.S., Holocaust deniers such as Bradley Smith, director of the self-styled *Committee for Open Debate on the Holocaust,* (CODOH) which is described as Holocaust *"revisionism,"* has become one of the most virulent voices for contemporary anti-Semitism.

Bradley's and others' strategies are simple and familiar. They distort, even fabricate, history and then broadcast their propaganda. They have learned from Hitler that *"a lie is believed because of the insolent inflexibility with which it is propagated."* Smith and his cohorts are engaged in what historian Deborah Lipstadt has termed an *"assault on truth and memory."*

While Holocaust denial and Jewish conspiracy theories are known to Americans as pure propaganda, to many in the Middle East, such lies are considered good media and are sold to the public as fact. What we in the West throw out as garbage is put to "good use" by the Middle Eastern newspapers and school authorities. One example is this statement from an article in the official Palestinian Authority newspaper Al-Hayat Al-Jadeedah, September 3, 1997:

"Since its establishment, the racist Zionist entity has been implementing various forms of terrorism on a daily basis which are a repetition of the Nazi terror...This also explains the cooperation between the Jews and the Nazis during World War II, through which were revealed the forged claims of the Zionists regarding alleged acts of slaughter perpetrated against the Jews during the same period..."

Or the following exchange from the official Palestinian Authority TV station, August 25, 1997:

"Moderator: It is well-known that every year the Jews exaggerate what the Nazis did to them. They claim there were 6 million killed, but precise scientific research demonstrates that there were no more than 400,000. Has the complex which the Jews have as a result of the Nazis' actions created within them psychological burdens which they are now releasing against the Palestinians?"

Palestinian author Hassan Al-Agha, responding:

> The truth is I do not think so. Psychological baggage after 40 or 50 years...I am skeptical...But I do think that we are talking about an investment. They have profited materially, spiritually, politically and economically from the talk about the Nazi killings. This investment is favorable to them and they view it as a profitable activity so they inflate the number of victims all the time. In another ten years, I do not know what number they will reach. Last year, for the first time, a statistic appeared according to which 1½ million children were killed by the Nazis. This number was not previously known...If this number was indeed correct, then someone would certainly have remembered it...In my opinion, it is an investment, and as you know, when it comes to economics and investments, the Jews have been very experienced ever since the days of the Merchant of Venice.[83]

"At the end of our period of imprisonment the time passed very slowly. We felt as if we were being burned. Imagine...the Jews are saying: "The Nazis burned us in gas chambers." That is a false tale, but at times I felt that we were those who were being burned up within the walls..." [84]

ARAFAT REVEALED

Yasser Arafat died on November 11, 2004, Veterans' Day in America, in a warm bed in a hospital in France.

His final days were nothing like those of his thousands of innocent Jewish victims who perished at his hand on the streets, in their homes, in their cafes and on the battlefield trying to defend their country from his unrelenting attacks. Nothing like the deaths of all those Palestinians, lost in battles he could have prevented years ago. Nothing like the horrible deaths of the suicide bombers, **many of whom were children, who blew themselves to pieces, confusing reality with hate.** His legacy is that he was one of the greatest terrorists of modern times. He was buried with the blood of thousands on his hands.

What the world must acknowledge is that Arafat *never wanted a Palestinian state because he never wanted the conflict to end.* If he did, he would have accepted the Barak agreement *that gave him everything he claimed he wanted.* He rejected this offer and all others. What does a nation do when it agrees to give the enemy nearly everything it demands but the enemy rejects the offer? So what then, *did* he want? Obviously there is no other answer but the destruction of Israel and the Jews.

Blaming Israel for the plight of the Palestinians, as Arafat and other Arab leaders did, is like turning reality upside down. Israel has done more for the Palestinians than the Arab leaders ever did. Israel built the Palestinians schools, hospitals, and apartments. Jordan and Egypt don't want them back and neither does any other Arab country.

The Palestinians lived in poverty for one reason: Arafat stole their money and their poverty kept them under his control. Millions in financial aid came flowing in. But he and his cabinet, who called the Jews thieves, pocketed much of the money, donated by American tax dollars and by the United Nations.

"Almost all of it was stolen or dribbled away. The Palestinian Authority's own auditors reported last year that nearly 40 percent of the annual budget—$323 million—was wasted, looted, or misused. In President Arafat's regime, bribery was endemic, services are nil, connections are everything, and might is the only right there is." [85]

Recent disclosures indicate the amount may be much greater. Arafat re-routed the money to dozens of banks and to his wife, who lived in luxury in France. While his people lived like peasants.

Yet, the United States Presbyterian Church and other protestant churches decided to punish Israel by divesting stock from companies that do business with her. This is madness. It is also a great injustice and perpetrates the long, ugly history of bigotry against Jews. These groups send leaders to Palestine to meet with a few leaders who tell them the Jews are to blame for everything, and then they fly home. No one can learn the truth that way. The Palestinian poverty exists because 1) Arafat stole millions from his own people 2) he would *never* come to any agreement with Israel and 3) other Arab leaders have a stake in filtering money to the PA to keep the conflict going and therefore keep the face of Israel as the villain on the world's billboard.

We've seen this madness before. The Nobel Committee awarded this murderer and long-time terrorist a peace prize.

Arafat: " No...no. Allah's messenger Muhammad accepted the al-Hudaibiya peace treaty and Salah a-Din accepted the peace agreement with Richard the Lion-Hearted. "

What Arafat was referring to is the permission by Allah to break treaties and agreements made with any enemy. Muhammad had a ten-year pact with the Koreish, which he broke within two years when the Islamic forces strengthened during the cease-fire. He then conquered the very people with whom he had a "peace agreement." Salah a-Din was a Muslim leader who, after a cease-fire, declared a jihad against the Crusaders and captured Jerusalem. This was the plan behind Arafat's "negotiations" for peace with Israel. Think back to how Arafat came smiling to every accord meeting, claiming he was ready to make peace. Yet he never honored any agreement and the killings continued. Finally, sick of the blood and tears, Barak offered him everything Arafat *claimed* he wanted: the land, money, sovereignty, and control of one-half of Jerusalem, a painful accommodation for Israel. Arafat turned it down.

On changing the PLO Covenant, which calls for the total destruction of Israel:

"We have no intention of changing or nullifying the Covenant, rather, we will adhere to it until our last breath since it embodies the essence of our demands."[86]

"Jerusalem is the capital of the state of Palestine whether someone likes it or not, and whoever does not like it, let him drink from the sea of Gaza."[87]

"The Israelis are mistaken if they think we do not have an alternative to negotiations. By Allah I swear they are wrong. The Palestinian people are prepared to sacrifice the last boy and the last girl so that the Palestinian flag will be flown over the walls, the churches and the mosques of Jerusalem."[88]

"Jenin is the first nail in Israel's coffin. We will agree to leave here only the dead Jews who are buried here. Like all Palestinians, I am happy that Arafat is here today in a liberated Palestinian city. With the help of Allah, all the land of Palestine will be liberated. The Jews must return to where they came from, to their Diaspora...Abu Ammar [Yasser Arafat] visited us and spoke with us...Abu Ammar also thinks as I do. In the long run, he will get all of Palestine. He will not give up on one inch of Palestinian land...I don't want to continue living in Gaza or Jenin. My place is in Palestinian Beersheba."[89]

On the liberation of Palestine: "The struggle will continue until all of Palestine is liberated."[90] The chameleon can change colors, but never its nature.

ARAFAT'S CONTINUED TIES TO TERRORISM

Arafat created a "mini Iraq" designed to gain world recognition, particularly from Israel's best ally, the United States. Then, he played the "leader who wanted peace" while continuing terrorist raids. And he had a terrific scapegoat: he would always point the finger at Hamas, yet he fully supported this terrorist group at all times, while he carried on his own brutal "campaign of peace."

Listen to the PA's Justice Minister Freih Abu Medein:

"The PA and the [Hamas] opposition complement each other...We regard Hamas and Islamic Jihad as national elements...The main enemy, now and forever, is Israel."[91]

The Hamas terrorist group enjoys more than full benefits in this new state. The families of terrorists killed in action in bus bombings and other civilian target attacks are awarded free air tickets, monthly allowances, and scholarships abroad. In addition, Hamas receives funding from Palestinian expatriates, from Iran, and from private benefactors in Saudi Arabia and other moderate Arab states. Some fundraising and propaganda activity takes place in Western Europe and North America.

The first lady, Suha, Arafat's wife, carries on the mission and gathers support. She and Arafat gave speeches and threw parties to honor the terrorists, and even named streets after them.

Hamas was created in 1987 in the Gaza Strip. By 1988, it was the PLO's primary rival, and it took advantage of the Intifada from which it had sprung. The Hamas plan was an immediate and unrelenting frontal assault against Israel. Hamas has known ties to Iran and suspected ties to individuals in the United States and Western Europe who are, at the very least, maintaining the group's financial existence. Hamas is one of the leading terrorist organizations of its kind.

Depending on the outcome of the peace process, if the PLO does not deliver the land to the Palestinians, Hamas is the likely candidate to take over Palestinian leadership. It has an armed militant wing known as Izudeen Al-Qassam, which carries out numbers of large-scale suicide bombings against Israeli targets. Primary targets are unarmed Jewish settlers. This makes Hamas even more appealing as it presents the opportunity for the greatest infliction of casualties.

The Hamas relationship to the PLO is complex. Before the Intifada, a number of Hamas members had joined the PLO and many current Islamists are former PLO nationalists.

Arafat refused to extradite Hamas killers to Israel, or to shut down Hamas training camps, or to outlaw Hamas, or even to publicly criticize Hamas by name. Col. Jibril Rajoub, chief of the Palestinian Authority's Preventive Security Service, said in a May 27, 1998 interview with Al-Jazeera television:

> "We view Hamas as part of the national and Islamic liberation movement. Outside of the 3 percent [of Judea-Samaria that is under complete PA control] they can do

as they wish. They can go to Jordan to carry out armed operations and they can also carry out such operations from Syria. At the top of my list of priorities is the [Israeli] occupation and not Hamas. We are not interested in arrests." [92]

Arafat said, 'Hamas, even its military wing, is a patriotic movement.' [93]

Arafat's Foreign Minister, Farouk Kaddoumi, said: 'Hamas is part of the national movement and it has its own style and approach to action. It is resisting the Israeli enemy.' [94]

From PA Cabinet Minister Hanan Ashrawi, "It is not up to Israel to decide or define who is our enemy. Hamas is not the enemy, it is part of the political fabric." [95]

Abbas Zakai of the Fatah Central Committee stated: "[attacks by Hamas] strengthen the Palestinian position...It would be dangerous to stop these actions, because the accords will crumble if there is nothing to make Israel go forward." [96]

Asked by a reporter about Hamas, Arafat replied, "There is no confrontation with Hamas and the Palestinian Authority." [97]

And PA Justice Minister Freih Abu Medein said: "The PA and the [Hamas] opposition complement each other...We regard Hamas and Islamic Jihad as national elements...The main enemy, now and forever, is Israel." [98]

Said PA Cabinet Minister Nabil Sha'ath, "We have a brotherly relationship with Hamas." [99]

Hisham Abdel-Razzak, Fatah leader in Gaza: "The dialogue with Hamas will not be broken off. Hamas is part of the Palestinian people." [100]

Listen to Arafat and his aides praise Hamas terrorists:

"The Engineer," Yahya Ayyash who led the military wing of Hamas and was well known for his proficiency as a 'bomb maker,' suspected of planning seven suicide bombings in Israel that killed as many as 70 people was then killed January 5th, 1996 by improvised explosive device contained within his cellular telephone. Israeli security officials have neither confirmed nor denied their involvement in Ayyash's death. After his death, Arafat praised him as a 'martyr' and had his name given to a public square in Arafat-controlled Jericho, and a street in Beit Lahiya.[101]

The New York Times reported in 1994 that Arafat called Hamas leader, Sheikh Ahmed Yassin, "my brother Ahmed Yassin the warrior."[102]

Following the death of Muhi-Deen Al-Shareef, another Hamas bomb-maker responsible for dozens of Israeli deaths, Yasser Arafat's wife, Suha, publicly praised him as "*a Palestinian martyr,*" as reported by the Jewish Telegraphic Agency, 1998.[103]

After the March 1997 suicide bombing of a Tel Aviv café, killing 3 Israeli women, the Palestinian Legislative Council sent condolences to the family of the bomber, Moussa Ghneimat, and praised him as a "*holy martyr,*" reported by Ma'ariv, 1997. Arafat even went as far as hiring Imad Falouji, a Hamas activist from Gaza, as a Minister without portfolio, and chose Talal Sidr, a Hamas activist from Hebron, as Minister of Youth.[104]

In a statement of June 2, 1998, the Israeli government said that these latest developments prove that "The Palestinian Authority has failed to wage a systematic campaign against terrorist groups. The terrorist infrastructure remains in place and the PA openly approves of terrorist attacks against Israel as long as they do not implicate the Authority."

- Arafat and the PA collaborated with Hamas
- Arafat publicly hugged and kissed Hamas leaders, Abd el-Rantisi and Sheikh Ahmed Yassin.
- Arafat refused to extradite Hamas killers to Israel, to shut down Hamas training camps, to outlaw Hamas, or even publicly criticize Hamas by name.[105]

"Arafat Permits 'Hamas Week' in PA-Controlled Nablus." In November 1997, Arafat permitted the Hamas terrorist group to stage a week-long exhibition glorifying terrorism and terrorists, at A-Najah

University, in PA-controlled Nablus. This was the headline and lead in a November 25, 1997 press release from the Zionist Organization of America. Verification? Arafat's own official newspaper, Al-Hayat Al-Jadeeda, published a report praising the exhibition in its November 23, 1997 edition:

The University's campus was turned into a Palestinian city during the Intifada—dozens of veiled-face individuals carrying [replica] submachine guns, five machine guns on the shoulders, swords and other sharp objects which created the Intifada's unique culture...At the entrance to the "Martyrs' Exhibit," enormous pictures of holy martyrs who ascended to heaven were drawn...as well as a huge drawing of a veiled-face youth, carrying a stone in order to throw it at an occupation patrol...Marking the opening of the "Struggle Week" activities, veiled-face youths blew up and burned an Israeli bus, symbolizing the suicide bombings carried out by Iz a-Din al-Qassam's squads. In one corner, there was a large tent called "The Shahid's Tent," which presented the clothes of holy martyrs who were killed during the Intifada...The body [effigy] of a man who was executed during the Intifada for collaborating with the occupation was hanging on the stem of a palm tree.

PLANTING ISLAM IN THE WEST

"Islam isn't in America to be equal to any other faith, but to become dominant. The Koran...should be the highest authority in America, and Islam the only accepted religion on earth." [106] Quran 86:17: "Be patient with unbelievers until you have strength."

Action is evidence.

Chapter Three
DISTORTING BIBLICAL TEXT

This section and many that follow was written primarily for Christians who claim to believe in the Bible, yet still support the Palestinian cause.

THE ORIGINS GAME

THE PALESTINIANS: ARE THEY ISHMAELITES OR PHILISTINES?

Common Palestinian claim:

"Today's Palestinians are the descendants of the Canaanites. In fact, it's in the Bible:

'Yea, and what have ye to do with me, O Tyre, and Zidon, and all the coasts of Palestine? Will ye render me a recompense? And if ye recompense me, swiftly and speedily will I return your recompense upon your own head...'" [1]

Palestinian claims vary, depending on the issue. If the claim concerns who was there first, then they are descendants of the Canaanites. If the goal is to prove who legally deserves it, then they are Arabs. Both claims are in great error. With the Biblical evidence confirmed by history and by decades of archeological research, the Bible has proven to be the most accurate book on Middle Eastern history. In it is recorded God's plan for Canaan and its peoples.

"Then the LORD said to Moses, 'Leave this place, you and the people you brought up out of Egypt, and go up to the land I promised on oath to Abraham, Isaac and Jacob,' saying, 'I will give it to your descendants. I will send an angel before you and drive out the Canaanites, Amorites, Hittites, Perizzites, Hivites and Jebusites.'" [2]

"Then made this vow to the LORD: 'If you will deliver these people into our hands, we will totally destroy their cities. The LORD listened to Israel's plea and gave the Canaanites over to them. They completely destroyed them and their towns; so the place was named

Hormah.' And today the Palestinian people cling to the idea that they are a descendant of the Canaanites, Jebusites, and Philistines." [3]

Why do Palestinians want to claim Canaanite ancestry anyway? The first occupation of Canaan (the Promised Land) by the nation of Israel, knew that God was One God: "Hear O Israel, the Lord thy God is One." This was a startling revelation in the midst of the nations who were worshipping innumerable *gods*, so holding onto the rejected heathen tribes prior to Israel's existence is no honor. So why did Yasser Arafat and his cabinet insist that they are of Canaanite and Jebusite origin? At the same time, they also insisted that they are Arabs, to the extent of making Jesus a Palestinian revolutionary.

How could Yasser Arafat and the Palestinians be Canaanites and Arabs at the same time? Even the Christian educators of today's Palestine are plagued with Replacement Theology propaganda; Bishara Awad, Dean of Bethlehem Bible College argues: *"You must try reading the New Testament, not the Old when looking at such things."* [4]

Joel 3:4, a Biblical verse that curses the Philistines, is often cited to prove the mention of Palestine. The Hebrew word translated in some versions for Palestine is *Palasheth* which is Philistia, the land of the Biblical Philistines, a non-Semitic people who lived in a small portion of land Southwest on the coast land that included only Joppa, Ashdod, Ashkelon, and Gaza. This presents a major problem, since today's Palestinians claim to originate from Semitic Arabs. To lay stake to a land of promise by misusing Scripture, attributing the land of promise to Ishmael, and claiming to be Philistines, are death blows for the Palestinian argument.

To call today's Israel the land of the Philistines would require a recreation of the other seven nations that made up the land of Canaan. How does one relate today's supposedly Semitic Palestinians to the non-Semitic Hevites, Perazites, and Jebusites? No one today can trace any culture, language, religion, or family origin to any Canaanites from Palestine, and there is ample historical evidence showing the "true" origin of today's Palestinians as we have shown.

In 135 A.D., Emperor Hadrian applied the term "Palestine" to the Land of Israel as a propaganda ploy to erase Israel, his enemy, and replace it with Israel's enemy instead: Philistines with a new Latin twist—Palestine. He replaced the shrines of the Jewish Temple and the Sepulcher of Christ in Jerusalem with temples to pagan deities. Hadrian was an enemy of the Bible, so the question should be, if we support Hadrian's changing the name to Palestine, why then not support his other changes, and convert the holy places to pagan shrines or at least the pagan names that he forced on these places?

Christian Arabs who focus on the New Testament instead of the Old ignore the fact that in the New Testament, the *term Palestine is never used, only Israel*, and no matter how they look at Scripture it always seems they have a problem fitting it to their political agenda. Even in the End-Times, believers in Israel are asked:

"But when they persecute you in this city, flee ye into another: for verily I say to you, Ye shall not have gone over the cities of Israel, till the Son of man shall have come." [5]

So the land is clearly Israel *before* the coming of our Lord, and while He came,[6] and just before His Second Coming, as we have seen in Matt 10:23.

As for Bishara Awad, the Dean of Bethlehem Bible College who asks believers to look to the New Testament since Israel is replaced by the church, the Lord says:

"Hath God cast away His people? God forbid. God hath not cast away His people whom He foreknew." [7]

> "Thus saith the Lord, who giveth the sun for a light by day, and the ordinances of the moon and of the stars for a light by night, who divideth the sea when its waves roar; The Lord of hosts is His name: If those ordinances depart from before Me, saith the Lord, then the seed of Israel also shall cease from being a nation before Me forever. Thus saith the Lord, If heaven above can be measured, and the foundations of the earth searched out beneath, I will also cast off all the seed of Israel for all that they have done, saith the Lord." [8]

This should put the matter to rest.

THE JEWS OF RUSSIA

Common opinion:

"The Jews of Russia and Eastern Europe are originally Khazars from Turkey who converted to Judaism in the 8th century."

"Most of the Khazars [a Turkish tribe that converted to Judaism in medieval times] are the Ashkenazic Jews who arrived in Palestine. As Allah is my witness, in my blood flows more of the Children of Israel and the ancient Hebrews than in the blood of Ariel Sharon and Benjamin Netanyahu."[9]

Response:

Jews existed in the Crimean Peninsula way before the Khazars. What's more notable was their success in this tolerant land.

"Of all the astonishing experiences of the widely dispersed Jewish people none was more extraordinary than that concerning the Khazars."[10]

> The Khazar people were an unusual phenomenon for medieval times. Surrounded by savage and nomadic tribes, they had all the advantages of the developed countries: structured government, vast and prosperous trading, and a permanent army. At the time, when great fanaticism and deep ignorance contested their dominion over Western Europe, the Khazar state was famous for its justice and tolerance. People persecuted for their faiths flocked into Khazaria from everywhere. As a glistening star it shone brightly on the gloomy horizon of Europe, and faded away without leaving any traces of existence.[11]

The Jews of Khazaria, by Kevin Alan Brook, recounts the eventful history of that Turkic kingdom, which was located in Eastern Europe and flourished as an independent state from about 650 to 1016.

Brook states that ancient communities of Jews existed in the Crimean Peninsula way before the Khazars moved to the area, a fact supported by much archaeological evidence. It is significant that Crimea came under the control of the Khazars later on. The Crimean

Jewish communities were later supplemented by refugee Jews fleeing the Mazdaq rebellion in Persia, the persecutions of Byzantine emperors Leo III and Romanus I Lecapenus.

Before the Khazars moved to Crimea, original Jews came to Khazaria from modern-day Uzbekistan, Armenia, Hungary, Syria, Turkey, Iraq, and many other places, as documented by al-Masudi, the Schechter Letter, Saadiah Gaon, and the Arabic writer Dimashqi.

Brook notes that the Jews from the former Russian Empire are descended from a mixture of Khazar Jews, German Jews, Greek Jews, and Slavs. This argument by no means defines the Israeli nation as being foreign. The Jewish people never assimilated into the gentile world while the Khazars were quite different, this was a gentile nation that assimilated to follow the Jewish faith.

If the Jews of Eastern Europe and Russia descended strictly from the Khazars, what can be said of the recent genetic research showing the lineage of the Kohanim? Prof. Karl Skorecki, a senior nephrologist (blood specialist) at Rambam Hospital in Haifa, is the head of molecular medicine at the Technion-Israel Institute of Technology Medical School. He and his colleagues published their findings in *Nature,* a respected British science journal. This new genetic research shows the vast majority of Kohanim, the Jewish priestly class, to be descended from a single ancestor, scientific confirmation of an oral tradition passed down through 3,000 years.

A worldwide project using cutting-edge genetic technology proved that at least 70 percent of Kohanim families (5% of Jewish men), have a common set of markers on their Y chromosome, the chromosome every male receives almost unchanged from his father, and, in effect, from his father's father before him. This genetic evidence was found in Kohanim from both the Ashkenazi (European) and the Sephardi (Spanish and Middle Eastern) branches of the worldwide Jewish population. This is strong proof that the Aaronic priesthood existed in the distant past as the Bible relates.

Further, this provides fascinating evidence that the Jewish priesthood predated the division of the Jewish people into the Ashkenazi and the Sephardi branches, the two major ethnic groups, which occurred approximately 1,000 years ago during the Middle Ages.

David Goldstein, an expert in the field of evolutionary genetics at Oxford University, stated: "It looks like this chromosomal type was a constituent of the ancestral Hebrew population. It was incredibly exciting to find something that could be tracing paternally-inherited traits over 40 to 50 generations, three or four thousand years of history. This is the first time ever we have been able to make a correlation with the ethnographic record over this time scale. Some people keep records that go back three, maybe four generations. But 50 generations!"

THE LAND OF ISHMAEL OR ISAAC?

Common opinion:

God promised the land to Abraham and his seed. Since Ishmael is his seed, they too have the right to the land of Israel.

Ishmael was Abraham's seed, according to Genesis 21:13. To whom was the promise of the land made? To Abraham and his seed, no exceptions, citing Genesis 12:17, 13:15, 15:18. Thus now, even from the Bible, the Arabs are included in the promise.

Does God play favorites? Is God a Zionist because He has been supernaturally assisting the Jews?

Response:

God uses the word *My* in two connections: "*My* people Israel" and "*My* land." In each case He, in a particular way, identifies Himself with them:

"I will establish My covenant as an everlasting covenant between Me and you and your descendants after you for the generations to come to be your God and the God of your descendants after you. The whole land of Canaan where you are now an alien, I will give as an everlasting possession to you and your descendants after you and I will be their God." [12]

God promises to give the whole land to Abraham and his descendants for an everlasting possession. This is established by a covenant of God and God declares in Psalm 89:34 "His covenant He will never break." But to which of his descendants? Ishmael? Isaac? Or both?

In his book, Chapman tries to connect the land to Ishmael, since he is a descendant of Abraham. However, the Bible answers the questions where God tells Isaac:

"Stay in this land (the land of Israel) for a while and I will be with you and bless you for to you and your descendants I will give all these lands and will confirm the oath I swore to your father Abraham. I will make your descendants as numerous as the stars in the sky and I will give them all these lands, and through your offspring all nations on earth shall be blessed." [13]

Later on, God restricts the same promise to Jacob (Israel) alone:

"The land I gave to Abraham and Isaac I also give to you and I will give this land to your descendants after you." [14]

The promise runs through a specific line: from Abraham to Isaac to Jacob and on to their descendants. In Psalm 105, the psalmist uses the following terms to describe the extent of God's commitment to this purpose: covenant, word, command, oath, decree and everlasting covenant. There is no language used in the Bible that could give stronger emphasis to God's commitment.

"He is the Lord our God; His judgments are in all the earth. He remembers His covenant forever, the Word He commanded, for a thousand generations, the covenant He made with Abraham, the oath He swore to Isaac, He confirmed it to Jacob as a decree, to Israel as an everlasting covenant: 'To you I will give the land of Canaan as the portion you will inherit.'" [15]

So all three connect: Abraham, Isaac, and Jacob (Israel) forever. The word "everlasting" makes null and void any other claim to the land. To say that the land is not an issue any longer contradicts God's word. If we believe the Bible to be the Word of God, there is no doubt as to God's purpose for the land. Further, nothing has changed God's purpose from the time that it was spoken until this time of restoration, which was predicted by Jeremiah:

"Write in a book all the words I have spoken to you. The days are coming, declares the Lord, when I will bring My people, Israel and Judah, back from captivity and restore them to the land I gave their forefathers to possess, says the Lord." [16]

If we look at the context of Scripture, we can easily see to whom this *seed* refers,

"But you, O Israel, my servant, Jacob whom I have chosen, you descendants of Abraham my friend, I took you from the ends of the earth, from its farthest corners I called you. I said, 'You are my servant; I have chosen you and have not rejected you.'"[17] ***Jacob was chosen, not Ishmael or the Arabs.***

"Thus saith the Lord, who giveth the sun for a light by day, and the ordinances of the moon and of the stars for a light by night, who divideth the sea when its waves roar; The Lord of hosts is His name: If those ordinances depart from before Me, saith the Lord, then the seed of Israel also shall cease from being a nation before Me forever."[18]

From this, we know that the seed of Abraham is Jacob, and the land is Israel, as they are specifically mentioned and fulfilled by most of the Biblical prophecy in both Old and New Testaments.

If Ishmael's advocates' very-confused argument is accepted, Jesus, the seed of promise, can end up being an Ishmaelite, since God told Abraham concerning the Messianic blessing that out of his seed the whole world will be blessed.[19]

Yet ignorance of Scripture is not an excuse with God, since the rest of Scripture directs us to the remaining story and to whom this seed belongs. The promises of the land in the Abrahamic Covenant are given strictly to Jacob, who was later called Israel. I don't need to quote more verses here, since the entire Bible is written with this promise in God's Mind.

> The Bible concentrates on Israel as the Chosen Nation, the repository of the Covenants, the channel of the Messianic Hope, the custodian of the divinely approved Temple, the keeper of the oracles of God, and the capital nation of the returning crucified and risen King of Kings. Thus, page after page, book after book in the Old and New Testaments deals with these issues that mean little or nothing to world powers or historians. Israel is the central theme of the Bible. "Thus saith the Lord God: Behold, I will take the children of Israel from among the

nations, to which they are gone, and will gather them on every side, and bring them into their own land."[20]

So these promises of land and return clearly involve Israel, not Ishmael. The question is, why are these Christians trying to distort the Bible to shore up Muslim claims? Even a book like the Quran was vague concerning the identity of the child of promise, but the Bible left no doubt. Therefore, what are the false seeds that Replacement Theology plants?

The statement by Pope John Paul II that the "shepherds of Bethlehem," when Christianity was founded 2000 years ago, were the "ancestors" of today's Palestinian Arabs is false. In fact, those shepherds were Jews, not Arabs.

THE NEW TESTAMENT ANSWERS THE QUESTION ABOUT THE LAND

Common opinion:

"Jesus never mentioned Israel being in the land, this is a Christian Zionist invention."

On page 136 of his book, Chapman writes: "He [Jesus] said nothing at all about what would follow the times of the gentiles, and didn't give any clue about the significance of Jerusalem coming once again under Jewish rule."

Response:

In Christian theology, Jesus is the author of all Scripture and every thing created: "All Scripture is given by inspiration of God, and is profit able for doctrine, for reproof, for correction, for instruction in righteousness: That the man of God may be perfect, thoroughly furnished unto all good works."[21] We cannot isolate Jesus' first mission (redemption) from the rest of Scripture, concluding that God did away with the rest of Scripture fulfillment.

Israel will be His focus prior to and after His Second Coming, written in much detail. In fact, the *entire* Bible, in both the Old and New Testaments with the prophets, and Christ and the apostles when they are speaking of Christ's Second Coming—in all Scripture—Israel is in the land, as they were in His First Coming.

Was not Christ to rule Israel?

"And thou Bethlehem, in the land of Judah, art not the least among the princes of Judah: for out of thee shall come a Governor that shall rule my people Israel..." [22]

So, when Christ is to rule Israel in this verse, where would Israel be? This *two-fold* prophecy regarding the rule over Israel is obviously about His Second Coming, with Israel in the land. Even the Replacement Theology advocates would agree that this is a two-fold prophecy, yet they will not accept the *other* two-fold prophecies. One could argue: "But these verses pertain to the Jews returning after Christ establishes His Kingdom, not before." That is not the case.

Matthew 10:23: "But whenever they persecute you in one city, flee to the next; for truly I say to you, you will not finish going through the cities of Israel until the Son of Man comes."

Another two-fold prophecy: when Jesus says "until the Son of Man comes," this pertains to His *Second Coming*, since He is already there talking to them. Why, then won't believers "finish going through" until "The Son of Man comes?"

And to whom is He telling them to witness? None other than Jews: "But he answered and said, I am not sent but unto the lost sheep of the house of Israel." [23] And where is Israel before "The Son of Man comes?" What did Jesus tell the Jews of their Diaspora?

"O Jerusalem, Jerusalem, thou that killest the prophets, and stonest them which are sent unto thee, how often would I have gathered thy children together, even as a hen gathereth her chickens under her wings, and ye would not! Behold, your house is left unto you desolate. For I say unto you, Ye shall not see me henceforth, till ye shall say, Blessed is He that cometh in the name of the Lord." [24]

Jesus was talking to them about Jerusalem while He was in Jerusalem, and He will not return to establish the Kingdom unless they are in Jerusalem crying. "Blessed is he that cometh in the name of the Lord." This return to Israel *with Jews in it* is emphasized by every prophet in the Old Testament and all the way to the Book of Revelation.

Matthew 19:28: "And Jesus said to them, 'Truly I say to you, that you who have followed Me, in the regeneration when the Son of Man will sit on His glorious throne, you also shall sit upon twelve thrones, judging the twelve tribes of Israel.'"

Where is Israel being judged in this verse? And where will His glorious Throne be?

"At that time they shall call Jerusalem the throne of the lord; *and all the Nations Shall Be Gathered Unto It*, to the name of the Lord, to Jerusalem; neither shall they walk anymore after the stubbornness of their evil heart." [25]

The Church will return with Christ to Israel, and will rule with Him for a thousand years.[26] Christ and the disciples will rule over the twelve tribes of Israel in the restoration. Israel was not forgotten in God's plan.

To add more confusion for his readers, Chapman states, regarding Luke's testimony in 24:21: "We had hoped that he [Christ] was the one who was going to redeem Israel." And quoting Luke 24:25-27 regarding the fulfillment of the Scripture in His Messiah role, Chapman concludes that "He wanted them to understand that all that the prophets had said about Israel and its redemption had been fulfilled in himself," yet the author provides no supporting verse. He isolates 24:25-27, taking it out of context. It has no mention of Israel's redemption, apparently, but incorrectly, making Israel's return to the land null and void.

How could Israel's return be invalid when Christ spoke of predictions of the future of Jerusalem?

"And they shall fall by the edge of the sword, and shall be led away captive into all nations: and Jerusalem would be trampled down by the Gentiles (non-Jews), until the fullness of the Gentiles be fulfilled." [27]

While Replacement Theology advocates claim that the "fullness of the Gentiles" means the end of Israel, Christ made this verse plain that a Jewish rule (non-gentile) is what is destined for Israel. Any attempt to make this fit the Church of Replacement Theology requires surgical procedures to Scripture, which will prove fatal to the faith.

Let's look at the context of the verse in Luke 21:24. Jesus is speaking of Jerusalem and of Israel, its destruction, desolation, Diaspora, and return. The part that the author ignores is the previous verse; in *context*, we see: "And they [Israel] will fall by the edge of the sword [destruction], and be away captive into all nations [Diaspora], and Jerusalem will be trampled by the Gentiles [desolation] until the times of the Gentiles are fulfilled [end of Gentile, beginning of Jew]."

This is confirmed in Romans 11:25-27:

"For I would not, brethren, that ye should be ignorant of this mystery, lest ye should be wise in your own conceits; that blindness in part is happened to Israel, until the fullness of the Gentiles be come in. And so all Israel shall be saved: as it is written, There shall come out of Zion the Deliverer, and shall turn away ungodliness from Jacob: For this is my covenant unto them, when I shall take away their sins."

"Oh that the salvation of Israel [were come] out of Zion. When God bringeth back the captivity of his people, Jacob shall rejoice, [and] Israel shall be glad." [28]

This national redemption is confirmed when the Times of the Gentiles is fulfilled. Reading the passage in context, and the previous verse in Romans 11, sheds much light. Jesus is giving them the "full" picture; He is showing them the "full circle" of events in one single sentence: fall, desolation, Diaspora, then Return. This "full circle" scenario is strictly and only for Israel and the Jewish people.

The gentile world will end in judgment; Joel chap. 3 is solely about Israel and its division. Matthew 25:32: "*All the nations [gentiles] will be gathered*," and this judgment is mentioned by Christ describing the treatment of the Jews during the Tribulation Period and the world's persecution of Israel's believers.

The problem with concluding that Jesus was "silent about the future of the land" is, again, the isolation of verses from the context of Scripture. The truth is that Christ, on His First Coming, came to die for our sins. Jesus instructed His disciples to "go only to the lost sheep of the House of Israel" and He reminded a gentile that "Salvation is through the Jews..."[29]

It became evident that salvation was designed for all humankind, beginning with Jerusalem.

The emphasis on salvation by no means negates the many other references to His Second Coming, when the land is mentioned. They are all part of the whole story. Isolating Scripture is like looking at one piece of a puzzle. We get the true picture only when we put all the pieces together.

Chapman, instead, rearranges the pieces, creating any sort of configuration to make his point stick. His mixing of "The Kingdom of Heaven" with the Restoration of the Jews to Israel, is a case in point. On page 127, he compares:

Matthew 8:10-12... "And I say unto you, That many shall come from the east and west, and shall sit down with Abraham, and Isaac, and Jacob, in the kingdom of heaven..." with Isaiah 43:5-6... "Fear not: for I am with thee: I will bring thy seed from the east, and gather thee from the west; I will say to the north, Give up; and to the south, Keep not back: bring my sons from far, and my daughters from the ends of the earth..."

Chapman argues that these verses speak of the same event, "The Kingdom of Heaven," concluding that Isaiah's description of Israel's return is invalid. No, it is not.

Matthew speaks of the "many," while Isaiah speaks strictly of Jacob's seed, Israel. Combining the two to mean a return *only* of the believers in the Kingdom of Heaven, and ignoring Israel's return before God sanctifies her, distorts the true intent of the verses.

The Kingdom of Heaven, as Unger's Bible Dictionary describes it: "The Kingdom of Heaven, more precisely 'The Kingdom of the Heavens,' is a term descriptive of any kind of ruler-ship God may assert on The Earth at a given period...According to Matt 13 the present gospel age represents the mystery form of the kingdom since the kingdom of heaven is no other than the rule of God on Earth..."

"Thou shall arise and have mercy on Zion; for the time to favour her, yes the set time, is come...When the Lord shall build up Zion he shall appear in his glory...This shall be written for the generation to come...to declare the name of the Lord in Zion, and his praise in Jerusalem...When the people are gathered together, and the kingdoms, to serve the Lord"[30]

Here the Lord (Christ) builds up (the land of) Zion, He shall appear in His glory (The Kingdom, the Second Coming), while the kingdoms [the world] come and serve the Lord in Jerusalem. In light of this verse and many others, Chapman continues: "Luke's version of the discourse therefore points to the same conclusions as the discourse in Mark: that Jesus was silent about the future of the land."

Common claim:

The Bible already fulfilled the "desolation and return" of the Jews after the Babylonian Captivity. The claims that some modern interpreters make regarding the recent establishment of the state of Israel have no foundation in the Bible, since all the prophecies they use pertain to the return after the Babylonian captivity, after which there will be a Diaspora with no return. Therefore, this modern state cannot be Biblical.

Response:

God calls Israel specifically "My Land." Out of all the land on the Earth, God has laid a special claim for His sovereign purpose to that little strip of territory which is Israel. In Ezekiel 38:16, He warns the northern invader:

"...to turn thine hand upon the desolate places that are now inhabited, and upon the people that are gathered out of the nations, which have gotten cattle and goods, that dwell in the midst of the land...In days to come, O Gog, I will bring you against My land so that the nations may know Me when I show Myself holy through you before their eyes."

Most Biblical scholars agree that the Gog and Magog prophecy has not been fulfilled but will occur in the End-Times, and Israel must be in the land prior to the fulfillment of this prophecy. This prophecy, and many others which are yet to be fulfilled, assure believers that Israel **will** have another return before the end.

In the Gog and Magog prophecy:

- Israel is described as God's land, desolate, then inhabited.
- Ezekiel and all the prophets describe a gathering *from the nations*, not from Assyria or Babylonia.
- Ezekiel 38 is a battle between Israel and many nations who never attacked Israel in the past.
- This re-gathering to a *desolate* land is an event in the future, far from Ezekiel's time.
- Today exist the very enemies which were mentioned by name: Libya, Persia, Ethiopia, and many others who hate Israel and are accumulating armaments and are likely to be invading Israel soon.

Again in Joel, God declares: "I will gather all nations and bring them down to the valley of Jehoshaphat (which means 'the Lord Judges'); then I will enter into judgment against them concerning My inheritance, My people Israel, for they scattered My people among the nations and *divided up My land*." [31]

This is our warning: the division of the land is taking place right now, after the 1993 Oslo Peace Accord. The extent of denial by the prophecy doubters is seen in Chapman's book, page 115, which provides an interpretation by the philosopher-theologian, *Philo*, who allegorizes the prophecies about Israel's final re-gathering to the land of Israel and changes the meaning from "promised land" to "fruitful wisdom."

Where in the Bible does it say that God intended that only certain scholars interpret Scripture? And with all the existing opposing views, what makes Philo's the correct interpretation?

I am not diminishing the role of scholars. But we need to examine carefully what certain scholars write. For example, there are "scholars" who deny the Holocaust ever existed.

In the time of Christ, there were rabbinical schools with their "common" and "expert" opinions that Jesus was the Messiah who had come to be King of the Jews (thus the Romans putting that name on the cross), yet other rabbis who held that the Messiah would come later.

To hold stubbornly to the "common" and "expert" interpretation is in opposition to the reasoning of Replacement Theology, since its advocates agree that, at times, this group of rabbinical schools was wrong and should have seen that Messiah came first to die for our sins, then would come again to be King and defeat the enemies of Israel. This is what the Bible describes. They should understand that there will be two Diasporas, after they have established Israel, and two re-gatherings.

The Jews would be re-gathered in unbelief at first, and then later, on His Second Coming, they would be redeemed. Why not use the same logic to interpret Messianic prophecies when looking at the land of Israel? Why not look at the Bible in light of occurring events? Isn't it possible "the many" have been incorrectly interpreting the prophecies?

Surely, there is no other way for the Jews to have returned to modern Israel outside of God's plan, as the prophets tell us. God sent Bible prophecy; He intended it to be understood as handed down, which we are able to do by simple cross-referencing the events and teachings and by studying the fulfillments:

"Let them bring forth and show us what will happen; Let them show us the former things, what they were, That we may consider them, And know the latter end of them; Or declare to us the things to come."[32]

So the "latter end of them" would be the fulfillment, and since we cannot see how God will fulfill prophecy in the future, we must wait. When the predictions come to pass, then we shall know that it was God's Will. Only then will we see how the plan of God is carried out.

Take a look at Zechariah 12 and 14. In 12:2-6, we learn of God's plan for Jerusalem:

Behold, I will make Jerusalem a cup of trembling unto all the people round about, when they shall be in the siege both against Judah and against Jerusalem.

The nations of the world will surround Jerusalem: people of the earth will be gathered together against it. And on that day will I make Jerusalem a burdensome stone for all people: all that burden themselves with it shall be cut in pieces, though all the people of the earth be gathered together against it. In that day, saith the LORD, I will smite every horse with astonishment, and his rider with madness: and I will open mine eyes upon the house of Judah, and will smite every horse of the people with blindness. And the governors of Judah shall say in their heart, The inhabitants of Jerusalem shall be my strength in the LORD of hosts their God. On that day will I make the governors of Judah like a hearth of fire among the wood, and like a torch of fire in a sheaf; and they shall devour all the people round about, on the right hand and on the left: and Jerusalem shall be inhabited again in her own place, even in Jerusalem.

How could there be governors of Judah unless we have Israel in the land? Especially when the verse emphasizes that Jerusalem Shall Be Inhabited Again in Her Own Place Even Jerusalem, while verse 3 warns "Though All the People of the Earth be Gathered Together Against It."

This can only be the future fulfillment. When did the "world" ever gather against Jerusalem while the Jews were in Israel? The gentiles will come against the Jews in a final showdown, but once more, and against all odds, the Jew will be triumphant:

In that day shall the LORD defend the inhabitants of Jerusalem; and he that is feeble among them at that day shall be as David; and the house of David shall be as God, as the angel of the LORD before them. And it shall come to pass in that day, that I will seek to destroy all the nations that come against Jerusalem. And I will pour upon the house of David, and upon the inhabitants of Jerusalem, the spirit of grace and of supplications: and they shall look upon Me whom they have pierced, and they shall mourn for Him, as one mourneth for his only son, and shall be in bitterness for Him, as one that is in bitterness for his firstborn.

In Zachariah 12:8-10, we learn that the "Lord" who was "pierced" (verse 10), will fight for Judah. When has the Lord who was pierced fought for Judah in a battle? This is obviously His Second Coming when Israel will be in the land. Then Christ will pour upon Israel His Holy Spirit and have mercy on them, thus a national redemption of Israel is fulfilled.

"And one shall say unto him, What are these wounds in thine hands? Then he shall answer, Those with which I was wounded in the house of my friends." [33] The pierced Messiah will have the signs left on His hands.

"Behold, the day of the LORD cometh, and thy spoil shall be divided in the midst of thee. For I will gather all nations against Jerusalem to battle; and the city shall be taken, and the houses rifled, and the women ravished; and half of the city shall go forth into captivity, and the residue of the people shall not be cut off from the city." [34] Again, *"all nations."*

In this battle, Israel will suffer rape and pillage, and half of Jerusalem will be taken. The world's mock trial and the sinister plots finally culminate in an attempt to execute the world's scapegoat.

> "Then shall the LORD go forth, and fight against those nations, as when he fought in the day of battle. And his feet shall stand in that day upon the mount of Olives, which is before Jerusalem on the east, and the mount of Olives shall cleave in the midst thereof toward the east and toward the west, and there shall be a very great valley; and half of the mountain shall remove toward the north, and half of it toward the south." [35] Israel's defender will finally intervene, and His feet, like a mighty judge's hammer, will strike the earth for His judgment. The Lord's feet will stand on the Mount of Olives? When did the Lord have feet?

Christ in the flesh at His Second Coming will defend Israel and assure its right to the land and its eternal existence; in fact, Christ comes to the aid of Israel to fulfill His promise:

"And I will bring again the captivity of my people Israel, and they shall build the waste cities and inhabit them...and I will plant them upon their land, and they shall no more be pulled up out of their land which I have given them, sayeth the Lord thy God." [36] "And They Shall No More Be Pulled Up."

144

Here's the final blow to the argument regarding Israel's restoration from the Babylonian captivity as the *only* Biblically supported re-gathering. How can it be true that there was a Diaspora after Christ's first coming, yet this verse strictly emphasizes that Israel *"Shall No More Be Pulled Up?"* At which re-gathering is Israel promised never to be scattered? This is the dilemma of the nations: Israel won all the wars waged against her. Even when the whole world goes against Israel, the plans will be destroyed when God (Christ) Himself intervenes.

Chapman causes more confusion, not edification, when on page 112, he doubts the authenticity of the Book of Isaiah: *"Whether the rest of the book [Isaiah] (chapter 40-46) was written by the same writer or by a later writer during the exile..."* which is an argument often pursued by atheists and agnostics. The argument became moot when the Dead Sea Scrolls revealed that the book of Isaiah had not even a break between the alleged "two Isaiahs."

On pages 117-118, Chapman references Ezekiel with only scattered comments and half sentences, ignoring much of the prophecy that does not support his views.

Ezekiel 11:17: "Therefore say, Thus saith the Lord GOD; I will even gather you from the people, and assemble you out of the countries where ye have been scattered, and I will give you the land of Israel."

Ezekiel 20:41: "I will accept you as a sweet aroma when I bring you out from the peoples and gather you out of the countries where you have been scattered."

Ezekiel 36:6-ll: "Prophesy therefore concerning the Land of Israel and say... I will settle you after your old estates, and will do better unto you than at your beginnings: and you shall know that I am the Lord."

First a re-gathering to the land, then a re-gathering back to God; "know that I am the Lord." This re-gathering in unbelief is confirmed in another verse:

"But I had pity for my holy name, which the house of Israel had profaned...therefore, I do not this for your sakes, O house of Israel, but for my holy name's sake...and I will sanctify my great name...and the heathen (Gentiles) shall know that I am the Lord when I shall be sanctified in you before their eyes. For I will take you from among the heathen, and gather you out of all the countries, and will bring you into your own land. THEN will I sprinkle clean water upon you...A new heart also will I give you..."[37]

God gathers Israel for His glory first, then to sanctify them.

> Ezekiel 34: 12-15, 28: "As the shepherd seeks out his flock on the day that he is among his scattered sheep, so will I seek out My sheep and deliver them from all the places where they were scattered. And I will bring them out from the peoples and gather them from the countries and will bring them to their own land. I will feed them on the mountains of Israel, in the valleys and all the inhabited places of the country...And they shall no longer be a prey to the nations. Nor shall other lands devour them. But they shall dwell safely and no one shall make them afraid."

God will feed them "on the mountains of Israel" and they "shall no longer be a prey to the nations" (gentiles). Nor shall other lands devour them. Is it not true that Israel for two millennia was prey to the gentiles? Then how can we exchange Israel for the Church and make sense of these verses?

> Again in Ezekiel 36:23 and 36: "And I will sanctify My great name which has been profaned among the nations, which you have profaned in their midst, and the nations shall know that I am the LORD, says the LORD God, when I am hallowed in you before their eyes...Then the nations which are left all around you shall know that I the LORD have rebuilt the ruined places and planted what was desolate. I the LORD have spoken it and I will do it."

And in Ezekiel 39:29: "I will not hide My face from them anymore; for I shall have poured out My Spirit upon the whole house of Israel, says the LORD God."

The Bible itself tells us whose promised land this is.

146

WHO SCATTERED THE PALESTINIANS?

Abu Mazen wrote in an article titled, Madha `Alamna wa-Madha Yajib An Na`mal, *What We Have Learned and What We* Should *Do*, published in Falastin eth-Thawra, Revolutionary Palestine, the official journal of the PLO, Beirut, March 1976:

"The Arab armies entered Palestine to protect the Palestinians from the Zionist tyranny but instead, they abandoned them, forced them to emigrate and to leave their homeland...The Arab states succeeded in scattering the Palestinian people."

Khaled al-Azm, who served as Prime Minister of Syria in 1948 and 1949, wrote in his memoirs that among the reasons for the Arab failure in 1948 was

"...the call by the Arab Governments to the inhabitants of Palestine to evacuate it and to leave for the bordering Arab countries, after having sown terror among them...Since 1948 we have been demanding the return of the refugees to their homes. But we ourselves are the ones who encouraged them to leave...We have brought destruction upon a million Arab refugees, by calling upon them and pleading with them to leave their land, their homes, their work and business..." [38]

Harry C. Stebbens, who was an official in the British Mandatory Government in Palestine in 1947-48, wrote:

"Long before the end of the British mandate, between January and April, '48, practically all my Arab Palestinian staff of some 200 men and women and all of the 1800 labor force had left Haifa in spite of every possible effort to assure them of their safety if they stayed. They all left for one or more of the following reasons:

1. The Arab terrorism engendered by the November, 1947, U.N. partition resolution frightened them to death of their imaginative souls and they feared Jewish retaliation.

2. Propagandists promised a blood bath as soon as the mandate ended in which the streets of all the cities would run with blood.

3. The promised invasion by the foreign Arab armies (which started on May 14, 1948, with the Arab Legion massacre of some 200 Jewish settlers at Kfar Etzion) was preceded by extensive broad-

casts from Cairo, Damascus, Amman, and Beirut to the effect that any Arabs who stayed would be hanged as collaborators with the Jews.

"It is true that the massacre of Deir Yassin (always quoted by the Arabs) caused some to be refugees. But the massacre of Kfar Etzion, the massacre of the hospital convoy which killed 48 Jewish doctors and nurses, and the continued shelling and blasting of Jewish settlements for more than 20 years, has not caused one single Israeli to move away. They sit tight, if necessary, in their shelters, while across the river where the shooting comes from, the towns and villages are deserted, last year's crops still rot on the trees and the refugees move still further away from any trouble." [39]

Jamal Husseini, in charge of the Palestine Higher Committee, told the Security Council on 23 April 1948, *"...we have never concealed the fact that we began the fighting..."*

On September 6, 1949, the Beirut Telegraph carried an interview with Emile Ghoury, Secretary of the Palestine Higher Committee, in which he said: *"The fact that there are these refugees is the direct consequence of the act of the Arab states in opposing partition and the Jewish state."*

The Jordan daily, Falastin, stated in February, 1949: "The Arab states which had encouraged the Palestine Arabs to leave their homes temporarily in order to be out of the way of the Arab invasion armies, have failed to keep their promises to help these refugees."

As late as October 12, 1963, the Cairo daily, Akhbar el-Yom, recalled: "15 May 1948 arrived...on that very day the Mufti of Jerusalem appealed to the Arabs of Palestine to leave the country, because the Arab armies were about to enter and fight in their stead..."

A British police report to Jerusalem Headquarters on April 26, 1948 attested:

"Every effort is being made by the Jews to persuade the Arab population to stay and carry on with their normal lives..."

In Haifa, on April 27, 1948, the Arab National Committee refused to sign a truce, reporting in a memorandum to the Arab League Governments:

...when the delegation entered the conference room it proudly refused to sign the truce and asked that the evacuation of the Arab population and their transfer to neighboring Arab countries be facilitated...The military and civil authorities and the Jewish representatives expressed their profound regret. The mayor of Haifa (Mr. Shabtai Levi) adjourned the meeting with a passionate appeal to the Arab population to reconsider its decision...

"The first group of our fifth columnists consists of those who abandon their houses and business and go to live elsewhere... At the first sign of trouble they take to their heels to escape sharing the burden of struggle." [40]

"The Arab streets are curiously deserted and, evidently following the poor example of the more moneyed class there has been an exodus from Jerusalem too, though not to the same extent as in Jaffa and Haifa." [41]

"The refugees were confident that their absence would not last long, and that they would return within a week or two. Their leaders had promised them that the Arab Armies would crush the 'Zionist gangs' very quickly and that there was no need for panic or fear of a long exile." [42]

"Of the 62,000 Arabs who formerly lived in Haifa not more than 5,000 or 6,000 remained. Various factors influenced their decision to seek safety in flight. There is but little doubt that the most potent of the factors was the announcements made over the air by the Higher Arab Executive, urging the Arabs to quit...It was clearly intimated that those Arabs who remained in Haifa and accepted Jewish protection would be regarded as renegades." [43]

All the above statements were written while the exodus of refugees-to-be was still taking place. Let's look at statements made *after* the fact:

"The Arab states encouraged the Palestine Arabs to leave their homes temporarily in order to be out of the way of the Arab invasion armies." [44]

"It must not be forgotten that the Arab Higher Committee encouraged the refugees' flight from their homes in Jaffa, Haifa, and Jerusalem." [45]

"The Arab exodus, initially at least, was encouraged by many Arab leaders, such as Haj Amin Al-Husseni, the exiled pro-Nazi Mufti of Jerusalem, and by the Arab Higher Committee for Palestine. They viewed the first wave of Arab setbacks as merely transitory. Let the Palestine Arabs flee into neighboring countries. It would serve to arouse the other Arab peoples to greater effort, and when the Arab invasion struck, the Palestinians could return to their homes and be compensated with the property of Jews driven into the sea." [46]

"We will smash the country with our guns and obliterate every place the Jews seek shelter in. The Arabs should conduct their wives and children to safe areas until the fighting has died down." [47]

"This wholesale exodus was due partly to the belief of the Arabs, encouraged by the boasting of an unrealistic Arab press and the irresponsible utterances of some of the Arab leaders that it could be only a matter of some weeks before the Jews were defeated by the armies of the Arab states and the Palestinian Arabs enabled to re-enter and retake possession of their country." [48]

"I do not want to impugn anybody but only to help the refugees. The fact that there are these refugees is the direct consequence of the action of the Arab states in opposing partition and the Jewish state. The Arab states agreed upon this policy unanimously and they must share in the solution of the problem." [49]

"The Secretary General of the Arab League, Azzam Pasha, assured the Arab peoples that the occupation of Palestine and of Tel Aviv would be as simple as a military promenade...He pointed out that they were already on the frontiers and that all the millions the Jews had spent on land and economic development would be easy booty, for it would be a simple matter to throw Jews into the Mediterranean... Brotherly advice was given to the Arabs of Palestine to leave their land, homes, and property and to stay temporarily in neighboring fraternal states, lest the guns of the invading Arab armies mow them down." [50]

"The Arab governments told us: get out so that we can get in. So we got out, but they did not get in." [51]

Chapter Four
ISRAEL AND THE LAND
CONTROVERSY

WHO RULED IT?

"For Zion's sake will I not hold my peace, and for Jerusalem's sake I will not rest, until the righteousness thereof go forth as brightness, and the salvation thereof as a lamp that burneth. And the Gentiles shall see thy righteousness, and all kings thy glory...I have set watchmen upon thy walls, O Jerusalem, which shall never hold their peace day nor night: ye that make mention of the LORD, keep not silence." [1]

The Bible describes Israel as "land upon which the eyes of God are always turned." [2]

The great American writer, Mark Twain, describing the Jews, wrote:

> If the statistics are correct, the Jews represent merely one percent of humanity—an irrelevant spark in the light of the Milky Way. Normally speaking, the Jews should hardly be heard of, and yet we heard and hear of them again and again. They can rival any people on earth in fame, and their significance in economy and trade are in no ratio to their population. Their contribution to the list of great names in literature, natural science, art, music, finance, medicine and profound learning is just as amazing. They have done extremely well in this world—with their hands tied behind their backs. They could rightly be proud of themselves. The Egyptians, Babylonians and Persians came into power, filled the earth with their glory, but perished. The Greeks and Romans followed, "made a lot of noise," and then disappeared. Other nations rose up, their torches burned for a while, and then they were extinguished, and today they sit in the twilight or have completely disappeared. The Jews saw it all. They beat them all, and are today what they always

were, showing no decay, no aging, no weakening, no decline of energy, no blunting of their wide-awake dynamic spirit. Everything is mortal except the Jew. All other powers perish but he remains. What is the mystery of his immortality?"[3]

Common Palestinian claims:

"We didn't kick out the Jews, the Romans did, and the Arabs came there later, so why do the Arabs have to take the heat?"

"The land was always ruled by Arabs, what gives the Jews the right to rule it?"

"The Arabs owned and governed the land for a millennium."

"The land was Arab with a majority Arab population from time immemorial."

"The land is Arab Palestine not Jewish Israel."

"The country was inhabited by Arabs throughout the centuries; in 1948 when Israel was established, there were thriving cities like Jerusalem, Yaffa, Hebron, Lud, and many others."

PLO TV: "all the events surrounding Kings Saul, David and Rehoboam occurred in Yemen, and no Hebrew remnants were found in Israel, for a very simple reason—because they were never here."[4]

Response: The Bible itself refutes all these claims.

Solomon Prov.18:17: "He who states his case first seems right, until the other comes and examines him."

Matthew 23: "Behold, your house is left unto you desolate…" "predicting the destruction of the Temple and the Diaspora..."

Ezekiel 36: "The desolate land shall be tilled instead of lying desolate in the sight of all who pass by. So they will say, 'This land that was desolate has become like a Garden of Eden, and the waste and desolate and ruined cities are now fortified and inhabited.'"

Chapman questions the validity of the Jewish claims. Perhaps you can't judge a book by its cover, but Chapman's cover title is an obvious play on the phrase long associated with Israel, "the promised land," and it is clear he is challenging that historical tie.

While the cover of the book suggests that both sides are examined, "What are the claims and counter claims?" an examination, as suggested by Solomon in Proverbs 18:17, shows a clear bias. Chapman presents an incomplete summary of the history of the land. To get to the truth, we have to look at the information he omitted.

For example, the very title of Chapter One, 16 1.6: "Palestine under the Babylonians, Persians, and Greeks." There never was a *Palestine* during any of these empires, yet Chapman presents it as historical fact.

DID THE ARABS RULE THE LAND?

To give the Arabs the credit for ruling the land for hundreds of years, Chapman sums up two dynasties, one in section 1.9 titled, "Palestine under the Arabs," and then "Seljuk Turks" (632–1096), stretching the period of "Arab rule" by combining the two.

"While the Palestinian Arabs cannot claim to be 'pure Arabs', they can maintain without any doubt that their ancestors—however mixed racially they may be—have been living in the land for thirteen centuries at the very least (i.e., since the seventh century AD)."

Historian David George Hogarth, who was described by Arab writers as "one of the greatest authorities of his time on Arabian history," said:

"Arabs governed Arabs through Arabs on an imperial scale for much less than a century. It is just the Umayyad Caliphate—the Damascus period and no more."

Chapman's exaggeration grows. Faisal Husseni, a right-hand man to Yasser Arafat, was interviewed on the Zola Levitt television program and bluntly claimed that the Palestinians originated from the Jebusites before Abraham moved to Israel. He clearly changed the historic facts for an American audience that he believed lacked knowledge of Eastern History.

Contrary to these arguments which plague the schools of the West Bank, today's Palestinians are immigrants from many nations,

"Balkans, Greeks, Syrians, Latins, Egyptians, Turks, Armenians, Italians, Persians, Kurds, Germans, Afghans, Circassians, Bosnians, Sudanese, Samaritans, Algerians, Motawila, Tartars, Hungarians, Scots, Navarese, Bretons, English, Franks, Ruthenians, Bohemians, Bulgarians, Georgians, Syrians, Persian Nestorians, Indians, Copts, Maronites, and many others."[5]

It was only in 1878, that harsh conditions forced many groups to immigrate into Palestine: "Circassians, Algerians, Egyptians, Druses, Turks, Kurds, Bosnians, and others. 141,000 settled Muslims living in all of Palestine (all areas) in 1882, at least 25% of those 141,000 were newcomers who arrived after 1831 from the Egyptian conquest."[6]

"The Arab Muslims took the land from the Byzantines, later came the Abbasids who entrusted the land to Iranians, who trusted mercenaries, at first Persian, then Turk, Circassian, Kurd—any race but the Arabians…"[7]

After the Turkish Ottomans, the British fought the Turks for supporting the Nazis, and legally created the state of Israel. There was never a call for a National Palestine except after the Jews got the land. The Arabs then, out of jealousy, attacked, in an attempt to wipe out all the Jews, which resulted in an Arab defeat, as the Bible predicted.

There is conclusive historical and archaeological evidence of an unbroken Jewish presence in Jerusalem since 438 AD, 200 years before the Arab conquest in 638 AD.

Since 1820, the Jews constituted the largest single community there. Despite persecution and oppression, the Jewish presence in Jerusalem was interrupted only twice: under Byzantine rule between 135 and 438 AD, and during the Crusader Kingdom, which lasted from 1099 to 1187 AD.

Despite volumes of historical accounts on Israel's desolation, Chapman concludes: "Given the situation of Palestine at the end of the nineteenth century—with 5 per cent Jews and 95 per cent Arabs living under the Ottoman Empire," he lashes at Theodore Herzl, "But I cannot see how he [Herzl] can be excused for describing Palestine to European audiences as 'a land without a people.'"[8]

In the entire history of Arab and Muslim conquest of the land, and with the claim for the Temple Mount as the third most holy place, never was any significant Islamic school established, or an Arab Jerusalem capital, or a valid state set up for the Arabs. The city of Jerusalem was never visited by any Arab leader besides the kings of Jordan, and the *Sunnah* requirement of the Haj to visit Jerusalem was not practiced by Muslims. Even running water and electricity were never installed. There was never a call for a Palestinian state in all Arab history—*only* after the Jews returned to Israel. Yet the Jews made all the "nevers" possible when they made this ignored land a nation. They made Jerusalem a capital, opened the holy places to all three religions, and built it like never before.

A LAND OF DESOLATION

Remember the prophecy about taking the desert and turning it into a Garden of Eden? The Diaspora of the Jews, which was prophesied by Christ and the prophets before Him, left Israel a land of desolation.

Prior to the 1800s, the land was not inhabited except for small impermanent pockets of people scattered throughout the country. History contradicts the propagandists of today; the land was not a thriving nation, ever, in the past 2000 years and never until the Jews made it so.

Here is just a sample of observations made by visitors of all backgrounds:

In 1697 Jews from Papal states, whose immigration was approved by a Papal bull, were resettling Tiberius. Nazareth was continuing its decline. A Franciscan pilgrim wrote "A house of robbers, murderers, the inhabitants are Saracens...it is a lamentable thing to see thus such a town. We saw nothing more stony, full of thorns and desert." [9]

As for population, in the mid 1700s, British archeologist Thomas Shaw wrote that the land in Palestine was "lacking in people to till its fertile soil." [10]

Count Constantine F. Volney claimed in 1793 that the population of Jerusalem was "less then 14,000; Hebron had 900 men, and Bethlehem had only 600 adult men."

J. S. Buckingham described his visit of 1816 to Jaffa, which "has all the appearances of a poor village, and every part of it that we saw was of corresponding madness."

And he described Ramle, "where, as throughout the greater part of Palestine, the ruined portion seemed more extensive than that which was inhabited."

After a visit in 1817—1818, travelers reported that there was not "a single boat of any description on that lake Tiberius..." [11]

French poet, Alphonse de Lamartine, in 1835 said: "Outside the gates of Jerusalem we saw indeed no living object. Heard no living sound. We found the same void, the same silence that we should have found before the entombed gates of Pompeii or of Greece. A complete eternal silence reigns in the town, in the highways, in the country; the tomb of a whole people."

The British Consul in Palestine reported in 1857, "The country is in a considerable degree empty of inhabitants and therefore its greatest need is that of a body of population."

In 1863, Mark Twain writes: "a desolate country whose soil is rich enough, but given over wholly to weeds—a silent mournful expanse ...Desolation is here that not even imagination can grace with the pomp of life and action...We never saw a human being on the whole route." [12]

Historian and writer De Haas records: "The real source of the interest in the problem was the condition of Palestine; empty, silent, waste, ruin between 1840 and 1880..." [13]

In 1840, Jerusalem's population was 15,000, of whom 8,000 were Jews, 4,500 Muslims, and the rest Christians.

The Arabs' unfounded claim that Jerusalem was always predominately Arab-Muslim territory is negated by the statistics: [14]

1844—Jews 7,120	Muslims 5,000	Christians 3,390
1896—Jews 28,112	Muslims 8,560	Christians 8,748
1922—Jews 33,971	Muslims 13,413	Christians 14,699
1948—Jews 100,000	Muslims 40,000	Christians 25,000
1967—Jews 195,700	Muslims 54,963	Christians 12,64
1983—Jews 300,000	Muslims 105,000	Christians 15,000

In 1880, the American Consul in Jerusalem reported the area was continuing its historic decline. "The population and wealth of Palestine has not increased during the last forty years," he said. These numbers are confirmed by the report of the 1863 British Consul in Jerusalem.

DeHass writes again, "The real source of the interest in the problem was the condition of Palestine; empty, silent, waste, ruin between 1840 and 1880…" [15]

Carl Herman Voss said: "In the twelve and a half centuries between the Arab conquest in the seventh century and the beginning of the Jewish return in the 1880's, Palestine was laid waste. Its ancient canal and irrigation system were destroyed and the wondrous fertility of which the Bible spoke vanished into desert and desolation…Under the Ottoman Empire of the Turks, the policy of (de)foliation continued; the hillsides were denuded of trees and the valleys robbed of their topsoil." [16]

1889—30,000 out of 40,000 people in Jerusalem are Jews.

Ernst Frankenstine: "It was in 1878, harsh conditions forced many groups to immigrate to Palestine; Circassians, Algerians, Egyptians, Druses, Turks, Kurds, Bosnians, and others. 141,000 settled Muslims living in all of Palestine (all areas) in 1882, at least 25% of those 141,000 were newcomers who arrived after 1831 from the Egyptian conquest." [17]

All these people came to this area no more than 150 years ago and were not even Arabs. The Arab immigrant clans like Al-Nashasheebi, Al-Khalidi, and Al-Husseni settled in Palestine in the same period and were given the status of "Efendi" which made them an upper class taking over the lands while the rest of the lower class *Falaheen* were exploited.

The great majority of what are called "the Palestinian Arabs" are of very recent origin, starting in the nineteenth century and immigrating from many nations, most of which are not even Arab. The Report of the Palestine Royal Commission quotes an account of the Maritime Plain in 1913:

> The road leading from Gaza to the north was only a summer track suitable for transport by camels and carts...no orange groves, orchards or vineyards were to be seen until one reached [the Jewish village of] Yabna [Yavne]...Houses were all of mud. No windows were anywhere to be seen...The ploughs used were of wood...The yields were very poor...The sanitary conditions in the village were horrible. Schools did not exist...The western part, towards the sea, was almost a desert...The villages in this area were few and thinly populated. Many ruins of villages were scattered over the area, as owing to the prevalence of malaria, many villages were deserted by their inhabitants.

Lewis French, the British Director of Development wrote of Palestine:

> We found it inhabited by fellahin who lived in mud hovels and suffered severely from the prevalent malaria...Large areas...were uncultivated...The fellahin, if not themselves cattle thieves, were always ready to harbor these and other criminals. The individual plots...changed hands annually. There was little public security, and the fellahin's lot was an alternation of pillage and blackmail by their neighbors, the Bedouin.

Surprisingly, many people who were not sympathetic to the Zionist cause believed the Jews would improve the condition of Palestinian Arabs. For example, Dawood Barakat, editor of the Egyptian paper "Al-Ahram," wrote:

"It is absolutely necessary that an entente be made between the Zionists and Arabs, because the war of words can only do evil. The Zionists are necessary for the country: The money which they will bring, their knowledge and intelligence, and the industriousness which

160

characterizes them will contribute without doubt to the regeneration of the country."

Even a leading Arab nationalist believed the return of the Jews to their homeland would help resuscitate the country. According to Sherif Hussein, the guardian of the Islamic Holy Places in Arabia:

> The resources of the country are still virgin soil and will be developed by the Jewish immigrants. One of the most amazing things until recent times was that the Palestinian used to leave his country, wandering over the high seas in every direction. His native soil could not retain a hold on him, though his ancestors had lived on it for 1000 years. At the same time we have seen the Jews from foreign countries streaming to Palestine from Russia, Germany, Austria, Spain, America. The cause of causes could not escape those who had a gift of deeper insight. They knew that the country was for its original sons (abna'ihilasliyin), for all their differences, a sacred and beloved homeland. The return of these exiles (jaliya) to their homeland will prove materially and spiritually [to be] an experimental school for their brethren who are with them in the fields, factories, trades and in all things connected with toil and labor.

Baedeker's Guide of 1911 reports Jerusalem's total population as 70,000: 45,000 Jews, 15,000 Christians and 10,000 Muslims.

King Hussein foresaw the regeneration of Palestine, and the growth of its population came only after Jews returned in massive numbers. The Jewish population increased by 470,000 between World War I and World War II while the non-Jewish population rose by 588,000. In fact, the permanent non-Jewish population increased 120 percent between 1922 and 1947.

This rapid growth was a result of several factors. One was immigration from neighboring states—constituting 37 percent of the total immigration to pre-state Israel by non-Jews who wanted to take advantage of the higher standard of living the Jews had made possible. The Arab population also grew because of the improved living conditions created by the Jews as they drained malarial swamps and brought improved sanitation and health care to the region. The Muslim infant mortality rate fell from 201 per thousand in 1925 to 94 per thousand in 1945, and life expectancy rose from 37 years in 1926 to 49 in 1943.

In fact, the non-Jewish population increased the most in cities with large Jewish populations that had created new economic opportunities. From 1922-1947, the non-Jewish population increased 290 percent in Haifa, 131 percent in Jerusalem and 158 percent in Jaffa. The growth in Arab towns was more modest: 42 percent in Nablus, 78 percent in Jenin and 37 percent in Bethlehem.

Within the last 40 centuries, Arabs ruled the land for less then one of them. I say to the Arabs, if your current claim to the land is based on the length of time you ruled historically, it's best to find another argument.

DID THE JEWS STEAL THE LAND?

Common Palestinian opinion:

"The Jews entered Palestine forcefully and stole the land."

Response:

How? Did they come carrying artillery or any weapons at all? Did they have a standing army? Was there a military front from which they entered? The answer to all of these questions is, of course, no. Here are the facts.

The Jews created Israel out of land they obtained in three ways:

1. *Government-owned land* which was legally given to them by the British Mandate.

2. *Jews bought the rest from Arabs who were more than willing to sell*. I know that my own grandfather sold land to the Jews, as did many, many other Arabs because they got good prices for it and it had little other value to them. We have the documents.

3. *All other land was acquired as the result of the unsuccessful attacks on Israel*, particularly the Six-Day War when the tiny new nation fought off the armies of 5 Arab nations, plus the

Palestinians and other guerrillas. And even much of that land was returned when an honest accord was reached. Israel returned control of the Sinai to Egypt, along with the very profitable Eilat resort area, as per the truce agreement with Anwar Sadat.

The weekly *Fasl al-Maqal*, owned by Arab-Israeli parliament deputy Azmi Beshara and based in the predominantly Arab city of Nazareth in north Israel, ran a list of 54 leading Palestinians who sold land to Jews from 1918-1945.

As'ad elShuqeiri, a Muslim religious scholar and father of PLO chairman Ahmed Shuqeiri, took Jewish money for his land. Even King Abdullah leased land to the Jews. In fact, many leaders of the Arab nationalist movement, including members of the Muslim Supreme Council, sold land to Jews.

The paper reported that Yasser Arafat's grandfather in Jerusalem sold land to Jews in the years before Israel's founding.

The paper ran a story titled "Our Fathers On The Take" that took the issue back to the era of the British mandate before Israel's founding in 1948, when the Zionist movement was seeking land in Palestine. The paper reports that some of the people highest in the Palestinian nationalist movement, which opposed the Jewish state, were, at the same time, selling land to the Jewish Agency, the body spearheading the Zionist drive. The weekly's editor-in-chief, Awad Abdel Fatah, reported that the names came from an official document dating back to the British mandate in Palestine, which the paper received from official sources in Jordan.

"We published only a partial list from the document, showing the role of the Palestinian leadership in the flow of lands to the Jewish Agency before the disaster of 1948," he said.

Besides Arafat's grandfather, one of the most prominent names on the list is *Muhammad Taher al-Husseni,* father of *Haj Amin Al-Husseni,* the mufti of Jerusalem and supreme head of the Palestinian nationalist movement. Another was *Kazem al-Husseni, grandfather on the mother's side of Faisal Husseni,* the top PLO official in Jerusalem. Kazem sold lands in Jerusalem, where he was mayor from 1918-1920. The list includes five other members of the Husseni family, one of the most prominent clans in pre-1948 Palestine and today.

Other leading Palestinian families also showed up on the list, as did members of the *High Arab Committee*, the *High Islamic Council* and the *Arab Executive Committee*, the main bodies that led the nascent Palestinian nationalist movement against Zionism. *Mussa al-Alami*, who headed the Palestinian delegation to the London Conference of 1939 that convened to discuss the future of mandate Palestine, sold 90 hectares (222 acres) to Jews in Bisan, now the north Israeli city of Beit Shean.

Ragheb al-Nashashibi, mayor of Jerusalem from 1920-1934 and head of the National Defense Party, sold over 120 hectares (296 acres) of land in Jaffa, outside Tel Aviv. Nashashibi also sold land in east Jerusalem upon which the Hebrew University was later built.

Yaakub al-Ghussein, who headed the Arab Fund that was created to gather money to support the Palestinian cause, sold land to Jews in Jaffa, what is now the Gaza Strip, for 4,000 Palestinian pounds, equivalent to British pound sterling at that era. Other elite Muslim and Christian families of Palestine were listed, including the *Abdel Hadi, Bseiso, and Fahum clans.*

Despite the growth in their population, the Arabs continued to assert they were being displaced. The truth is that from the beginning of World War I, part of Palestine's land was owned by absentee landlords who lived in Cairo, Damascus and Beirut. About 80 percent of the Palestinian Arabs were debt-ridden peasants, semi-nomads and Bedouins.

In 1946, the British Mandate Government surveyed the land. Ownership was as follows:

70%—owned by the British government, in trust for the Jewish National Homeland, transferred by international law to Israel

8.6%—owned by Jews

3.3%—owned by resident Arabs

16.5%—owned by non-resident Arabs

When Jews started to buy Arab lands, they actually went out of their way to avoid purchasing property in areas where Arabs might be displaced. They sought land that was largely uncultivated, swampy, cheap and, most important, without tenants.

In 1920, Labor Zionist leader David Ben-Gurion expressed his concern about the Arab fellahin, whom he viewed as "the most important asset of the native population."

Ben Gurion said, "under no circumstances must we touch land belonging to fellahs or worked by them."

He advocated helping liberate them from their oppressors.

"Only if a fellah leaves his place of settlement," Ben Gurion added, "should we offer to buy his land, at an appropriate price."

It was only after the Jews had bought all of this type of available land that they began to purchase cultivated land. Many Arabs were willing to sell because of the migration to coastal towns and because they needed money to invest in the citrus industry.

When John Hope Simpson, British civil administrator and author of early books on the refugees, arrived in Palestine in May 1930, he observed:

"They [Jews] paid high prices for the land, and in addition they paid to certain of the occupants of those lands a considerable amount of money which they were not legally bound to pay."

In 1931, Lewis French conducted a survey of landlessness and eventually offered new plots to any Arabs who had been "dispossessed." British officials received more than 3,000 applications, of which 80 percent were ruled invalid by the Government's legal adviser because the applicants were not landless Arabs. This left only about 600 landless Arabs, 100 of whom accepted the Government land offer.

In April 1936, a new outbreak of Arab attacks on Jews was instigated by a Syrian guerrilla named Fawzi Al-Qawukji, the commander of the Arab Liberation Army. By November, when the British finally sent a new commission headed by Lord Peel to investigate, 89 Jews had been killed and more than 300 wounded.

The Peel Commission's report found that Arab complaints about Jewish land acquisition were baseless. It pointed out that

"...much of the land now carrying orange groves was sand dunes or swamp and uncultivated when it was purchased...there was at the time of the earlier sales little evidence that the owners possessed either the resources or training needed to develop the land..."

Moreover, the Commission found the shortage was *"due less to the amount of land acquired by Jews than to the increase in the Arab population."*

The report concluded that the presence of Jews in Palestine, along with the work of the British Administration, had resulted in higher wages, an improved standard of living and ample employment opportunities.

In his memoirs, Transjordan's King Abdullah wrote:

"It is made quite clear to all, both by the map drawn up by the Simpson Commission and by another compiled by the Peel Commission, that the Arabs are as prodigal in selling their land as they are in useless wailing and weeping."

Even at the height of the Arab revolt in 1938, the British High Commissioner to Palestine believed the Arab landowners were complaining about sales to Jews in hopes of driving up prices for lands they wished to sell. Many Arab landowners had been so terrorized by Arab rebels they decided to leave Palestine and sell their property to the Jews.

The Jews were paying exorbitant prices to wealthy landowners for small tracts of arid land. By 1947, Jewish holdings in Palestine amounted to about 463,000 acres. Approximately 45,000 of these acres were acquired from the Mandatory Government; 30,000 were bought from various churches and 387,500 were purchased from Arabs. Analyses of land purchases from 1880 to 1948 show that 73 percent of Jewish plots were purchased from large landowners, not poor fellahin. Those who sold land included the mayors of Gaza, Jerusalem and Jaffa.

The Jews, before the wars, who were already living as peasants, bought lands and cultivated them after years of neglect. The Jews restored the land and made it what it is today, with an economy ten times the size of that of Egypt, Jordan and Syria combined, while the Arabs have been plotting wars against her since the 1920s and instead of getting rid of the Jews, they displaced one-half of the Palestinians in 1948.

The Arab opposition to an Israeli state began after the Balfour Declaration 1917, which supported the idea of a Jewish national homeland. In the 1920s there were anti-Zionist riots in Palestine, then governed by the United Kingdom under a League of Nations mandate.

In 1936, an Arab revolt led to a British Royal Commission that recommended partition approved by the United Nations in 1947, but rejected by the Arabs.

When it became clear that the British intended to leave by May 15, leaders of the Yishuv decided to implement that part of the partition plan calling for establishment of a Jewish state.

In Tel Aviv on May 14, the Provisional State Council, formerly the National Council,

"...representing the Jewish people in Palestine and the World Zionist Movement, proclaimed the establishment of the Jewish state in Palestine, to be called Medina Israel (the state of Israel)..."

There was no time to celebrate. On May 15, the armies of Egypt, Jordan, Syria, Lebanon, and Iraq joined Palestinian and other Arab guerrillas who had been fighting Jewish forces since November 1947 and attacked Israel, an event known as the War of Independence. The Arabs failed to prevent establishment of a Jewish state, and the war ended with four United Nations-arranged armistice agreements between Israel and Egypt, Lebanon, Jordan, and Syria. The frontiers defined in the armistice agreements remained until they were altered by Israel's repeat victory against attackers during the Six-Day War in 1967.

The wars that were intended to annihilate the Jews ended as Israel's victories. With their losses, the Arabs became defensive. That is expected; all those large countries waging five wars to annihilate tiny Israel, along with hundreds of terror attacks, and she triumphed. Wars always have repercussions and Arabs are not immune from the bad taste of their own medicine. Hafez al-Assad, Syria's then-Minister of Defense, vowed at the start of the 1967 war:

"Our forces are now entirely ready...to initiate the act of liberation itself and to explode the Zionist presence in the Arab homeland... The time has come to enter into a battle of annihilation."

President Nasser of Egypt declared, *"Our basic goal is the destruction of Israel."* [18]

Still, many Westerners believe that the Arabs actually want peace. The truth is that the evil saga of the "final solution" will continue as planned by Satan. Westerners forget who it was that supported Hitler in World War II, the Soviet Union during the Cold War and Saddam Hussein in the Gulf War. Instead, they rallied behind Arafat who, until his death, still refused to change the PLO Charter calling for the destruction of Israel.

Chapter Five
ISRAEL—BLAMED NO MATTER WHAT

THE MASSACRED ACCUSED OF MASSACRES

Common Palestinian opinion:

"The Jews conducted massacres of Qana, Sabra, and Shatella and other."

Response:

Israel, the very nation mentioned more then any other in the Bible, the very people that are the heart and means to carry the message and the Messiah, must be eliminated, destroyed, and we must reinterpret Biblical verses to justify such these goals. The end justifies the means, and by all means, Israel must be destroyed.

To that end, we must put the Jews on trial whenever there is a death, a war, or even a housing project like Har Homa near Jerusalem. If they kill in defense, we ignore the motive. If one aberrant person goes on a shooting rampage, we accuse the whole nation. If Israelis get fed up with terrorism and close the roads, we accuse them of imprisoning the masses; and if they guard their attackers, they are accused of tyranny, dictatorship, and occupation.

Conversely, Israel, in order to be accepted, needs to be sinless, and every Jew needs to be as pure as the Messiah. Their government must be perfect, and all Jewish citizens must be flawless. Never can the Jewish society, which fills in the bell curve just like every other group, produce an extremist group or trigger-happy mad man. Jews are not allowed to be human.

There are, of course, some people in Israel such as Rabbi Yaacov Perrin who says, "One million Arabs are not worth a Jewish fingernail."[1] And when a Jew says such things, we find that every anti-Israel website posts it.

Even the Human Rights Watch group joined the masses of accusers. In one report, it concludes:

the government of Israel shares blame for the state of human rights in the Gaza Strip and Jericho. Israel's still-considerable control over the lives of Palestinians in these areas entails significant obligations that Israel has failed to fulfill...Since August, the Palestinian Authority has arrested hundreds of members of the political opposition with little semblance of due process: arrest warrants are the exception rather than the rule, and suspects have been held without charge for several days or longer without being brought before a judge.[2]

This is simply not true. Israel is a humane nation. She acts only to protect her people. However, what Israel *did* do wrong was to allow Yasser Arafat back in power. Whatever this terrorist did, Israel got the blame. If a flowchart of abuses were to be drawn, the arrows would always point to Israel, even though it was the Palestinian Authority at fault. The Sabra and Shatella Massacres in Lebanon were blamed on Israel, even though they were carried out by the Lebanese. You would rarely read condemnation for Arabs killing Arabs, even though Arabs killed hundreds of thousands of other Arabs.

In all the years I lived there, I watched the Palestinians do nothing but try to destroy Israel, to exterminate the Jews like city rats. I watched the ongoing, heartbreaking saga that has continued through the ages. I know many "final" solutions were carried out, causing unspeakable suffering, yet the Jews and Israel have survived against all odds.

Tragically, plans for another "final solution" are in the hearts and minds of the Muslim extremists today.

# # #

Israel has suffered from a few of its own extremists.

On October 24, 1993, two such organizations, Kach and Kahane Chai, set off two small bombs near the French embassy in Tel Aviv, saying the attack was carried out to protest PLO leader Yasir Arafat's visit to France and the agreements he signed there.

In July 1999, three Israeli soldiers were expelled from the Israeli army for affiliating or sympathizing with the Kach and Kahane Chai organizations. It was feared that these groups were plotting the assassination of high-level Israeli politicians in the summer of 1998 following the murder of Jewish settlers in Hebron.

In September 1999, an Israeli court convicted Uri Amit of belonging to and supporting a terrorist organization. The ruling declared that the Noar Meir youth group, named after Kach founder Meir Kahane, is affiliated in fact and not just in name with the Kach organization. Specifically, Uri Amit was found to have distributed flyers that lauded the murder of Arabs and praised the assassination of Prime Minister Yitzhak Rabin apparently for being "too liberal" with the Arabs. Another flyer urged people to contribute to the "Baruch Goldstein Fund" to honor the settler who massacred 29 Muslim worshippers in Hebron in 1994. According to Judge Hanoch Feder, "It appears that what characterizes Kahane Chai and Noar Meir is violence as an ideology, at times as a religious commandment."

Ami Ayalon, head of Israel's General Security Service, indicated his concern by dissuading politicians from participating in public events, given reports that radical elements may have tried to kill key figures in order to stop the peace process. Based on certain data collected by Israel's security services, a meeting convened by then-Prime Minister Netanyahu on August 28, 1998, determined that special precautions were needed to preempt assassination attempts on the Prime Minister, President Ezer Weizman, and then-Defense Minister Yitzhak Mordechai, among others.

Jewish terrorist attacks like Yehida, the Khisas, Qazaza, and few others, are not condoned, and are but a tiny speck of violence when compared with hundreds of terrorist attacks by Arabs against Israelis, including several wars of intended annihilation. No one argues that a Jewish terrorist killed 60 in Hebron's Abraham Shrine.

The difference between Israel and the Palestinians is that Israel condemns such criminal acts. The criminals go on trial and, if found guilty, they are punished. Jews don't cheer in the streets, parading body parts. One cannot blame an entire nation for a few lawless individuals who carry out acts of violence against Palestinians. No one blames America for Timothy McVeigh bombing the Murrah government building in Oklahoma.

All of these acts were committed by individuals going against the mainstream society, unlike the terrorist attacks against the Jews that are planned and supported by the entire Palestinian community. The world has yet to hear the Arab nations condemn the terror carried out against the Jews by Muslim Arabs from time immemorial.

The unspeakable treatment of Christians and Jews by Muslims is suppressed in today's modern history and media. The Fall of Christianity, by Bat D'or, consists of hundreds of detailed, well-researched pages on the persecution carried out by Islam throughout history—and it is a revelation. They called the accidental death toll during Israeli bombings on Lebanon "massacres," a term generally given to the deliberate rounding up of civilians and killing them indiscriminately. No one can deny that 70 people died in Qana, and Israel admitted that it was in error while trying to bomb terrorist areas, and while there were hundreds of websites condemning the incident, there were hardly any that talked about the hundreds of terrorist attacks against Israel that truly were "massacres."

The great tragedy of all wars is that innocents will be killed; unintended destruction will take place. War is not neat.

Most nations do everything possible to protect their civilians. So why do Hezbollah and the rest of the Arab terrorists in Lebanon intentionally base their camps in the middle of civilian populations? Incidents similar to Qana happened during the Gulf War, yet the world correctly blamed Saddam Hussein, not America.

Whatever happened to all the Ketusha rockets that landed on targets like Keriat Shmona, killing many more civilians than in Qana? They hit these targets with the deliberate intention of killing civilians in order to terrorize the Jewish population. The perpetrators admitted their intention was to kill civilians and not armed troops.

Jews are blamed for Sabra and Shatila, but it was the Lebanese Kataeb and Ahrar who carried it out. The massacre was a result of the civil war in Lebanon, when the Lebanese militia rounded up Palestinian refugees and indiscriminately killed them. Since the Jews did not come to the rescue of these Palestinians, the Jews must take the blame?

The Al-Aqsa Mosque incident was another tragedy started by Arab rioters throwing heaps of stones down on the Jewish worshippers on the Wailing Wall; the result was the death of about 20 Palestinians as the Israeli Police opened fire on the rioters.

Why do the Arab masses maintain refugee camps while Israelis always house their immigrants? Why is the Al-Ibrahimi Mosque Massacre, committed by one individual, blamed on every Jew in Israel? Why must a whole nation take the blame for a single mad man? Yet state-supported incidents carried out by Arabs receive praise from the Arab masses. Arafat even named a street after a murderer, and every terrorist who kills Israelis and Americans is free on Palestinian streets. Where are all the websites to cry to the heavens about the Hebron Massacre of Jews? Click on a Yahoo search engine for the Hebron Massacre of Jews by the Arabs. Know what you'll get? Hundreds of articles on the Hebron Massacres of *Palestinians* on the Ibrahimi Mosque. And that horror against the Jews did not spring from one mad man, but from the Arab masses, attacking, looting, raping, and indiscriminately killing every Jew in Hebron.

Such lies should shake the mountains.

DEIR YASEEN—A HISTORY OF A LIE

Common Palestinian's opinion:

"Israel killed 250 people at Deir Yassin in cold blood—of them 25 pregnant women were bayoneted in the abdomen while still alive and 52 children were maimed under the eyes of their own mothers, and they were slain and their heads cut off."

A Palestinian activist's opinion:

"254 Arabs died at Deir Yassin."[3] "an estimated 100-250 Arab villagers were slaughtered."[4] "over 100 Palestinian men, women and children were killed."[5]

Response:

These atrocities never occurred.

Beir Zeit, a Palestinian University student who interviewed every Arab survivor, admitted that the number was 110. The story has been exaggerated and conflicting testimonies cloud the facts, but the best study on this issue is <u>The History of the 1948 War</u> by Professor Uri Milstein, one of Israel's most distinguished military historians. It's meticulous, detailed and accurate.

In 1952, a hearing was conducted in Israel during which Israeli judges heard eyewitness testimony on the events at Deir Yassin and issued a ruling that has important implications for understanding what happened in that battle. How often did the Arabs issue any ruling from any court, or hold any hearing for the countless massacres of Jews in any Arab country?

Long before Deir Yassin, Arab and Jewish armies were already battling. An "Arab Liberation Army," sponsored by the Arab League and manned by volunteers from various Arab countries, had always attacked civilian Jewish communities in Palestine prior to 1948. My own father witnessed Arab villagers, along with Arab soldiers, raid Jewish communities. Even the religious leader, Haj Amin Al-Husseni, who collaborated with Hitler, had SS trained graduates battle the Jews; some of their bodies, lying alongside the corpses of dead Palestinian fighters, were found with their SS identifications.

The facts are that every Arab village in Israel participated in attacking Jewish settlements in order to destroy the Jews. The Arab attackers faced the consequences of their actions; raids on civilians will always have repercussions.

Deir Yassin was a heavily armed nest of terrorists who, in 1947-1948, had been attacking nearby Jewish neighborhoods and traffic on the Jerusalem-Tel Aviv highway. Mordechai Ra'anan, leader of the Jewish soldiers who fought in Deir Yassin, deliberately exaggerated the number deaths as 254 in order to undermine the morale of the Arab forces. No body count was conducted to tally the dead.

Despite Ra'anan's *clear admission of the lie,* the figure 254 was circulated by Palestinian Arab leader Hussein Khalidi and was the basis for a widely re-printed article in the New York Times which became the permanent reference for the story from then on.

A tally of Jewish losses revealed 42 Israeli wounded and 6 dead out of an attacking force of 132 soldiers. One of the commanders of the

Jewish forces, Ben Zion Cohen, says *"(The Arabs were) shooting from every house."*

While the Jewish soldiers with loud speakers warned in advance to "Lay down your arms! Run for your lives," the Arabs fired at the vehicle and the battle erupted.

The claims of rape and other atrocities were fabricated to incite Arab violence against Israel. Arab eyewitnesses interviewed in a PBS documentary revealed that they were told by Dr. Hussein Khalidi, a prominent Palestinian Arab leader, to fabricate claims of atrocities at Deir Yassin in order to encourage Arab regimes to invade the Jewish state-to-be.

Deir Yassin resident Abu Mahmoud recalls: "Jerusalem at the Hebron Gate. We checked who was missing, and who we had gathered in survived. Then the [Palestinian] leaders arrived, including Dr. Khalidi."

Hazem Nusseibeh, an editor of the Palestine Broadcasting Service's Arabic news in 1948, and a member of one of Jerusalem's most prominent Arab families, admitted that he too was told by Hussein Khalidi, the originator of the massacre story, to fabricate claims of atrocities in order to encourage Arab regimes to invade the Jewish land. According to a Jerusalem Report, Nusseibeh:

"...describes an encounter at the Jaffa Gate of Jerusalem's Old City with Deir Yassin survivors and Palestinian leaders, including Hussein Khalidi...'I asked Dr. Khalidi how we should cover the story,' recalled Nusseibeh. He said, 'We must make the most of this.' So we wrote a press release stating that at Deir Yassin, children were murdered, pregnant women were raped. All sorts of atrocities."

Abu Mahmoud, a survivor declared: "We said, 'There was no rape.' (Khalidi) said, 'We have to say this, so the Arab armies will come to liberate Palestine from the Jews.'"

The PBS narrator says, "Arab radio stations passed on the false reports, ignoring the protests of the witnesses."

The famed syndicated columnist Sid Zion, whose articles originate in the New York Daily News, wrote on March 23, 1998, calling the "massacre" claims "one of the great hoaxes of the 20th century."

Deir Yassin has ever since been the rallying call for the Arabs and the enemies of Israel and of the Jewish people. Arafat compares it to Auschwitz. It is one of the great hoaxes of the 20th century; comparable to the libel that Jews drank Christian blood...The fight for Deir Yassin was part of the war and a necessary battle for Jewish survival. The Irgun, under Menachem Begin, warned the Arabs and asked them to evacuate their women and children. Hundreds left, but hundreds stayed. A pitched battle ensued, and when the smoke cleared, 120 Arabs were killed, 40 Jews were seriously injured and four Jews were dead...The Israeli government and every other historical study have long since discredited the 'massacre' claim. But like all libels, it stands off truth and proof.

The Palestinian Arabs left voluntarily, overreacting to their own leaders' fabricated atrocity reports. They were not expelled, as Arab propagandists claim. *I was there. I witnessed the Six-Day war and, afterwards, the Jews did no harm to us.* They committed no massacres on the West Bank and in general behaved righteously. It is our hate drug that fuels these terrible wars.

Chapter Six
THE CHURCH-REPLACEMENT THEOLOGY AND OTHER ABUSES OF GOD'S WORD

MARTIN LUTHER, THE EX-CATHOLIC MONK

Martin Luther caused a religious earthquake when he claimed that Christendom, which was then all Catholic, had always persecuted the Jews. He had an agenda: to taint the Catholic Church. And he admitted that he was not the first who tried to reform the Church:

"We are not the first to declare the papacy to be the kingdom of Antichrist, since for many years before us so many and so great men…have undertaken to express the same thing so clearly…" [1]

True. Luther, who unfortunately inherited many false Replacement Theology ideas taught by the Catholic Church, was certainly not the first Christian who tried to reform Catholicism. Many centuries before Luther, a movement began among priests and monks calling for a return to the entire Bible, both the Jewish Old Testament and the New Testament. In reality, the first reformer was the Priscillian Bishop of Avila who was falsely accused of witchcraft by a Synod in Bordeaux, France in 384 A.D. Seven of his recently discovered writings in the University of Germany's Wurzburg Library can easily refute the false charges.

Priscillian and six others were beheaded at Trier in 385 A.D. and many martyrs followed. These persecutions continued into the late 1300s when John Wycliffe, who was given the title "morning star of the Reformation," championed the authority of the Scriptures, translated and published them in English and preached and wrote against the evils of the popes and transubstantiation. Influenced by Wycliffe was Jan Hus, a fervent Catholic priest and rector of Prague University. He was later excommunicated in 1410, and burned at the stake as a "heretic" in 1415.

Despite Luther's writings, it is not fair to blame all the divisions of Christendom for persecuting the Jews. Many throughout the centuries who fought the evils of the Catholic Church tried to stop the killings and denounce the Church. During the tenth century, a council at Rheims, ordered by the Bishop of Orleans, called the Pope *"The Antichrist."* In the eleventh century, Rome was denounced as *"the See of Satan"* by Berenger of Tours. The Waldensians identified the Pope as Antichrist in an 1100 treatise titled "The Noble Lesson." In 1206, an Albigensian conference indicted the Vatican as the woman "drunk with the blood of the martyrs."

Many also blame anti-Semitism on Martin Luther's writings against the Jews. It is true that in the last few years of his life, Martin Luther changed his position on the Jews and wrote condemning essays about them. However, at the beginning of his career, Luther was apparently sympathetic to Jewish resistance to the Catholic Church:

"The Jews are blood-relations of our Lord; if it were proper to boast of flesh and blood, the Jews belong more to Christ than we. I beg, therefore, my dear Papist, if you become tired of abusing me as a heretic, that you begin to revile me as a Jew."[2]

In 1523, Martin Luther wrote, "Jesus Christ was born a Jew" and made reference to the origins of Christianity; later, the aging reformer did not see this 'return to the right path' and he turned bitter. He wrote strong polemic works at this point, such as "The Jews and their Lies." Another reason for Luther's anti-Semitic position, other than his disappointment with the Jews for not accepting his "true belief," could be that his education was still based on the Replacement Theology as taught by Augustine, which was prevalent in the Catholic Church.

Luther wrote many anti-Semitic statements; however, his infamous piece, "On the Jews and their Lies," takes top honors for vile, anti-Jewish ranting:

Their breath stinks for the gold and silver of the heathen; since no people under the sun always have been, still are, and always will remain more avaricious than they, as can be noticed in their cursed usury. Therefore know, my dear Christians, that next to the Devil, you have no more bitter, more poisonous, more vehement an enemy than a real Jew who earnestly desires to be a Jew...Do not their Talmud and rabbis write that it is no sin to kill if a Jew kills a heathen, but it is a sin if he kills a brother in Israel? It is no sin if he does not keep his oath to a heathen. Therefore, to steal and rob—as they do with their money lending—from a heathen, is a divine service...Now what are we going to do with these rejected, condemned Jewish people?...

...set fire to their synagogues or schools and to bury and cover with dirt whatever will not burn...I advise that their houses be razed and destroyed...I advise that all their prayer books...in which such idolatry, lies, cursing, and blasphemy are taught, be taken from them...that their rabbis be forbidden to teach henceforth on pain of loss of life and limb...that safe-conduct on the highways be abolished completely for the Jews...that all their treasure of silver and gold be taken from them...But if the authorities are reluctant to use force and restrain the Jews' devilish wantonness, the latter should, as we said, be expelled from their country and be told to return to...Jerusalem where they may lie, curse, blaspheme, defame, murder, steal, rob, practice usury, mock, and indulge in all those infamous abominations which they practice among us, and leave...our Lord the Messiah, our faith, and our church undefiled and uncontaminated with their devilish tyranny and malice.

THE PERSECUTION OF JEWS BY CHRISTENDOM

Sadly, there are many respected resources documenting the long and terrible persecution of the Jews by Christendom. One of the classic studies is by renowned historian, James Parkes, The Conflict of the Church and Synagogue: a Study in the Origins of Anti-Semitism. From his works, we learn of the following major decrees and events:

306 A.D. Synod of Elvira prohibited intermarriage and sexual intercourse between Christians and Jews, and prohibited them from eating together. During the 4th and 5th centuries synagogues were burned by Catholics and the first synagogue was destroyed as ordered by Catholic bishop Innocentius of Dertona in Northern Italy.

388 A.D. The first synagogue known to have been burned down was near the river Euphrat, on command of the bishop of Kallinikon.

527–564 A.D. The Justinian Code was an edict of the Byzantine Emperor Justinian. A section of the code negated civil rights for Jews. Once the code was enforced, Jews in the Empire could not build synagogues, read the Bible in Hebrew, gather in public places, celebrate Passover before Easter, or give evidence in a judicial case in which a Christian was a party.

533–541 A.D. Council of Orleans prohibited marriages between Christians and Jews, forbade the conversion to Judaism by Christians, banned contact with Jews, forbid the reading of the Torah exclusively in Hebrew.

553–545 A.D. Confiscation of Jewish property and the prohibition of the sale of Christian property to Jews.

692 A.D. Trulanic Syno prohibited Christians from being treated by Jewish doctors.

694 A.D. Council of Toledo, Jews were enslaved, their property confiscated, and their children forcibly baptized.

1010 A.D. The Bishop of Limoges (France) had signs posted in the city; Jews who would not convert to Christianity must be expelled or killed.

1050 A.D. Synod of Narbonne prohibited Christians from living in Jewish homes.

1078 A.D. Synod of Gerona required Jews to pay taxes to support the Church.

1096 A.D. First Crusade. 12,000 Jews slaughtered in Mainz, Cologne, Neuss, Altenahr, Wevelinghoven, Xanten, Moers, Dortmund, Kerpen, Trier, Metz, Regensburg, Prague and others (all locations are in Germany except Metz/France, Prague/Czech.)

1147 A.D. Second Crusade where hundreds of Jews were slain in Ham, Sully, Carentan, and Rameru (all locations in France).

1179 A.D. Third Lateran Council prohibited certain medical care to be provided by Christians to Jews.

1189 A.D. Third Crusade: English Jewish communities sacked in Fulda/Germany.

1215 A.D. Fourth Lateran Council required Jews to wear special clothing to distinguish them from Christians.

1235 A.D. 34 Jewish men and women slain.

1267 A.D. Jewish communities of London, Canterbury, Northampton, Lincoln, Cambridge, and others exterminated.

1290 A.D. in Bohemia (Poland) 10,000 Jews were killed.

1337 A.D. Starting in Deggendorf Germany a Jew-killing frenzy reaches 51 towns in Bavaria, Austria, and Poland.

1348 A.D. All Jews of Basel/Switzerland and Strasbourg/France (two thousand) burned.

1349 A.D. In more than 350 towns in Germany, all Jews murdered, mostly burned alive (in this one year more Jews were killed than Christians had been in 200 years of ancient Roman persecution of Christians.)

1389 A.D. In Prague 3,000 Jews were slaughtered.

1391 A.D. Seville's Jews killed led by Archbishop Martinez. 4,000 were slain, 25,000 sold as slaves. Their identification was made easy by the brightly colored "badges of shame" that all Jews above the age of ten had been forced to wear.

1431–1443 A.D. Council of Basel forbade Jews to attend universities, or to act as agents in the conclusion of contracts between Christians, and required that they attend church sermons, and decreed the removal of former religious and governing privileges, the curtailment of rabbinical jurisdiction, and prohibition of missionary work. Jews were no longer allowed to hold high office, or to have military careers (legislation in 537 A.D. prohibited local Jewish people from serving on municipal bodies).

1492 A.D. In the year that Columbus set sail to conquer a New World, more than 150,000 Jews were expelled from Spain; thousands died on their way.

1648 A.D. Chmielnitzki massacres in Poland; approximately 200,000 Jews were slain.[3]

DIVIDING ISRAEL—THEOLOGICAL OR POLITICAL ISSUE?

A Common Palestinian theological argument:

"Palestine is for the Arabs, Jesus was Palestinian, so Palestine belongs to us."

"The Bible does not mention an exclusive Jewish state."

Response:

Let's start with the End-Times verses of Scripture:

"For behold, in those days and at that time, when I bring back the captives of Judah and Jerusalem, I will also gather all nations, and bring them down to the valley of Jehoshaphat; and I will enter into judgment with them there on account of My people, My heritage Israel, whom they have scattered among the nations; they have also divided up My land."[4]

This is the end of Israel's ongoing trials. God the Just and Great Judge does not favor the majority, but comes to save a very small minority. He is coming to judge the world over this small people, and over this tiny piece of real estate, a fraction of a percent of all the land on earth. How strange then it is to dismiss or re-interpret these verses. How is it that when this judgment is made, Israel will be in her land? How can people dismiss the Bible Prophecy of Israel as being fulfilled already, way in the past before Jesus came? Could it be that this is the only way to deny what is coming by shuffling the timeline of these events?

Also in Joel 3, *"In those days"* obviously refers to the verses before it in chapter 2:30:

"And I will shew wonders in the heavens and in the earth, blood, and fire, and pillars of smoke to be judgment day [where] all havoc breaks loose." How is Israel there, at that time, way in the future? There must be a re-gathering and a division of land prior to judgment day.

DIVIDING ISRAEL—WHAT THE NATIONS ARE DOING

The division is taking place; the entire world seems in support of the division and the United Nations is standing against Israel, pressuring her to give up Judea. Joel's declaration of judgment to the nations is on its way. The Bible suggests strongly that we not be found guilty of hating Israel or Jews, or contributing to the division of Israel. To interpret Joel accurately: to hate Jews is to hate God, and to stand against Israel is to be on the side of Antichrist. Those who question Joel's prophecy must answer to the amazing accuracy of the portions that were fulfilled, and to the countless other verses by other prophets. And as predicted, the "nations," in the form of the United Nations, are carrying out the evil plan.

Morris B. Abram, Chairman of the United Nations Watch, writes

"Emergency Special Sessions of the United Nations General Assembly are rare. No such session has ever been convened with respect to the Chinese occupation of Tibet, the Indonesian occupation of East Timor, the Syrian occupation of Lebanon, the slaughters in Rwanda, the disappearances in Zaire or the horrors of Bosnia. In fact, during the last 15 years they have been called only to condemn Israel."[5]

In April 1997, an "emergency special session" of the United Nations General Assembly, which condemned Israel's construction of a new Jewish neighborhood in Jerusalem, has raised serious questions about the world body's function and bias.

The session was called under the "Uniting for Peace" resolution adopted by the General Assembly in 1950, a formula enabling members "to act in a case where there appears to be a threat to the peace, breach of the peace or act of aggression." The formula was used just ten times since 1950 where 93 member states felt that building apartments in Jerusalem were a breech of the Oslo Peace Accord.

Israel's construction of homes in Jerusalem was not a violation of the Oslo Accords, since there was no change in the status of the territory.

Therefore, why was the United Nations so alarmed over a *legal* housing unit project when tens of thousands of refugees in central

Africa faced death by starvation or disease as civil war raged in Zaire; as hundreds of Algerians, including women and children, were being butchered by Islamists; as enslavement of Christians in the Sudan continued; as a German court implicated the Iranian regime in sponsoring terrorism abroad; as new reports emerged of chemical weapons being manufactured by several Middle Eastern states; as the Irish Republican Army stepped up its bomb-threat campaign; as Albanian anarchy persisted; as the civil war and accompanying refugee crisis reached new proportions in Afghanistan; and as the separatist struggle in China's Xinjiang province became ever more violent?

The General Assembly resolution demanded the "immediate and full cessation" of construction at Har Homa, Jerusalem, and urged all states to stop "all forms of assistance and support for illegal Israeli activities," notably in building settlements in disputed areas. It requested UN Secretary-General Kofi Annan to report within two months whether Israel had stopped the work in Jerusalem.

One hundred and thirty-four nations supported the resolution. Three opposed it: Israel, the United States and the tiny Pacific island federation of Micronesia. Eleven abstained: Germany, Australia, Canada, Latvia, Liberia, Lithuania, Marshall Islands, Norway, Romania, Rwanda and Uruguay.

All this denunciation, yet Yasser Arafat's Palestinian Authority had financed the illegal construction of thousands of Arab homes in the Old City section of Jerusalem and *"Faisal Husseni, Arafat's cabinet minister, announced that Saudi Arabia has donated $19 million "to build 600 Arab homes in Jerusalem and strengthen their hold over parts of the city."* [6] Aharon Domb, the Secretary General of the Council of Jewish Communities in Judea, Samaria and Gaza, released photographs, video surveillance, and maps showing that during June-December 1996, Palestinian Arabs had built more than 1,000 illegal buildings in "Area C," which is the area that is under Israeli control in the administered territories. [7]

The Bible is very clear on this issue, "I am about to make Jerusalem a cup of reeling to all the peoples round about; it will be against Judah, also in the siege against Jerusalem." [8]

Jerusalem is the only city in the world that could cause uproar over a housing project, yet as the Bible predicted; today it is indeed a burdensome stone to the world:

"On that day I will make the clans of Judah like a blazing pot in the midst of wood, like a flaming torch among sheaves; and they shall devour to the right and to the left all the peoples round about, while Jerusalem shall still be inhabited in its place, in Jerusalem." [9]

Yet, Jerusalem shall remain inhabited.

ZIONISTS—CHRISTIANS AND JEWS

After the Diaspora and the destruction of the Jewish Temple in 70 AD, Jews began the first Zionist movement, which is simply defined as the longing and striving to restore the Jewish people back to Israel. This longing, which was based on the Bible and held close by the Jewish people for two millennia, was finally given life after the establishment of The Zionist Organization in 1897, the year of the first Zionist Congress.

Before the Zionist Congress took root, there was always a sizeable minority of Christians who supported a Jewish return, but when the Jews were expelled from the Promised Land under Hadrian in 135 AD, those same Christians began to focus on the quick return of Jesus and laid the Jewish issue to rest.

Christian writers throughout history supported the Zionist idea. The historian, Frederick M. Schweitzer, in his work, A History of the Jews Since the First Century AD wrote,

"Scots are very proud that unlike 'the kingdom to the south' their homeland has never been desecrated by anti-Semitism, expulsions, confiscations, or ill-feeling of any kind toward [the] Jews…This happy condition is due to their Calvinist heritage." [10]

John Calvin (1509-1564) was one of the foremost leaders in the Protestant Reformation in Europe. John Knox (1515-1572) perpetuated Calvin's teaching in Scotland. Hence, Calvin's principles of theology are embodied in the creeds and practices of the Presbyterian Church of Scotland. "To follow Calvin meant to live a high degree of holiness, seeking to know and follow the will of God." [11]

As early as 1650 A.D., hundreds of books were written regarding the Jewish return to the land in light of Bible Prophecy. Peter Jurieu, the "Goliath of the French Protestants," wrote in 1687 regarding the fulfillments of Bible prophecies for the Jewish return:

"To the Nation of the Jews...I desire of that people, that they would please to read this book attentively, and without prejudice...I confess the hopes they conceive of a Kingdom of the Messiah...is built upon express and unquestionable prophecies; that even their Jerusalem should be rebuilt, and that they should be again gathered together in their own land." [12]

Restorationist Joseph Eyre, published a scholarly essay in 1771 titled "Observations upon Prophecies Relating to the Restoration of the Jews." He made his readers aware of the ancient Biblical promises from the Creator to Abraham concerning the area which the descendants of Abraham would occupy, known as the "Promised Land" [Genesis 15:18-21; 17:7-8]. Concerning the return of the Jews from the lands of their dispersion, Eyre quoted at length from the Book of the Prophet Ezekiel, in the Hebrew Scriptures, chapters 36 and 37. Here is pictured a major prophecy that the "whole House of *Israel*" would experience a resurrection from the "*graves.*"

Holger Paulli (1644-1714), a Danish pietist, believed whole-heartedly in the Jewish Return to the "Promised Land" as a condition for the Second Coming of Christ. He would have been motivated by Jesus' own promise to return [John 14:1-3], and by the promise of angelic messengers who, at Jesus' ascension, declared..."this same Jesus which is taken up from you into heaven, shall so come in like manner as you have seen Him go into heaven." [Acts 1:9-11] The Apostle Paul also wrote that the Deliverer, meaning the Messiah, would come to Zion, and all Israel would be saved [Romans 11:26]. Paulli published books and memoranda, which he dispatched to the kings of France and England calling on them to help the Jews in their desire to return and regain their statehood.

John Toland of Ireland (1670-1722), was an active participant in the theological and political debates of contemporary England. In 1714, he published his "Reasons for Naturalizing the Jews in Great Britain and Ireland on the Same Footing with All Other Nations." He was a forerunner of the modern human rights movement. He spoke against the backdrop of Jewish ghettos in Europe. "Jews having no official status in England until 1866, when the House of Commons admitted Lionel de Rothschild, the first Jewish Member of Parliament."

The most famous English Jew of the 19th century was, of course, Benjamin Disraeli, whom Queen Victoria made noble as Lord Beaconsfield, who twice became the Prime Minister of England, first in 1868. The first world leader of great reputation to acknowledge the Jewish claim to the Promised Land, Napoleon, in 1799 made this statement:

"Jews! Unique nation of the world! For thousands of years the tyranny of the world has succeeded in depriving you of your ancestral lands but it has not eradicated your name, nor your national existence...Legitimate heirs of the Land of Israel! Hurry! The moment has arrived to claim the return of your rights among the nations of the world. You must claim for yourselves a national existence as states among states, and your unencroachable right to bow down before God according to your faith, publicly and forever." [13]

Lord Palmerston, British Foreign Secretary, wrote in 1840:

There exists at the present time among the Jews dispersed over Europe a strong notion that the time is approaching when their nation is to return to Palestine. It would be of manifest importance to the Sultan (Turkey) to encourage the Jews to return and settle in Palestine because the wealth that they would bring with them would increase the resources of the Sultan's dominions, and the Jewish people if returning under the sanction and protection at the invitation of the Sultan would be a check upon any future evil designs of Egypt or its neighbors. I wish to instruct your Excellency strongly to recommend to the Turkish government to hold out every just encouragement to the Jews of Europe to return to Palestine.

Lord Shaftesbury (Anthony Ashley Cooper, 1801-1885) was a man of unshakeable faith who based his life on literal acceptance of the Bible. His guiding principle in life was the old Judeo-Christian Bible decree: *"Love thy neighbor as thyself."* The Jews he always called *"God's ancient people,"* and *he accepted them in the same way that he accepted the Bible,"* wrote Dr. Pragai. It was the era when Christians of the Western culture were taking an interest in Biblical lands.

In 1890, Viennese activist and Jewish nationalist, Nathan Birnbaum, supported the return of the Jewish people to Israel and is credited with coining the term *Zionism*. From 1896, the term "Zionism" referred to the political movement founded by Theodore Hertzel, whose goal was to establish a Jewish state in Israel.

William H. Hechler (1845-1931), a British clergyman, met Dr. Herzl in 1896, and became a sympathizer and close friend. Hechler said:

"All that this remarkable movement now requires is the public recognition and protection of the Sovereigns of Europe . . . the Jewish state is successful, which it must be according to the Bible, for the Jews are then to be a blessing to the nations."

Hechler personally wrote to the German Emperor. Towards the end of 1898, Kaiser Wilhelm II, wrote in reply:

"I have been able to notice that the emigration to the land of Palestine of those Jews who are ready for it is being prepared extremely well and it is even financially sound in every respect...I am convinced that the settlement of the Holy Land...will soon bring blessing to the land."

That same year the Kaiser made a formal visit to Jerusalem and met Dr. Herzl and members of the Zionist organization just outside the Jaffa Gate. "It amounted to a clear act of recognition of the Zionist Movement by the Sovereign of a crucially important Protestant European power," Pragai noted in his book.

When Mehemet Ali of Egypt threatened the Sultan in 1838, Palmerston and Ashley influenced the Turkish Government to permit the establishment of a British Consulate in Jerusalem. Ashley's delight over the achievement is reflected in his diary:

"The ancient city of the people of God is about to resume a place among the nations, and England is the first of Gentile kingdoms that ceases "to tread her down.""

Yitzchak Ben-Zvi, who became the second president of the State of Israel, commented:

"We are witnessing today the wondrous process of the joining of the tribes of Israel bone to bone and flesh to flesh; the merging of them into one nation. I pray that the Rock and Redeemer of Israel may prosper our ways and that in our days Judah may be saved and Israel dwell securely."

Of course, the single most miraculous event that has forced many theologians to re-examine their suppositions concerning the Jews is the physical rebirth of the unexpected nation of Israel in 1948. Yet before that, many others had foreseen this as they studied and trusted the Bible:

"And it shall come to pass in that day, that the Lord shall set His hand again the second time to recover the remnant of His people...and He shall set up an ensign for the nations, and shall assemble the outcasts of Israel, and gather together the dispersed of Judah from the four corners of the earth." [14]

"And I will bring again the captivity of my people Israel, and they shall build the waste cities and inhabit them...and I will plant them upon their land, and they shall no more be pulled up out of their land which I have given them, sayeth the Lord thy God." [15]

"At that time they shall call Jerusalem the throne of the lord; AND ALL THE NATIONS SHALL BE GATHERED UNTO IT, to the name of the Lord, to Jerusalem; neither shall they walk anymore after the stubbornness of their evil heart." [16]

"Yet will I set my King upon my holy hill of Zion" [17]

"Hear the Word of the LORD, O ye nations. Declare it and say, He that scattered Israel will gather him, therefore, they shall come and sing again in the heights of Zion." [18]

"...to the brightness of thy rising. The wealth of the Gentiles shall come to thee Israel. Thou shalt suck the milk of the Gentiles and thou shalt know that I am the LORD, thy Saviour, thy Redeemer, the Mighty One of Jacob. They (the Gentiles) shall call thee (Israel) the City of the LORD, the Zion of the Holy One of Israel." [19]

The Apostle Paul also wrote that the Deliverer (meaning the Messiah) would come to Zion; and all Israel would then be saved. [20]

At the end, we will reconnect with the Jewish heritage of our Christian faith and understand that true Christians, in reality, are "spiritual Jews," connected to the God of the Bible.

GENTILE CHRISTIANS—SHOULD THEY BE ZIONISTS?

The Word of God makes it clear that He who scattered Israel will gather them, Jeremiah 31:10, and He will use gentiles to help carry them home:

> But the LORD will have compassion on Jacob and will again choose Israel, and will set them in their own land; and aliens will join them and attach themselves to the house of Jacob. And the nations will take them and bring them to their place, and the house of Israel will possess the nations as male and female slaves in the LORD's land; they will take captive those who were their captors, and rule over those who oppressed them. [21]

> Thus says the Lord God: I will soon lift up my hand to the nations, and raise my signal to the peoples; and they shall bring your sons in their bosom, and your daughters shall be carried on their shoulders. Kings shall be your foster fathers, and their queens your nursing mothers. With their faces to the ground they shall bow down to you, and lick the dust of your feet. Then you will know that I am the LORD; those who wait for me shall not be put to shame. Can the prey be taken from the mighty, or the captives of a tyrant be rescued? But thus says the LORD: Even the captives of the mighty shall be taken, and the prey of the tyrant be rescued; for I will contend with those who contend with you, and I will save your children. I will make your oppressors eat their own flesh, and they shall be drunk with their own blood as

with wine. Then all flesh shall know that I am the LORD your Savior, and your Redeemer, the Mighty One of Jacob.[22]

Israel was first in the Bible, and she has gone through that long journey and finally come to be a nation. The Jews in the Diaspora, the dispersion, have always been in danger and Satan still seeks to destroy them. Many horrors, along with the Holocaust, have taken place and most people hope that history will not be repeated. However, Jews outside Israel are still in danger of assimilation, anti-Semitism and even annihilation. The difference between past generations and those living today is that the Jews have a home. Since 1948, Israel is a fact. Unfortunately, in the wake of this miracle, chaos looms.

The breakup of the former Soviet Union, with the resulting economic and political instability, left Ukraine with the highest density of Jewish people as well as the most tragic history of anti-Semitism. Centuries ago, God said through the prophet Zechariah, *"Come, come, flee from the land of the north."* Not only from Russia (the land of the north) but out of more than a hundred different nations.

Romans 15:27: "You Gentiles owe it to the Jews to help them in Earthly matters."

This command reveals the increasing opportunities to reach out to the Jewish people and speak a prophetic word concerning God's desire for them. The Scripture is clear in many passages, such as Ezekiel 37, that God's plan is the physical restoration of Israel, followed by a spiritual worldwide revival.

REPLACEMENT THEOLOGY—HISTORY

Opinions:

"My opinion is the same as most Arab Christians, Orthodox or Catholic, and they believe in Replacement Theology."

Response:

This is one of the most evil concepts promoted throughout the centuries, yet I doubt that many Christians even realize it. Many misguided church fathers eliminated the lessons of Peter, Paul, Timothy and

John in order to follow Saint Augustine and his path of errors. It was Augustine, around 400 A.D., who ultimately articulated the idea, principally in his well-known work, "The City of God."

Augustine had, at one time, espoused the doctrine of Chiliasm, (from the Greek chiliasmos, meaning "a thousand years") which was a belief in a future millennium when Christ would return and the righteous (the Church and redeemed Israel) would reign with Him for a thousand years.

But which of Augustine's doctrines is more credible, the original one or the one that came later? One would think that the original supersedes, as it is closer to what both the Apostles and Jesus Christ taught. And why did Augustine abandon the earlier apostolic views? These questions are difficult to answer by Replacement Theology supporters.

One thing is clear, Replacement Theology is not a conviction based on research and study of Scripture, but a state of mind plagued with centuries of dependence on tradition that is clouded with half-truths. This twisted history put thick scales on Middle Eastern eyes. Arab students are never taught Jewish history and they seldom look at Scripture for themselves; they are programmed by repetition of old propaganda to the point where they end up believing that they themselves hold divine truth.

One would think that the Palestinians who live in the midst of the conflict would be experts on the situation, but the opposite is true; their schools are infested with hate-filled lies, their mosques preach hatred from the pulpit, and their priests call out for the destruction of Israel. Christians and Muslims alike in Israel are victims of this brainwash.

They have chosen to live in isolation from the Jew. The Jew, on the other hand, is so afraid of Arab attacks that he too is isolated. You have barbed-wire fenced Jewish settlements on the hilltops and Arab villages in the valleys, and no one communicates.

The Arab Christians, on the other hand, are unaware of their blind stand against the Jew. They walk with Muslims on the same path of struggle; they are unaware, or maybe look the other way, at much of the evidence of repeated history, that Islam holds an "extreme" position and a different form of Replacement Theology than their "Christian" brothers. This Replacement excludes not only Israel from the land, but the Christians as well. Islam has no problem using anyone to oppose an arch enemy until it reaches power; then any other theologies must be eliminated, including any faiths that supported it in the past.

Just as the beast, mentioned in Revelation, uses the whore, then turns on her to destroy her.

History proved this through the ages, but the only way Arab Christians can see it is to study hundreds of historical events from time immemorial showing the atrocities committed by Muslims toward the Christians. They overlook the slaughter of 1.5 million Armenian Christians, the Sudan Muslims' destruction of one million Christians, annihilation of almost all Nubian Christians, and the forced conversions of almost every Christian nation in the East.

In Sudan during the last few years alone, the Muslim terror has become fiercest since the coming power of dictator General Haasan El-Bashi. The Muslims attacked Christian villages. Children between the ages of 13 and 20 were shot without judgment. United Nations reports say that others were burned alive in their huts. Many churches were closed or destroyed. Sudan is forcibly Islamized. Males get circumcised. Leaders of animist tribes were invited by the authorities to a "conference," and then they were shot. Crucifixion and stoning of Christians and torture with red-hot iron bars is a horrifying reality that, accompanied with mass expulsions and starvation, was carried out right next door to a silent world that only recently has heard their cries. To many in the West, Arab oil has become more valuable than Christian blood.

Only the future will show that history did repeat itself and that Islam was able to conquer, not Jewish communities only, but entire Christian nations as well. Christian Arabs may not know that Egypt, Syria, Turkey, and even many parts of Saudi Arabia, were once Christian. The Jews were eventually destroyed or exiled, and the Christians put to the sharp Islamic sword, given the choices of "Shahadatan" or death. The East was lost to Islam, due to its weakness and lack of adherence to Scripture, and its beliefs in saints, substituting apostolic teachings for a world full of icons. Unfortunately, even my plea would be viewed as a betrayal based on the old principle of "divide and conquer." The Middle East is plagued with supposed conspiracy theories that everything malignant must have been generated by Zionist ideas. However, those perversions came not from Zionists but from enemies of the Jews long ago, springing up again in the 20th century as Communism and Nazism and yet again, as I write, in the Middle East. These perversions had the full support of the late Yasser Arafat, Hanan Ashrawi, George Habbash, and the rest of the corrupt political spectrum of Palestinian Authorities.

The whole story of Scripture is the story of the fallen man who is in need of redemption and a loving creator who sends His Son through a chosen nation, Israel. God had promised an everlasting covenant, that through them a redeemer would come. For some of them would betray Him, yet in the end He will come back to them, as He remembers His eternal covenant, and rescues them in Jerusalem from the gentile world that attacks His beloved chosen people from every nation and from every side.

Instead, His Will is pushed aside by the recent Ecumenical Movement and the one behind the vale of Satan, riding all the way to Mystery Babylon on the back of the demonic beast of world alliance.

Unfortunately, Satan is always at work, as The Lord told us, to deceive even "the very elect," and Christendom canonized Augustine's contemptible ideas by making him a saint, while theologians throughout the Roman Empire accepted his false doctrine.

The Chiliasts were branded as holding "aberrant and heretical views," and Augustinian Replacement Theology, along with other false theologies, became the cornerstones of the Roman Catholic Church. Later in the Eastern Orthodox Church, the European Reformation and the Anglicans split, and Replacement Theology continued essentially untouched. It was an important part of the standard Christian view of Israel, the world, and prophecy. This view, which "evolved," had no basis in the teachings of the Apostles; on the contrary, instead of being Biblical, it became anti-Biblical, as cursing Israel in reality is cursing God's chosen people. Roman persecution, the Holocaust, the Russian pogroms and the various inquisitions used this theology to try to destroy the Jew.

How can anyone claim to support both Biblical Christianity and Replacement Theology and not see the contradiction? Worse, the effect of all of this on Christian attitudes about Israel has been devastating. In truth, Replacement Theology disenfranchised Israel from having a continuing covenant relationship with God. Instead of looking at Jerusalem as the "City of the Great King," in which Christ will reign for a thousand years upon His return, they saw Jerusalem's perpetual desolation as much a confirmation of Christianity as the destruction of Pharaoh's army in the Red Sea was a confirmation of Moses.

The Marcion heresy expressed the extreme form of this view. Marcion, the first century theologian, proposed that the Old Testament be abandoned, something that many Arab Christians stand by, but that was unacceptable to the Church. They felt a better way to de-Judaize the Hebrew Scriptures was to Christianize them, which would spiritualize the text and incorporate New Testament concepts. That view is still prevalent today.

To argue that we should follow what certain Church fathers teach is a contradiction of what Replacement Theology advocates themselves teach, since they tell the Jews to ignore the errors of their rabbis and seek the Word of God and the original Hebrew Prophets. Replacement Theology's misguided approach to the Bible "has not only led millions of Christians astray over the years but it has, in addition, birthed evil of the most horrific proportions. Replacement Theology played a role in the persecution of Jews by the church through the centuries, including the Holocaust," [23] since all the promises and blessings and Israel's entire inheritance now belongs to the Church, while Israel gets to keep the curses.

This false theology instituted originally by Rome was a great stumbling block for the Jews, as it prevented them from recognizing their own Messiah, "Remove the obstacles out of the way of my people." [24]

God has in no way either rejected or replaced Israel or the Jewish people. His covenant with them is unconditional and non-transferable. God's covenants and promises were never based on Israel's good behavior, but were based on God's faithfulness toward His people. Although the Jewish people have suffered the consequences of breaking God's Laws, just as we all do, they have not been replaced or rejected. The Scriptures make that quite clear.

REPLACEMENT THEOLOGY—THE OPINION OF THE MASSES

Opinion:

"What I believe is what all Christians believed in until the 19th century and what the majority of Christians believe in today."

Response:

This opinion is rooted in blindness more than fact and, like a magnet, attracted errors and false doctrines along the way. It does not recognize that reformation was necessary to keep Christians on track and to protect believers from many false teachings of the Church fathers.

Replacement Theology is still the majority view among professing Christian theologians, but pre-millennialists are largely considered a legitimate and vocal minority, at least in Evangelical Protestant circles.

Organizations such as the Roman Catholic Church and the World Council of Churches, which include both Protestant and Catholic faiths have, for the last half-century, taken positions favoring the Arab and Muslim enemies of Israel. It is with considerable reluctance that the Vatican finally recognized Israel, and the Church's primary interest is in asserting its influence in maintaining its Holy Places in Jerusalem. Similarly, the World Council of Churches has consistently pled the cause of Palestinians against the claims of Israel.

Thus, Christianity, because of its various theological views, has divided opinions about Zionism and the revived State of Israel. In Numbers 14, the option of Replacement Theology is flatly rejected. The idea was that God would kill all the Israelites because of their sinfulness and He would start over again from the beginning. He would not discard the idea of a chosen people, but He would destroy those who were descended from Abraham and start a new people with Moses. Again, this theory is rejected. God listened to Moses' prayer for His sinful people. God the Father has surely listened to the prayer of Jesus.

WHO IS A JEW?

The very verse that anti-Zionists and Replacement Theology advocates use to support their position that God had no more plans for the Jew, that God replaced them by others, in reality, backfires:

"For he is not a Jew, which is one outwardly; neither is that circumcision, which is outward in the flesh: But he is a Jew, which is one inwardly; and circumcision is that of the heart, in the spirit, and not in the letter; whose praise is not of men, but of God." [25]

Since this verse never stated that God is done with the Jews or replaced them, I wonder why Replacement Theology advocates don't change their title from Christians to Spiritual Jews? That is what this verse, one that they advocate, calls for, especially when it is a New Testament verse intended for Christ's followers. If this verse means that we are a new breed of faith, why would the One God dictate more than one faith?

God has only one faith to which he has called us, that is of being Spiritual Jews or Jews at "heart" and "spirit," as the Bible puts it in the following verse. Paul was telling Christ's followers, who were Jews, that what mattered to God was not being circumcised in the flesh, but seeking the heart and the spirit of God, to follow His ways in obedience to His Word, to love the Lord your God with all your heart and with all your might; this is the first commandment.

The Bible tells us clearly that God wants us to be "spiritual Jews."

"But he is a Jew, which is one inwardly; and circumcision is that of the heart, in the spirit." [26]

To some, that sounds like a detested title, but God chose the title of "Jew" for Christ, for the apostles, for the prophets before them, and for His followers as well. Today's term, *Christians*, is nowhere to be found in Scripture. I agree that we are to follow Christ, yet the Bible states that we are to be followers of the Messiah who came for the Jew first, then to the Gentile. I am by no means arguing that we cannot call ourselves "Christians," but only that the Church has not replaced the Jew. For how long will we deny God His ways?

Replacement Theology advocates claim that *they* are now God's chosen, since they are the ones after God's heart, not these abandoned, divorced Jews in the flesh. Instead of loving these Jews by heart and spirit until death, witnessing to them by God's truth, and setting the perfect example for them to find their Messiah, a new era of the faith has begun: a Christian era with the Marys, icons, and Crystal Cathedrals. To them, there is no need for God to fulfill His plans for Jerusalem, or establish David's seat on Zion. For how long will they deny God's Will?

What happened to the God who said, "I bring back the captives of Judah and Jerusalem?" He makes it clear that Israel will be first in unbelief and in her land, when Gentile rule is finished:

> "For I would not, brethren, that ye should be ignorant of this mystery, lest ye should be wise in your own conceits; that blindness in part is happened to Israel, until the fullness of the Gentiles be come in. And so all Israel shall be saved: as it is written, There shall come out of Zion the Deliverer, and shall turn away ungodliness from Jacob." [27]

Isn't the following verse clearly the Will of God?

> "And it shall come to pass in the last days, that the mountain of the *Lord's* house shall be established in the top of the mountains, and shall be exalted above the hills; and all nations shall flow unto it. And many people shall go and say, Come ye, and let us go up to the mountain of the LORD, to the house of the God of Jacob; and he will teach us of his ways, and we will walk in his paths: for out of Zion shall go forth the law, and the word of the LORD from Jerusalem." [28]

Can we replace Zion and Jerusalem with the Vatican, the seat of Christ which is now in Rome? Where are all the verses about Rome?

In reality, nothing changed in the Christian world from the Jewish era. The same verses that Replacement Theology advocates use regarding the "fleshly-circumcised Jew" and the "Spiritual Jew" fits them. From time immemorial we have had "fleshly Christians" (Christians by tradition) and "Spiritual Christians" (Christians who follow Scripture). There were many wars between the two with millions of casualties for the "Spiritual" Christians. Those who claim to be Christians, yet say they hate Jews at the same time, are in contradiction of their faith. The Nazis, the Ku Klux Klan, Replacement Theologists, anti-Zionists and anyone who is anti-Jew is not abiding by the prescription set by God.

Indeed, anti-Israel advocates will not be able to enjoy heaven, whose twelve gates bear the names of the twelve tribes of Israel. How will we ever be healed? How is it that we are so blind? Where are the verses that say, "We the Spiritual Jews have replaced God's plan for the circumcised Jews?"

Doesn't God have plans for them? Doesn't God have hundreds of verses describing their plan to become Spiritual Jews as well? Hasn't God supplied us with abundant Scripture to show that He loves the Jews and has a plan for them? How could we be so determined to dismiss this Scripture that we would isolate one or two verses and twist them like pretzels to fit our narrow views? Why would God choose the word *Jew* if He, all of a sudden, abandoned and divorced them forever?

"Disguised believers" isolate a few verses and then contrive a new theology. This includes the Faith Theology, Jehovah's Witnesses, Mormons, Modern Day Prophets Movement, The Mother Mary cult, The Goddess Cult, David Koresh, The Hour of Power, and many others. There is always a new one, fulfilling what the Bible predicted, that in the later times, false prophets will arise to deceive. Replacement Theology advocates use the same tactics as do cults.

In Matthew 8, we see that Christ will rule the earth and all believers, Jew and Gentile, will be with him while the rest of the unbelieving world will be cast out. Christ will have His seat. The subjects of the kingdom are by no means the Jews of Israel, but all the unbelievers in the world as described in Matt 13:38:

"The field is the world; the good seed are the children of the kingdom; but the tares are the children of the wicked one."

199

The good seed are the "Children of The Kingdom" from the "field" which is the world. While the Kingdom of Heaven has *nothing* to do with re-gathering the children of Jacob (Israel), Replacement Theologists try to equate the two, since both gatherings are from the east and the west.

This kingdom will come as Zechariah predicted in his vision of the messianic era. He foretold that in the end of days, "It shall come to pass that every one that is left of all nations that came against Jerusalem, shall go up from year to year to worship the King, the LORD of hosts, and to keep the Feast of Tabernacles." [29]

Several thousand Christians trek annually to Jerusalem to worship the King. In 1996, during the Jewish Succot, more than 5,000 such pilgrims participated from more than 100 gentile nations. Leaning on their distorted interpretations of Scripture, Replacement Theologists claim that the prophecies of Israel's return have been fulfilled already, after the Jews came out of the Babylonian captivity. In Joel, chapter 3, we see that the facts are:

- The Jews were never disbursed throughout every nation until the Diaspora.
- Currently, and since the early twentieth century, they have been brought back to Israel from every corner of the globe, and almost half of the world's Jews are in Israel.
- Jerusalem today is Israel's capital. *"I bring back the captives of Judah and Jerusalem."* What is left of this strange declaration is that on Christ's Second Coming, there will be a judgment of the nations for disbursing the Jews and for dividing Israel with her enemies.

On page 124 of his book, <u>Whose Promised Land?</u> Chapman emphasizes, *"The Meek...will inherit the Earth,"* and he offers a re-translation of the Greek word "ge'en" to mean "land." Even if we accept the translation, it is not specific to Israel. It is obvious that this re-translation is intended to make the Bible fit the Replacement Theology doctrine, and is therefore invalid in light of the rest of Scripture which clearly makes Israel a non-gentile ruler of the land, especially when there will be a rule of the whole world by Israel at the time of Messiah's rule.

WHO IS "ISRAEL OF GOD?"

Argument:

The term "Israel of God," is found only in Galatians 6:16, where Paul writes: *"Peace and mercy to all who follow this rule even to the Israel of God."* It is Paul, writing to the Galatians, who says that the Church could now assume a title that had formerly belonged solely to the Jewish people.

Response:

This is contrary to what Paul was actually saying. I refer to a previous verse:

"Neither circumcision, nor un-circumcision means anything, what counts is a new creation." Who is Paul talking about? There are five candidates mentioned by Paul in this letter:

1 - Gentile Christians tempted to desert to a different gospel (1:6ff)

2 - The Church of God (1:13)

3 - The Gentiles to whom Paul was called to preach (2:7)

4 - The Jewish circumcision believers (2:11-13), and

5 - The Jewish circumcision party (2:11-13)

By process of elimination, "Israel of God" cannot refer to the Gentile believers, tempted by the circumcision party, because it is they who Paul is warning about being pressured to be circumcised, the *"you"* in 6:11,12,13.

Paul is not calling them "Israel of God;" thus he must be referring to a group different from these *"foolish Galatians."* Nor is he referring to the circumcision party. He has already addressed them as *"those who want to make a good impression,"* in 6:12.

We can rule out the gentiles to whom Paul brings the Gospel. Circumcision is of no relevance to them. Therefore, does "even the Israel of God" mean "the Church of God," the title that Paul used in 1:13?

Remember that the letter is written, "to the churches in Galatia," made up of Jewish and gentile believers. However, the thrust of the letter is to expose the folly within the Church[30] of the Galatian Christians being persuaded by the Judaising party[31] that they should be circumcised in order to be righteous.[32] Why expose their folly, and then confuse the whole situation by calling the Gentile-dominated church in Galatia "the Israel of God?"

He was condemning Israel as being "in slavery with her children." Why confuse the church that he labored so hard for[33] by trading one clear collective noun "Israel", denoting a distinctive ethnic group of people, for the Christian Church, which is distinctly not the nation of Israel?

There is one other problem in transferring Israel's title to the Church, and it is the word *even—even to the Israel of God*.[34]

The Greek word is "kai" and is usually translated as "and." Thus it would read, "Peace and mercy to all who follow this rule..." (e.g., all you gentiles who resist the pressure to be circumcised to obtain righteousness) *and* to the "Israel of God," a separate group. This is how the Authorized Version, Revised Version, Douay, New English Bible, and New American Standard versions translate "kai."

Paul addresses Gentiles in this passage as *"you."* We dismiss the title as referring to "the Church" for the reasons just stated. Believing Jews needed to hear this too, since they had already been circumcised and might be tempted to believe circumcision provided righteousness based on the Jewish law. It makes much more sense to see that Paul refers to them in 6:16 as *"the Israel of God,"* the believing remnant of Israel to which Peter and Barnabas belonged[35] and who themselves had been led astray.[36] They were "of Israel" and also "of God."

This is the *only* reference to this title, and a basic rule of exegesis is that doctrine is developed not from a single text, but from the broad teaching of Scripture. If we replace the word "Israel" with the word "Church" anywhere else in the New Testament, the context makes no sense. The Amplified Bible cross-references this verse with Psalms 125:5, *"Peace be upon Israel."*

Further, the theft of the title by the Church implies that all the promises that were made to Israel are now promised to the Church. Ezekiel says in 36:8-12,

"But ye, O mountains of Israel, ye shall shoot forth your branches, and yield your fruit to my people of Israel...Yea, I will cause men to walk upon you, even my people, Israel."

Doesn't this prophecy clearly mean Israel? Wasn't Israel's land replenished? Aren't the Jews walking on one of the finest cultivated areas in the Middle East? Tell me, what Church mountains will shoot forth branches and have men walk upon her?

The word "Israel" or "Israelites" occurs about 75 times in the New Testament. In at least 70 of these entries, the name Israel is used in precisely the same way as it was in the Old Testament. This includes nine distinct quotations of Old Testament Scriptures. In every one of these New Testament quotations, the meaning of "Israel" is exactly the same as it was in the Old Testament.

In perhaps four instances in the New Testament, the apostle Paul uses "Israel" in a special, restricted sense to denote only those Israelites who have continued in the faith of their forefather Abraham, and for this reason have acknowledged Jesus as their Messiah.[37] However, not once in the New Testament is Israel used as a synonym for the Church as a whole. In Romans 11:25-26, Paul sums up his analysis of the relationship between Israel and the Gentiles in one comprehensive statement:

"Hardening in part has happened to Israel until the full number of the Gentiles has come in. And so all Israel will be saved."

BIBLE PROPHECY—WHO SHOULD INTERPRET IT?

A Palestinian argues:

"Why should we accept your interpretation of the Bible? You already *cited 'no prophecy of the Scripture is of any private interpretation...*'" [38]

Response:

The statement is a contradiction in itself. If we assume that that passage above means that average people cannot have "private interpretation(s)," then which "experts" can interpret it?

For the answer: "For no prophecy was ever made by an act of human will, but men moved by the Holy Spirit spoke from God." [39]

Matthew Henry, the 17th century minister and famous Bible commentator says,

"The gospel message was also foretold by the prophets and penmen of the Old Testament, who spoke and wrote under influence, and according to the direction, of the Spirit of God."

Therefore, Scripture was not created by man but by God. The verse does not say to follow the "majority" interpretation. The Bible was written to be understood by everyone who reads it.

ISRAEL—BY DIVINE RIGHT

Zionism is simply the return of the Jewish people to Zion, to the land of Israel, to the land promised by God to Abraham and his descendants forever. These promises are found throughout all of Scripture, the first one in Genesis 12:1-3; expanded by Genesis 15:7:

"God said unto Abraham, I am the LORD who brought you out of the land of Ur of the Chaldees to give this land to you to inherit it. And Abraham said, Lord God, how shall I know that I will inherit it?"

Then God makes a covenant with Abraham through the sacrificial system, and in verse 13 He said to Abraham,

"Know of a surety that thy seed shall be a stranger in a land that is not theirs (that is Egypt) and shall serve them and they shall afflict you there four hundred years. But in the fourth generation you shall come out for the iniquity of the Amorites is not yet full."

The Amorites were then residents of the land that was to become the Promised Land. "In the same day the LORD made a covenant with Abraham saying, unto thy seed have I given this land from the River of Egypt unto the great river, the River Euphrates." [40] Then He tells us who is going to be moving out: the Kenites, the Kenizzites, the Kadmonites, the Hittites, the Perizzites, the Rephaim, the Amorites, the Canaanites, the Girgashites, and the Jebusites.

This is of particular interest, because the Jebusites occupied the city of Jebus, which later became Jerusalem. Therefore, Zionism is the fulfillment, in flesh and blood, of God's promise to Abraham; and the promise depends completely on the faithfulness of God rather than on the faithfulness of Abraham and his descendants.

After the first Jewish captivity in Babylon, about 600 BC, the Persian leader, Cyrus, allowed the Jewish people to return to rebuild Jerusalem and re-establish their religion. That was the initial application of Zionism—the first return of the Jewish people to the Promised Land some 530 years before the time of Christ.

Twenty-five hundred years later, we witnessed World War II and that unspeakable time—of which we must speak—called the Holocaust. From the depths of despair to the height of triumph in 1948: the return of the Jews from all the nations to the modern State of Israel.

"Therefore say, Thus says the Lord God: 'I will gather you from the peoples, assemble you from the countries where you have been scattered, and I will give you the land of Israel.'" [41]

Never in history was a nation so scattered throughout the world and later re-gathered. And Jerusalem will become the central city for Israel:

"I will bring them back, and they shall dwell in the midst of Jerusalem. They shall be My people and I will be their God, in truth and righteousness." [42]

Thus says the Lord: "Against all My evil neighbors who touch the inheritance which I have caused My people to inherit—behold, I will pluck them out of their land and pluck out the house of Judah from among them. Then it shall be, after I have plucked them out, that I will have compassion on them and bring them back everyone to his heritage and everyone to his land."[43] "Therefore behold, the days are coming," says the Lord, "that it shall no more be said, 'The Lord lives who brought up the children of Israel from the land of Egypt, but The Lord lives who brought up the children of Israel from the land of the north and from all the lands where He had driven them. For I will bring them back into their land which I gave to their fathers.'"[44]

The exodus from Egypt in the time of Moses, great as it was, cannot compare to the re-gathering of the Jewish people from all over the world. The mighty God of Israel is still bringing them from all the lands and from the land of the north (former Soviet Union). Jeremiah tells us about this:

Behold, I will bring them from the *north country*, and gather them from the farthest parts of the earth, among them the blind and the lame, the woman with child and her who is in travail, together; a great company, they shall return here. With weeping they shall come, and with consolations I will lead them back, I will make them walk by brooks of water, in a straight path in which they shall not stumble; for I am a father to Israel, and Ephraim is my first-born. Hear the word of The Lord, O nations, and declare it in the coastlands afar off; say*, 'He who scattered Israel will gather him*, and will keep him as a shepherd keeps his flock.'[45]

Russia (the north) has persecuted the Jews since the time of the Czars until the recent breakup of the Soviet Empire. What a victory is this new state of Israel!

It is simply arrogant for man to dictate how God, his Maker, should operate the world or write His Bible; it is He who chooses the way He wants to be honored. The following prophecies should ring true to anyone who witnessed the recent historical events in Israel.

"I will bring them from *the coasts of the earth*, and with them the blind and the lame, the woman with child together: a great company shall return thither." [46]

Isaiah 35:10: "And the redeemed of the Lord shall return and come with singing unto ZION and everlasting joy shall be upon their heads; they shall obtain gladness and joy; and sorrow and sighing shall flee away."

Until now, this prophecy has not been fulfilled because the joy of return has never lasted. The Jews were always driven out.

Jeremiah 16:14: "Therefore, behold, the days come, says the LORD, that it shall no more be said, 'the Lord liveth, that brought up the children of Israel out of the land of Egypt;' but, 'the Lord liveth that brought up the children of Israel from the land *of the north*, and from all the lands whither He had driven them,' and I will bring them again into their land that I gave to their fathers."

Amos 9:14-15: "And I will *return* My people Israel out of captivity, and they will rebuild the waste cities and inhabit them, and I will plant them upon their land, and they shall never again be plucked up out of their land which I have given them, says the Lord your God."

In Acts 10, we read of the acceptance of non-Jews into the family of believers. The first example was particularly hard to accept: an officer of the pagan Roman occupation army, Cornelius, and his family. Yet, after intense discussion among Jesus' Jewish followers, he was accepted graciously and with a spirit of amazement at God's generosity.

Note: In the Hebrew Bible, there are stories of the killing of conquered enemies and stories of conquered enemies being fed and freed. Israelis have, without exception, followed the second alternative.

Note: In the Synoptic Gospels, the chief use of the word "Jews" is in reference to Jesus as "King of the Jews" with only three exceptions.

"Fear not, O Jacob My servant, says the Lord, for I am with you. I will make a full end of all the nations to which I have driven you, but I will not make a full end of you, but correct you in measure, yet I will not leave you wholly unpunished." [47]

TYRE: AN AMAZING PROPHECY

For thus says Yahweh God: "Behold, I will bring against Tyre from the north Nebuchadnezzar king of Babylon, king of kings, with horses, with chariots, and with horsemen, and an army with many people. He will slay with the sword your daughter villages in the fields; he will heap a siege mound against you, build a wall against you, and raise a defense against you. He will direct his battering rams against your walls, and with his axes he will break down your towers. Because of the abundance of his horses, their dust will cover you; your walls will shake at the noise of the horsemen, the wagons, and the chariots, when he enters your gates, as men enter a city that has been breached.

With the hooves of his horses he will trample all your streets; he will slay your people by the sword, and your strong pillars will fall to the ground. They will plunder your riches and pillage your merchandise; they will break down your walls and destroy your pleasant houses; they will lay your stones, your timber, and your soil in the midst of the water. I will put an end to the sound of your songs, and the sound of your harps shall be heard no more. I will make you like the top of a rock; you shall be a place for spreading nets, you shall never be rebuilt, for I Yahweh have spoken."[48]

The facts:

Nebuchadnezzar laid waste to the mainland city three years after the prophecy. The Encyclopedia Britannica notes "After a 13 year siege (585-573 B.C.) by Nebuchadnezzar II, the city came to terms and acknowledged Babylonian suzerainty." When he broke the gates down, he found the city almost empty. The majority of the people had fled by ship to an island about half a mile off the coasts and fortified a city there. The mainland city was destroyed in 573, but the island city of Tyre remained powerful for several hundred years.

Alexander later attacked Tyre and, possessing no fleet, he demolished old Tyre on the mainland, and with the debris, built a moat 200 feet across the straits, separating the old and new towns, erecting towers and war engines at the further end. The old city of Tyre did supply stones and dirt to build the causeway.[49]

Tyre was a mainland city divided from the Alcatraz-like island fortress, and a causeway, which still exists. Philip Myers, a secular historian and theologian called it, *"uniting the rock with the mainland."* When the city at last was taken after a seven-month siege, 8,000 of the inhabitants were slain and 30,000 were sold into slavery.

Myers also wrote, "Alexander the Great reduced the city to ruins (332 B.C.). She recovered in a measure from this blow but never regained the place she had previously held in the world. The larger part of the site of the once great city is now bare as a top of a rock, a place where the fisherman that still frequent the spot spread their nets to dry."

Historian John C. Beck noted, "The history of Tyre does not stop after the conquest of Alexander. Men continue to rebuild her and armies continue to besiege her walls until finally, after 1600 years, she falls never to be rebuilt again."

Joseph Michaud, the 18th century French historian, described how the Muslims destroyed Tyre: "Their houses, their temples, the monuments of their piety, their valor and their industry, everything was condemned to perish with them by the sword or by fire."

Guy LeStrange quotes Abu'l fiela (1321 A.D.): "The city was reconquered by the Muslims in 690 (1291)…and then was laid in ruins, as it remains down to the present day." [50]

Today Tyre is a fishing community. Nina Jidejian writes:

"The Sidonian port of Tyre is still in use today. Small fishing vessels lay at anchor there. An examination of the foundations reveals granite columns of the Roman period which were incorporated as binders in the walls by the Crusaders. The port has become a haven today for fishing boats and a place for spreading nets."

This small fishing village called Tyre, the mistress of the seas, the trade and commercial center of the world for centuries, passed away *never* to rise (re-build) again. The fishermen drying their nets upon the rocks that once formed the foundation of that ancient metropolis are the last link in the chain of prophecy that Ezekiel gave over 25 hundred years ago.[51]

Jidejian concludes:

> Tyre's stones may be found as far away as Acre and Beirut. Yet evidences of a great past are abundant and recent excavations have revealed successive levels of this proud Phoenician seaport...The great ancient city of Tyre lay buried under accumulated debris. The ruins of an aqueduct and a few scattered columns and the ruins of a Christian basilica were the only remains found above ground...looking down into the water one can see a mass of granite columns and stone blocks strewn over the sea bottom. Until recently the ruins of Tyre above water were few.[52]

> Although Tyre is still an excellent site for a city, it has never been rebuilt, even though it has fresh springs producing 10 million gallons of fresh water daily. True, the prophecy was written after the events occurred, when Alexander destroyed the city; however, the Muslims fulfilled the prophecy by destroying everything, leaving just bare rock.[53]

WHO CAUSES DIVISION?

Argument:

"Christian supporters of Israel advocate division."

An anti-Israel man stated, "Usually the person who causes division is the one who comes at a later date with a new opinion which the majority never held to. With all due respect, your views are the new, later views, thus you cannot say that the earlier views, which most Christians adhere to, caused the division."

Response:

It was Augustine who came later on, cancelled Chiliasm and created Replacement Theology by writing the "City of God." This would qualify him as one who "comes at a later date with a new opinion."

The founders of Replacement Theology, particularly Augustine, agreed with Christian Zionists that the New Testament apostles, who believed in a future for Israel and the literal Second Coming of Christ, would later change their views, effectively saying that the apostles were mistaken!

Replacement Theology is simply absurd. God, throughout the ages, has used only a few people to fulfill His plans: Daniel, Moses, Esther, a handful of the twelve Apostles, and the twelve tribes of Israel to show His will. Whether we like it or not, God uses the minority. And His Will is not to be replaced by man.

IS GOD THROUGH WITH THE JEWS?

The Jews in the Bible are indestructible. This unassimilated people have gone through long, intense and awful suffering. The Egyptians tried to finish them by enslaving them and forcing them to kill their children, then the Assyrians, then Nebuchadnezzar in 588 B.C. In 170 BC, Antiochus Epiphanies sought to destroy them and failed. Titus destroyed the Temple in 70 AD, killed over one million Jews and carried 97,000 into captivity to Rome. Christ made the startling prophecy: *"Verily I say unto you, there shall not be left here one stone upon another, that shall not be thrown down..."* [54] Which, to the amazement of His followers, was figuratively fulfilled. The Jewish blood flowed down the temple steps like water. Instead of stones, thousands upon thousands of Jews perished and the studded crosses on the mountains of Jerusalem were as far as the eye could see.

For several centuries, Jews were called Christ killers and burned on the stake or enslaved by the orders of dictators and tyrants. And no one can effectively describe the horror of the Holocaust. The world has always tried to destroy the Jews. Even King Ferdinand and Queen Isabella, revered in history for equipping Columbus for his journey, also made 500,000 Jews homeless.

The Soviet Union conducted many pogroms of torment, terror and death. No single nation or people in history have suffered a fraction of what the Jews have endured. The irony is that almost all of this inhuman behavior was conducted in the name of God, except for the Holocaust. Nothing in the Bible justifies this hatred of the Jews. Who could expect them to survive? From small remnants, and with half the Jews of Europe murdered by Hitler, the Jewish population has grown to approximately 15 million, fulfilling God's promise in the Bible:

"Hath God cast away His people? God forbid. God hath not cast away His people whom He foreknew..." [55] In fact, God settled the question Himself:

> Thus saith the Lord, who giveth the sun for a light by day, and the ordinances of the moon and of the stars for a light by night, who divideth the sea when its waves roar; The Lord of hosts is His name: If those ordinances depart from before Me, saith the Lord, then the seed of Israel also shall cease from being a nation before Me forever. Thus saith the Lord, If heaven above can be measured, and the foundations of the earth searched out beneath, I will also cast off all the seed of Israel for all that they have done, saith the Lord.

Many civilizations rose, prospered and died: Babylon, Greece, Rome. However, the nation of Israel persisted against all odds. The Arabic nations occupy an area five hundred times larger than Israel, but they insist on conquering the tiny spot of land she claims. Her validity is proven, not only by hundreds of ancient prophecies that came to pass, but by one ancient word created by God from the time of Jacob until our generation, and that word was and still is "*Israel.*"

Israel's existence today, and the re-gathering of the Jews from all parts of the world, is irrefutable proof that the Holy Bible is the true Word of God, as God scattered them throughout the whole world, and re-gathered them again from ALL nations back to their original land in fulfillment of his promises.

However, how do we reconcile God's prophecy with the concentration camps of Auschwitz and Treblinka? We cannot question God's eternal and unchangeable Bible, the very living and speaking God who never ceased to talk to the whole world. He is the same God who parted the Red Sea, destroyed the walls of Jericho, and gathered his scattered Jews from all over the globe.

Exactly what happened when 850,000 Jews were forced to flee Arab Muslim lands for Israel? On the other hand, 450,000 Arabs left

Israel after the Arab media urged them to go to allow the Arab armies to enter and annihilate the Jews. This was the great "exchange plan" God orchestrated.

"Therefore behold, the days are coming says the Lord, that it shall no more be said, 'The Lord lives who brought up the children of Israel from the land of Egypt,' but 'The Lord lives who brought up the children of Israel from the land of the north and from all the lands where He had driven them. For I will bring them back into their land which I gave to their fathers.'" [56]

Again, Replacement Theology advocates intentionally ignore prophecy in order to justify their claims, and many Christians who witness to Muslims ignore the direction given by God for fear of offending them; to them, Israel is an offense. Yet they would not hesitate to use Bible prophecy to prove Jesus was The Messiah. We can never excuse a contradiction of goals and a twisting of the Word of God. If Israel is an offense to cults, so is Christ crucified and His Lordship. Must we not speak of Christ? Must we not trust God that *"All Scripture is given by God...good for teaching...?"*

God affirmed in the next verses of Jeremiah:

"Thus saith the Lord, If heaven above can be measured, and foundations of the earth searched out beneath, I will also cast off all the seed of Israel for all that they have done, saith the Lord." [57]

"How can I give you up Ephraim? How can I hand you over, Israel? For I am God and not man." [58]

There are no other people chosen to reveal God's truth:

"He has revealed his word to Jacob, his laws and decrees to Israel. He has done this for no other nation." [59]

"The LORD will not reject his people; he will never forsake his inheritance." [60]

"I ask then: Did God reject his people? By no means!" [61]

"Remember that at one time you were separated from Messiah, excluded from citizenship in Israel and foreigners to the covenants of the promise...Consequently, you are no longer foreigners and aliens,

213

but fellow-citizens with God's people and members of God's house-hold..." [62]

"The law, introduced 430 years later, does not set aside the covenant previously established by God and thus do away with the promise. For if the inheritance depends on the law, then it no longer depends on a promise; but God in his grace gave it to Abraham through a promise." [63]

"Hear the Word of the LORD, O ye nations. Declare it and say, He that scattered Israel will gather him, therefore, they shall come and sing again in the heights of Zion." [64]

When was the Church ever scattered? Again in Isaiah 60:

"The Gentiles shall come to thy light," declared the prophet Isaiah. "And the Kings to the brightness of thy rising. The wealth of the Gentiles shall come to thee Israel. Thou shalt suck the milk of the Gentiles and thou shalt know that I am the LORD, thy Saviour, thy Redeemer, the Mighty One of Jacob."

Ezekiel 36:24-28 sums up the story of Israel's return and redemption:

> For I will take you from among the heathen, and gather you out of all countries, and will bring you into your own land. Then will I sprinkle clean water upon you, and ye shall be clean: from all your filthiness, and from all your idols, will I cleanse you. A new heart also will I give you, and a new spirit will I put within you: and I will take away the stony heart out of your flesh, and I will give you a heart of flesh. And I will put my spirit within you, and cause you to walk in my statutes, and ye shall keep my judgments, and do them. And ye shall dwell in the land that I gave to your fathers; and ye shall be my people, and I will be your God.

God named the land, and anyone who changes this name or harms His people will end up paying a heavy price, for He said speaking of Israel:

"For thus says the Lord of hosts: He sent Me after glory, to the nations which plunder you; for he who touches you touches the apple of His eye." [65]

It is indeed a warning to anyone who harms the Jews. Notice He says, "He sent Me." How could God send God? It is God the Father who sends God the Son. As He continues in verse 10:

"Sing and rejoice, O daughter of Zion! For behold, I am coming and I will dwell in your midst, says the Lord." [66]

This is a literal coming of the Lord (God in the flesh) to dwell in Jerusalem. This was prophesied by Zechariah long before Christ appeared. How could the Jews today, who do not believe in Christ, ever be accused of corrupting His Word, since they hold dearly onto these verses?

As in Micah 5:2, here is a two-fold prophecy: first a return in unbelief, then the Messiah's Second Coming and belief. Hebrew, the language Israel spoke thousands of years ago and thought to be a dead tongue, is very much alive and the official language of Israel today. No other nation in history lost its language then later restored it.

"For then will I turn to the people a pure language, that they may all call upon the name of the Lord, to serve Him with one consent." [67]

They eventually will call on God when Christ comes the second time. The Jews turned a wasteland into a Garden of Eden, and Israel's abundance makes up 90% of Europe's citrus fruit market. God said through Isaiah,

"He shall cause them that come of Jacob to take root: Israel shall blossom and bud, and fill the face of the world with fruit..." [68]

Israel made the desert blossom. With the help of a 10% increase in rainfall measured every decade, and the Israelis' incredible irrigation systems, millions of trees were planted, farms and orchards prospered and God transformed the whole environment of the land, which He prophesied through Isaiah:

"Be glad then, ye children of Zion, and rejoice in the Lord your God: for He hath given you the former rain moderately, and He will cause to come down for you the rain, the former rain, and the latter rain in the first month..." [69]

The laws of probability would never predict such fulfillment of prophecy by God. There can be no doubt that God exists and His name is Jehovah the Redeemer of Israel as He declared:

- On the destruction of the city of Tyre—Ezekiel 26
- On the destruction and rebuilding of Amman, Jordan—Jeremiah 49:3-6
- On the desolation of Petra—Jeremiah 49, fulfilled
- On Babylon—Jeremiah 50, fulfilled

THE EASTERN GATE

In the book of Ezekiel, 44:1-3:

"Then He brought me back to the outer gate which faces toward the east, but it was shut. And the Lord said to me, This gate shall be shut; it shall not be opened, and no man shall enter by it, because the Lord God of Israel has entered by it; therefore it shall be shut."

Now see Ezekiel 43:1:

"Afterward he brought me to the gate, the gate that faces toward the east. And behold, the glory of the God of Israel came from the way of the east."

And in chapter 43: verse 4:

"And the glory of the Lord came into the temple by way of the gate which faces toward the east."

These passages refer to the beautiful Eastern or Golden Gate, located 1,035 feet north of the Southeast corner of Al-Harm or Temple Mount area. When Muslim Khaleefeh Abdel-Malek bin-Marwan built the Dome of the Rock in 691 A.D., the gate had been sealed almost a thousand years. According to these verses, this gate is reserved for the coming Messiah. Many people have tried to open it.

In 1917 Muslim leaders, in control of Jerusalem, tried and failed to break the prophecy and open the gate. Each time, on the exact day the workmen were preparing to demolish the ancient stone, the hand of God intervened and the city of Jerusalem passed out of Muslim control into the hands of the British.

In 1967, the same attempt was made. However, Israel took over Jerusalem on the same day. These verses are referring to The Lord God of Israel who entered by the Eastern Gate. And again he will enter by that Gate a second time. This prophecy can be speaking about no other than the Messiah (Al-Maseeh).

It plainly calls Him the God of Israel. He is declared *"The God."* The Bible declares that He is God in the Flesh Who came to the Temple, left, and will come back again. The Gate He entered by shall be reserved for Him just before the Second Coming.

Muslims disclaim the Bible by accusing the Jews or the Pharisees of corrupting the Old Testament. That would be impossible, since the Jews, like the Muslims, do not believe God came or will come in the flesh. The Jews always regarded their sacred texts of the Bible to be Holy. They never changed them, and the existence of these verses is proof. This concurs with the Book of Zechariah, chap. 14 verses 3 to 4:

> Then the Lord will go forth and fight against those nations, As He fights in the day of battle. And on that day His feet will stand on the Mount of Olives, which faces Jerusalem on the east. And the Mount of Olives shall split in two, from east to west, Making a very large valley; Half of the mountain shall move toward the north and half of it toward the south.

When did "The Lord God" have feet? The Mount of Olives, which directly faces the Eastern Gate, will be opened by His coming. These prophecies are remarkable and astonishing. How did these prophets predict all of this, even down to the sealed Eastern Gate?

On the rebuilding of the Third Temple in Jerusalem (Future), read Amos 9:11 and Revelation 11:1-2. Christ will enter in the Eastern Gate to go into the Temple and the Bible clearly promises that Israel will build the Third Temple. Yet the Muslim Dome of the Rock is on the Temple Mount (Al-Haram Al-Shareef). Despite all the problems concerning the holy sites, *a Jewish Temple will be built* according to God's promise. Many question the possibility of the Jewish Temple being rebuilt side-by-side with the Muslim Dome of the Rock, since The Tomb of Abraham (Machphella) in Hebron includes worship sites for both Muslims and Jews. The prophet John (Yahya) was given a vision of the rebuilt Temple during the Tribulation:

"Rise and measure the temple of God, the altar, and those who worship there. But leave out the court which is outside the temple, and do not measure it, for it has been given to the Gentiles. And they will tread the holy city under foot for forty-two months." [70]

Since the Dome of the Rock was built in the area called the Court of the Gentiles, it is possible that the Temple will be side by side with a wall separating the two. When the Messiah comes, He will descend on the Mount of Olives, cross the Kidron Valley, enter the Eastern Gate, and go into the Temple.

ISRAEL—A PROPHECY IN THE QURAN

The Quran speaks to the restoration of Israel:

"And after him (Moses), we said to the children of Israel, dwell Ye in the Promised Land, and when the time of the promise of the latter days comes, we shall bring you out of various peoples."

Mustafa Mahmud, in The Quran: A Modern Understanding, explains a Quranic verse, Al-Isra 17:4, concerning Israel:

"And We gave (clear) warning to the children of Israel in the Book, that twice would they do mischief on the land and be elated with mighty arrogance (And twice would they be punished!)"

According to Mahmud, this verse is a prophecy:

"And here we see today the Jews reaching might and power and doing iniquity in the land for the second time..."

Mahmud, like many Muslim apologists, ignored the fact that the Quran was simply speaking about history; that Israel had two well-known historical events where they did iniquity, and both events are well recorded, and God made them pay for both by allowing the destruction of Israel.

The first was the Babylonian destruction by Nebuchadnezzar in 586 BC. The Israelites were taken into captivity. This was their punishment for rebelling against God and disobeying his commandments. This was the *first* destruction of the Temple in Jerusalem.

The second was the Roman destruction by Titus in 70 A.D. They disobeyed again, and the Temple was destroyed. The Jews were dispersed throughout the world (the Diaspora). This was the *second* destruction of the Temple in Jerusalem. Twice disobeyed, and twice destroyed. This is clearly not a prophecy but repetition of what the Bible and history already told us.

EMEU, AL-SABEEL, AL-BUSHRA, ABUNA CHACOUR: WHAT ARE THEIR GOALS?

Anti-Israel Christians and most Muslims in Palestine point to a political agenda of Christian Zionists. While Christian Zionists support Israel and the Jews' right to live there, Christian organizations like Evangelicals for Middle East Understanding (EMEU), Al-Sabeel, Al-Bushra, and others in Palestine and abroad have only small differences with Islamic fundamentalist groups in their hard-line politics against Israel.

Christian Zionists substantiate their claims by close adherence to Bible prophecy. There is an abundance of Scripture to support their views. It is only fair that their opponents support theirs.

Take, as an example, the works of Labib Qubti and the volumes of articles on his website called *Al-Bushra (The Good News)*, and its statement of faith:

> Al-Bushra stands pro-Truth, pro-Justice and pro-Peace & prays God, Allah, HaShem, Adonai, the Most Holy for Mankind. Al-Bushra is asking you to pray for Peace and Justice in the World. Its purpose is not a political purpose but one of prayerful purpose. He pleads with people to go to their churches, synagogues, mosques or temples and say a private prayer on behalf of Peace and Justice—as we believe in ONE GOD, that GOD, ALLAH, ADONAI, HaSHEM, the Most Holy is One for all of us.[71]

The goal is prayer? Read the website to see the *real* goal…

In cooperation with the Palestinian Authority, formerly led by Yasser Arafat, they've been engaged in what they call "The Phased Plan," which calls on Palestinians to accept *any* peace proposal in order to gain as much land as possible. In one statement, they cry out to Yasser Arafat:

"We call upon Arab governments and the Palestinian Authority to unify their positions concerning Jerusalem, a historical trust for the Arabs and all people of faith throughout the world, and to intensify their defense of the Arab character of Jerusalem and its religious pluralism raising it to the stature befitting this blessed site." [72]

"Please, stand with the Right of the Palestinians to have their own independent Country Palestine and their Capital East-Jerusalem." [73]

If this is not a political agenda, what is it?

This is an expensive campaign. In fact, so expensive that they are willing to call on non-Christians for support. Even their "prayers" are answered without the need of Jesus Christ. The Palestinian Charter and government have similar goals: first, the division of Israel, then its destruction.

# # #

Instead of acknowledging the persecution of Jews in Christian history, and the persecution by Muslims of Christians and Jews, these "Christians" claim that it is "Israel" that persecutes Christians to the point that they are moving out in droves. They champion the Palestine Authority.

The facts are that Christians in the Holy Land are persecuted by Muslims, not by Jews. The Jews of Israel have never persecuted Arab Christians for their faith, though it has served Palestinian propaganda purposes to pretend that it has happened. What Arab Christians call persecution is simply the outcome of Israeli border closures to stop *Palestinian terrorism*. It was not something the Jews wanted to do, but were forced to do by the constant Palestinian attacks against Jewish civilians, particularly those "suicide bombings" we read about too often. These closures affected everyone in the Palestinian territories, Jews, Christian and Muslims.

220

Labib Qubti, Emil Salayta, Elias Chakour and others who get their support from the Catholic and Greek Orthodox churches, follow the commands of the Pope who favored Arafat over Jewish administrators of Israel. The Vatican ignored Muslim persecution of Arab Christians in Israel and elsewhere, but bent to Arafat, an Islamic terrorist. Biblically, the Jews are Jesus Christ's own family. The Muslims have no relationship with Him whatsoever. These key people have been used simply as a tool for political agendas of Arafat and the Vatican. In the 1970s, the Greek Melkite Archbishop, Hilarion Capucci, was deported to Brazil. He was a convicted terrorist who was smuggling explosives for the Palestine Liberation Organization.

Jerusalem patriarch Michael Sabbah also promotes Islamic loathing of Jews in Palestinian churches. Following a theological map created in 1983 by the al-Liqa Catholic center and a Catholic Justice and Peace Commission pamphlet, "Muslims and Christians on the Road Together," Sabbah supported the Sabeel's Ecumenical Liberation Theology Center, whose very name suggests a Christian brand of jihad. In language "stuffed with expressions of compassion, justice, and peace toward an evil Israel," Sabeel director, Naim Ateek, refined his perverse jihad ideology, which Palestinian churches now export to the U.S. at every opportunity.

I grew up with people like Ghasson Andoni and George Rishmawi, the co-founders of the Rapprochement Center. They also co-founded the International Solidarity Movement (ISM) with Huwaida Arraf and Adam Shapiro, a Jewish self-hater. Both organizations are driven by the malevolent jihad ideology. Indeed, at the third annual Palestine Solidarity Conference at Ohio State University, ISM featured such radical speakers as Khalid Turaani, executive director of American Muslims for Jerusalem. According to respected author Steven Emerson, AMJ is a radical group that "routinely invokes 'Zionist' conspiracies and has called at its conferences for the killing of Jews..." In May 2004, the ISM held a $40 per plate dinner co-sponsored by an Islamist group, the Muslim Public Affairs Council.

Another sponsor was the American Friends Service Committee.

The goal of the Arab and Muslim masses towards Israel is obvious, a political agenda for "the weak" until they become strong enough to take on their enemies. Allah of Islam, with whom many professing Christians are uniting, is so different from the God of the Bible. Allah's messenger stated that:

"The Last Hour would not come till the Muslims fight against the Jews, and the Muslims will kill them until the Jews hide themselves behind the stones and trees, and the stones and trees would speak up saying: "O Muslim! O slave of Allah! There is a Jew hiding behind me; come and kill him." The Gharqad tree would speak, for it is the tree of the Jews." [74]

Must we as Christians unite with Islam against the Jews? One glance at their material will quickly uncover their religion, convictions, and goals:

"Eastern Churches were the first to discover the love of Mary. Eastern Marian theology leads us to discover the real face of Mary." [75] "For Christians she is the all-holy Theotokos, the mother of God." [76] and as far as God's calling to evangelize Muslims,

> They [the Muslims] adore one God, living and enduring, merciful and all-powerful, maker of heaven and earth and speaker to humankind...They also honor Mary, his virgin mother; at times they call on her too with devotion. What a propitious moment it is, therefore, that finds Christians and Muslims together on a major feast of the Virgin Mary to celebrate the mutual esteem for one another which befits men and women in the faith tradition of Abraham. [77]

In their view, since Abraham is the father of all three religions, the main goal should be religious unity, and not evangelism.

In a conference in 1999 for Peace and Middle East Understanding, held in Walnut Creek, California, Emil Salayta, a speaker at EMEU, a Parish priest of Bir-Zeit Palestine, and the General Director of the Latin Patriarchal Schools for all of Palestine was asked, "What do you think of Israel?" He responded, "It should be eliminated." And when he was asked "By putting bombs in Jewish buses and killing Jewish children?" He responded, "By whatever means, they should be eliminated."

222

Claiming to carry out God's calling, Salayta was asked: "Do you evangelize the Muslims in your school?" He responded "No, because evangelizing would not be respecting the convictions of others and creating a problem for the other side." The question Christians should ask is, what would Christ say? If Salayta's agenda is not to evangelize Muslims, then what are the group's religious goals and convictions?

Christian Zionist establishments, like the Christian Embassy in Jerusalem, do not have any support or sympathy for the Christian Arabs. Daud Kuttab, a prominent Palestinian journalist, writes:

> Unlike what its name implies, the International Christian Embassy doesn't represent the world's Christians; it doesn't even represent Protestant or Evangelical Christians which comprise the majority of the people that attend its annual feast of the tabernacle festival. The U.S.-based Evangelicals for Middle East Understanding, which is holding its annual conference next month in Chicago, has distanced itself from this embassy...The local Arab Christian population, both in Israel and Palestine, has had nothing to do with this organization. Local Christian leaders (both Arab and foreign) have not only disagreed with their theology, but they have regularly denounced its one-sided and biased political activities on behalf of right-wing Israelis.[78]

The opposite of what Mr. Kuttab wrote is true for EMEU, which is unknown in America and does not represent Evangelicals anywhere in the world; in reality; EMEU members are hardly evangelical in nature. Mr. Kuttab concludes his article:

"What is worrisome is that the International Christian Embassy is not really interested in converting people to Christianity but rather in converting apolitical Christians...to their brand of Christian Zionism."

If we are to accept EMEU and Al-Bushra as true representatives, which Kuttab promotes, we can interchange the words "Christian Embassy" and "EMEU," and "Christian Zionism" with "Palestinian Cause" and the results would be the same. What is worrisome is that EMEU is not interested in converting people to Christianity but converting a political Christian to the Palestinian cause.

Their aims are not much different from those of the Arab Muslim masses. Both Muslims and Christians alike in Palestine are called to fight against the main enemy: Israel. They are willing to set aside their differences to achieve this goal and to deny historical facts about the decades of persecution of Christians by Islam. Emil Salayta was asked:

"Do you face persecution as a Christian here in a Muslim context?" Mr. Salayta responded: "I think what the West thinks is part of a Western propaganda against Islam. We've lived with Islam for centuries and centuries." [80]

Salayta avoids "rocking the boat" but feels free to condemn former Israeli Prime Minister Benjamin Netanyahu, calling him a "liar," and accusing Israel of suppressing freedom of speech. If Salayta expressed his opinion in any Arab country the way he does in "oppressive" Israel, he would probably be condemned to death for calling any Arab leader a "liar." Salayta does not report the true history of persecution committed by Islam; instead, he glorifies Islam, and intentionally omits the fact that Islam declared the Jews to be Dhimmis, an act that placed the Jews under the Omar Charter.

This covenant was applied by Islam to Jews and Christians from time immemorial, yet he claims that for "centuries and centuries" Christians lived in peace and harmony with Muslims. Ignored are the million Armenians butchered by Muslims in Fez, Turkey, with blood that flowed through the streets. Ignored are the 1.5 million Sudanese Christians annihilated in the past few years by Muslims, the massacres in Bosnia, and the persecution of millions of Christians around the world. Anti-Israel Christians would rather spend their energies marching with pitchforks when Jews build 6,500 houses in Jerusalem.

To see an Arab nation replace Israel, these groups go so far as to change history to support their claims. The majority of Palestinians cling to the idea that their ancestors are the Canaanites and Jebusites. The Arab Christian view regarding God's promise of the land to Abraham is that the land is for all the children of Abraham, including the Arabs, and that Arabs inhabited the land of Israel for thousands of years before the modern state was established. To them, any Christian who uses Bible prophecy to support Israel is a Christian Zionist liar. Labib Qubti writes:

"...the Christian Zionists are not truthful about the Holy Land or Jerusalem. A simple reading of history shows their claims are not well founded."[81]

Are the Palestinians who they claim to be? Are the Canaanites the original church? The Bible and history answer the questions.

ISLAMIC ESCHATOLOGY

1 - The Lesser Prophetic Signs
(1) The decay of faith and the rise of sensuality.
(2) Tumults and sedition everywhere.
(3) A great war with the Turks and great distress throughout the world.
(4) The rebellion of Iraq and Syria.
(5) The expansion of the sacred city of Medina.

2 - The Greater Prophetic Signs
(1) Heavenly signs; sun rising from the west, moon eclipse, and smoke filling the earth.
(2) A war with the Greeks, and the capture of Constantinople by seventy-thousand Jews; during the victory the Antichrist will arise.
(3) The Antichrist (Al-Masih al Dajjal), with one eye, and the letters (CFR) or infidel on his forehead, he will appear near Iraq and Syria riding a colt, and followed by 70,000 Jews and will be killed by Jesus.
(4) A war with Jews involving Muslims and barbarians (Yajuj and Majuj), Gog and Magog.
(5) Jesus descending on Damascus to kill the Antichrist.
(6) The Arabs returning to pagan worship.
(7) Gold discovered under the Euphrates River.
(8) The Kaaba destroyed by the Ethiopian army.
(9) Fire in Yemen.
(10) The Mahdi's coming (descending from the prophet Muhammad).
(11) The final trumpets and the end.

According to Islam, this "Dajjal" (literally means 'the liar') will have already appeared. This will be a very great calamity. The Muslim ummah (nation) will be in great fear during that period of time. Some will follow him and regard him as a god. Jesus will eventually kill Dajjal with his spear at Lydda, which is in Palestine. The Jews will be targeted and assassinated. *Trees and boulders will speak to the Muslims informing them of any Jew seeking shelter and protection by them. The Gharqad tree will however conceal the Jew; hence, this tree is being planted by the thousands in Palestine.* Those Christians who will repent and accept Islam will be saved from any persecution or massacre. Others who choose to disbelieve, will be put to death. Thereafter the entire world will be ruled by Muslims.

Chapter Seven
GOG AND MAGOG WAR

IS IT SEPARATE FROM THE FINAL BATTLE OF ARMAGEDDON?

Common Argument:

Gog and Magog is a battle that comes just before the battle of Armageddon between Russia and Israel and is separate from the final battle of Armageddon.

Response:

Ezekiel 38 and 39 are the same battle of Armageddon for several reasons:

1. The great earthquake happens in Messiah's presence

In Ezekiel 38:19, the earthquake is the greatest in history and matches Zechariah 14:4. This earthquake is definitely the mark of the Messiah's presence on earth at the moment of His touch-down. He will descend from heaven to fight the enemy, Gog, to save his heritage, Israel, when they cry out *"blessed is He who comes in the name of the Lord"* [1] upon their infliction. Zechariah 14:3 states, *"the Lord will go forth and fight...His feet will stand in that day upon the Mount of Olives..."*

There can be no doubt that in Christian theology, the Lord will come in the flesh. Then we have the greatest earthquake:

> "For in my jealousy and in the fire of my wrath have I spoken, surely in that day there shall be a great shaking in the land of Israel; So that the fishes of the sea, and the fowls of the heaven, and the beasts of the field, and all creeping things that creep upon the earth, and all the men that are upon the face of the earth, shall *shake at my presence,* and the mountains shall be thrown down, and the steep places shall fall, and every wall shall fall to the ground." [2]

This *"presence"* can be demonstrated further within Christian theology to prove that Ezekiel 38-39 is the showdown between Christ and Antichrist (Gog). This is indeed "touchdown," with Messiah scoring the great victory. Ezekiel 39:22 confirms a day of redemption for Israel:

"Israel will know that I AM the Lord their God from that day onward." "(The) nations will know that I am the Lord, the Holy One *in* Israel"[3]

Note that the Holy One is *in* Israel; the rest of Scripture uses the phrase "Holy One *of* Israel," hence Messiah will be on Earth.

These passages agree with Revelation 19:17:

"And I saw an angel standing in the sun; and he cried with a loud voice, saying to all the fowls that fly in the midst of heaven, Come and gather yourselves together unto the supper of the great God; (18) That ye may eat the flesh of kings, and the flesh of captains, and the flesh of mighty men, and the flesh of horses, and of them that sit on them, and the flesh of all [men, both] free and bond, both small and great."

Scavenging birds are harbingers of death and symbolize judgment; these birds that eat the armies are found in both Revelation 19:17 and Ezekiel 39:

"Thou shall fall upon the mountains of Israel, thou, and all thy bands, and the people that [are] with thee: I will give thee unto the ravenous birds of every sort, and [to] the beasts of the field to be devoured." There's further confirmation that Ezekiel 38-39 is the Armageddon of Revelation 20:8.

2. All the prophets have spoken of Gog.

Ezekiel 38:17 states, *"Are you not the one of whom I have spoken in former days, by the prophets of Israel?"* We are unable to find any use of *Gog* in the prophets prior to Ezekiel or after, but if Gog is the Antichrist, we have little problem finding him. Prophets mention him prior to Ezekiel. In fact, Isaiah, Jeremiah, Zechariah, Joel and David, and the New Testament Revelation, Thessalonians, Jude, and Matthew all spoke of the same figure—the Antichrist.

3. Gog must be Satan in the flesh:

"Is the battle of Gog and Magog before or after the Millennium?" Both. Once we understand that Gog is Satan incarnate, we will see that Ezekiel 38 is the same Gog of Revelation 20:8, unleashed in the world twice, once at Armageddon and once after the Millennium. How else can he come into the world twice in such a span of time? He cannot, unless he is Satan. This refutes the notion that the Magog war is separate from the final battle of Armageddon.

Gog is simply another word for the Antichrist, the Assyrian, the Son of Perdition, and Lucifer. Satan is also referred to as "the devil" and as "the proud one," as he tried to exalt himself as God. They are one and the same. Since he will be loosed after the thousand years, he is still *Gog* and *Satan* as described in Revelation 20:7 *"And when the thousand years are expired, Satan shall be loosed out of his prison..."*[4]

The characteristics that the Bible attributes to Antichrist are opposite of the characteristics of the one true God. Christ is called The Truth, while the Antichrist is called The Lie. Christ is called the Holy One, and the Antichrist is called The Lawless One. Christ is The Son of God, while the Antichrist is The Son of Perdition. Christ is called "The Mystery of Godliness," and Antichrist is called "The Mystery of Iniquity." God will allow Satan to continue his deception for a time and then Jesus Christ will finally destroy Satan, the Son of Perdition, The Antichrist, *"by the brightness of His coming."*[5] Satan's main tactic to destroy God's plan is to counterfeit the Biblical prophecies. He doesn't necessarily have to have the same name, but does bear similar attributes.

God gave us many warnings in the Bible concerning Satan and his work.

"Then the king shall do according to his own will: he shall exalt and magnify himself above every god, shall speak blasphemies against the God of gods, and shall prosper till the wrath has been accomplished; for what has been determined shall be done."[6]

The Antichrist's will is the will of Satan, while Christ's Will is His Father's Will (The God of Truth). In Christian theology, the mystery of God's nature is presented in the Bible as One God—Father, Son and Holy Spirit: *"Hear O Israel, the Lord our God, the Lord is One."*[7]

For Jews, this passage is the bedrock of their belief in a single God, a one true God and none other. Christian doctrine teaches that the trinity of God is supported in both the Old and New Testaments.

ARE GOG AND MAGOG REALLY RUSSIA?

Many prophecy students picked Russia as the prime candidate for Magog until the Russian Communist nation split. Today we have the Commonwealth of the Independent States in Southern Russia (C.I.S.), which are mostly Islamic and not ethnically related to the Slavic Russians. The fear of Communism encouraged this interpretation, catching the church sleeping at the guard tower regarding the real threat: fundamentalist Islam.

However, most historians and sources such as the Macmillan Bible Atlas, Oxford Bible Atlas, the Moody Atlas of Bible Lands, and others, all locate Magog, Meshech, Tubal, Gomer and Beth Togarmah in *Asia Minor, not Russia.*

> This region of Asia Minor includes Turkey, Uzbekistan, Tajikistan, Girgestan and this was the heart of the vast Islamic Ottoman Empire for many centuries. Russians did not migrate north from Asia Minor, which is where they should have originated if this argument is true. Hesiod, the father of Greek didactic poetry, identified Magog with the Scythians and southern Russia in the 7th century B.C. Hesiod was a contemporary of Ezekiel. Flavius Josephus records that the Greeks called the Magogians "Scythians." Philo, in the 1st century, identifies Magog with Turkey and southern Russia—that entire northern region is described in Ezekiel 38 as the *"remote parts of the north."* The Bible does not say "farthest north," it simply says *"the house of Togarmah of the north quarters"* in Ezekiel 38:6 *"And thou shalt come from thy place out of the north parts"* in Ezekiel 38:15. The word used for "parts," "quarters" is the Hebrew 'twot' which means: "Side, coasts, parts, border, quarters, flank, side, extreme parts, recesses, side, sides, recesses.[8]

Gomer is the founder of the Cimmerians who settled originally on the shores of the Caspian Sea. The Assyrians referred to them as the Gimirraya. Esarhaddon (681-668 B.C.) records his defeat of the Gimirrai, while King Ashurbanipal tells us in his records of the Cimmerian invasion of Lydia in the days of the Lydian king Gugu (Gygez) around the year 660 B.C. This is perhaps the name preserved in Scripture as 'Gog' (Ezek. 38:2). 'Gog' is the reference used in the past to refer to 'Gugu' of Lydia (Turkey). In this case, the Bible refers to a future 'Gugu.' It is plausible, since Gugu or Gygez was a real historic figure from Lydia (Turkey).

In fact, the Gomer were Turkic peoples who were descendants of tribes people recorded in history as the Oguz. They founded the Gokturk Empire in the 6th century, 522 CE, and were defeated in 745 CE by the Uygurs, an ethnically related Turkic tribe. "Gokturk," with the "Gok" part being the distinguishing name of this particular Turkic tribe, is remarkably similar to "Gog" and again reinforces the point that the Biblical Gog may well be a Turkic region in Asia Minor.

After several conquests among the diverse Turkic tribes, the Ghaznavids, under the leadership of Sevuktekin in 963 A.D., established the first Muslim Turkish state. The Oguz Empire emerged once more upon the defeat of the Ghaznavid dynasty in 1040 CE and was assimilated by the Oguz. After the expansion of Islam, the empire came under the leadership of Tugrul Bey and Cagry Bey, grandsons of Seljuk, and the name was adopted for the Seljuk Dynasty. The Empire covered the region of Anatolia, Northern Iran, Syria, Iraq, Southern Caucasus, and Azerbaijan under Turkish rule under the leadership of Alp Arslan and Malik Shah in the 11th century. The Seljuk Dynasty declined steadily during the 13th century and the land of Seljuk Sultanate was divided among chieftains. The Mongol conquest in 1243 A.D. marked the end of the Seljuk Dynasty. Ertugrul Gazi ruled the lands around Sögüt, a division of the Seljuk Sultanate. Upon his death in 1281 A.D., his son, Osman, expanded the territory known as the Ottoman Empire.

Archaeology can sometimes be the best forensic science when examining prophecy. In the case of Gog, the Bible uses past names, past leaders, and past locations to be introduced in the future. Gyges was first known to the Greeks as 'tyrant' and the one who introduced "tyranny" to the Greeks: he was called "tyrannos" or the tyrant one.

Archagetes means to be "further" and is applied both to divinities and to military leaders—in other words, a military leader who makes himself to be further, or greater than he is, a god, exactly as portrayed in the Bible regarding Antichrist. Gyges of Lydia, the first to be called a tyrant, acquires a particular significance. There seems to be no doubt about the Phrygian or Lydian origin of the word τυραννο|σ.[9]

The name of the Phrygian *Moon-god Men* is often followed by the epithet τυραννο|σ in Greek inscriptions of Attica and Phrygia, and the name of some divinities is followed by the epithet *bd turan* in Etruscan inscriptions.[10] Gygez was also called "*the King of Lydia*" similar to what the Bible called Gog "*chief prince of Meshech and Tuba.*" Today Lydia is called Turkey.

Regarding Gomer, Herodotus gave us a more detailed account of the Kimmeri:

"...The wandering Scythians once dwelt in Asia, and there warred with the Massagetae, but with ill success; they therefore quitted their homes, crossed the Araxes, and entered the land of Kimmeria. For the land which is now inhabited by the Scyths was formerly the country of the Kimmerians."[11]

Magog is the region of Gog, the second of the sons of Japheth.[12] In Ezekiel 38:2 and 39:6, it is the name of a nation, probably some Scythian or Tartar tribe descended from Japheth. They are described as skilled equestrians and expert in the use of the bow. The Latin Father Jerome says that this word denotes "Scythian nations, fierce and innumerable, who live beyond the Caucasus and the Lake Maeotis, and near the Caspian Sea, and spread out even onward to India, which represents the Assyrian Mat Gugi, or 'country of Gugu,' 'the Gyges of the Greeks.'"[13]

Perhaps this is why the Bible addresses him as "The Assyrian." The Schaff-Herzog Encyclopedia of Religious Knowledge, citing ancient Assyrian writings, places the location of Magog in the land mass between ancient Armenia and Media; in short, the Republics south of Russia and north of Israel which were comprised of Azerbaijan,

Afghanistan, Turkistan, Chechnya, Turkey, Iran and Dagestan. Significantly, all of these nations are Muslim nations today.

Why is it that the only people the Messiah is going to fight with in these battles are the Islamic nations? Why is it that they all come up against Israel? There is no need for Him to fight people who want no harm for Israel since he is coming back when Israel cries out "Baruch Haba B'Shem Adonai" (Blessed is He who comes in the name of the Lord.) They seek for their Messiah to come and save them from an overwhelming invading army.

Why is it that the only nations today that want to annihilate Israel and drive the Jews into the sea are the Islamic nations? Why can't prophecy students see this? Muslims pretend to make peace just as Muhammad, their prophet, did in 628 CE with the treaty of Hudabiya, when he was weak. However, he broke that treaty two years later and slaughtered the Meccans—when he was in a much stronger position to do so.

The Russians of the far north (Moscow) are unrelated to the people in the southern parts of today's C.I.S. nations, which are mostly Turkic. In reality, the Russians of today are Scandinavians. The Vikings' ventures into Eastern Europe were to a great extent trade-related. They established trade routes along the Great Russian Rivers, such as the Volga and Dnieper, and, since some of the major Russian cities were located on those rivers, they came into direct contact with the Slavs living there. Despite the controversy on the question of the Russian origins, the sources seem to point out "that Russia had its origin in the Rus who were Scandinavians."[4] Rurik I settled in Novgorod and the other two, Sineus and Truvor, settled in Beloozero and Izborsk. It is apparent that the Kievan dynasty was of a Viking origin. Oleg (Helgi), Igor (Inguar) and his wife Olga (Helga) were of Scandinavian descent.

"Igor and Olga's son Sviatoslav (957-73 A.D.) was the first ruler to have a 'slav' name. In 998 A.D. his son Vladimir adopted Orthodox Christianity. In the reign of his son Yaroslav the Wise (1014-54 A.D.) the connection with Scandinavia was sealed by royal marriages."[14]

In the 7th century B.C., nomadic Scythians migrated north into fertile Russian territories. Herodotus the Greek, who visited southern Russia in the 5th century B.C., observed that

"Some tribes cultivated the land; the builders of the Parthenon would have gone hungry without Russian wheat; but the ruling element remained nomads, living in tents, yet not altogether eschewing the arts of civilization." [15]

These people also began trading furs and honey with Constantinople; eventually, the merchants acted as intermediaries between other settlements in the far north (inhabited by Finnish tribes) and the Roman Empire. As these early Slavic people began to cultivate the land, villages and towns sprang up, protected by wooden citadels, or *kremlins*, cut from the abundant forest timber. The inhabitants gradually occupied an area from St. Petersburg to Kiev and spoke a language (originating from Greek) quite similar to modern Russian.

The numerous tribes united in the 8th and 9th centuries, when the Scandinavians, Vikings known as Varangians, migrated south and began establishing trade settlements with the Slavs, along with their own strongholds. Many of these settlements were situated along the Neva River and Lake Ladoga. When the Norseman Rurik defeated the strongest Slavic settlement, Novgorod, in 862 A.D., the Varangians became the rulers of northern Russia. In the south, the Slavic Prince Kii had formed the Kievan territory. In 880, Rurik's successor, Oleg, conquered the Slavic-ruled Kiev and made the city his capital two years later. With the two areas united, the state of Rus (its name derived from the Viking word ruotsi, meaning "oarsman") became one of the largest kingdoms in the world. The Bulgars and the Mongols, who moved from the Balkans and into Russia, respectively, were not Slavs. The people of Finland are very much like the Slavs, and the ties between the Fins and the Slavs have always been close. They even share a genetic predisposition to alcoholism and depression.

Grant Jeffrey, who wrote several books on prophecy, argues that Russia is Magog: "The areas described by Professor Rawlinson that were ruled by the Scythians are located *south of Russia* and in the *southern republics of the Commonwealth of Independent States* (the former USSR)." Grant quotes Rawlinson correctly that Magog is the Islamic C.I.S. (states) of Southern Russia (former USSR). Yet he insists on making Russia proper to be Magog.[16] C. Marvin Pate and Calvin B. Haines, Jr. in <u>Doomsday Delusions</u> posed an interesting theory: "It is quite unlikely, for instance, that Ezekiel had either Russia or China in mind when he prophesied about Gog and Magog—indeed, he would likely have been surprised to hear of such correspondences, since neither country existed in his time." [17] Finally, historian Edwin Yamauchi notes that even if one transliterated the Hebrew *ro's* as a proper name (as the Septuagint does), it can have nothing to do with modern Russia. He writes,

"This would be a gross anachronism, for the modern name is based upon the name *Rus*, which was brought into the reign of Kiev, north of the Black Sea, by the Vikings only in the Middle Ages.". . . (We) cannot positively identify the antecedents of these historical names. However, the identifications of *Mesech* and *Tubal* are not in doubt. Few scholars today equate them with Moscow and Tobolsk. Rather, combined ancient testimony attests to the fact that Meshech and Tubal were located in central and eastern Anatolia (Asia Minor), respectively." [18]

Chapter Eight
MARRIAGE SUPPER

There is debate that the *"marriage supper of the lamb"* and the *"marriage supper of the Great God"* are two different events, with the first taking place in heaven and the second taking place while the earth endures its tribulations. This supports the theory that the Rapture occurs, and we are gone and do not need to endure any hardship. The Messiah's coming is imminent, but no one knows for certain whether the Rapture is pre, mid, or post Tribulation.

However, Scripture shows they are the same: a battle with believers (Bride of Messiah) lead by The Lamb (Messiah Himself). It is likely not to be a wedding in heaven with feasting at a supper with the King Messiah. Islam supports such a concept as heaven, but not the Bible. These cannot be two separate events, since both are within the same context of Revelation 19. In fact, there is not a single reference mentioning our being in heaven during this event.

It is error to believe the Rapture means God taking the believers to be with Him in heaven. In the text, there is no mention of heaven:

> Behold, I show you a mystery; We shall not all sleep, but we shall all be changed, In a moment, in the twinkling of an eye, *at the last trump*: for the trumpet shall sound, and the dead shall be raised *incorruptible,* and we shall be changed. For this *corruptible must put on incorruption, and this mortal [must] put on immortality.* So when this corruptible shall have put on incorruption, and this mortal shall have put on immortality, then shall be brought to pass the saying that is written, Death is swallowed up in victory. O death, where [is] thy sting? O grave, where [is] thy victory? But thanks [be] to *God, which giveth us the victory* through our Lord Jesus Christ.[1]

The Book of Joel describes a single event—the Day of the Lord and the Battle of Armageddon. In Joel, we see agreement with 1Cor. 15 regarding the incorruptible body, yet in Joel, it appears that it is given for war. In Joel chap. 2, this incorruptible body is fighting on the Day of The Lord:

"Blow ye the trumpet in Zion, and sound an alarm in my holy mountain: let all the inhabitants of the land tremble: for the day of the LORD cometh, for [it is] nigh at hand"[2]

Here we have a trumpet, possibly the same as 1 Cor. 15 on the day of the Lord. Joel describes it as:

A day of darkness and of gloominess, a day of clouds and of thick darkness, as the morning spread upon the mountains: a great people and a strong; there hath not been ever the like, neither shall be any more after it, [even] to the years of many generations. Fire devoureth before them; and behind them a flame burneth: the land [is] as the Garden of Eden before them, and behind them a desolate wilderness; yea, and nothing shall escape them." (Joel 2:2-4) "Neither shall one thrust another; they shall walk every one in his path: and [when] they fall upon the sword, they shall not be wounded."[3]

Here these fighters cannot be wounded or killed, since they have incorruptible bodies as described in 1 Cor 15. Joel presents these people as super-human and this event as a definite tribulation:

They shall run to and fro in the city; they shall run upon the wall, they shall climb up upon the houses; they shall enter in at the windows like a thief. The earth shall quake before them; the heavens shall tremble: the sun and the moon shall be dark, and the stars shall withdraw their shining. And the LORD shall utter his voice before his army: for his camp [is] very great: for [he is] strong that executeth his word: for the day of the LORD [is] great and very terrible; and who can abide it?[4]

"The sun and the moon" being dark are none other than The Day of The Lord. Yet on that day, He speaks to His army in preparation for this battle of the Day of the Lord. Messiah is here in person, leading the defense of Jerusalem. This confirms that believers will fight physically in Jerusalem. Our fight in this world may be against spiritual forces, against powers and philosophies, but this struggle will confront us in the physical realm too; Scripture makes that explicit.

This declaration of the Lord before His army is supported in Revelation 19:15:

"And out of his mouth goeth a sharp sword, that with it he should smite the nations: and he shall rule them with a rod of iron: and he treadeth the winepress of the fierceness and wrath of Almighty God."

This "sharp sword" coming out of His mouth is *the proclamation of war* as written in Joel 2:11: *"And the LORD shall utter his voice before his army."* Some people claim that this "sword" is simply God destroying the enemies miraculously. Yet, the utterance from Messiah's mouth is a command:

"I beheld till the thrones were cast down, and the Ancient of days did sit, whose garment [was] white as snow, and the hair of his head like the pure wool: his throne [was like] the fiery flame, [and] his wheels [as] burning fire. *A fiery stream issued and came forth from before him: thousand thousands ministered unto him, and ten thousand times ten thousand stood before him*: the judgment was set, and the books were opened." [5]

It's a command, an order, a proclamation. Revelation 19:14 speaks of the Lord's army:

"And the armies [which were] in heaven followed him upon white horses, clothed in fine linen, white and clean."

Joel 2:16 describes it: "Gather the people, sanctify the congregation, assemble the elders, gather the children, and those that suck the breasts: let the bridegroom go forth of his chamber, and the bride out of her closet."

Here is the Rapture in which the bridegroom (Messiah) meets the bride (Messiah's followers) to participate in The Marriage Supper of The Lamb. The text continues to tell us what is to come:

"Let the priests, the ministers of the LORD, weep between the porch and the altar, and let them say, Spare thy people, O LORD, and give not thine heritage to reproach, that the heathen should rule over them: wherefore should they say among the people, Where [is] their God?" [6]

We find the same idea in Psalm 74:10 and in Joel 2:18:

"Then will the LORD be jealous for his land, and pity his people."
And in Joel 2:20: "But I will remove far off from you the northern
[army], and will drive him into a land barren and desolate, with his
face toward the east sea, and his hinder part toward the utmost sea, and
his stink shall come up, and his ill savor shall come up, because he
hath done great things..."

Similar to the Gog and Magog battle from the north:

"And the LORD shall utter his voice before his army: for his camp
is very great: for he is strong that executeth his word: for the day of
the LORD is great and very terrible; and who can abide it?" [7]

"The sun shall be turned into darkness, and the moon into blood,
before the great and terrible day of the LORD come." [8]

"And it shall come to pass, that whosoever shall call on the name
of the LORD shall be delivered: for in mount Zion and in Jerusalem
shall be deliverance, as the LORD hath said, and in the remnant whom
the LORD shall call." [9]

RAPTURE, THEN WAR

The word used for Jesus Christ's return is "parousia" in 1
Thessalonians 4:16-17, which talks about His Second Coming and
nothing more. Christian scholars use this text to identify the Rapture:

"For the Lord himself shall descend from heaven with a shout, with
the voice of the archangel, and with the trumpet of God: and the dead
in Christ shall rise first: Then we which are alive and remain shall be
caught up together with them in the clouds, to *meet the Lord in the air*:
and so *shall we ever be with the Lord.*"

We will meet Him as He comes down. From that moment on, we
will be with Him forever, yet this by no means assures an ascension
back to heaven. The text simply does not support this. The same scene
is described in Matt 24:27:31:

> "For as the lightning cometh out of the east, and shineth
> even unto the west; so shall also the *coming of the Son of
> man be.* For whosesoever the carcass is, there will the
> eagles be gathered together. Immediately after the tribula-

tion of those days shall the sun be darkened, and the moon shall not give her light, and the stars shall fall from heaven, and the powers of the heavens shall be shaken: And then shall appear the sign of the Son of man in heaven: and then shall all the tribes of the earth mourn, and they shall see the Son of man coming (parousia) in the clouds of heaven with power and great glory. And he shall send his angels with a great sound of a trumpet, (same trumpet as in 1 Thes. 4:16) and they shall gather together his elect from the four winds, from one end of heaven to the other."

What links do we see in these passages?

Matt. 24:30 Jesus descends from heaven
Matt. 24:27 Coming (Parousia)
Matt. 24:31 Sound of trumpet heard
Matt. 24:31 Angels present

1 Thes. 4:16 Coming (Parousia)
1 Thes. 4:16 Sound of trumpet heard
1 Thes. 4:16 Archangel present
1 Thes. 4:16 Jesus descends from heaven

It's pretty clear that this is the same event, not the Rapture as popularly believed, but "the Coming of Christ" in both verses, and it indeed could happen before the Great Wrath.

The true Christians meet Jesus Christ in the air, but what happens after that? We cannot find any verse in Scripture that says that after Rapture, people are going to be lifted up into heaven. In fact, Rev. 20:5 tells us *"it is the first resurrection."*

Revelation 19:13 goes further: *"And He was clothed with a garment sprinkled with blood; and his name is called The Word of God."*

"And the armies that were in heaven *followed him* upon white horses, clothed in fine linen, *white and clean.* And out of his mouth goeth a sharp sword, that with it he should smite the nations, and he shall rule them with a rod of iron; and he treadeth the winepress of the fierceness and wrath of Almighty God. And he hath on his vesture and on his thigh a name written, KING OF KINGS, AND LORD OF LORDS." [10]

The armies followed Him to where? Heaven? Or earth? It must be earth, since they will "smite the nations." We cannot have unbelievers anywhere but on earth. Notice, the armies are *"clothed in fine linen, white and clean."* According to Revelation 19:7-8, this is the attire of the bride of Christ. It is said that His armies are angelic hosts, yet Scripture could allude to the believers:

> "And when he had opened the fifth seal, I saw under the altar the souls of them that were slain for the word of God, and for the testimony which they held: And they cried with a loud voice, saying, How long, O Lord, holy and true, dost thou not judge and avenge our blood on them that dwell on the earth? And *white robes* were given unto every one of them; and it was said unto them, that they should rest yet for a little season, until their fellow servants also and their brethren, which should be killed as they [were], should be fulfilled."[11]

The believers, who are with the Lord, are given white robes, the same garments in which the armies are dressed. Messiah will come for battle with His army (the believers).

> "Who is this that comes from Edom, from Bozrah in garments stained crimson? Who is this so splendidly robed, marching in his great might?" "It is I, announcing vindication, mighty to save." "Why are your robes red, and your garments like theirs who tread the wine press?" "I have trodden the wine press alone, and from the peoples no one was with me; I trod them in my anger and trampled them in my wrath; their juice spattered on my garments, and stained all my robes. For the day of vengeance was in my heart, and the year for my redeeming work had come. I looked, but there was no helper; I stared, but there was no one to sustain me; so my own arm brought me victory, and my wrath sustained me. I trampled down peoples in my anger, I crushed them in my wrath, and I poured out their lifeblood on the earth." [12] "I (the Lord) will send a fire into Teman: and it shall devour the houses of Bozrah."[13]

Yet most Christians believe that a sword will come out of His mouth and poof! the enemy is gone. Not so. The big metal blade protruding from His mouth is symbolic, representing the Messiah's judgment upon the nations, and the crimson or scarlet color represents sin,[14] too costly or royal raiment signifying wealth[15] and blood. Zechariah 14:4 states that the Messiah will stand on the Mount of Olives with an earthquake, as he comes for the battle in Jerusalem.

According to Christian doctrine, the nation of Israel was punished with 2000 years of Diaspora for not paying attention to *"the time of thy visitation"* [16] It is possible that the same problem will occur on His Second Coming. The issue was ignorance: *"my people are destroyed from lack of knowledge"* [17] This is the attitude of some people today, "We will find out when He comes" or "We'll know the truth when we die."

It could be argued that they did not recognize His First Coming because they didn't care how He was to come; they simply followed the mainstream interpretations of famous rabbis who said that the Messiah would defeat Rome. Noah preached for 120 years and not one person outside his family listened to him,

> "And spared not the old world, but saved Noah the
> eighth person, *a preacher of righteousness,* bringing in
> the flood upon the world of the ungodly." [18]

Every word regarding Messiah's Second Coming is crucial. How else could we distinguish between the Antichrist, who performs signs and wonders, and the Messiah, who also performs signs and wonders? Most Christians' attitude towards Israel is, at best, lukewarm, and so they must meditate on the written word of God to recognize that the Messiah is coming back *for Israel* and He will fight for her, so we ought to decide which side we are on right now. Do we sit by while her enemies try to crush her and say, "God will take care of it?"

The Church today relies on the Rapture, yet there is not a single verse that confirms a definite position; moreover, *the word is not even mentioned* in the Bible. Indeed, all church history up until the last hundred years or so generally supported the Rapture after the mid point of the tribulation. The Rapture is likely to occur when believers are caught up

in the air to meet the Lord as *He is coming down to the Mount of Olives.*
That is what the text appears to say and when you link the new covenant
writings with the prophets of Israel then we see its true meaning:

"Then we which are alive [and] remain shall be caught up together
with them in the clouds, to meet the Lord in the air..." [19]

The Lord captures the believers literally in the clouds to descend on
earth to fight for Israel in the battle of Armageddon:

"For the Lord Himself shall descend from heaven with a shout, with
the voice of the archangel, and with the trump of God: and the dead in
Christ shall rise first." [20]

The Bible says that we ought to focus on His coming again and our
meeting Him and being with Him. Messiah is simply coming for
Israel to save his people, the Jewish nation, with his saints, and these
saints are no other than the true Christians who rise up to meet him in
the air and then descend down to fight the enemy on the ground:

"So the angel that communed with me said unto me, Cry thou, saying, Thus saith the Lord of hosts; I am jealous for Jerusalem and for
Zion with a great jealousy." [21]

The Lord is greatly concerned for Jerusalem his holy city and his
people of Israel, to the point where He is jealous for His people and
will fight for them in the last days.

"And I am very sore displeased with the heathen that are at ease: for
I was but a little displeased, and they helped forward the affliction." [22]

The Lord is very angry that the people round about have made the
lives of Jewish people very hard and bitter, and other nations did nothing about it. In light of this, we need to consider:

- The Muslim nations are bent on destroying Israel and driving
  her people into to the sea.
- Most western nations sit there trying either to negotiate impossi-
  ble peace deals or to force sanctions on Israel through the United
  Nations.
- Most Christians are lukewarm and don't really care.

- Many of these Christians believe in Replacement Theology—the church replaces Israel and the Jews are simply not God's concern anymore.
- Only a few Christians truly understand and stand up for the Jewish nation, zealous for God's people and voicing a loud concern for Israel's safety.

"Therefore thus saith the Lord; *I am returned to Jerusalem* with mercies: my house shall be built in it, saith the Lord of hosts, and a line shall be stretched forth upon Jerusalem." [23]

The Lord is going to return to JERUSALEM. And the house he is going to build is the THIRD temple in Jerusalem. It is clear that the Messiah descends to Jerusalem. "Then shall the Lord go forth, and fight against those nations, as when he fought in the day of battle." [24]

The Lord fights those nations that try to destroy Israel or attempt to possess its land, and they will be no more:

"And this shall be the plague wherewith the Lord will smite all the people that have fought against Jerusalem; Their flesh shall consume away while they stand upon their feet, and their eyes shall consume away in their holes, and their tongue shall consume away in their mouth." [25]

A supernatural plague will kill the people who come up to fight Israel and take Jerusalem. The only people who want to take Jerusalem are the Islamic nations. They are no other than the countries "round about"…"*and the wealth of all the heathen round about shall be gathered together…*" [26]

Those that survive will go to Jerusalem to pay their homage to the God of Israel in His Temple:

"And many nations shall come, and say, Come, and let us go up to the mountain of the Lord, and to the house of the God of Jacob; and he will teach us of his ways, and we will walk in his paths: for the law shall go forth out of Zion, and the word of the Lord from Jerusalem." [27]

The Law, God's commandments, shall go forth from Zion (greater Israel and Jerusalem where God's Holy Mountain is), where His third Holy Temple will be built. Many Christians claim that the Torah (The

Law) is invalid, but how can it be when Jews live by it each day? We need to learn from the Jews that "Torah is forever."

"Sing and rejoice, O daughter of Zion: for, lo, I come, and *I will dwell in the midst of thee*, saith the Lord." [28] God dwells in our midst as Messiah once again, in Jerusalem.

"Have mercy upon me, O Lord; consider my trouble which I suffer of them that hate me, Thou that liftest me up from the gates of death: That I may show forth all Thy praise in the gates of the daughter of Zion: I will rejoice in Thy salvation." [29]

The Lord will have mercy upon his people who are hated for having his witness.

"And many nations shall be joined to the Lord in that day, and shall be my people: and I will dwell in the midst of thee, and thou shalt know that the Lord of hosts hath sent me unto thee." [30]

Many countries who confess Jesus as their Saviour will be among God's people, called as his people, and will all personally know the Lord Jesus Christ. Quite clearly this is not a metaphor, but God among us who is revealed in the person of Jesus the Messiah sent by His Father in heaven: "And the Lord shall inherit Judah his portion in the holy land, and shall choose Jerusalem again." [31]

Jerusalem, God's holy capital, will once again be used for His purposes, where all people will flow for supplications and blessings:

> "But I [God] have chosen Jerusalem; that my name may be there for ever: and mine eyes and mine heart shall be there perpetually" [32] "For now have I chosen and sanctified this house, that my name may be there forever: and mine eyes and mine heart shall be there perpetually." [33] "And he set a carved image, the idol which he had made, in the house of God, of which God had said to David and to Solomon his son, In this house, and in Jerusalem, which I have chosen before all the tribes of Israel, will I put my name forever." [34]

246

Chapter Nine
TURKEY AND THE END-TIMES

"The simmering Islamic volcano in the villages of Anatolia and in the poor neighborhoods of the sprawling cities makes us wonder not 'if' but 'when.' If and when Turkey becomes a fully-fledged democracy, that instant it will become Islamic and anti-Western..."[1]

Turkey has the largest standing army of the European NATO powers[5]. Aechariah, an ancient prophet of Israel, confirms the concerns of Serge Trifkovic, foreign affairs editor for Chronicles, that the showdown led by Messiah between Israel and Turkey is clear in the Bible:

"and I will stir up thy sons, O Zion, against thy sons, O Greece (Javan)"[2]

The Hebrew translation of "Greece" is Javan and in the Hebrew lexicon, it's stated as "Ionia." Josephus, citing the Hebrew Bible, notes that Javan (Hebrew Iawan), associated with the Greek Ionia, is a province in modern western Turkey. The Encyclopedia Britannica states it as *"Any member of an important eastern division of the ancient Greek people, who gave their name to a district on the western coast of Anatolia (now Turkey)."*[3]

This prophecy refers to Messiah's Second Coming:

And the LORD shall be seen over them, and his arrow shall go forth as the lightning: and the Lord GOD shall blow the trumpet, and shall go with whirlwinds of the south. The LORD of hosts shall defend them; and they shall devour, and subdue with sling stones; and they shall drink, [and] make a noise as through wine; and they shall be filled like bowls, [and] as the corners of the altar. And the LORD their God shall save them in that day as the flock of his people: for they [shall be as] the stones of a crown, lifted up as an ensign upon his land.[4]

This refers to the Time of the End. So this battle between Israel, lead by Messiah, *(and the LORD shall be seen over them,)* and the revived Grecian empire, occurs right before the Messianic kingdom is established. Here the Messiah moves with "whirlwinds of the south," since He is traveling north to fight Gog (Ezekiel 38), the chief prince of Meshech and Tubal in the northern quarters.

Therefore, "the sons of Zion" (Israel)[5] will fight the "children of *Ionia*" (Turkey). This is a geographic reference. Many insist on using a tribal tracking of peoples to support a European migration of Javan. If this were true, the text would have said *"whirlwinds of the west."* But this is not the case, because Messiah is attacking towards the North, which is the direction of this invading army. This interpretation agrees with Ezekiel 38 regarding the area of the "north quarters," where Gomer, Magog, Tubal, Meshech, the brothers of Javan, settled, and *not* Western Europe.

Even if this migration theory were correct, how can we interpret *"children of Zion?"* Is *"Zion"* a person or a place? Nowhere in Scripture is *"Zion"* a person. How can we understand that the descendants of "Javan" will fight the descendants of Zion? We must conclude that this battle is between Zion (Israel) and Ionia (Turkey). Turkey also bears the historical taint for killing the saints. The following is a partial list of Turkish massacres from 1822 up until 1904:

1822 Chios, Greeks 50,000
1823 Missolongi, Greeks 8,750
1826 Constantinople, Jannisaries 25,000
1850 Mosul, Assyrians 10,000
1860 Lebanon, Maronites 12,000
1876 Bulgaria, Bulgarians 14,700
1877 Bayazid, Armenians 1,400
1879 Alashguerd, Armenians 1,250
1881 Alexandria, Christians 2,000
1892 Mosul, Yezidies 3,500
1894 Sassun, Armenians 12,000
1895-96 Armenia, Armenians 150,000
1896 Constantinople, Armenians 9,570
1896 Van, Armenians 8,000
1903-04 Macedonia, Macedonians 14,667
1904 Sassun, Armenians 5,640
1909 Cilician Armenians killed 30,000

1915-1923 Armenian Massacre 1.5 million

1974 Massacre of Cypriots 4000

It is estimated that Muslim Turks have slaughtered 2.8 million Christians.

Turkey has the largest standing army in the North Atlantic Treaty Organization and has been viewed by the U.S. and its allies as a bastion against nationalism in Russia and fundamentalism in Iran and other neighboring countries. As stated in the Guardian, August 1996, "the scope for conflict, were Turkey, like Iran, to 'go Islamic' would be immense."[6]

A Turkish professor of political science says "if you read the Islamists' newspapers, you'll see that what they're telling their voters is: 'You haven't given us enough votes to govern alone. We have to act like this.' Their argument is, 'Give us more power and then see what we can do.' "[7]

Western appeasement of Islam in Turkey is based on the false assumption that Turkey, with its Kemalist views, is moderate. This view provoked fighting against Christian Serbs and Macedonians in order to support Bosnian and Albanian Muslims in Bosnia and Kosovo. These groups were aided by Iranian Islamists and Chechens in an attempt to re-Islamize the Balkans.

There is a general but incorrect belief that these nations were peaceful and friendly with Israel, because the newly liberated Muslim Republics of Central Asia (C.I.S.), which split from Russia and Communism, seemed to embrace a pro-Western policy, reinforced by diplomatic ties with Israel and the West.

Against all hopes, expectations, and predictions of the "experts," Necmettin Erbakan, the head of the Islamist Party, won a plurality of the vote in 1996. The Turkish government today is openly pro-Islamic and is awaiting control over the military machine, which is still pro-Western.

The Islamists, in contrast, look increasingly to the Muslim states for economic and security assistance. Although Erbakan's stated intentions were not to replace NATO membership or hoped-for participation in the European Union (EU), he visited Libya and Iran soon after taking office, concluded an agreement to purchase Iranian gas, and was instrumental in creating the so-called Developing Eight, whose members include Egypt, Libya, Iran, Pakistan, Indonesia, Malaysia, Nigeria, and Turkey.

Erbakan denounced Israel and joined with Saudi Arabia and other Muslim states and organizations in opposing the peace process. Prime Minister Tayyip Erdogan, following Erbakan, with his newly created Islamic Party, which ran for elections in 2002, won a sweeping majority of the vote. The Islamic party in Turkey today is the most popular since the times of Kemal Attaturk.

Contrasting Turkey's Islamists and its Generals

Issue	The Islamists	The Generals
National identity	New Ottomans; Muslim first, then Turk.	Preservers of Ataturkism; Turks first, European second, then Muslim.
Government	Democratic state based on Islam and shariat law; profess belief in separation of religion and the state.	Secularism with strong state control of religion.
Foreign Policy	Economic and security ties with Muslim states (Iran, Pakistan, Nigeria, Egypt, Malaysia, Libya, Indonesia); oppose Arab-Israeli peace process; play on growing popular resentment of exclusion from EU.	Agreements with Israel on training, intelligence, aircraft upgrades, joint exercises; accuse Iran, Syria of supporting PKK terrorism; favor close ties with U.S., cooperation with NATO, EU membership.
Social Issues	Reintroduce dress codes, expand religious schools, build mosques in secular centers of Ankara and Istanbul.	Oppose any encroachment of religion into public life; favor enforcing secular dress and social codes and eight-years compulsory secular education with religious schools primarily for training clerics.
Threat Perception	PKK terrorism, western culture	Claim internal (Islamists) threat more serious than PKK, Syria.
U.S. Security Relationship	Oppose economic sanctions on Iraq and isolation of Iran; have muted long-time opposition to U.S., NATO military ties.	Favor strong political and military ties to the United States despite misgivings on U.S. policy toward Iraq, Iran, perceived arms embargo.

Similar to what the Bible predicted that the Antichrist would do, Turkey's Prime Minister, Abdullah Gul's moderate statements about peace and his desire to fight terrorism and maintain economic ties with Israel duped the world. Everything changed in March 2003, during the preparations for the Iraq War, when Turkey decided to ban the United States from using its territory, and openly show favor to the Palestinian cause. In time, the Islamists will appoint their own leaders in the Turkish military. Keep in mind Turkey's former Prime Minister, Tayyip Erdogan's, famous remark in 1999:

"The minarets are our bayonets, the domes [of the mosques] our helmets, the mosques our barracks."

Stanley Cohen, Professor of Criminology at the Hebrew University in Jerusalem called Turkey

> The nearest successful example [of collective denial] in the modern era is the 80 years of official denial by successive Turkish governments of the 1915-17 genocide against the Armenians in which 1.5 million people lost their lives. This denial has been sustained by deliberate propaganda, lying and cover-ups, forging documents, suppression of archives, and bribing scholars.

> In 1974, Turkey invaded Cyprus, moved in Muslims, and ordered the Greeks to move out within 24 hours. Churches went up in flames or were converted into mosques. Seventy percent of its industry is now under Turkish control. Yet it's still considered part of NATO and a "friend" of the US regardless that Turkey's past is rising up, as from a wounded beast, and turning into a ravishing monster. It is no wonder that The CIA's 1997 *State Failure Task Force* report identified Turkey as a nation in danger of collapse. The West needs to come to grips with the realization that Turkey is not a democracy, and any efforts to establish a democracy in it will prove fatal since democracy, like the attempts in Iraq, will only be used for electing an Islamic Sharia-driven system.[8]

The revival of the defunct Ottoman Beast is on its way.

Despite its acceptance as a full-fledged member of the world community, Turkey today is backsliding, and its rejection by the European Union can be exploited by both Islamic and secularist forces in Turkey. It will be nearly impossible for the United States to deal with Iran's nuclear weapons, the Iraq War, and Turkey's decline into Islamism—all at the same time.

SHIPS OF TARSHISH QUESTION

Many teachers of Christian prophecy claim that the European Union is the Antichrist's dominion by pointing to Tarshish in the Bible as being Spain or Britain, without any Biblical or historic support. They claim that the *"merchants of Tarshish and all the young lions thereof"* [9] refer to other European countries.

It is important to distinguish between "ships of Tarshish" and the *"merchants of Tarshish"* as nations that simply traded. One such verse is in Isaiah 23:1:

"The burden of Tyre. Howl, ye ships of Tarshish; for it is laid waste, so that there is no house, no entering in: from the land of Chittim it is revealed to them." In this verse, 'Ships of Tarshish' point to Tyre (Lebanon).

Tarshish is cited in several passages. Many writers point to Ezekiel 27:12, noting that since only Britain or Spain manufactured tin, and since Britain manufactures tin, then it must be Tarshish. This theory has several serious flaws:

1. For this to be true, Britain and Spain must also manufacture silver, lead and iron.

2. "Tarshish [was] thy merchant by reason of the multitude of all [kinds of] riches; with *silver, iron, tin, and lead*, they traded in thy fairs."

3. Only Turkey was renowned for silver, iron, tin, and lead altogether.

For the next argument, we turn to Jonah who, in attempting to flee to Tarshish from Israel, boarded a ship at the port of Joppa (on the Mediterranean coast).[10] This would indicate that Tarshish lies west. This is true, but the ships could also sail to Turkey and Lebanon westwards. In fact, historically, Turkey is renowned for its *silver, iron, and lead*. Even so, many modern authors are divided between Tartessos in Iberia and Tarsus in Cilicia (Turkey). Cilicia was the ancient name of southern Turkey. Göltepe was associated with tin mining; Kestel, located in the central Taurus Mountains of Turkey, also produced tin. Josephus cites *"Tharsus"* in Turkey:

"...Tharsus to the Tharsians, for so was Cilicia of old called; the sign of which is this, that the noblest city they have, and a metropolis also is Tarsus..."[11]

Josephus, citing from the Hebrew Bible, notes that Tarshish is a descendant of Japheth (Greek Iapetos/Japetus) and Javan (Hebrew Iawan), associated with the Greek Ionia, a province in modern western Turkey. The ancient Greek historian Athendorus, a citizen of Tarsus, ascribes a genealogy from Japetus, the ancestor of Javan, for Tarsus:

"Athendorus, the Tarsian, said that the city was originally called Parthenia, from Parthenius, son of Cydnus, the grandson of Anchiale, daughter of Japetus..."[12]

Charles F. Pfeiffer, editor of The Biblical World, a Dictionary of Biblical Archaeology, states:

"Ancient Anatolia was famous for its metals, which were carried in Phoenician ships as trade items to other parts of the ancient Near Eastern world. Phoenician inscriptions have been found at Karatepe, in Cilicia." Silver heads the list of precious metals associated with Tarshish, and ancient Assyrian sources noted that the Taurus Mountains above Tarsus were referred to as the Silver Mountains. In fact, modern metallurgy maps indicate that every single metal associated with Tarshish, can be found in the Taurus Mountains. "...Silver beaten into plates is brought from Tarshish..." [Jeremiah 10:9][13]

Harper's Bible Dictionary describes Tarsus:

Tarsus, the capital of Cilicia...The city was built on the banks of the swift Cydnus River, 10 miles from the Mediterranean and 30 miles south of the Taurus

("Silver") mountains, which were veined with lead and silver. "Archaeologists found evidence of smelters in the vicinity of Tarsus in antiquity," as noted by MacQueen: "The final shaping into tools and weapons was done locally, and areas devoted to this have been found at Bogazkoy and Tarsus marked by the presence of large quantities of slag." Tarsus also produced a clay crucible with bronze adhering to it.[14]

Since Bronze is an alloy of tin and copper, the natives of ancient Tarsus had to have had access to tin in order to make the bronze. Hodges notes that the Assyrians were interested in controlling the tin resources of Eastern Anatolia (Turkey)

There can be little doubt that Sargon's chief concern in this enterprise was to attempt to control the sources of supply of his raw materials, and one is tempted, therefore, to suppose that much of the tin required for bronze making came from the mountains of Syria and Turkey... No later than Early Bronze Age times, Anatolian bronze objects were utilizing tin. The Larousse Encyclopedia of Prehistoric describes bronze production "...it seems certain that bronze and bronze-working originated in the Middle East, where Anatolia and Armenia were mining regions...between 2300-2000 B.C...the quantity of the bronze with an already remarkably high tin content is impressive."[15]

Aslihan Yener, assistant professor at the university of Chicago's Oriental Institute, discovered an Early Bronze Age tin mine, 60 miles north of Tarsus.

Aslihan Yener believes that a mine and ancient mining village she has found in the central Taurus mountains of Turkey shows that TIN MINING was a well developed industry in the area as early as 2870 B.C...the mine at a site called Kestel—some 60 miles north of Tarsus, on the the Mediterranean coast—has two miles of tunnels... nearby stands the mining village of Goltepe, which was probably occupied by 500 to 1,000 persons more or less continuously between 3290 and 1840 B.C...the site contains no evidence of copper metallurgy...it did not produce bronze; instead it produced tin for export...Yener and her colleagues have analyzed tin-rich slag from 50 crucibles discovered at Goltepe. Within the total one metric ton of metallurgical debris in the form of crucible and vitrified materials, she has excavated some that have 30 percent tin content (a high percentage) still intact in the crucible.[16]

If the peoples of Cilicia were capable of mining tin in the Early Bronze Age, they certainly did not need to sail to Spain to get tin to make bronze!

Ezekiel 38:13 describes merchants of Tarshish:

"Sheba and Dedan and the merchants of Tarshish with all its villages will say to you, 'Have you come to capture spoil? Have you assembled your company to seize plunder, to carry away silver and gold, to take away cattle and goods, to capture great spoil?'"

While this statement does not conclude which side Sheba, Dedan, and the Merchants of Tarshish are on, it is clear that grabbing booty was an Islamic trait which these nations would enjoy copying. Isaiah, however, tells us about the judgment of the ships of Tarshish, as we refer, once again, to:

"The burden of Tyre. Howl, ye ships of Tarshish; for it is laid waste, so that there is no house, no entering in: from the land of Chittim it is revealed to them. Be still, ye inhabitants of the isle; thou whom the merchants of Zidon, that pass over the sea, have replenished." [16]

Isaiah 23:10 calls Tyre/Lebanon a "daughter" of Tarshish.

"Pass through thy land as a river, O daughter of Tarshish: [there is] no more strength." And 23:6 says, "Pass ye over to Tarshish; howl, ye inhabitants of the isle."

This place is somewhat related to Tarshish and is in close proximity to her in order to "pass over" to her. If Tarshish is Spain, how is Tyre to pass over such a far place?

There was some claim that made Tarshish out to be Europe, noting that in Isaiah 60:9, it was western ships that carried immigrant Jews to Israel.

"Surely the isles shall wait for me, and the ships of Tarshish first, to bring thy sons from far, their silver and their gold with them, unto the name of the LORD thy God, and to the Holy One of Israel, because he hath glorified thee." [18]

However, this is fulfilled in the Messianic Kingdom, since all the nations that hated Israel will participate:

"The multitude of camels shall cover thee, the dromedaries of Midian and Ephah; all they from Sheba shall come: they shall bring gold and incense; and they shall shew forth the praises of the LORD. All the flocks of Kedar shall be gathered together unto thee, the rams of Nebaioth shall minister unto thee: they shall come up with acceptance on mine altar, and I will glorify the house of my glory." [19]

It is obvious that the Arabs will participate. If Europe today is the candidate for the "ships of Tarshish," which carry Jews back to the homeland, then when did the Arabs (Midian, Kedar, Sheba) ever do such thing? If anything, the Arabs today would rather drown the Jews in the sea than extend assistance to carry them to the land of Israel.

Biblical Tarshish is lumped up together with Turkic regions. Isaiah clarifies the issue:

"And I will set a sign among them, and I will send those that escape of them unto the nations, [to] *Tarshish, Pul, and Lud, that draw the bow*, [to] *Tubal, and Javan*, [to] the isles afar off, that have not heard my fame, neither have seen my glory; and they shall declare my glory among the Gentiles." [20]

Here, Tarshish, Pul, Lud, Tubal, and Javan are thrown together in one "that draw[s] the bow," and all these are in Turkey. Why should only Tarshish be identified as Spain or England?

THE ETHIOPIA QUESTION

Ezekiel 38 mentions Ethiopia, which is traditionally interpreted as modern Ethiopia, the predominately-Christian nation that joined with

Muslims in the attack against Israel. This interpretation poses several problems:

According to the Encyclopedia of the Orient, Cush is the "Ancient kingdom of Nubia in today's northern Sudan, whose rulers conquered southern Egypt in the 8th century B.C. and established a capital at Napata."

The Sudan is one of the most strident, fundamentalist Islamic states. Two million Christians have been slaughtered or starved in the last twenty years there in a Christian holocaust, carried out by the Arab Muslims—in the name of Islam. Even though Sudan is prominently Catholic, Muslims see no difference between Protestants or Catholics. Yet the Catholics are accused of being part of the Harlot of Revelation. A study of Scripture shows this to be pure conjecture, based on an old interpretation that depended on the animosity between Protestants and Catholics.

Cush borders Egypt. Isaiah describes the destruction of Egypt from the Aswan Dam (Syene) to the borders of 'Cush' "Behold, therefore I [am] against thee, and against thy rivers, and I will make the land of Egypt utterly waste [and] desolate, *from the tower of Syene even unto the border of Ethiopia.*" [21]

If Egypt has a "Cush" border, and Egypt is adjacent to Sudan, then Cush would definitely stand for the nation of Sudan. Many authors, such as Dr. Arnold G. Fruchtenbaum, in The Footsteps of the Messiah, have, without evidence, interpreted Cush to be other nations; Fruchtenbaum describes Cush as "Somaliland or Somalia" without any historic or Biblical basis.

THE KINGS OF THE EAST QUESTION

China has been accused of being the Kings of the East with the 200 million-man army invading Israel, based on the following verse:

"And the sixth angel poured out his vial upon the great river Euphrates; and the water thereof was dried up, that the way of the kings of the east might be prepared." [22]

Yet not a single reference connects "Kings of the East" with China.

"Now when Jesus was born in Bethlehem of Judea in the days of Herod the king, behold, there came wise men from the east to Jerusalem." The Scripture tells us that these Kings from the east are from a Muslim region.

Others conjecture "Sinim" or China (note Isaiah 49:12), by referring to those people living to the farthest east of the known world. However, Isaiah 49:12 does not refer to any wars, punishments, or tribulation against that country, but rather the return of the Jewish people from there to Israel:

"Behold, these shall come from far: and, lo, these from the north and from the west; and these from the land of Sinim." [23]

ANTICHRIST FROM THE WEST (EUROPE) OR THE EAST?

Argument:

In Daniel 9, the *"people of the prince who is to come,"* speaks of a Roman Antichrist, and since Titus is the fulfillment, then it must be a revived Roman Empire from Europe. Since Europe is in the West, then the Antichrist must be a western leader.[24]

Response:

There is much evidence to demonstrate why the Antichrist *cannot* be from Western Europe:

1. Daniel 9 does not point to a western leader.

Titus is considered a fulfillment for the first part of the prophecy. Even if that were true and Titus is the fulfillment, it is important to note that he led *The Eastern Legion of the Roman Empire,* not the Western. After Vespasian emerged as the head of the Eastern Legions to challenge Vitellius, Julius Alexander, the Prefect of Egypt, then proclaimed Vespasian to be Emperor. He and Titus became consuls in 70 A.D.

Titus was a *type* of the one who will come (the prince); *"the people of the Prince"* in Daniel 9:26a, are the ancestors of the future Antichrist *"and the <u>people</u> of <u>the prince that shall come</u> shall destroy the city and the sanctuary."* The *"prince that shall come"* refers to the future, in the End-Times. The *"people of the prince"* are simply his ancestors who destroyed the city and sanctuary in Titus' time. This was the composition of the tenth Roman legion in Palestine:

A - Thracum Syriaca
B - IV Cohort Thracia-Bulgaria and Turkey
C - Syria Ulpia Petraeorum-Petra (Edom) Nabataean Arabs
D - IV Cohort Arabia-Arabia
E. - Syria

Therefore, these were a mixture of peoples, Syrian, Arabs, and Turks, and that describes today's nations as mentioned in Prophecy.

2. Grammar discounts Titus as the person of Daniel 9:25.

This is the entire text of Daniel 9:25-27:

> Know therefore and understand, [that] from the going forth of the commandment to restore and to build Jerusalem unto the Messiah the Prince [shall be] seven weeks, and threescore and two weeks: the street shall be built again, and the wall, even in troublous times. And after threescore and two weeks shall Messiah be cut off, but not for himself: and the people of *the prince that shall come* shall destroy the city and the sanctuary; and the end thereof [shall be] with a flood, and unto the end of the war desolations are determined. And *he* shall confirm the covenant with many for one week: and in the midst of the week he shall cause the sacrifice and the oblation to cease, and for the overspreading of abominations he shall make [it] desolate, even until the consummation, and that determined shall be poured upon the desolate.

The word that proves that this refers to the ancestors of Antichrist is *"he"* in verse 27: "And he shall confirm the covenant with many for one week…" This he is referring to the same person in verse 26 "the prince that shall come." This he cannot be Titus.

3. Titus never committed an "abomination" but a "destruction."

4. Titus never established a seven-year treaty.

This is none other then the Antichrist. Again, what Daniel 9:27 is speaking of is the "people of the prince [Antichrist] who is to come [way in the future] shall destroy the city and the sanctuary." [70 A.D.]

In fact, that specific reference is often debated. How could Titus be both here and in the future? Some people claim the grammatical reference is clear: if "he," in verse 26, is referring to Titus, then Titus must be coming back from the dead.

No. The "prince" is the Antichrist whose ancestors (eastern legions of the Roman Empire) destroyed Jerusalem and the Temple in 70 A.D.

Daniel 11 and Matthew 24 agree that the Temple is desecrated, not destroyed. Daniel 9:26 cannot be referring to the End-Times, since the Temple at that point is already completely destroyed. Therefore, the short-term fulfillment of the *destruction of the Temple* in Daniel 9 cannot be the same as the *abomination of desolation* done by the *"little horn"* of Daniel 8 and 11.

5. The Temple of End-Times is not destroyed

When armies surround Jerusalem again, the Temple will be saved, since Messiah must enter it:

"Then He brought me back to the outer gate which faces toward the east, but it was shut. And the Lord said to me, this gate shall be shut; it shall not be opened, and no man shall enter by it, because the Lord God of Israel has entered by it; therefore, it shall be shut." [25]

Turning to Ezekiel 43:1: "Afterward he brought me to the gate, the gate that faces toward the east. And behold, the glory of the God of Israel came from the way of the east."

And in chapter 43:4: "And the glory of the Lord came into the temple by the way of the gate which faces toward the east."

This refers to the Golden Gate, which is located 1,035 feet north of the southeast corner of the Temple Mount area, on which Muslim Khaleefeh Abdel-Malek bin-Marwan built the Dome of the Rock in 691 A.D.

6. Christ confirmed desolation not destruction

Christ Himself ends the arguments. In Matthew 24:15, we read, "When ye therefore shall see the abomination of desolation, spoken of by Daniel the prophet, standing in the holy place."

This reference cannot be to Daniel 9:26, but Daniel 9:27, since in Daniel 9:26, no *abomination* took place but a *destruction.*

7. The traditional interpretation ignores a 'type' fulfillment

This reference by Christ cannot be referring to Antiochus Epiphanies, as Daniel 11 has been traditionally interpreted. Therefore, Antiochus, like so many fulfillments in prophecy, is a *type*, not a specific person, especially since Antiochus lived before Jesus' time, and Jesus, in Matthew 24:3, is speaking of the end and the *"signs of your [His] coming and the end of the world."*

8. Traditional interpretation forces a contradiction

We cannot have contradictions in the Bible, which insists on a Grecian Antichrist. For this, we need to examine the only references in Daniel regarding an abomination—Daniel 11:31, 12:11, 19:27, and 8:13. Daniel 8:13 is clearly referring to one horn from the Grecian four horns of Alexander's Grecian Empire:

"And out of one of them came forth a little horn, which waxed exceeding great, toward the south, and toward the east, and toward the pleasant [land]." Most Bible scholars agree on this.

Then we have in verse 10: "And it waxed great, [even] to the host of heaven; and it *cast down [some] of the host and of the stars to the ground,* and stamped upon them." These "stars" (fallen angels) are "cast down" to earth in the Tribulation.

Thus, the Antichrist must come from the Grecian regions of the Roman Empire. This interpretation has no contradictions and the text fits like a glove.

If this were a reference to Antiochus, then how did he "*cast down [some] of the host of heaven* (fallen angels)?" This is definitely a reference to End-Times. Again, why would Jesus refer to a man who was long dead before Jesus' birth?

In Daniel 11:21, the one who is a *type* of the Antichrist comes on the scene from the north, and this is believed to be Antiochus Epiphanies who came from the Seleucid division, one of the four divisions of the Grecian Empire. The *"little horn,"* prophecy is described as, *"the vision is for the time of the end."* [26] The *little horn* of chapter

261

seven must be the end time Antichrist who causes one-third of the angels to fall:

"And it waxed great, even to the host of heaven; and some of the host and of the stars it cast down to the ground, and trampled upon them. Yea, it magnified itself, even to the prince of the host; and from him the continual burnt-offering was taken away, and the place of his sanctuary was cast down."[27]

How is this Antiochus casting down heavenly stars (angels), and in verse 25, "And through his cunning he shall cause craft to prosper in his hand; and he shall magnify himself in his heart, and in time of security shall he destroy many; he shall also stand up against the prince of princes; but he shall be broken without hand."

This is a showdown between Messiah and Satan. Science tells us that the stars are asteroids that fall on earth. Whether God intended a double meaning for fallen angels and asteroids remains to be discovered, but in Scripture, Satan is depicted as a star:

"And he said unto them, I beheld Satan as lightning fall from heaven."[28]

In conclusion, Jesus, in Matthew 24:15, placed Daniel 11:31 into the future, pointing to the Antichrist as this "abomination of desolation" before His Second Coming and not in the Maccabean period. Daniel 11:5-20 is a broad sketch of post-Grecian Empire history[29] which leads right up to the time of the Antichrist (little horn) in Daniel 11:21. This shows, to a certain degree, that many Bible prophecies use the device of a *type* for fulfillment, Antiochus being an excellent example. We must never assume that the Bible is all history.

So, the confirmation of Jesus' clear plan for the future is found in Daniel. Here we must follow Jesus' instructions carefully. The abomination of desolation is the one described by Daniel[30] The precise expression "abomination of desolation" occurs in Daniel 11:31, with a further reference to its appearance in the holy place in Dan 12:11. Dan. 9:27 contains a third reference, as does Dan. 8:13.

9. The Bible speaks of a king coming from the North (Eastern Roman Empire) not west.

The Bible does not once mention any future leader coming from the West. Daniel 11:31 describes a final evil ruler, the "*King of the North*," who sets "the abomination of desolation" and puts an end to temple sacrifices.

Therefore, in accordance with Matthew 24 and as the Bible states in Daniel 8:9, we must conclude that Antichrist is *"From one of the prominent horns came a small horn whose power grew very great. It extended toward the south and the east and toward the glorious land of Israel."* He must come from the Grecian part of this Roman Empire i.e., the Eastern part of the Roman Empire and north of Israel. Since he is going south (*It extended toward the south*), he must be coming from the north parts in relation to Israel, exactly as specified in Ezekiel 38, Joel 3 and many others.

In Daniel 8 and 11, the Antichrist is seen rising up in one of the four kingdoms formed by the splintering of Alexander's Greek Empire (little horn).

"Therefore the goat waxed very great: and when he was strong, the great horn was broken; and for it came up four notable ones toward the four winds of heaven."

These four kingdoms were:

1. The Greek/Macedonian region ruled by Cassander (Macedonia is a Muslim majority state today).

2. The Thracia/Turkey region (Bulgaria and Turkey today), ruled by Lysimachus and later called the Byzantine Empire (Muslim today).

3. The Babylonian/Persian region, including Southern Russia (Muslim today) Afghanistan (Muslim today), Iran (Muslim today), Syria (Muslim today), Lebanon (Muslim today), Arabia (Muslim today) and all the coastland to the city of Tyre, Lebanon (majority Muslim). This region was known as the Seleucid Dynasty.

4. The whole of Egypt, which in prophecy includes Libya and the Nubians and are Muslim regions today. Thus, the Antichrist comes from the Grecian Empire and most likely Asia Minor and not Syria. That he comes from the north is again confirmed in Daniel 8:9:

"And out of one of them came forth a little horn, which waxed exceeding great, toward the south, and toward the east, and toward the beauteous land." He can only go south if he is coming from the North.

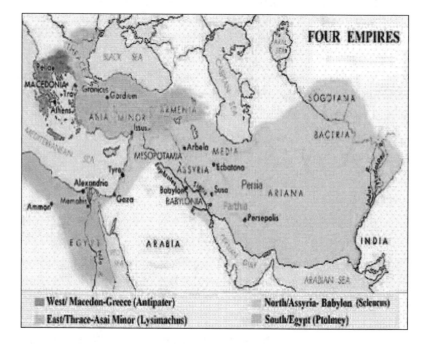

Fig. 2: The map, figure 2, shows the four divisions of Alexander the Great's Grecian empire. Note that the only portion in the West is Greece and the rest of the divisions are all in the East. This makes it more plausible that the Antichrist will be from Turkey or Turkic peoples of the CIS nations south of Russia, as they were part of the Grecian empire.

Argument:

If Antiochus the Syrian was from the Seleucid Dynasty, how do we link him with Gog of Ezekiel 38, which points to Central Asia?

Response:

Central Asia seems plausible since it too was part of the Grecian Seleucid Empire:

"Seleucus, who became king of the eastern provinces—more or less modern *Afghanistan, Iran, Iraq, Syria, and Lebanon, together with parts of Turkey, Armenia, Turkmenistan, Uzbekistan, and Tajikistan.*" [31]

Revelation 13 describes the End-Times beast in terms of regions: Leopard (Grecian), Lion (Babylonian), and Bear (Medo-Persian), because all three Empires ruled the region of Asia Minor, i.e., the Seleucid portion of the Grecian Empire. Scripture places the land of Gog north of Israel, and Asia Minor is north of Israel. All prophetic writings must pinpoint the region, and indeed they do. The question is, is this "King of the North" a separate person from the Antichrist?

"And at the time of the end shall the king of the south push at him and the king of the north shall come against him like a whirlwind, with chariots, and with horsemen, and with many ships; and he shall enter into the countries, and shall overflow and pass over." [32]

Many students of prophecy conclude that there are three parties involved in this prophecy: the Antichrist, the king of the north, and the king of the south. This is incorrect. Daniel 11:40 is speaking of only *two* parties fighting, the *king of the north* and *king of the south*. The king of the south is considered to be Egypt because Egypt is south of Israel and this is the land that the King of the north comes up against. The "king of the south" is the Antichrist attacking Egypt which falls to him, along with Libya (Phut) and Sudan (Cush) [see Daniel 11:43].

"...at the time of the end shall the king of the south (Egypt) push at him (Antichrist) and the king of the north (Antichrist) shall come against him (king of the south/Egypt) like a whirlwind, with chariots and with horsemen, and with many ships; and he shall enter into the countries, and shall overflow and pass over."

Bear in mind that in Daniel 9:27, Antichrist does not make a peace treaty as traditionally claimed; the text simply has Antichrist *confirming* a covenant which is broken in the middle of the week (a week representing 7 years) with Israel, and this, together with the abomination of desolations, marks the beginning of the Tribulation period. Today, Turkey and Egypt have established a peace agreement with Israel.

Chapter Ten
THE CRESCENT CONNECTION

Islamic art depicting the Quran and crescent moon
(Al-Hilal) engulfing the whole earth

THE CRESCENT IN ISAIAH

Questions: Isaiah's subject?
Satan's rebellion in the heavenly realm?
Fulfillment in the King of Babylon
(Nebuchadnezzar)?
The Antichrist?

The prophets gave the Antichrist different names: "Gog,"[1] "The Assyrian,"[2] "The Antichrist,"[3] "Son of Perdition,"[4] "Lucifer,"[5] and more. It is essential to point that the Hebrew text for the word "Lucifer" in Isaiah 14:12 is *"Hilal ben Sahar."*

Hilal also means "the brightness" and in Aramaic/Arabic it means "Crescent Moon." Satan is also an angel of light (2 Cor. 11:14). Studying these two words, "Hilal" and "Sahar," we find:

267

1 – "Helel, or Heylel (morning star) have possible links with Akkadian elletu (Ishtar) and *Arabic hilal* (new moon)."[6] "The worship of the moon is also attested to by proper names of people such as *Hilal*, a crescent; *Qamar*, a moon; and so on."[7] "Hilal" means "the shining one" in Hebrew and Arabic, and in Ethiopian it means "Moon-crescent." He is a Moon-god.[8]

2 – "Sahar" or "Shahar" is Hebrew for dawn or morning star. The two combined make up his symbol—crescent moon and star, and as described later in chapter 13.

The Quran mentioned the "rising of the dawn" in a night called "The Night of Vision:"

"We have sent it to thee in the Night of Vision, what do you know of this Night of Vision. The Night of Vision is better then a thousand months. The *angelic hosts descend* [to earth] in it with *the Spirit* by command of *their Lord*. Peace shall it be until *the rising of the Dawn* (Morning star)"[9] The morning dawn and crescent moon are important symbols to Muslims everywhere. When terrorists from over 40 different organizations assembled in Tehran, they gave the name of the summit "Ten Days of Dawn."[10]

The italicized words could very well have come out of Scripture regarding Satan (Dawn, The spirit, their Lord), cast out of heaven, and the fallen angels.

These verses refer to *Ramadan* when Muslims fast when the crescent moon appears with Venus (morning star), which is the symbol of Satan, as written by Isaiah. Muslims wait until the late hours of the night, gazing at the sky, waiting to see the sky open and the angelic host descend.

As a Muslim, prior to my conversion, I would go up on the roof with the family during the "Night Vision" and gaze at the sky and wait for this heavenly sight. Another reference to the God of Islam as one who brings evil is in Surah 113:

"Say: 'I seek refuge in the Lord of the *Daybreak*, from *the evil of what He has created*; and from the evil of the night when it comes on; and from the evil of the witches who blow upon knots, and from the evil of the envious when he envies.'" Here he is the lord of the "day-break," or of the morning, or son of the morning.

The most well known Islamic song, which came from Islam's founders, is called "Tala'a Al-Badr."[11] I have provided the English translation: [O you who were raised amongst us is Muhammad]

ARABIC	ENGLISH
Tala'al-Badru 'alayna	O the White glowing Moon rose over us
min thaniyyatil-Wada'	From the Valley of Wada'
wajaba al-shukru 'alayna	And we owe it to show gratefulness
ma da'a lillahi da'	Where the call is to Allah
Ayyuha al-mab'uthu fina	O you who were raised amongst us
Ji'ta bi-al-amri al-muta	Coming with a work to be obeyed
Ji'ta sharrafta al-Madinah	You have brought to this city nobleness
marhaban ya khayra da'	Welcome! Best Call to Allah's Way

In Isaiah 14, the *"king of Babylon"* is identified as Satan:

"O shining star, son of the morning! How you have fallen from heaven," and to him the Bible says, "You shall be cast from your grave" and, "You shall not be united with them [the other kings of the earth] in burial, because you ruined your land and you have slain your people."[12]

This agrees with Revelation 19, where we see the Antichrist thrown alive into the Lake of Fire. It is the embodiment of Satan as the Antichrist, Satan in the flesh deceiving people as the false Messiah.

"I will break the Assyrian in My land, and tread him underfoot."[13] Here, Satan [Lucifer] is addressed as a man. "They that see thee shall narrowly look upon thee, [and] consider thee, [saying, is] this is the *man* that made the earth to tremble, that did shake kingdoms."[14] The question is, when did this angelic 'Lucifer' become man? Clearly, this is Satan-in-the-flesh.

Thus, the Babylonian king is not Nebuchadnezzar or any other ruler of ancient Babylon. Isaiah 14:14, all the way to verse 23, is about Satan, and then suddenly verses 24 and 25 use End-Time terminology:

"As I have purposed, it shall rise; to break Assyria in My land, and on My mountains I will trample him...this is the purpose that is purposed on all the earth, and this is the hand that is stretched out on all the nations."

The text suddenly goes from describing the Antichrist's destruction to describing the destruction of Assyria without any apparent break. In Isaiah, "the king of Assyria," is very descriptive of the Antichrist. Isaiah 30:30-31 confirms this:

"Yahweh will make the majesty of his voice heard; the lowering of his arm he will show, with raging anger, and a consuming flame; cloudburst and storm and hailstones. For by the voice of Yahweh, Assyria is crushed."

It's that unmistakable terminology signifying the Day of the Lord, where "his arm" is referring to Jesus, as is the case throughout Isaiah, including Isaiah 3:1. This is not the Assyria of the moment, but an End-Time Assyria which is destroyed at the fiery coming of Jesus on dark and tempestuous clouds, when He destroys Satan by a "breath of His mouth" and "Sword out of His mouth."

Isaiah reveals the outcome for the man who would be a modern "Nebuchadnezzar" and threaten all of creation with his terrible weapons: "For I will rise up against them, says the Lord of hosts, and cut off from Babylon its name and remnant, and offspring and posterity, says the Lord...I will sweep it with the broom of destruction..." [15]

The broom of destruction. Anyone who has seen footage of a nuclear bomb explosion knows how the ominous cloud sweeps up everything in its path.

CRESCENT MOON AND MYSTERY BABYLON

Revelation 17 presents a snapshot of the entire Babylonian influence and of human sin, stretching over time to encompass the empires of Daniel with their false religions. Islam's crescent moon, in reality, stems from Babylonia, modern day Iraq. In 217 A.D., Emperor Caracala was killed after he was returning from visiting the Temple of the Moon God in Harran, Iraq. In 363 A.D., Emperor Julian paid his respects to the temple of Sin. The Moon God, in fact, was the most worshiped god in Roman times. It is reasonable to connect the Roman Empire's religious worship from Babylon to Islam, which adopted this symbol. The Moon-god at Haran was described by the Doctrine of Addai, Jacob of Searug, and others.

Pic 1

Pic 2

Pic 3

\# 1-2 — (Stella) Exalts the crescent moon on a high place as seen in minarets.

\# 3 — (Coin) Even Hadrian the Roman emperor worshiped the Moon god at Ur (Haran).

271

Pic 4

4 — (Stones) we can see hands extended upwards in prayer form towards the Moon god,[15] a position used today by Muslims in Du'aa (prayer)

Islam is simply a revival of a Babylonian religion. The Moon god with the crescent moon and star symbol originated in Babylon (Iraq) and was one of the 360 idols in the Kaaba (Mecca) before Muhammad destroyed them. In Babylon, the Moon god was called "Sin."

G. Caton Thompson's book, The Tombs and Moon Temple of Hureidha, discusses the uncovering of a temple of the Moon-god in southern Arabia. The symbols of the crescent moon and no less than twenty-one inscriptions with the name "Sin" were found in this temple. An idol, which may be the Moon god himself, was also discovered. The Arabic word for 'god' is 'Ilah' and the Moon god became synonymous with "al-Ilah," meaning "the god;" pagan Arabia believed that the Moon god was the greatest of all the gods, hence the phrase "Allahu Akbar," meaning "Allah is greater."

This is what led Muhammad to go one step further and proclaim in the Quran that "la ilaha ila Allah" (there is no god but Allah). Inscriptions of "al-Ilah" have been found on an idol with the crescent moon and star symbols. The pagan Arabs used "Allah" in naming their children. For example, Muhammad's father was called Abdullah, meaning "servant of Allah."

The killing of converts was not unusual in pre-Islamic practice in Arabia, just as it is not unusual today. There is the story of Sylleus the

Arab, who fell in love with Salome in Herod's kingdom, but he would not convert at her request for fear of being stoned by his people, the Arabs.[16]

Sir Leonard Woolley excavated a temple of the Moon-god in Ur (Babylon). His findings are displayed in the British Museum. In the 1950's, a major temple of the Moon-god was excavated at Hazer in "Palestine." Two idols of the Moon god were found. Each was a statue of a man sitting upon a throne with a crescent moon carved on his chest, and the inscriptions confirm the items were idols. They also found several smaller statues bearing inscriptions identifying them as the "daughters" of the Moon-god.[17]

In Saudi Arabia, the three daughters, al-Lat, al-Uzza and Manat, were depicted together with Allah, the Moon-god, represented by a crescent moon above them. The daughters themselves have the symbol of a star. Even the Quran, in Surah 53:19-20, mentions them by name, not to mention the abrogated "Satanic verses" which give more weight to the fact that Allah was the Moon-god. Idols of al-Lat, al-Uzza and Manat were also worshiped in the Kaaba and, lo and behold, Surah 53 is titled "An-najm," meaning "the star."

This "Mystery Babylon" stemmed from Babylon and lived throughout history in every empire in the east. The fall of "Mystery Babylon" as prophesied could likely mean "the fall of Islam."

Dr. Arthur Jeffrey, professor of Islamic and Middle East Studies, one of the world's foremost scholars on Islam, said that the name "Allah," and its feminine form, "Allat," were well known in pre-Islamic Arabia and were found in inscriptions uncovered in North Africa: it "is a proper name applicable only to their peculiar god." He adds,

"Allah is a pre-Islamic name...corresponding to the Babylonian god known as Bel."[18] "Bel" simply means "lord" and this is a title of reverence to the Moon-god "Sin."

And the name *Sanballat the Arab* is a derivative of two words, the Sin (Moon-god), and Allat, the feminine of Allah, one of his three daughters. This shows that such names existed way before Muhammad, just as his father's name, Abd-*Allah,* meant "slave of Allah," the Moon-god.

The worship of the Moon-god came from Ur of the Chaldees in Babylon. Abraham is the first to mention it in his account of his journey in Genesis 12:1.

Nabodnidus elevated the Moon-god, Sin, to the top of the Babylonian pantheon in an effort to make the Babylonian religion more acceptable to the Arabs and Armadas. The emblem for the god Sin, *the Controller of the Night,* was the crescent moon, which became the primary religious symbol of Islam. The Islamic calendar is based on the lunar cycle, and may have relevance to Moon-god worship. In Arabia, he was known as "Hubbell," *al-Allah,* "the god."

In Surah 106, the Quran commanded Quays, Muhammad's clan, to *"worship the Lord of this shrine"* (i.e., the Kabana) which can mean only the Moon-god. It is only after this Surah was revealed that Muhammad came back to destroy the idols in the Kabana and fight the people that refused to accept his status as prophet. There is no mention in the Bible of God ordering anyone to erect a shrine in Arabia, so who really is *"the Lord of this shrine?"*

WILL MESSIAH BREAK THE CRESCENT MOON OR THE CROSS

One hint is in Psalm 83:11: *"Make their nobles like Oreb, and like Zeeb: yea, all their princes as Zebah, and as Zalmunna."*

What happened in the story of Zeeb and Zalmunna? The answer is in Judges 8:21:

"Then Zebah and Zalmun'na said, "Rise yourself, and fall upon us; for as the man is, so is his strength." And Gideon arose and slew Zebah and Zalmun'na; and he took the *crescents* that were on the necks of their camels."

Gideon is a *type* for King Messiah, and instead of Messiah taking away the crosses as predicted by Islamic prophecy, the opposite was true—all the crescents on the highest places (minarets) will be taken away, just as Israel had to remove the Ashera from the high places. The word used for crescent in Judges 8:21, *Saharon,* which literally means crescent moon, is from the root *Sahar,* and is used for the name of Satan in Isaiah 14 (Hilal ben Sahar).

Yet Islam teaches the opposite:

"The final battle will be waged by Muslim faithful coming on the backs of horses...carrying black banners. They will stand on the east side of the Jordan River and will wage war that the earth has never seen before. The true Messiah who is the Islamic Mehdi who will kill the pig and will break the cross and will defeat Europe...will lead this army of <u>Seljuks</u>, He will preside over the world from Jerusalem because Mecca would have been destroyed..." [19]

The Seljuk Empire was a Turkic enterprise that preceded the Ottomans who arose from the division of the empire. It covered the region of Anatolia (Turkey), Northern Iran, Syria, Iraq, Southern Caucasus, and Azerbaijan. Many Islamic scholars believe that the Mehdi is the Messiah who leads an army of Turkish Seljuks, and that Mecca, the spiritual headquarters of Islam, will be destroyed, exactly what the Bible foretells for the Harlot city. It is incorrect to say that Muhammad was not a prophet; he's just not a prophet sent by the God of the Bible.

ABADDON—THE ANGEL OF THE BOTTOMLESS PIT

"They have as king over them, the angel of the abyss; his name in Hebrew is <u>Abaddon</u>, and in the Greek he has the name <u>Apollyon</u>." [20]

Abaddon means destroyer and encompasses two of the 99 names for Allah. The 62nd name of Allah in the Quran is 'al-Mumit' (the Destroyer, the one who causes death). The 92nd name of Allah is 'Al-Darr' (the Spoiler). In fact, Islamic terrorism today is exactly that: taking what is beautiful and spoiling it. Not only does Muslim jihad destroy lives and shatter families, it aims to destroy great buildings such as the World Trade Center and other critical state structures, to aim the blow where it will hurt the most: the government and its economy.

In Israel, the name of Allah is invoked by Muslims in a war cry, "Allahu Akbar," which preceded the murders of innocent Jews in restaurants, or on religious holidays such as the Yom Kippur war, which was waged on Israel on October 6, 1973 by Egypt and Syria on the most sacred day of the Jewish calendar, the Day of Atonement. That is the level of respect Islamism has for the freedom of religion.

The first woe is past; behold, two woes are still coming after these things. Then the sixth angel sounded, and I heard a voice from the four horns of the golden altar which is before God, one saying to the sixth angel who had the trumpet, "Release the four angels who are bound at the great river Euphrates. And the four angels, who had been prepared for the hour and day and month and year, were released, so that they would kill a third of mankind.[21]

Euphrates is in Babylon. Bear in mind that Mystery Babylon (Islam) with its government is unleashed at this time. In other words, God will not restrain the Muslims from unleashing war on the world. That is when the killing and destruction will take place.

Satan's fall to earth in his last attempt to control the world is described in Isaiah 14. This is the angel of the bottomless pit:

"He opened the bottomless pit, and smoke went up out of the pit, like the smoke of a great furnace; and the sun and the air were darkened by the smoke of the pit."[22] This is confirmed in Isaiah 14:31: "Howl, O gate; cry, O city; thou, whole Palestine, [art] dissolved: for there shall come *from the north* a smoke, and none [shall be] alone in his appointed times."

Here, "the north" is confirmed by Isaiah, as well as this "smoke" which causes a worldwide catastrophe. Obviously, this "smoke" is symbolic of war and destruction caused by the Antichrist. After all, Abbadon/Appolyon in Revelation literally means destroyer, so his purpose is destruction:

"Then out of the smoke came locusts upon the earth, and power was given them, as the scorpions of the earth have power. They were told not to hurt the grass of the earth, nor any green thing, nor any tree, but only the men who do not have the seal of God on their foreheads."[23]

When Yazid was marching with his army to invade Syria, Abu Bakar, the first Muslim Caliph after Muhammad, charged him with this:

"Destroy no palm trees, nor burn any fields of corn; cut down no fruit trees, nor do any mischief to cattle, only such as you kill to eat."

The "locusts" attacked idolatrous Christians who did *"not have the seal of God on their forehead."* The Saracens worked mainly in those countries where corruption of Christianity prevailed, i.e., the Greek Orthodox and Roman Catholic churches. Verses 7-9 describe the Saracens outfits. They were renowned for their horsemanship. Obviously, these are the weapons of war unleashed by the Antichrist on the rest of the world that is not saved. It could be that the ones with the mark of the beast are the ones who will do this task.

It was Satan who energized the Muslim hordes (the 7th head of Rev 17:10), which came like locusts from the east and swarmed towards the west. Incidentally, the Hebrew word for locust is *Arbei* and in Arabic is *Arbi*; also, the Arabian Desert is teeming with locusts because of its climate. Therefore, this is a befitting image. Islam does not permit the destruction of trees or green things. The "locusts" were not allowed to "hurt the grass, or green things, etc." The Saracen Muslim (first beast/7th head) armies were under orders, which, *as a type,* match this.

"crowns of gold" —	They wore yellow turbans
"hair like women" —	They had long hair
"teeth like lions" —	They were extremely fierce
"breastplates" —	They wore metal armor. Their horses were also armored, and made a loud, clattering noise when they galloped.

"Tails like scorpions"—they were very dangerous and deadly. Their king's name was "Abaddon" and "Apollyon" which means "destroyer." The Arabian climate sustains scorpions as well as locusts, and it is interesting that the zoology depicted in Revelation fits the Arabs and the Arab climate perfectly.

Perhaps it is difficult to see how this armor compares to anything we have today, but *"the sound of their wings was like the sound of chariots"* can relate to airplanes and the *"sound of many horses rushing to battle"* to jet engines. Today, missiles are weapons of war and Revelation paints a picture of *"tails like scorpions, and stings; and in their tails is their power to hurt men for five months"* which would be an adequate description of warplanes and missile launchers, albeit without the time limit.

"And they were not permitted to kill anyone, but to torment for five months; and their torment was like the torment of a scorpion when it stings a man…And in those days men will seek death and will not find it; they will long to die, and death flees from them." [24]

The goal of the Antichrist is to get people to surrender, to place his mark on them, take them with him to eternal damnation. Islam offers its enemies a choice: accept Islam or suffer the sword. The horsemen will kill one-third of the earth's people. This prophecy says that these weapons will not unleash death at first, but later they will destroy that portion of the population.

"They have as king over them, the angel of the abyss; his name in Hebrew is Abaddon, and in the Greek he has the name Apollyon." [25]

"The number of the armies of the horsemen was two hundred million; I heard the number of them. And this is how I saw in the vision the horses and those who sat on them: the riders had breastplates the color of *fire and of hyacinth and of brimstone*; and the heads of the horses are like the heads of lions; and out of their mouths proceed fire and smoke and brimstone." [26]

The description of the breastplates' colors of "fire," "hyacinth" and "brimstone"—red, blue and yellow—are the colors of the Ottoman Empire, the Ottoman warriors' military uniforms and the "war flag," as prescribed by Sultan Mahmoud II [1834-1859].

"For the power of the horses is in their mouths and in their tails; for their tails are like serpents and have heads, and with them they do harm and out of their mouths proceed fire and smoke and brimstone." [27]

These could be the modern jet fighters. The explosive charge, whether nuclear or otherwise, is in the missiles. A missile fitted under the tail wings would look much like a snake with a head. It is the missile that does the harm and not the planes. Of course, in John's time, there was no concept of "jets" or "nuclear force," but the metaphors for weapons of destruction, "snake" and "scorpion," well described the devastating effects of their "sting." What John saw were indeed lethal weapons and he gave a graphic description of what is today technological warfare. Jeremiah was describing precision bombing when he wrote about the destruction of End-Times Babylon: *"their arrows [shall be] as of a mighty expert man; none shall return in vain.* "[28]

"A third of mankind was killed by these three plagues, by the fire and the smoke and the brimstone which proceeded out of their mouths."[29] What a perfect description of modern "shock-and-awe" warfare. We also need to see Rev 8:8 in perspective:

"And the second angel sounded, and as it were a great mountain burning with fire was cast into the sea: and the third part of the sea became blood."

Besides the plausible interpretation of cosmic hail, a "mountain" is also symbolic of an empire or kingdom, and "sea" is always symbolic of peoples, nations, and tongues.[30] Or, the "great mountain burning with fire" is an asteroid.

THE "BLACK STONE" AND THE FALLEN STAR

Rev 8:10, "And the third angel sounded, and there fell a great star from heaven, burning as it were a lamp and it fell upon the third part of the rivers and upon the fountains of waters."

Besides a literal star (asteroid), the fallen star is synonymous with Satan and his fallen angels. A metaphorical interpretation would be that Satan (morning star, angel in heaven) appears as a lamp (angel of light) and is cast down to deceive the world (Isaiah 14). Since the death of one-third of the population will occur by rise of the eighth empire, which will be Islamic, we must correlate these verses with this Scripture. The fallen star, the destroyer who is unleashed, must lead the "mountain" (empire), causing one-third of mankind to die.

An asteroid is a logical assumption, since the Black Stone itself is evidently a meteorite and undoubtedly owes its reputation to the tradition that it fell from the "heavens." It is doubly ironic that Muslims venerate this piece of rock as that given to Ishmael by the angel Gabriel to build the Kaaba, since it is, to quote Margoliouth,

"...of doubtful genuineness, since the Black Stone was removed by the...Qarmatians in the fourth [Muslim] century, and restored by them after many years: it may be doubted whether the stone which they returned was the same as the stone which they removed."[31]

This asteroid stone caused a great portion of mankind to be spiritually poisoned, and all Muslims, when they pray, bow towards it in worship to Allah five times a day. Yet the Bible offers a similar symbol for Satan being cast out to dwell on earth and demand worship as he sits in the Temple.

This is a most interesting story. According to Muslim writers, the Kaaba was first built in heaven, (where a model of it remains), two thousand years before the creation of the world. Adam erected the Kaaba on earth but it was destroyed during the Flood. Abraham was instructed to rebuild it and he was assisted by Ishmael. While looking for a stone to mark the corner of the building, Ishmael met the angel Gabriel, who gave him the *Black Stone, which was then whiter than milk; it was only later that it became black from the sins of those who touched it.*

This veneration of an asteroid would be blasphemous in Christian theology, since Jesus was the only one who took upon Himself the sins of the world. In other words, the black stone is believed by Muslims to have come down from heaven and took upon itself the sins of mankind. This story is nothing new; long before, the Book of Acts spoke of this very issue:

"At last the mayor was able to quiet them down enough to speak. 'Citizens of Ephesus' he said. 'Everyone knows that Ephesus is the official guardian of the temple of the great *Artemis, whose image fell down to us from heaven.*'" [32]

Artemis with the crescent moon on her forehead.

Artemis, in Ephesus, was often depicted with the crescent of the moon on her forehead and was sometimes identified with Selene (goddess of the moon) who the people in Ephesus (Turkey) worshiped. It is likely that Turkey's crescent symbol is a throwback to these ancient times. Could *"the image of the beast"* be a crescent moon? Only time will tell.

MIRACLES FROM HEAVEN

The Antichrist will come to deceive the world once more with *"all power and signs and lying wonders."* [33] Just as Muhammad presented the miraculous sign of Quranic revelations allegedly received from the angel Gabriel, so the awaited Mahdi of the Islamic world will bring similar signs and wonders to seduce the world unto condemnation. How else did Muhammad know about the "Night Vision," "dawn" and "morning star?" How interesting are the numerous similarities among different cults, even though the cult leaders never met.

Here's an interesting comparison of Islam with the Mormon Church:

Islam Created: Dissatisfied with the world of different beliefs, Muhammad regularly attended and meditated at *Ghar-Hira'a,* a cave near Mecca, seeking God's will. He saw a magnificent bright Angel of Light, Gabriel. The Islamic traditions record that his excitement looked like a trance or vision. The *Wahi* or Angel, overtook him and he underwent a trance-like experience, then the Wahi instructed him to "arise and preach." The Angel taught him that all Christians and Jews were wrong in their beliefs and so Islam was established.

Mormonism Created: Joseph Smith, as recorded in his testimony, was dissatisfied with the world of different beliefs, regularly attended the same place alone, and began to offer up his desires to God. Then he encountered a bright Angel of Light, "Moroni," and he immediately seized upon some power, which caused Smith to undergo a trance-like experience. He was taught that all the current beliefs of the world were wrong and Mormonism was established.

Islam's Holy Book: Muhammad received revelations from originals *engraved on tablets of stone in heaven.* (Al-Lawh Al-Mahfuth). A new book, the Quran, was created. It supersedes all the previous God-inspired books.

The Book of Mormon: Joseph Smith got his revelation from originals engraved on <u>tablets of different metals</u> and delivered by the "Angel of Light." A new book was established, <u>The Book of Mormon.</u> It supersedes all the previous God-inspired books.

Islam's New Holy City: The Islamic religion that Muhammad promoted re-directed the "holy city" from Jerusalem to Mecca, with the Kaaba as the holiest place.

Mormon's New City: Joseph Smith changed the coming of Christ from Jerusalem to Independence, Missouri, and promoted "Salt Lake City" as the central headquarters for Mormons.

Islam Geographical Moves: In the Quran, geography is changed so that the countries where the prophets live fit God's choice for His message. Abraham is found living in Mecca, and building the Kaaba on its original foundation with his son Ishmael. The Arabs who are descendants of Ishmael are chosen to reveal the truth to a lost world. And the people of the prophet, their language and their city, became significant. Israel has been replaced as the chosen people of God. Israel has no more significance, and Arabic is now God's chosen heavenly language, with the Quran superseding the Bible. Muslims now are God's instrument to deliver truth to the world.

Mormon Geographical Moves: Joseph Smith's <u>Book of Mormon</u> has the tribes of Israel moving to America. Jesus, however, will come back to Independence, Missouri. The Book of Mormon supersedes the Bible, which was corrupted; Mormons are now the chosen people of God to deliver truth to the world.

Islam: The main arguments the Quran has with the Judeo-Christian faith go to Muhammad's prophecies and his new revelations. True Christianity was lost, and all of today's Christians are "kuffar" or unbelievers, and are full of error. Muhammad accused the Judeo-Christian believers of twisting God's word, which led the Christians and Jews astray.

Mormonism: The main arguments Joseph Smith had with the Judeo-Christian faith stemmed from his own role as prophet, and his new revelations. He believed all of today's Christians are full of error.

Islam and Polygamy: Muhammad received revelations from the Angel of Light, Gabriel, to take the wife of his adopted son, Zaid. He promoted polygamy, and married at least 22 women: Khadija, Sawda, Aesha, Omm Salma, Hafsa, Zaynab of Jahsh, Howarya, Omm Habiba, Safia, Maymuna of Hareth, Fatema, Hind, Asma of Saba, Zaynab of Khozaymia, Habla, Asma of Muman, Maria Al-Kibtia, Rayhana,

Omm Sharik, Maymuna, Zaynab (the 3rd one), and Khawla. Polygamy was promoted in Islam for the believers (four wives for each man). The prophet's marriage privileges were limitless.

Mormonism and Polygamy: Joseph Smith received revelations from the Angel of Light, Moroni, when he desired to take a woman. He practiced polygamy and married many women: Louisa Beman, Fanny Alger, Lucinda Harris, Zina D. Huntington, Prescindia L. Huntington, Eliza Roxey Snow, Sarah Ann Whitney, Desdemona Fullmer, Helen Mar Kimball, Eliza M. Partridge, Emily D. Partridge, and many others. Polygamy was promoted in Mormonism. (State laws and modern lifestyles have severely cut back the practice, although there are still some Mormon polygamists.)

Could their inspiration be from the same source? Both books claim to believe in the Bible; in truth, both reject the most essential Biblical teachings.

Fire From Heaven

Acclaiming holy books, signs, and wonders is nothing new. According to the New Testament, the Antichrist will

"doeth great wonders, so that he maketh fire come down from heaven on the earth in the sight of men, And deceiveth them that dwell on the earth by the means of those miracles which he had power to do in the sight of the beast" [34]

The question is, how will bringing fire [to] come down from heaven be accomplished?

Let's keep in mind these verses use both metaphor and allegory. Simple cross-referencing in Scripture can prove that allegoric or metaphoric fire is just that—not a literal burning. Here are other examples:

"As the fire burneth a wood, and as the flame setteth the mountains on fire; so persecute them with thy tempest, and make them afraid with thy storm." [35] This is not a literal fire, but a metaphor for trouble, strife and fear.

"A fire goeth before him, and burneth up his enemies round about." [36] "Who maketh his angels spirits; his ministers a flaming fire..." [37]

Here, the ministers are so persuasive that they are described as "flaming fire." So the Antichrist will be effective in deluding the world with his signs.

"He gave them hail for rain, [and] flaming fire in their land." [38]

"And a fire was kindled in their company; the flame burned up the wicked." [39]

In the Bible, God commands fire and brimstone from heaven on Sodom and Gomorrah "Then the LORD rained upon Sodom and upon Gomorrah brimstone and fire from the LORD out of heaven." [40]

In Sodom, it was actual fire and brimstone, but in Revelation, is it really fire? Alternatively, is it symbolic? Satan cannot create fire, so what is this satanic blaze?

Fire destroys, and this "fire from heaven" will destroy the ones who see it and believe.

Chapter Eleven
MYSTERY BABYLON

ROME VS SAUDI ARABIA

Common Arguments for Rome:

The seven hills only exist in the Vatican, which is part of Rome (Italy).

The false prophet/beast is believed to be the Roman Catholic Church in Revelation 13, 14 and 17.

In Revelation 17:4, *"the woman was arrayed in purple and scarlet color"* means the Catholic cardinals who are arrayed in scarlet clothes and *"...having a golden cup in her hand full of abomination..."* is the golden cup used to offer up the Eucharist.

The Catholic Church also is *"drunken with the blood of the saints, and with the blood of the martyrs of Jesus"*—the death of so many Protestants is ample evidence that the Catholic Church can be the only candidate.

Response:

While the Catholic Church today openly admits and regrets the persecutions of Jews and Christians in the past, *the deaths in Scripture* regarding End-Times come by *beheading*. This form of punishment has never been used by the Catholic Church. Also, Vatican City is not built on seven hills, but only one, Vatican Hill, which is *not* one of the seven upon which ancient Rome was built. Those hills are on the east side of the Tiber River; Vatican Hill is on the west.

There is no argument that the color scarlet represents the Catholic Church. Same thing for the golden cup of wine used for Communion, but purple and red are *not* the dominant colors of Catholic clerical vestments. White is. All priests wear white (including bishops and cardinals when they are saying Mass) as well as the Pope. Scarlet yarn and wool are used in ceremonies.[1] God also commanded that the priests' vestments be made with purple and scarlet yarn.[2]

We must also ask how *"the merchants of the earth are waxed rich through the abundance of her delicacies."* We will show this is *not* the Catholic Church; Mecca and Medina are better candidates than the Vatican.

SAUDI ARABIA AS THE MYSTERY BABYLON

Saudi Arabia correlates with the prophecy much better than does Rome:

1) Saudi Arabia is mentioned for destruction in the text several times, while Rome is not mentioned even once.

Certain European countries are specifically mentioned in the Bible, yet not with a single reference to destruction. *Spain* is mentioned in Romans 15:24,28 and *Rome* in Acts 2:10, 18:2, 19:21, 23:11, 28:14, 28:16; Romans 1:7, 1:15; Galatians 6:18; Eph 6:24; Ph 4:23; Col 4:18; 2 Tim 1:17; 2 Tim 4:22; and Ph 1:25.

The prophets never mentioned the destruction of Rome by name, yet *Arabia is* mentioned by name in several areas:

2) Isaiah 21 confirms the destruction of Saudi Arabia

"The burden of the desert of the sea" in verse 1 refers to Saudi Arabia.

The term "desert of the sea" in Isaiah 21 is similar to the term used today for Arabia as "The Arab Island," a desert island that sits on the seas. This corresponds with other references in Jeremiah and Revelation regarding this "harlot/city" to which John is taken to in the wilderness (desert). What nation fits that description better than Arabia?

The prophecy mentions locations that exist only in Arabia, not Rome. Saudi Arabia is mainly desert and it sits on many seas and thus this matches the prophecy's geography perfectly.

Dumah is located in Saudi Arabia near Yathrib (Medina), today called "Dumat el-Janda..." Dumah was one of the sons of Ishmael. Kedar was also a son of Ishmael, the line from which Muhammad descended.

The use of *"burden of Dumah,"* "burden upon Arabia," and *"the glory of Kedar shall fail..."* What would be the "glory of Kedar?" Could this be Mecca?

3) Saudi Arabia has been in the forefront of the move to export Islamic ideology to bring about a revival of Islam that will take over the world:

Revelation 13:3: "And I saw one of his heads as it were wounded to death; and his deadly wound was healed: and all the world wondered after the beast."

Islam once controlled the ancient world; it will try to heal its wound and revive the Islamic Empire.[3]

Saudi Arabia has been the leader of the move to spread jihad by funding it throughout Afghanistan, Algeria, the former USSR (C.I.S.), Chechnya, Kosovo, the Philippines, Bosnia, Pakistan, the Middle East, and many other parts of the globe. This bears a distinct Wahhabi imprint that is none other than ancient Islam revived.

4) Saudi Arabia has influence via oil over the kings of the earth [Rev 17:18]

The political conflict is about oil, the commodity the whole world is dependent on, especially the Western nations. And the Arabs have a monopoly on the oil market.

5) Corrupts the nations [Rev 17:2; 18:3; 19:2] with Islamic influence

Islam is the only other overtly evangelistic religion aside from Christianity, and the extent of Arab imperialism in non-Arab Islamic countries is transparent. *It is the only religion that defies the word of God at the core.* Islam maintains that we all worship the same God but makes charges of corruption against the Bible. The Jews may also disagree with the Christian perspective, but the Old Testament is something that all Christians revere and uphold as divine revelation; therefore Christians attest to Biblical Judaism as far as Scripture itself is concerned.

6) "The City of Seven Hills"

Revelation 17:18: "the woman which thou sawest is that great city, which reigneth over the kings of the earth."

Chapter 19:2 speaks of Babylon as a real city that will be judged by God and destroyed. Using the common tools of Biblical interpretation, we see that Babylon is indeed the seat of power for the final empire of the Antichrist. In Revelation 17:9, it says that the woman sits on seven hills, or mountains. Many interpreters believe this city is Rome, which is famous for its seven hills. However, the Greek word "epi" which translates as "on," can just as legitimately be translated as "near." Given this alternate reading, and surrounded by seven hills, Mecca qualifies. Also, in Revelation 17:18, the allegoric word "mountain" is intended to mean kingdom.

7) Persecutes the Saints

There is no persecution in Rome today. It is *Saudi Arabia* that the Islamic decrees come from, calling for the beheading of Christians exactly as *Revelation 20-4b stated:*

"And I saw the souls of those who had been beheaded for their witness to Jesus and for the word of God."

Saudi Arabia is mentioned in Jeremiah 49:33 by the name of Hezor and Kedar, a descendent of Ishmael, the father of the Arabs. We should note that Muhammad was a descendent of Kedar. In Jeremiah, God's wrath is kindled against the descendants of Kedar and Hazor. Iran (Persia or Elam) will suffer destruction as well;[4] this fits the Gog of Ezekiel 38, which includes Persia, modern day Iran.

8) Offers a commodity necessary for the whole world

Oil again. Revelation 18:3:

"For all nations have drunk of the wine of the wrath of her fornication, and the kings of the earth have committed fornication with her, and the merchants of the earth are waxed rich through the abundance of her delicacies."

Through the abundance of oil (delicacies) all the nations have prospered; their wealth is dependent on the availability of oil, the lifeblood of the industrialized world. What delicacy (commodity) does the Vatican offer?

9) Needs oil to burn

In Isaiah 34, Edom is used to represent all the nations against whom God's judgment is set. While Edom was a short-term fulfillment, the text of Isaiah was speaking of a greater, long-term fulfillment:

"For [it is] the day of the LORD'S vengeance, [and] the year of recompenses for the controversy of Zion. Its streams [nachal, Heb] shall be turned into pitch and its dust into brimstone; its land shall become burning pitch. It shall not be quenched night or day; its smoke shall ascend forever." [5]

Incredibly, Isaiah, almost three millennia before the discovery of fuel oil, predicted the burning of pitch, bitumen, and tar, which means crude oil. Note that the land shall not be "like" burning pitch but shall *become* burning pitch; no simile here. This prophesy could only be fulfilled in an oil rich region which, in our world, is predominantly Arab. The word for "streams" is not to be taken literally to mean "water" since the Hebrew "nachal" means "torrent" "torrent-valley," "wadi /valley" or a "mine." In other words, the terrain will turn into a river of burnt petroleum.

Recall the "scorched earth" response of Saddam Hussein in the first Gulf war, as he set thousands of oil wells on fire.

Therefore, the kings of the Earth shall cry for oil, but the oil will go up in flames. Again, Arabia is one such oil-rich region, so much so that Saudi Arabia oil export revenues make up more than 90% of its export earnings. This one nation alone has control over 26% of the world's oil reserves. All this is what the Bible declares to be "the LORD'S vengeance, [and] the year of recompenses for the controversy of Zion." God Himself finally resolves the question with this great destruction. Similarly, Ezekiel 25:12-13 says:

"Thus saith the Lord GOD; 'Because that Edom hath dealt against the house of Judah by taking vengeance, and hath greatly offended, and revenged himself upon them. Therefore thus saith the Lord GOD; 'I will also stretch out mine hand upon Edom, and will cut off man and beast from it; and I will make it desolate from Teman; and they of *Dedan* shall fall by the sword.'"

This future destruction is not restricted to Jordan alone, since "Dedan" is an Arabian location situated between Medina and Tabuk in central Saudi Arabia. This land mass includes the Nabataean Empire which was ruled by the Arabs from Arabia who began acquiring wealth and building a merchant empire. Their camel caravans crossed Arabia and their ships plied the Red Sea, the Mediterranean Sea, and even the Indian Ocean. Eventually Nabataean merchants and explorers would visit almost every known place on the globe. The "Inner Nabataean Kingdom" was located in the Middle East, on the edge of the great Arabian deserts. This crescent-shaped area was defined by three distinctive geological barriers. It was these peoples who built Petra for which the Bible predicted desolation and addressed them as people who "dwell in the clefts of the rock."

"And the merchants of the earth will weep and mourn over her, for no one buys their merchandise anymore..."[6]

Clearly, this Scripture indicates that this country is one that relies heavily on imports. Again, Saudi Arabia's only real export income is from oil, over 90%, and thus it depends greatly on imports, especially foods such as livestock and grains. It even imports water, as it has little or no source of its own. According to a 2004 report by the World Bank Group, Saudi Arabia's Gross Domestic Product (GDP) in 2003 was $214.7 billion US Dollars, with its export trade estimated at $46.9 billion US Dollars, 90% of which is oil revenue. Its import stocks are estimated at $29.7 billion. *Therefore, the surrounding nations are dependent on her oil, but their economic stability depends on the established trade traffic to flow freely.*

Oil is the principle commodity driving the global economic market. Therefore, oil-rich countries have an economic monopoly. However, crude oil is not a renewable resource, and as the supply diminishes, not only Saudi Arabia but all nations will suffer an economic crisis. If the nations can't produce goods, *"and so the merchants will mourn for no one buys their merchandise anymore..."* Saudi Arabia cannot import them. In contrast, most European countries' export revenue is not based on a single commodity, and are significantly more diverse.

10) Saudi Arabia has a tremendous foreign work force:

"We would have healed Babylon, but she is not healed: forsake her, and let us go every one into his own country."[7]

Nearly all laborers in Saudi Arabia are foreigners, constituting two-thirds of its population. Some are from Arab lands and many are from underdeveloped Asian countries such as Pakistan and Sri Lanka. Today the Saudi labor force is dominated by foreign nationals. There are approximately three million foreigners in Saudi Arabia's total population of 16.7 million. About 60% of the Saudi workforce is foreign nationals, and over 90% of workers in the private sector are non-Saudis. These workers have no rights to obtain citizenship, so it's understandable why they would flee each "into his own country."

"Thus shall they be unto thee with whom thou hast labored, even thy merchants, from thy youth: they shall wander every one to his quarter; none shall save thee."[8]

11) No other people live in such luxury with hidden sin:

"How much she hath glorified herself, and lived in luxury."[9]

The Saudis boast great wealth and live very affluent lives. Their homes are made of marble, adorned with artifacts and designed with the architecture of prominent cities to represent their prosperity.

"Therefore hear now this, thou that art given to pleasures."[10]

"For thou hast trusted in thy wickedness: thou hast said, *none seeth me*."[11]

Saudi Arabia is a deeply entrenched, patriarchal society where the authority bestowed on men by nature and by God is abused to an extreme.

Saudi Arabia is the spiritual headquarters of all Muslims. Males dominate public life. The treatment of women and foreign workers is shameful and their respective roles are proscribed not only by the society but also by the Quran. Women are restricted in dress and lifestyle, supposedly to prevent lewdness and to prevent husbands from straying. However, the men in this society live very different private lives than the public behavior they display. Their hearts are far from godliness.

There is little respect for free will or civil liberties, let alone human life; it is a culture without remorse or compassion, a country where there is little chance of justice unless you hold an influential position of power. There are no elections or political parties because the House of Saud rules autocratically, based on an extremist interpretation of Shari'a law. Non-government organizations that could give a voice to the people, such as trade unions or other associations, are forbidden or constrained. Torture and inhumane and degrading treatment are common practices and many a prisoner has not had a fair trial. And there is little chance of penetrating a culture that is so introverted and yet united in religion; international human rights organizations may be able to highlight issues, but they can barely scratch the surface...and so the country continues to sin in secret.

"...And the kings of the earth, who have committed fornication and lived deliciously with her, shall bewail her, and lament for her, when they shall see the smoke of her burning." [12]

12) Saudi Imports matches Revelation 18 and Ezekiel 27:

Notice that the merchandise in Revelation 18 is almost identical to that in "Tyre" of Ezekiel 27—persons of men (slaves), and vessels of brass (verse 13), ivory and ebony (verse 15), gemstones and fine clothes (verse 16), oil and balm (verse 17), wine (verse 18), iron and cassia wood (verse 19) cedar (verse 24), animals (verse 20), spices and precious stones (verse 21). This Mystery Babylon is also described as Tyre with the merchants being identical to the nations that deal with Mecca. As I have stated, Persia, Lud, and Phut were the armies of this merchant city [Ezekiel 27:10]. Indeed, Phut (North Africa), was populated by the Moors who were the soldiers of Islam, and who captured Spain and occupied it for hundreds of years. Lud (Turkey) was the Ottoman Empire, which expanded Islam, and the Janissaries were the military might of Islam. Ezekiel 27 indeed has a long-term fulfillment and cannot be speaking exclusively of ancient Tyre, since it did not encompass these nations as "men of war" serving that city.

"The merchandise of gold, and silver, and precious stones" [13]

The Asian and Arab cultures are renowned for their appetite for gold, silver, and precious stones since these treasures are linked to social position and are important for personal adornment. In fact, gold is the largest bulk of Saudi imports and was estimated at a whopping $909.203 million US Dollars in 2001.

"And of pearls"

Saudi Arabia imports pearls from other Arab countries and from Japan. In 2001, pearls and precious stones imports came to millions of US dollars. How curious, since Islamic law supposedly renders the fashion and cosmetic industries dead, so this is a significant amount for an extremist Islamic country.

"And fine linen, and purple, and silk, and scarlet"

Saudi Arabia imports luxurious fabrics from many nations. With a hot climate and the strict code of dress that Islamic law imposes, fine delicate fabrics such as silk are popular.

"And all thy wood, and all manner vessels of ivory, and all manner vessels of most precious wood, and of brass"

Saudi Arabian culture is known for its lavish lifestyle and a love of collecting artifacts. Ivory swords and dagger handles are exquisite in Arabia. Incidentally, when the Arabs invaded Zanzibar they took control over the ivory and the slave trade, since there was great demand for both at the time and it proved to be highly profitable. They were sent on ships bound for Saudi Arabia, India and China, where most of Saudi Arabia's ivory originates. Artifacts made of precious metals with arabesque calligraphy decorations and patterns are plentiful among the rich Arabs and are characteristic of Islamic art and sculpture.

"And iron and marble"

Iron is used in construction and marble for the flooring and building exteriors.

Who else uses so much marble in architecture as the Arabs of Saudi? Although Saudi Arabia is self-sufficient in marble, graphite and other ornamental stones, it imports additional materials, especially marble from Turkey, Pakistan, Jordan and Italy to meet its demand, approximately 12.4 million US Dollars worth in recent years.

The Medina Mosque is made entirely of marble with gold mosaics for design, Masjid al-harem is also made predominantly of white marble. In fact, marble is used so much in architecture that most of the petrol stations are made of it.

"And cinnamon, and odors, and ointments, and frankincense"

Essential oils are very popular, since commercial perfumes contain alcohol. As noted previously, the cosmetic industry is practically non-existent so natural scents are highly favored.

"Wine"

The following article on Saudi alcohol consumption appeared in the Christian Science Monitor: "*Saudi bomb attacks have whiff of illicit alcohol trade*" Special to the Christian Science Monitor:

"A series of mysterious bomb attacks against Westerners in Saudi Arabia has thrown an uncomfortable spotlight on the oil-rich kingdom, which craves an image of stability. The latest came last week when Gary Hatch, an American doctor, was maimed by a parcel bomb that exploded in his face at his hospital office in the eastern city of Al-Khobar. He was the first US victim since the bombings began in November, claiming the life of one British man and injuring several other foreigners."

Who's behind this spate of bombings, and whether they are even connected, is still unclear. But they have disrupted a period of relative tranquility in Saudi Arabia that had lasted since June 1996, when the port city of Al-Khobar was the target of one of the most devastating terrorist attacks against American targets abroad. A suicide bomber drove a truck packed with explosives into a US military barracks, killing 19 and wounding more than 500. That attack is still under investigation.

The Saudi authorities say those behind some of the recent attacks are connected to a bloody turf war between rival gangs of foreigners over the multimillion-dollar trade in alcohol, which is outlawed in this Muslim country. No evidence, however, suggests the victims are involved in the trade. Dissidents dismiss the accusation as a cover-up. The perpetrators, they claim, are small groups of Saudi Islamic extremists attempting to embarrass the regime and drive "unholy" Westerners from the Arabian Peninsula.

Gangland-style turf war over bootleg alcohol in a supposedly dry Islamic state? Or Middle Eastern terrorism against Westerners? Either explanation is embarrassing for the Saudi authorities, who have volunteered little information on their investigation. The arrest of three Westerners, who confessed on Saudi state television to a bombing that killed a British engineer, has failed to stop the bombings. Since the February confessions, there have been four more bomb attacks. The three, a Briton, a Belgian and a Canadian, have been in police custody for several months. Friends of the three accused say their confessions were extracted under duress, and British survivors of one bombing say they have difficulty believing the three were guilty.

The continuation of the attacks after the detention of the accused confirms it is not a matter of a fight over alcohol," says Saad Al-Fagih, a leading Saudi dissident based in London. Those responsible were Saudi fundamentalists, he alleges. "They want to keep the matter of the Western presence in the country as a hot subject, and send a message to Westerners that they are not wanted in the Arabian peninsula," added Dr. Fagih, director for the Movement for Islamic Reform in Arabia, which is committed to change through peaceful means.

While the authorities have not implicated any Saudis in the investigation, Fagih says at least 70 suspected Saudi Islamic fundamentalists have been arrested since the bombings began. They were from small groups which did not have the ability to launch more spectacular terrorist attacks against US military targets, such as the suicide bombing that killed 17 American sailors on board the USS Cole in Yemen.

"They want to hit the big US military bases [in Saudi Arabia] but they cannot reach them because they are like formidable fortresses," Fagih says. If Islamic rebellion is growing, it appears, then, to be in isolated pockets. Alcohol flows in, over land and over sea. Those who believe home-grown anti-Western terrorists are responsible [believe] that the reason few Americans have been targeted so far is that they are more security conscious and mix less with the locals than do the British expatriates.

If, however, the bombings are linked to the underground trade in alcohol, that also raises serious public relations problems for the Saudi authorities, especially because of suspicions of official complicity in the boot-legging business. While alcohol is banned, the local authorities have always held a benign tolerance toward foreign workers who drink discreetly. As long as they do not flaunt their activities or cause problems after drinking, bars on workers' compounds are allowed to flourish.

The bootlegging prize is huge. By conservative estimates, 150,000 cases of spirits, most of it Scotch whisky, are smuggled into the country every year, with resulting profits of $200 million. Industry experts believe that 70 percent is consumed by Saudis and the rest by expatriates.

Despite draconian penalties that can include public floggings for those found guilty of alcohol offenses, the spectacular profits appear to have made prohibition [no] more effective than it was in America in the "Roaring Twenties."

Experts say 80 percent of the smuggled alcohol comes from the United Arab Emirates. Another 18 percent arrives by the tiny Persian Gulf island of Bahrain, via the causeway linking it to Saudi Arabia.

Some used to be ferried in by private jet, a method that has become less popular because jets can be spotted by American military surveillance aircraft over Saudi Arabia.

With a bottle of Johnny Walker Black Label selling for as much as $200 in Saudi Arabia, a 20-ft. container with 1,100 cases brings in $2,640,000. Some $2 million of that is profit, although there are expenses to be paid all down the supply line. The scale of alcohol smuggled into Saudi Arabia would be impossible to sustain without some official complicity involving customs agents and higher-level patrons.

"Who is likely to have the sort of influence to ensure that two patrol boats happen to be pointing in opposite directions to allow a fast launch into the coast?" says one alcohol salesman with long experience in the Middle East.

"You also hear stories about sheikhs being rung up in the middle of the night by very worried people at the port saying, 'Sorry to bother you, sir, but your container of spare parts is leaking,'" he adds.

Less lucrative is the moonshine business, which caters to those reluctant to pay large sums for bootlegged whisky or who do not have access to the privileged diplomatic cocktail circuit. (Foreign embassies are allowed to serve alcohol on their grounds.) A litre and a half of raw alcohol known as "uncut" sells for about $40. Several large Western companies in Saudi Arabia even provide booklets informing workers how to make their own moonshine in kitchen distilleries without poisoning or blowing themselves up—while at the same time advising readers it is illegal.

Some expatriates claim to make as much as $3,000 a week producing it, although this business, like the bootlegging trade, has suffered because of a police crackdown following the bombings. More than 15 foreigners, including at least seven Americans, have been arrested on alcohol charges in a wide-ranging sweep, although Western diplomats say none of them have been implicated in the bombing campaign.[14]

"beasts, and sheep, and horses"

Arabs import a great deal of livestock as they have little of their own. Farming is not feasible in Saudi Arabia, since a substantial portion of the country is desert.

"Chariots"

They import all their cars and cars parts, and this forms the second largest group of imports.

"Slaves"

In the 18th century, there was an emphasis on rebuilding the cities and re-establishing the once thriving trade routes. Under the leadership of the Sultan of Oman, Seyyid Said, the Arabs worked to regain economic and political supremacy over the region. The island of Zanzibar quickly became the center of a very lucrative trade in slaves and ivory from the interior, and spices from the island itself.

Slavery was officially banned in Saudi Arabia in 1968, but reports filed by human rights organizations maintain that a situation akin to slavery persists in Saudi society. Leading affluent lives, many households employ foreign nationals as servants to do household chores such as cooking and cleaning, etc. Many of these foreign workers come from poorer Asian countries and some even from Arab lands. A large number of servants are hired from Sri Lanka in particular. Their employment is subject to a contract which allows the "master" to hold their passports throughout the duration of the contract and the workers in turn are paid very low wages. Also, the worker cannot leave the country without the sponsor's permission and females may not leave the country without a male escort. There have been many reports of female servants being sexually harassed and even raped. A Saudi Sheikh, Sheikh Saleh Al-Fawzan announced that "slavery is a part of Islam."

"And souls of men"

They corrupt the souls with Islam. Who else fits that bill more than Mecca and Medina? Saudi Arabia funds almost every movement to Islamize the world; it is the only other evangelistic religion that strikes at the root of Christian principles such as the trinity, original sin, atonement for sin and the death and resurrection of Christ. Paul declared in 1 Cor. 15:14 that "if Christ be not risen, then is our preaching vain, and your faith is also vain."

Islam challenges every one of these precepts, the *raison d'etre* of the Messiah. Saudi is the heart of Islam and no other religion churns out as much propaganda and as many hate campaigns to promote shahada (martyrdom) as does Islam. Look at the world today and ask yourself why Islamist fundamentalism has reached this height. In the Quran and in the mosques, it is openly preached from the pulpits that it is the duty of every Muslim to take part in jihad, which is directed at the "infidels" i.e., the West and Israel, *especially* Israel.

"The merchants of these things, [all of] whom were made rich by her, shall stand afar for the fear of her torment, weeping and wailing…"[15]

To review, more than 90% of Saudi Arabia's export revenue comes from oil, so it is heavily dependent on a single source of income. Most of the land mass is unfit for farming or for raising livestock, and water shortages have prompted Saudi Arabia to become the leading country in desalinating water, an expensive process. Twelve percent of the workforce is in the agricultural sector and does not produce enough to meet general demand, so, much is imported from other countries. Saudi imports are widely diverse, a stark contrast to its exports, and it is foreseeable why the merchants will "mourn for the country" that bought their goods and caused them to prosper. Nearly all nations are dependent on the established oil trade system, and their economies will be sorely affected by the destruction of Mecca.

"...their arrows shall be as of a mighty expert man; none shall return in vain."

Precision bombing will be the method of destruction; not one rocket is lost. This is exactly what modern, specialized equipment is designed to do.

"And they cast dust on their heads, and cried, weeping and wailing, saying, Alas, alas, that great city, wherein all were made rich that had ships in the sea by reason of her costliness! For in one hour is she made desolate."[16]

The Port of Jeddah is the Saudi Arabian commercial capital and so most of the import ships dock there. The commercial capital was established after oil was discovered in that region and tankers carry oil through that port as well. Jeddah is one of Saudi Arabia's largest cities, but unlike others in Saudi, it has managed to preserve many of its older buildings. It is also an extensively developed, modern city with a dazzling array of high-rise buildings and luxury hotels that line the shores of the Red Sea. The merchants of the ships may well see the smoke from her burning in the sky upon her destruction.

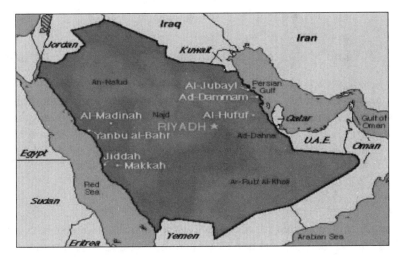

Fig 1. Jiddah, Al-Madina, and Mecca can be seen close to the Red Sea. They would be seen easily from "afar" burning.

301

Today, there are many nations that commit harlotry with Saudi Arabia and Islam because of oil. When President Bush stated to the world "Islam is peace" in the wake of September 11, the worst attack ever within our borders, had he forgotten that 15 of the 19 hijackers were Saudis? President Ronald Reagan called the Communist USSR "The Evil Empire," yet would any leader today dare call Islam evil in this politically correct society? The Bible says that "by their fruits you shall know them" and the fruits of Islam have proven sour, beginning a long time ago.

13) Revelation 18 concurs with Ezekiel 27:

Ezekiel 27 refers to merchandise of persons of men (slaves), and vessels of brass (verse 13), ivory and ebony (verse 15), gemstones and fine clothes (verse 16), oil and balm (verse 17), wine (verse 18), iron and cassia wood (verse 19) and cedar (verse 24), animals (verse 20), spices and precious stones (verse 21). *All this merchandise is remarkably similar to the merchandise of Babylon in Revelation 18.*

Ezekiel 27 is speaking of nations that today are all Muslim. We must then interpret Revelation 18 by looking at Ezekiel 27. If Revelation 18 meant "Rome," then we must ask, why are all these nations Muslim? Since Ezekiel 27 is speaking of Tyre, and the Bible confirms that the Antichrist is also called "prince of Tyre," then it is plausible to state the "King of Babylon" is the Antichrist leading "Mystery Babylon."

14) Saudi Arabia is destined to burn, even according to Islamic teaching

Medina, Islam's second holiest site, is predicted for destruction by Islam. Muhammad the prophet of Islam made an interesting statement:

"The flourishing state of Jerusalem will be when Yathrib is in ruins, the ruined state of Yathrib will be when the Great War comes, and the outbreak of the Great War will be at the conquest of Constantinople and the conquest of Constantinople when the Dajjal (Antichrist) comes forth. He (the Prophet) struck his thigh or his shoulder with his hand and said: This is as true as you are here or as you are sitting." [17]

"Medina will be destroyed and become the shelter of the savage people." "The greatest war, the conquest of Constantinople and the coming forth of the Dajjal (Antichrist) will take place within a period of seven months." [18]

Yathrib is Medina, one of the holy places of Islam. Constantinople is the modern Istanbul in Turkey. We are told that the Antichrist will be revealed to the world *after* the conquest of Constantinople and within a period of seven months, and presumably, this person would have full control over all the Turkic territories. Yathrib or Medina will be in ruins after this event, a consequence as prophesied by Muhammad. This would suggest that all these events are interdependent. This agrees with our deduction that the Antichrist power is Turkic. In addition, Rev. 2:13 confirms this by placing the seat or throne of Satan in Pergamon, Turkey.

Some people assert that the seat of Satan has moved from Turkey to Europe, but they fail to recognize that this is not a physical or even symbolic seat, but the spiritual abode of Satan and his power.

According to Islam, this "Dajjal" (literally means 'the liar') will have already appeared. This will be a very great calamity. The Muslim ummah (nation) will be in great fear during that period of time. Some will follow him and regard him as a god. Jesus will eventually kill Dajjaal with his spear at Lydda, which is in Palestine. The Jews will be targeted and assassinated. Trees and boulders will speak to the Muslims informing them of any Jew seeking shelter and protection by them. The Gharqad tree will not, however, conceal the Jew; hence, this tree is being planted by the thousands in Palestine. Those Christians who will repent and accept Islam will be saved from any persecution or massacre. Others who choose to disbelieve, will be put to death. Thereafter the entire world will be ruled by Muslims. [19]

MUSLIMS HAVE ATTACKED MECCA IN THE PAST

Centuries ago, Al-Hajjaj bin Yousef Al-Thaqafi (a Muslim) attacked Mecca with catapults and laid siege of her. Time has not changed the disregard for holy sites. Remember when Saddam Hussein sent scuds flying over Saudi Arabia, disregarding the high risk it would pose to the Islamic "holy land?" So far there has been little objection from Islamic nations regarding this careless firing of scud missiles over Saudi Arabia, Islam's holiest place.

Let's not forget that Turkey, although it is an Islamic state, is also a very secular state. Kemal Ataturk, who governed Turkey after the defeat of the Ottoman Empire, reacted very strongly to Islamic imperialism; he forbid the practice of veiling and changed the language from the Persian script, which is very similar to the Arabic. And he changed the calendar from the Islamic to the Gregorian. It is feasible that a nation such as this may attack even Saudi Arabia and relive the glory days of the Ottoman Empire.

The state of affairs in Saudi Arabia during World War I was very telling. The Ottomans were occupying Saudi Arabia and had control over the region. They resented the Arab imperialism that had spread through the vast Islamic empire and consequently they attempted to circumvent this by putting restrictions on Arab culture and language. This was so severe that the Arabs were persuaded by the British through their envoy, T. E. Lawrence, also known as "Lawrence of Arabia," to revolt against the Ottoman occupation and help the Allies in return for independence, and this dealt the final blow to the weakening Ottoman Empire. That Turkey is a secular state is crucial, as Daniel 7:25 states that the Antichrist will change times and laws, and as the beast is the Islamic kingdom, the times will change from the Gregorian to the Hijrah dates and the laws to Islamic Law, the Shari'a.

For those who find it incredulous that Muslims should attack the spiritual headquarters of Islam, read the following from With Lawrence of Arabia by Lowell Thomas, (Arrow Books 1962, Hutchinson & Co. Publishers Ltd, 1925):

> Hussein supervised the attack on Mecca, [and] while Faisel and Ali were in command of the force directed against Medina, the Grand Shereef was successful at Mecca. The forts on the three hills overlooking that forbidden and sacred city were garrisoned by the sultan's most faithful Circassian mercenaries and by picked Turkish troops. On the day of the attack, the Arabs swept through the gates and captured the main bazaar, the residential section, the administration buildings, and the

sacred mosque of the Holy Kaaba. For a fortnight the battle raged around the two smaller forts, which were finally taken. During all this fighting the aged Shereef remained in his palace directing operations in spite of scores of Turkish three-inch shells that riddled his residence. The Turks might have been able to hang on for many months had it not been for their own folly. The Ottoman seems to be a Muhammadan in theory only, occasionally adhering to the ritual and even less frequently adhering to the spirit of the Koran. Heedless of the deep set religious feelings of their enemies and co-religionists, they suddenly began to bombard the mosque of the Kaaba, the most sacred shrine of all Islam. One shell actually hit the black stone burning a hole in the holy carpet and killing nine Arabs who were kneeling in prayer. Hussein's followers were so enraged by this impious act that they swarmed over the walls of the great fort and captured it after desperate hand-to-hand fighting with knives and daggers.

JERUSALEM AS THE MYSTERY BABYLON?

Argument:

"Mystery Babylon is clearly the Jerusalem just before the Second Coming of Christ. It will be the center of a world empire and the capital of the false Christ with the false Elijah. Pay heed to the truth of God regarding these matters." "Behold, I have told you before."[20]

Some argue that Jerusalem is this Mystery Babylon. They point to a verse in Revelation where Jerusalem is called "the great city." According to this view, this correlates with "the woman" in "Mystery Babylon:"

"And the woman which thou sawest is that great city, which reigneth over the kings of the earth."[21]

"Their corpses will lie in the main street of the great city, which has the symbolic names 'Sodom' and 'Egypt,' where indeed their Lord was crucified."[22]

Yet this view ignores the fact that the Bible has 17 references to the "great city" such as "Resen" [23] and "Gibeon." [24]

An allegoric city is not necessarily a single place. Jeremiah 22:6, combines all of Judah as a "great city:"

"For thus saith the LORD unto the king's house of Judah; Thou [art] Gilead unto me, [and] the head of Lebanon: [yet] surely I will make thee a wilderness, [and] *cities* [which] are not inhabited."

It goes on to refer to Judah being this symbolic "Gilead" and one "great city:"

"And many nations shall pass by this city, and they shall say every man to his neighbor, Wherefore hath the LORD done thus unto this *great city*?"

This usage is nothing new; Jonah 1:2 refers to Nineveh as "that great city."

If the "great city" is a hint to link it to the Mystery Babylon, then why would the Bible use the word "Mystery" and "unknown," in one reference, yet "where our Lord was crucified [Jerusalem]" in another? This by no means leaves it a Mystery.

WHO IS "THE MOUNT OF ESAU"?

"Shall I not in that day, saith the LORD, even destroy the wise [men] out of Edom, and understanding out of the mount of Esau?" [25]

We are definitely talking about a time prior to the Kingdom age:

"And saviors shall come up on mount Zion to judge the *mount of Esau*; and the kingdom shall be the LORD'S."

"The mount of Esau" cannot be a literal mountain, but a kingdom or nation.

"As thou didst rejoice at the inheritance of the house of Israel because it was desolate, so will I do unto thee: thou shalt be desolate, O *mount Seir*, and all _Idumea_, [even] all of it: and they shall know that I [am] the LORD." [26] Mount Seir is what the Bible calls *All-Idumea*.

"God came from Teman, and the Holy One from mount Paran. Selah. His glory covered the heavens, and the earth was full of his praise." [27] This is definitely Messianic, pertaining to the Second Coming.

"He beheld, and drove asunder the nations (Midian); and the everlasting hills (nations) did bow" (vs. 6), *"Thou didst thresh the heathen in anger..."* (vs. 12)

So, "Mount Seir, and all Idumea" is the collective title of all the nations mentioned in Ezekiel. We get further clarification in Isaiah 34:2:

"For the indignation of the LORD [is] upon all nations, and [his] fury upon all their armies: he hath utterly destroyed them, he hath delivered them to the slaughter."

A group of nations is summed up with a reference to a specific region that is used to depict a judgment on them collectively:

"...for the LORD hath a sacrifice in Bozrah and a great slaughter in the land of Idumea." [28]

Idumea again encompasses *all nations* and *all their armies* in Isaiah 34:2. Bozrah and Idumea are located in Edom and are descendants of Esau.

"For [it is] the day of the LORD'S vengeance, [and] the year of recompenses for the controversy of Zion." [29]

This is the day of the Lord for Zion. Finally, Messiah will solve this conflict between Islam and Israel.

THE CHURCH IN ROME

Argument: 1 Peter 5:13 refers to the church in Rome as "she who is in Babylon." This phrase may indicate that the Epistle was written in Babylon. Some commentators take this as a literal Babylon, while others see it as a code word for Rome. Many believe that Peter was martyred in Rome.

However, there is no record in Scripture that Peter was ever in Rome. The argument that Peter intended a literal Babylon is plausible even if Babylon was destroyed. In Peter's day, Babylon was still a territory, even after its destruction. "The ancient city of Mesopotamia, an area which was then a center of pure and uncompromising Judaism..." Act 2:9 tells us they were in the Pentecost crowd. "After the fall of Jerusalem in 70 A.D. Babylonia became, and for centuries remained, a seat of Jewish Schools devoted to the study and interpretation of the law."

Traditional Christians want to support the idea that Peter was the first to establish the Church in Rome. The writings of Irenaeus and Eusebius are filled with error and contradict the Bible. Paul, who wrote much of the New Testament either near or from the city of Rome itself, commented on many Christians by name, but made not one mention of Peter. This is notable, particularly because in the tradition of the Church of Rome, Peter was supposed to be there from 42 to 67 A.D. Paul wrote the Book of Romans in 58 A.D. All this without even a greeting to Peter, the leader of the Church in Rome?

Then in Romans 1:11, "For I long to see you, that I may impart unto you some spiritual gift, to the end you may be *established*." Peter spends 16 years in Rome while Paul is still "establishing" the Church? It is quite plausible that on Pentecost, with the Romans there, (Acts 2), they went back to Rome to found the Church. If Peter were in Rome from 42 to 67, then why was there no mention of him by Paul who was also taken to Rome to serve in prison? Visitors were allowed to see him while he was under house arrest. Also, 2 Timothy 4:10-11 states:

"Only Luke is with me. Take Mark, and bring him with thee: for he is profitable to me for the ministry."

Did Paul forget Peter? No, *Peter was never in Rome.* Many Protestants reject the establishment of the Papacy by Peter in Rome, so why cling to the illogical use of "Babylon" as a code word for Rome?

Chapter Twelve
The One-World Government

Argument:

The whole world under Antichrist will gather against Jerusalem, and that will require a one-world government. The Bible clearly states that "...all the people of the earth [shall] be gathered together against it." [1]

Response:

Other than the account of the great flood, there is not a single reference in the entire Bible to "the whole earth" or "the whole world" that literally encompasses every part of earth. For example, when Alexander the Great ruled the lands from Greece to India, the Bible describes this area as "the face of the whole earth." The Bible frequently uses phrases such as "all nations" or "the whole world" as a figurative expression for an entire region.

"And as I was considering, behold, (a) male goat came from the west on the face of the whole earth." [2]

Alexander's empire, the male goat, never touched Western Europe, yet the Bible uses the phrase the "whole earth." We see a similar usage in I Kings:

"And all the earth sought to Solomon, to hear his wisdom, which God had put in his heart." [3]

The Hebrew word used in this passage from I Kings, *vkol ha'eretz,* means "the whole world." But did "the whole world" come to King Solomon? That is, did those that came to Solomon include the Chinese, the Aborigines in Australia, Africans, and all Indians? Obviously, the context is *all the world that was known then*—not all of *today's* known world. So, in context, kings from different regions of the then-known world would have come to meet King Solomon, not every individual person living in every city.

We see how critical it is to have the accurate interpretation of Biblical prophecy. When we read in Revelation 13 that "no man can buy or sell, save he that had the mark…," we do not conclude "all men in the world" but rather all those men living in the dominion of the Antichrist.

> "The burden of the word of the LORD for Israel, saith the LORD, which stretcheth forth the heavens, and layeth the foundation of the earth, and formeth the spirit of man within him. Behold, I will make Jerusalem a cup of trembling unto all the people round about, when they shall be in the siege both against Judah and against Jerusalem. And in that day will I make Jerusalem a burdensome stone for all people: all that burden themselves with it shall be cut in pieces, though all the people of the earth be gathered together against it."[4]

Note that in verse 1, those for whom Jerusalem is a "cup of trembling" are identified: "all the people round about" (KJV), "near by nations" (NTL), "peoples around" (NASB), "surrounding peoples" (NKJV), and finally "round about" (RSV). Further reading reveals that the nations "round about" Jerusalem are Muslim nations; these are the nations that receive the wrath of God. Since the rebirth of Israel in 1948, there have been five wars, all of them waged and lost by the surrounding Islamic nations.

> "Therefore I make a decree, That every people, nation, and language, which speak any thing amiss against the God of Shadrach, Meshach, and Abednego, shall be cut in pieces, and their houses shall be made a dunghill: because there is no other God that can deliver after this sort."[5]

Nebuchadnezzar's decree quite clearly cannot be taken literally to mean every person, nation, and language. It is obvious that Nebuchadnezzar could issue decrees only for those people under his authority—that is, the Babylonian Empire of that time but not the whole earth.

> "Howbeit every nation made gods of their own, and put [them] in the houses of the high places which the Samaritans had made, every nation in their cities wherein they dwelt."[6]

Did the inhabitants of every nation have Samaritan gods in their homes? Of course not. This passage concerns a local area where such practices were the norm. "All" is simply used to add emphasis.

In Isaiah 37:18, we read that "the kings of Assyria have laid waste *all the nations,* and their countries." Did King Sennachrib of Assyria actually destroy all nations on the face of the earth? Again, "all" is used as an emphatic statement of might and power.

Return to the passage in Zechariah 12,

> "The burden of the word of the LORD for Israel, saith the LORD, which stretcheth forth the heavens, and layeth the foundation of the earth, and formeth the spirit of man within him. Behold, I will make Jerusalem a cup of trembling unto *all the people round about,* when they shall be in the siege both against Judah and against Jerusalem. And in that day will I make Jerusalem a burdensome stone for *all people:* all that burden themselves with it shall be cut in pieces, *though all the people of the earth be gathered together against it.*"[7]

Verse 1 identifies who the 'all the people' are in that category; that is, those who are "round about" Jerusalem. Also, consider:

"And it shall come to pass in that day, that I will seek to destroy all the nations that come against Jerusalem."[8]

The use of "all" in the above passage applies only to those nations that come up against Jerusalem.

> And it shall come to pass, that every one that is left of all the nations which came against Jerusalem shall even go up from year to year to worship the King, the LORD of hosts, and to keep the feast of tabernacles.[9]

Here, *all* does not mean literally the entire world; this passage obviously refers to Messiah's millennial reign following His return to the earth. In this context, "all the nations" refers to the survivors of nations, those nations that *did not* come up against Jerusalem. And although the nations that come up against Jerusalem will be destroyed, that does not mean that every individual that shares some affinity with that nation will be destroyed. Interestingly, the 'End-Times Empire' is set to resemble the Greek Empire:

"When I have bent Judah for me, filled the bow with Ephraim, and raised up thy sons, O Zion, against thy sons, O Greece, and made thee as the sword of a mighty man." [10]

Islam is represented in many nations today, including Great Britain and France. Loosely speaking, Islam does have a presence in nearly the whole world. Until recently, Pakistan was considered the only Muslim nation with extensive nuclear capabilities, including the atomic bomb, and there are suspicions that Pakistan has sold nuclear weapons to Libya, Iran, and North Korea. However, Iran is now a major focus of concern regarding nuclear armament.

Scripture also identifies those who would come up against the Antichrist as the ships of Kittim, which refers to the islands and coastline of the Mediterranean and, in a wider sense, the Roman legions. Ararat, Minni, and Ashkenaz also have been identified as those who will oppose the Antichrist. Now that we have learned *who*, the following passages identify the weapons of His (God's) indignation against Babylon.

"Behold, a people shall come from the north, and a great nation, and many kings shall be raised up from the coasts of the earth." [11]

> "For, lo, I will raise and cause to come up against Babylon
> an assembly of great nations from the north country: and
> they shall set themselves in array against her; from thence
> she shall be taken: their arrows [shall be] as of a mighty
> expert man; none shall return in vain." [12]

Many prophecy experts identify the lands from the north as Great Britain and the United States; these two nations have been strong allies against Iraq (Babylon). Concerning the principle of dual fulfillment of this prophecy, these nations will be key players in the last days. They have demonstrated that they do not fear waging a battle against a national threat or for humanitarian intervention—regardless of how the international community views their actions.

Of course, if we were to believe that a revived Roman Empire is the kingdom of the Antichrist, then Britain would have to be part of that empire and thus capable of producing the Antichrist. This theory, however, does not stand in light of the above passages.

When have the British people ever wanted to drive the Jews to the sea? In fact, it was Lord Balfour who mandated that the Land be given back to the Jews. Indeed, Britain returned a portion of the land to the Jews, helping to establish the state of Israel. Britain was our ally in the first Gulf War when Iraq threatened the state of Israel by firing scud missiles at her, and our ally again in the current war against Iraq. We have seen Britain help Israel, and Britain shall rise up again and be used as an instrument of God.

THE NATIONS ROUND ABOUT

Argument:

"All the people round about" refers to "all the people of the earth gathered together against it [Israel]" (around it) and not strictly the nations around Israel.

Response:

This cannot be true when we examine other related passages of Scripture.

> "And render unto our *neighbors* sevenfold into their bosom their reproach, wherewith they have reproached thee, O Lord." [13]

> "Thou makest us a strife unto our *neighbors*: and our enemies laugh among themselves." [14]

> "Thus saith the LORD against all mine evil *neighbors*, that touch the inheritance which I have caused my people Israel to inherit; Behold, I will pluck them out of their land, and pluck out the house of Judah from among them." [15]

THE QUESTION OF THE JEWISH ANTICHRIST

For years, the Christian world pointed a finger at the Jews as the origin of the Antichrist; however, the Bible suggests the Antichrist will likely be Muslim. The sole basis for a Jewish Antichrist stems from *one* verse in Daniel, chapter 11:37: [ASV]

"Neither shall he regard the gods of his fathers, nor the desire of women, nor regard any god; for he shall magnify himself above all." [KJV]

"He will have no regard for the gods of his ancestors, or for the gods beloved by women, or for any other god; for he will boast that he is greater than them all." [NTL]

"He will show no regard for the gods of his fathers or for the desire of women, nor will he show regard for any [other] god; for he will magnify himself above [them] all."[NASB]

"He shall give no heed to the gods of his fathers, or to the one beloved by women; he shall not give heed to any other god, for he shall magnify himself above all." [RSV]

"Neither shall he regard the gods of his fathers, nor the desire of women, nor regard any god; for he shall magnify himself above all." [HNV]

In this passage, the Hebrew word used for God is not *Elohim* (the God) but rather *elohai* (gods). The difference is crucial. *Elohei* means gods in the sense of idols, as used in Deuteronomy. The verse states that the Antichrist will not worship the idols his father worshiped. The King James translators, living in particularly anti-Semitic times in England, must have fallen into temptation to use the ancient Jewish expression "*God* of his fathers." Unfortunately, the indictment of a Jewish Antichrist has persisted for centuries. The aversion of the King James translators to Judaism is obvious in Acts 12:4, where "Easter" is substituted for "Passover." The idea of a gentile Antichrist is much more supportable. Throughout the Bible, those who persecuted the Jews were gentiles, from the pharaoh to the foreign kings to Nero and the Caesars.[16]

Chapter Thirteen
The Antichrist, the Beast, and the Mark

IS THE BEAST THE ANTICHRIST?

Argument:

The beast is the Antichrist himself. He will be killed then revive from the dead.

Response:

Imagine Antichrist reviving himself. If this could happen, it would mean that Satan has the ability to revive the dead. This cannot be; Satan does not possess the attributes of God. He is not a giver of life, cannot create life, and cannot revive the dead.

Further, try to imagine a seven-headed beast[1] as the Antichrist. One would have to concede that this being is, at the very least, an odd looking ruler, and consider that one of the heads receives a death wound.[2] It is time to put this notion to rest forever.

There are many erroneous interpretations of the beast and the Antichrist because of the failure to grasp fully the meaning of "beast" as it is used in prophecy. The question is whether references to "beast" were actually references to Satan, to a man, or to an empire. Throughout Scripture, *beast* or *animal* is used to symbolize an empire or kingdom; the king or ruler of the empire is symbolized by a horn. So, a beast in the context of Scripture could be an empire with Satan as its head (or horn).

> "And there appeared another wonder in heaven; and behold a great red dragon, having seven heads and ten horns, and seven crowns upon his heads."[3]

We must understand the use of these symbols in Scripture: the dragon is Satan, the heads are his kingdoms, and the horns are the rulers of those kingdoms.

There is a great deal of misunderstanding of the following passage:

"And the beast was taken, and with him the false prophet that wrought miracles before him, with which he deceived them that had received the mark of the beast, and them that worshiped his image. These both were cast alive into a lake of fire burning with brimstone."[4]

A common assumption is that the beast is a man. However, it is clear from Scripture that a single entity does not necessarily represent a single being. For instance, in Revelation 19:7, we read "Let us be glad and rejoice, and give honor to him: for the marriage of the Lamb is come, and his wife hath made herself ready."

Just as the "wife" (bride) of Revelation 19:7 represents many people from different nations and tongues, so does the "beast" of Revelation 19:20 represent tribes and nations. The metaphorical use of the beast and the bride is consistent with the use of figures of speech throughout Scripture. We have already seen that the beast symbolizes a kingdom or empire. Every instance of the word *beast* in Daniel, chapter 7, verses 5, 6, 7, 11, 19, and 23, is a reference to an empire— with rulers or kings represented by horns.

"These great beasts [empires] are four in number are four kings [horns] who will arise from the earth."[5]

The beast also represents a group of people from every nation, tribe, and tongue that follows a false religion and its leader (horn). So, when the beast is taken and the "false prophet" with him, we understand that the empire and its leader (horn) are removed.

We know from Scripture that Satan seeks to be like God, to rule the earth, to have his own kingdom. With this in mind, we see that an Islamic revival is quite plausible as Satan attempts to woo followers. Jesus, our Messiah, desires His Bride (the saints) for love, and Satan desires his kingdom for destruction—parallels at opposite ends of the moral spectrum. Just as the Bride awaits the coming Bridegroom, Islam is waiting for the leader they call *Mahdi* who will lead them in the footsteps of his predecessor Muhammad. Thus we see the beast of Revelation 13:3 waiting and determined to follow the previous beast whose "deadly wound was healed."

Another common misunderstanding concerning the prophetic use of beasts is found in the interpretation of the "four beasts"[6]

> "And I beheld, and, lo, in the midst of the throne and of the four beasts, and in the midst of the elders, stood a Lamb as it had been slain, having seven horns and seven eyes, which are the seven Spirits of God sent forth into all the earth."[7]

The four beasts in the above passage are often confused for Cherubim; however, they actually represent the four beasts of Daniel 7, awaiting judgment at the feet of Messiah. The whole world throughout history is revived for Judgment Day. The four beasts in this passage symbolize all kingdoms and their final submission to, and worship of, the Lamb (Christ). "Every knee shall bow and every tongue confess that Jesus Christ is Lord."[8]

WHAT IS THE NAME OF THE BEAST?

The Bible provides three choices for the name of the beast, that is, three indications of allegiance:

> "And he causeth all, both small and great, rich and poor, free and bond, to receive a mark in their right hand, or on their foreheads: And that no man might buy or sell, save he that had the mark, or the name of the beast, or the number of his name. Here is wisdom. Let him that hath understanding count the number of the beast: for it is the number of a man; and his number is Six hundred threescore and six."[9]

The three means of indicating allegiance to the beast are the mark, the name, and the number.

> "And the smoke of their torment ascendeth up for ever and ever: and they have no rest day nor night, who worship the beast and his image, and whosoever receiveth the mark of his name."[10]

Now, what does the word "name" mean in this context?

"And upon her forehead [was] a name written, MYSTERY, BABYLON THE GREAT, THE MOTHER OF HARLOTS AND ABOMINATIONS OF THE EARTH."[11]

In Scripture, a name indicates the nature and character of the one who possesses it.

"And he [was] clothed with a vesture dipped in blood: and his name is called The Word of God."[12]

"And he hath on [his] vesture and on his thigh a name written, KING OF KINGS, AND LORD OF LORDS."[13]

"And I stood upon the sand of the sea, and saw a beast rise up out of the sea, having seven heads and ten horns, and upon his horns ten crowns, and upon his heads the name of blasphemy."[14]

So "the name of blasphemy" is simply a title that reveals the nature of the Antichrist. Consider the Islamic statement of faith, the Shahada: *La ilah ha il Allah, Muhammadan Rasul-Allah*, which means, "There is no God but Allah and Muhammad is the one sent by Allah." This declaration is blasphemous in its attempt to assign an importance to Muhammad that belongs only to Messiah. *In fact, according to Islamic theology, Muhammad is greater than Jesus.*

THE ANTICHRIST DENIES THE FATHER AND THE SON

"Who is a liar but he that denieth that Jesus is the Christ? He is Antichrist that denieth the Father and the Son."[15]

To blaspheme God is to deny His attributes—to deny that He is the Father, that He has a Son, and that Christ, the Word of God, took on human flesh. Islam is actually a polemic against Christianity. It is the only religion with the central purpose of denying that God is our Father and that He has a Son who came in the flesh.

The claim of a Jewish Antichrist can have no validity, since the Antichrist comes to destroy Israel. Further, Jews worship the one true God of the Bible. The theory of a Jewish Antichrist was spawned by anti-Semitic Christendom.

The idea of a Catholic Antichrist cannot stand up to the scrutiny of this passage from 1 John. In fact, church creed professes the doctrine of Father and Son. The Roman Catholic Church is indeed vindicated by this passage.

The issue of Father and Son is actually not an issue at all in Hinduism, Buddhism, or other religions. Among all world religions, only the tenets of Islam deny the Father and the Son. In fact, if you ask Muslims why they reject Christianity, they will happily tell you that God is not the Father of Jesus, God never became flesh, God does not have a Son, and Jesus was never crucified and did not rise from the dead. These are the leading arguments expressed in the Quran and the most frequently voiced by Muslims.

> "And they say, The All-merciful has taken unto Himself a son. You have indeed advanced something hideous. As if the skies are about to burst, the earth to split asunder and its mountain to fall down in the utter ruin for that they have attributed to the All-merciful a son; and behaves not the All-merciful to take a son. None there in the heavens and earth but comes to the All-merciful, as a servant." [16]

THE QUESTION OF "666"

Consider the English translation of the verse:

"Here is wisdom. Let him that hath understanding count the number of the beast: for it is the number of a man; and his number is Six hundred threescore and six." [17]

An examination of the original manuscript provides insight into this formula for the number of man. Some fragments of the Oxyrhynchus Papyri of the New Testament did not count the number of the beast as 666, but instead, 616 in one manuscript and 646 in another. How can we determine which one is correct?

Figure 1 The newest volume of Oxyrhynchus Papyri (P.Oxy. LVI 4499) contains a fragmentary papyrus of Revelation which is the earliest known witness to some sections (late third / early fourth century). The number—chi, iota, stigma (hexakosiai deka hex)—is in the third line of the fragment.

In the fragment shown here, we can see a vertical Allah inscribed in Arabic calligraphy as it appears in some Muslim writings.

It is possible that the Apostle John's revelation appeared as Arabic text with the two words *Bism Allah* and that John faithfully recorded what he saw.

Did John see a "sideways Allah," or did the scholars who copied the manuscript simply change it, making it appear to be the Greek letter *digamma* which no longer exists?

The Greek letters are *chi xi stigma*; however, the last letter no longer exists in modern Greek. Some experts in ancient Greek even argue that the last letter is not *stigma* but *stigma score*.

The translators no doubt transliterated word for word, then ascribed the interpretation that was most logical for the context of the verse:

Hode	here
Esti	is
Sophia	wisdom
Echo	let him that
nous	understanding
Psephizo	count/decide
Arithmos	the number/multitude
Therion	of the beast
Gar	for
Esti	it is

Arithmos	the number/multitude
Anthropos	of a man
Kai	and
Autos	his
Arithmos	number/multitude
chi xi stigma	

Revelation 13:18

It is plausible that the characters *chi xi stigma* are not actually Greek characters at all but rather a *symbol* that John saw and inscribed on the manuscript. Compare the "X" in the third line of Figure 1 (previous page) with Image 4 below, which is actually the Islamic symbol of two crossed swords.

The next word in the fragment appears to be "Allah" written vertically in Arabic script. It is impossible to know whether the scholars who copied the original text simply did not recognize the Arabic, and, in an attempt to make sense of it, inscribed what appears to be the Greek letter *Xi*. It is quite possible that John actually saw the mark of the beast—*Bism Allah*, which is translated "in the name of Allah"—and that he simply recorded it as accurately as he could.

Also, consider that the Greek word *Psephizo* can be translated "to decide" and that *Arithmos* can simply mean a "multitude." With this in mind, an alternate translation would read:

Here is wisdom. Let him that hath understanding decide [who] the multitude of the beast [is], for it is the multitude of a man [that is, Muhammad] and his multitude [are] "In the Name of Allah."

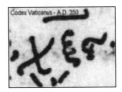

Compare this with the following passage concerning the multitude of the beast.

"And he saith unto me, the waters which thou sawest, where the whore sitteth, are peoples, and multitudes, and nations, and tongues." [18]

321

The whore sitting on the beast controls the "multitudes," which are peoples and nations.

> "And he causeth all, both small and great, rich and poor, free and bond, to receive a mark in their right hand, or in their foreheads: And that no man might buy or sell, save he that had the **mark** [Greek *charagma*], or the **name** of the beast, or the **number**/[multitude] of his name." [19]

Here, we see the three variations of the name of the beast: mark, name (title), or multitude (follower of this multitude).

THE BADGE OF SERVITUDE

The Greek word *charagma* used for "mark" is actually a "badge of servitude" or of allegiance and servanthood. *Strong's Hebrew Lexicon* defines *charagma* as "the mark stamped on the forehead or the right hand as the badge of the followers of the Antichrist." Note that the phrase "right arm" is from the Greek *dexios*, which could also be translated "right side."

The Islamic Shahadatan is actually a declaration of allegiance and servitude to Allah and Muhammad; the inscription of this declaration is worn by millions on the forehead or right arm. It can be seen among Muslim demonstrators and jihadists (See Images 9-12). There is absolutely nothing in the text of Revelation 13 to suggest that followers of the Antichrist will be required to have a chip implanted on their foreheads or their arms/hands.

Image 2
"*Bismillah*" in Arabic.

Image 2
A smaller version of
bismillah.

Image 1
The two swords of Islam on a
note with "*Bismillah Alrahman
Alraheem*" on the header. This is
common on all stationery used
throughout the Islamic world.

Image 3
The crescent moon, the Quran and
the two swords as emblems of the
Islamic resistance movement.

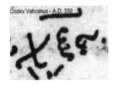

Image 4
Codex Vaticanus, AD 350.
Bismillah (In the name of
Allah) is clearly visible.
The word "Allah" is at an
upward angle and the two
swords are clear.

Image 5
Bismillah Alrahman Alraheem. The first two words are the same as in John's manuscript. Again, the "Allah" is vertical in the Codex.

Image 6
(similar to image 5)

Image 7
The two swords on the Dome of the Rock. The two swords have always been the symbol of Islam.

Image 8
(similar to Image 7) From Nusseibeh's university, Al-Quds Sari Nusseibeh.

The above images illustrate the Bismillah, the same Arabic text that can be seen on the original manuscript fragments of John's Revelation. The Bismillah is commonly used at the beginning of all books, letters, speeches, agreements, etc.

Note Image 8, the symbol for Nusseibeh's university, Al-Quds Sari Nusseibeh. The crossed swords of the Bismillah are used in the emblem of this university, generally claimed to be "moderate" by many left-wing Israeli politicians. In fact, Israeli Foreign Minister Shimon Peres once called Nusseibeh "courageous." However, in a study released by Palestinian Media Watch (PMW), Itamar Marcus documents Nusseibeh's use of "moderate" language during diplomatic encounters in English, while he continues to support terrorism and anticipate the destruction of Israel when speaking in Arabic. As evidence, Marcus cites an interview broadcast on Al Jazeera TV in which Nusseibeh, along with a Hamas leader and the mother of a suicide terrorist, expresses admiration for terrorists and their families.

Images 9 and 10: Chechnyan fighters proudly displaying the two crossed swords on their foreheads, the same symbol seen in the Revelation manuscript fragment.

Image 9: This picture was published in most Western newspapers only once. A few short TV stories on the subject were aired. Compare that to the daily barrage of anti-Serb propaganda from the same media outlets.

Image 10: The Times, December 11, 1995, page A10

One of the Bosnian Army Muslim brigades marches through Zenica in a demonstration of strength by 10,000 soldiers.

WHAT IS THE IMAGE OF THE BEAST?

We have a plausible explanation for the mark and the name of the beast, but what about the "image of the beast?"

"...that the image of the beast should both speak, and cause that as many as would not worship the image of the beast should be killed." [20]

Keep in mind that Revelation is allegorical.

> "And I stood upon the sand of the sea, and saw a beast
> rise up out of the sea, having seven heads and ten horns,
> and upon his horns ten crowns, and upon his heads the
> name of blasphemy." [21]

Reading the symbolism in prophetic passages, we see an empire coming out of (the waters, sea) the nations, multitudes, tribes, and different tongues. The empire is made up of seven countries that represent all past empires that have ruled the Middle East. And the empire which emerges is blasphemous.

> "And the beast which I saw was like unto a leopard, and
> his feet were as [the feet] of a bear, and his mouth as the
> mouth of a lion: and the dragon gave him his power, and
> his seat, and great authority." [22]

326

The emerging empire is composed of past empires: the lion (Babylon), bear (Persia), leopard (Greece). Satan gives this empire its seat of power (the seat of Satan).

> "And I saw one of his heads as it were wounded to death; and his deadly wound was healed: and all the world wondered after the beast."[23]

The empire fell and was revived. A popular theory is that Antichrist is killed then revived from the dead; however, we know that this cannot be so, because Satan does not have the power to give life.

> "And they worshiped the dragon which gave power unto the beast: and they worshiped the beast, saying, Who [is] like unto the beast? Who is able to make war with him?"[24]

They followed Satan who revived the empire; and they were filled with pride, calling for war.

> "And there was given unto him a mouth speaking great things and blasphemies; and power was given unto him to continue forty [and] two months. And he opened his mouth in blasphemy against God, to blaspheme his name, and his tabernacle, and them that dwell in heaven."[25]

The blasphemy of the one true God will continue for three and one-half years.

> "And it was given unto him to make war with the saints, and to overcome them: and power was given him over all kindreds, and tongues, and nations."[26]

This system persecuted God's people. The empire was given power to control those who speak different languages within his dominion.

> "And all that dwell upon the earth shall worship him, whose names are not written in the book of life of the Lamb slain from the foundation of the world."[27]

Everyone on earth, except those redeemed by the Lamb and whose names are written in His book, worshiped him, the Antichrist.

"If any man have an ear, let him hear. He that leadeth into captivity shall go into captivity: he that killeth with the sword must be killed with the sword." [28] The final outcome is destruction.

"Here is the patience and the faith of the saints." [29]

The following passage speaks of the tribulation for the true believers.

"And I beheld another beast coming up out of the earth; and he had two horns like a lamb, and he spake as a dragon." [30]

The empire is re-created and it emerges with two systems (possibly Shia and Sunni).

"And he exerciseth all the power of the first beast before him, and causeth the earth and them which dwell therein to worship the first beast, whose deadly wound was healed." [31]

This final empire resembles the one before it: revived Islam perhaps?

> "And he doeth great wonders, so that he maketh fire come down from heaven on the earth in the sight of men, and deceiveth them that dwell on the earth by [the means of] those miracles which he had power to do in the sight of the beast; saying to them that dwell on the earth, that they should make an image to the beast, which had the wound by a sword, and did live." [32]

So we have the revival of the false miracle, *Satan's* creation of the false miracle is the Quran. Satan called on his followers to revive the old religion of Islamic fundamentalism, which was wounded by the the sword yet survived to regain power and influence.

> "And he had power to give life unto the image of the beast that the image of the beast should both speak, and cause that as many as would not worship the image of the beast should be killed." [33]

Those who do not adhere to this revived system will be killed. Everyone within his dominion who refuses to declare this blasphemous title will be put to the sword. That is, all will be required to put a mark (banner of servitude) on their foreheads or right arm, and those who do not wear the mark cannot participate in commerce.

The word "image" is used once in the Bible in relationship to kingdoms:

"For the children of Israel shall abide many days without a king, and without a prince, and without a sacrifice, and without an image, and without an ephod, and [without] seraphim."[34]

How could Israel be "without an image?" Obviously, Israel can have no emblem if it has no kingdom.

We see in Revelation, the Antichrist will revive a kingdom, an emblem, and a banner. This empire, which was wounded and destroyed, will attempt to regain its former power. The mark is also the emblem/image of the beast/empire. The Islamic emblem imprinted on arms and foreheads is an excellent example of what is happening today all over the Muslim world. To make an image of a kingdom is to revive it and give it life. As we find in Revelation 13:14: "that they should make an image to the beast, which had the wound by a sword, and did live."

To make or carry an image (emblem) of something is akin to expressing allegiance to whatever the image or emblem represents; that is, they submit to the will of the beast/empire.

It is fascinating that the crescent moon was an emblem used by Babylon and Rome as well as by Islam. The crescent moon is also the emblem of Satan or Lucifer, *Helel ben Shachar* (Isaiah 14). The literal meaning of *Helel* is "crescent moon" and the sign of the "dawn." And the false miracle is the unleashing of Satan into the body of a man (the Antichrist), who will come from the north of Israel.

We find support for this interpretation in the words spoken by Jesus as recorded in Revelation 2:12-13:

"And to the angel of the church in Pergamos write; These things saith he which hath the sharp sword with two edges; I know thy works, and where thou dwellest, even where Satan's seat is: and thou holdest fast my name, and hast not denied my faith, even in those days wherein Antipas was my faithful martyr, who was slain among you, where Satan dwelleth."

Pergamos (Pergamon) was and is in Turkey—north of Israel. This passage alone names symbols representative of Satan/Lucifer, "son of the morning," a crescent moon and a star (Venus). Interestingly, these symbols appear on the Turkish flag and were part of an emblem on the uniform of the Ottoman Turks.

The Quran speaks of the Dawn, when the angelic host came down from heaven (Quran, Surat Al-Qadr). Once again, let's look at the Night of Vision:

> "We have sent it to thee in the Night of Vision, what do you know of this Night of Vision. The Night of Vision is better than a thousand months. The **angelic hosts descend** [to earth] in it with the **Spirit** by command of **their Lord**. Peace shall it be until the rising of the **Dawn** (Morning star)."

According to tradition, this event occurred on the 27th day of the month of Ramadan; that is, Muhammad had his encounter with the angel who revealed the Quran. Ramadan is the same month during which Muslims fast from dawn to dusk, basing the fasting season on the appearance of the moon. These words, in fact, parallel Scripture regarding Satan (the Dawn) being cast out of heaven, and the fallen angels.

EUROPE WILL FIGHT THE ANTICHRIST

Daniel 11:30 says that Roman ships (out of the west) will come against the Antichrist: "For the ships of Kittim shall come against him" (the Antichrist). How can we determine the origin of the ships and who has control?

In Numbers 24:24, Balaam foretold "that ships shall come from the coast of Kittim, and afflict Eber." Daniel also prophesied in chap. 11, verse 30 that the ships of Kittim would come against the king of the north. Josephus identifies Cyprus as Kittim, whose ancient capital was called Kition by the Greeks. Cyprus extended to include lands west of Syria, all of Greece, and as far as Illyricum and Italy (which supports Israel). Note that none of these lands is Muslim. The name was first used to identify the Phoenician port of Citium in Cyprus. In fact, *Kittim* actually appears in the Dead Sea Scrolls and was also used by the Romans in the Septuagint, Daniel 11:30. Again, we see that if Antichrist were to come from Western Roman Empire of Europe, the ships of Kittim would not come against him.

In general, the term Kittim (Chittim) was used to refer to all the islands and settlements along the seacoasts, as well as to the people who succeeded them when the Phoenician power decayed. Thus, Kittim generally refers to the islands and coasts of the Mediterranean and the races that inhabit those areas. The Dodanim, who were leaders of a race that descended from Javan (Genesis 10:4), were known in history as the Dardani; they originally lived in Illyricum and ethnically are related to Kittim. In I Chronicles 1:7, the Dardani are referred to as Rodanim. Both the LXX and the Samaritan Version render Rodanim as Rhodii, so some conclude that the Rhodians are the inhabitants of the island of Rhodes.

Are the European nations mentioned in the Bible? Yes. "The ships of Chittim" in the Septuagint is literally Romans, which included all the nations from Cyprus to Spain. According to the prophecy of Daniel 11, they attacked Antiochus; and if we are correct regarding a dual fulfillment, they will also attack the Antichrist. No European country is featured in End-Times prophecy as receiving a judgment of wrath.

Chapter Fourteen
HOW TO INTERPRET END-TIME PROPHECY

This is the part of prophecy study that can cause the most civil of men or women to go for the jugular. That's partly because we all want the story to have the ending we envision, a very human defense against the fear of our own annihilation.

But the larger issue is that no one wants his or her religion, nation or people to be revealed as the ultimate bad guy, the one that turns out to be the harlot city or the beast or the Antichrist. That would overturn centuries of religious doctrine and could mean the death of an organized faith.

But prophecy study isn't a cafeteria; you can't pick and choose what you'd like for that particular day. Instead, the Bible lays out the menu. You cannot get to truth through pre-conceived notions.

For true Biblical study, you must use the tools and resources accepted by honest students and scholars, not those who would twist the text into a Biblical pretzel. So where do we start?

With Accurate History Books. We need to understand the time and place of the people who wrote down God's word. For that, we need history books that share *evidence*, not propaganda. Consider Bible study to be like an archaeological dig. You may start out to find the metal icons of an ancient pagan marketplace, but your shovel brings up bones from an old Jewish burial ground. No amount of wishing can change those bones to metal. Like a good archaeologist, you accept that they are bones. Evidence commands authority.

When the prophecy warns that the invader will come from the north, we can easily find out who that invader is by looking at ancient maps that show what nation or nations were north of Israel at that time. Names of nations change over time, but their physical locations on the earth do not. Neither do compasses.

Don't Make it Rocket Science. I was shocked when I encountered the Bible's relatively simple style. True, the language is old, and it is packed with beautiful figurative language and allusion, but it is still quite understandable. God not only gave us a wonderful gift, he made sure we could understand it.

"The Lord answered me and said: Write the vision and make it plain on tablets, that he may run who reads it."[1]

To aid in that understanding, you need to collect some tools, kind of like your own Biblical Home Depot.

Inductive Study. This means that we have to research *all* the ways a particular word or phrase is used throughout the Bible, not just one or two instances. Again, this requires that we throw off our hopes and preconceived ideas, remain objective and be willing to accept what we find. In other words, let the Bible do the teaching.

A Bible Dictionary and a Bible Search Engine are extremely helpful. Commentaries and lexicons are necessities for the layman. I have found that **www.blueletterBible.org** is a great internet resource; it also provides access to the Hebrew and Greek texts.

Understanding of Literary Tradition. The Bible is fine literature, enlivened by the same oral and written traditions that humankind has used since Adam and Eve. It is filled with gorgeous figurative language, poetry and historical allusions.

Trained literary critics bring their knowledge of metaphor, simile, allegory, personification, symbol and allusion to the task, as well as a thorough knowledge of the times in which the author lived. Otherwise, literary criticism would be like the lazy student who refuses to study and claims, "the poem means whatever I want it to mean." No, the poem means what its author says.

Beyond that, the Bible is, of course, God's Word and He means for us to understand what He says, not what we would like Him to say.

"Knowing this first, that no prophecy of Scripture is of any private interpretation."[2]

> "The Jews from Berea were more fair-minded than those in Thessalonica, in that they received the word with all readiness, and searched the Scriptures daily to find out whether these things were so."[3]

The Bible is constant and does not change meaning with every altering wind. For the last two hundred years, the prevailing wind has suggested that the Antichrist will come out of the Roman Catholic Church and that we are somehow moving toward a one-world government. Close examination of the Scriptures totally disproves this theory.

Let's look at the use of figurative language in the Bible.

Symbolism

The symbols used in antiquity, commonly understood then even across cultures, are not so understandable to us, so we need background information. For example, one student might claim that "Mystery, Babylon the Great" in Revelation 17 is evidence that the Vatican is the only candidate to be the Harlot of Babylon. Why? Because it is the one city on earth that matches the Biblical description of having the symbolic seven mountains (Revelation 17:9). But the truth is, modern Rome actually encompasses *more* than seven hills. And Vatican Hill was *not* counted as one of the original seven.[4]

Ancient Babylon did have seven *artificial* hills within its walls. Constantinople, often called the "Second Rome," also had seven hills within its boundaries. And Mecca in Saudi Arabia is a city of seven hills—Mounts Abu Siba, Safa, Marwah, Milhah, Ma'aya, Hulayah, and Abu Ghuzlan. Therefore, there is more than one candidate. Also, Revelation 17:9 is not speaking of literal mountains.

"Here is the mind which has wisdom: The seven heads are seven mountains on which the woman sits. They are also seven kings."[5]

The seven mountains are used symbolically to represent seven kings. It is the same in the Greek text.

Some commonly used symbols are keys to understanding Biblical meaning:

1. Mountains Represent Kingdoms or Empires

My sheep wandered through all the mountains, and upon every high hill: yea, my flock was scattered upon all the face of the earth, and none did search or seek [after them].[6]

God's sheep (the Jews) were scattered in the Diaspora into many different nations. The word "mountain" is a symbol for nation, empire, or kingdom.

> "Behold, I [am] against thee, O destroying *mountain*, saith the LORD, which destroyest all the earth: and I will stretch out mine hand upon thee, and roll thee down from the rocks, and will make thee a burnt *mountain*."[7]

> "Then was the iron, the clay, the brass, the silver, and the gold, broken to pieces together, and became like the chaff of the summer threshing floors; and the wind carried them away, that no place was found for them: and the stone that smote the image became a great mountain, and filled the whole earth."[8]

> From the stone (Messiah), will come the Kingdom of God.

> [1]God is our refuge and strength, a very present help in trouble.
> [2]Therefore we will not fear, though the earth should change, though the mountains shake in the heart of the sea;
> [3]though its waters roar and foam, though the mountains tremble with its tumult. Selah
> [4]There is a river whose streams make glad the city of God, the holy habitation of the Most High.
> [5]God is in the midst of the city; it shall not be moved; God will help it when the morning dawns.
> [6]The nations are in an uproar, the kingdoms totter; he utters his voice, the earth melts.
> [7]The LORD of hosts is with us; the God of Jacob is our refuge.
> [8]They shall not hurt nor destroy in all my holy mountain: for the earth shall be full of the knowledge of the LORD, as the waters cover the sea.[9]

The above passage in Isaiah 11:6–9 is referring to the Millennium. The "mountain" means God's kingdom on earth, as Messiah rules the world. (Incidentally, only chapter 11 of Isaiah speaks of the Messianic kingdom.)

The primary and ultimate source for understanding the meaning of a word or symbol is always the text itself. A search engine makes this task an easier process.

2. Waters in Biblical Allegory are Always Peoples and Tongues

In addition to mountains symbolizing nations, Revelation 17:5 tells us explicitly that waters and rivers represent the flow of nations, peoples, and tongues.

"And he saith unto me, The waters which thou sawest, where the whore sitteth, are peoples, and multitudes, and nations, and tongues." [10]

> Oh that thou wouldest rend the heavens, that thou wouldest come down, that the mountains might flow down at thy presence, as [when] the melting fire burneth, the fire causeth the waters to boil, to make thy name known to thine adversaries, [that] the nations may tremble at thy presence! When thou didst terrible things [which] we looked not for, thou camest down, the mountains flowed down at thy presence. [11] ["Waters to boil" means the nations will rage.]

"I will make waste mountains and hills, and dry up all their herbs; and I will make the rivers islands, and I will dry up the pools." [12]

That He will make *the rivers islands, and...will dry up the pools* tells us that peoples, tribes, and tongues will cease to exist.

We can now apply some of these symbols to this passage from Isaiah:

> "When you pass through the waters, I [will be] with thee; and through the rivers, they shall not overflow thee: when you walk through the fire, you shall not be burned neither shall the flame kindle upon you." [13]

Interpretation: When you [Israelites] "pass through waters" (face the people against you) you will prevail. And when you walk through fire (the agonies of war and hate) and they declare war against you, you will not be hurt; you will prevail.

> "But I will put hooks in thy jaws, and I will cause the fish of thy rivers to stick unto thy scales, and I will bring thee up out of the midst of thy rivers, and all the fish of thy rivers shall stick unto thy scales." [14]

Interpretation: I will cause you to fall into a trap like a fish caught on a hook, and your people (all the fish of thy rivers) will follow you and fall.

> "And I will leave thee [thrown] into the wilderness, thee and all the fish of thy rivers: thou shalt fall upon the open fields; thou shalt not be brought together, nor gathered: I have given thee for meat to the beasts of the field and to the fowls of the heaven." [15]

Interpretation: You will fall in the desert (wilderness) with all your people (fish of thy rivers), and you will not be redeemed (not be brought together, nor gathered.)

> "And I will make the rivers dry, and sell the land into the hand of the wicked: and I will make the land waste, and all that is therein, by the hand of strangers: I the LORD have spoken [it]." [16]

Interpretation: I will make the land empty of people (the dry river) and a wicked stranger will destroy them.

Review the passage below from Daniel then compare it with the following passage from Psalm 72:8.

> "And there was given him dominion, and glory, and a kingdom, that all people, nations, and languages, should serve him: his dominion [is] an everlasting dominion, which shall not pass away, and his kingdom [that] which shall not be destroyed." [17]

He shall have dominion also from sea to sea, and from the river unto the ends of the earth. [18]

These two passages carry the same message; however, the passage from Psalms refers to peoples, nations, and tongues as waters, seas, and rivers.

3. A City is a Region or a Country

"…the woman which thou sawest is that great city, which reigneth over the kings of the earth." [19]

Again, as allegory, a "city" doesn't always denote a single place. For instance, the nation of Israel is also called *Medinat Yesrael*; in Aramaic and Arabic, the word *Medinat* is translated as city. In the following passage from Jeremiah, Gilead actually speaks of all of Judah as one city. The same is true for "house" which is not a single house but all the people of Judah.

> "For thus saith the LORD unto the king's house of Judah; Thou [art] Gilead unto me, [and] the head of Lebanon: [yet] surely I will make thee a wilderness, [and] cities [which] are not inhabited." (Judah itself will be a wilderness and like cities devoid of their people.) [20]

4. Trees (Other than Olive Trees) Represent Satanic Powers and Fallen Angels

> Behold, the Assyrian [was] a cedar in Lebanon with fair branches, and with a shadowing shroud, and of a high stature; and his top was among the thick boughs. The waters made him great, the deep set him up on high with her rivers running round about his plants, and sent out her little rivers unto all the trees of the field. [21]

Interpretation: The Assyrian (Satan) was made the greatest among all the angels, (a great cedar tree of beauty and importance) and the peoples and nations made him great, and they streamed to worship him and sent out ambassadors to serve him (waters, rivers running round about, little rivers.)

Above: Left, the Kaaba in Mecca   Above: Right, Pilgrimage

I have questioned the meaning of the "shadowing shroud" in this passage. Is it the black cloth that covers the Kaaba in Mecca? Or perhaps it refers to the hordes of people from all over the globe that come to worship Satan who is hidden in the black-shrouded Kaaba?

"The first angel sounded, and there followed hail and fire mingled with blood, and they were cast upon the earth: and the third part of trees was burnt up, and all green grass was burnt up." [22]

"A third of the trees" here refers to the one-third of the angelic host being cast from heaven.

"Though thou exalt [thyself] as the eagle, and though thou set thy nest among the stars, thence will I bring thee down, saith the LORD." [23]

Satan's pride "exalt [thyself]; set thy nest among the stars," will be punished.

Next, we have to address the sometimes-confusing "dual" fulfillments: events that are fulfilled both in the past and that will be fulfilled again in the future. For example, the destruction of ancient Babylon and the destruction of a future Babylon. Or Tyre and Edom. Or Israel of old and the prophesied Israel that has been realized in our lifetime. The Prophets spoke both of their own times and of what was to come.

THE BIBLE IS NOT SIMPLY A HISTORY BOOK

Daniel 9 talks about Titus, and chapters 8 and 11 discuss Antiochus Epiphanies. However, the references go beyond these two characters to the forces of good and evil, to Satan and Messiah. For instance, in Daniel 8:10 we see that he "cast down [some] of the host of heaven [fallen angels]," which is clearly a reference to the personification of Satan as the Antichrist, an End-Time prophecy. Antiochus represents the Antichrist. It is clear that the "little horn" of chapter 7 is the End-Time Antichrist who causes one-third of the angels to fall:

> And it waxed great, even to the host of heaven; and some of the host and of the stars it cast down to the ground, and trampled upon them. Yea, it magnified itself, even to the prince of the host; and from him the continual burnt-offering was taken away, and the place of his sanctuary was cast down.[24]

Antiochus is incapable of casting down heavenly stars (angels). Verse 25 of this same chapter also points to the Antichrist:

> "And through his cunning he shall cause craft to prosper in his hand; and he shall magnify himself in his heart, and in time of security shall he destroy many; he shall also stand up against the prince of princes; but he shall be broken without hand."[25]

Chapter Fifteen
The Revived Roman Empire and End-Times

UNDERSTANDING THE SEVEN MOUNTAINS OF REVELATION

Let's apply the study tools discussed in the last Chapter to understand the symbolic use of "mountains" in Scripture generally, and the meaning of the seven mountains of Revelation 17 specifically. Once done, we will see that speculation that the Vatican is the harlot city is invalid.

"So he carried me away in the Spirit into the wilderness. And I saw a woman sitting on a scarlet beast which was full of names of blasphemy, having seven heads and ten horns." [1]

"Here is the mind which has wisdom: The seven heads are seven mountains on which the woman sits. They are also seven kings." [2]

"Here is the mind which has wisdom" indicates we will learn truth or understanding. No need to struggle with the rest, since Scripture tells us that the *heads* are *mountains* (kingdoms/empires) and kings ("seven kings.")

"And there are seven kings: five are fallen, and one is, [and] the other is not yet come; and when he cometh, he must continue a short space." [3]

FIVE FALLEN EMPIRES

These are kingdoms or empires that have ruled over the land God gave to Israel and the whole Middle East. The five fallen empires are:

First	Egyptian Empire
Second	Assyrian Empire
Third	Babylonian Empire
Fourth	Persian Empire
Fifth	Grecian Empire

It's been suggested that Chinese dynasties could meet the definition of empires; however, because none of these dynasties actually controlled any portion of Israel, they do not qualify. However, Egypt does. Thutmose III of Egypt conquered Canaan in 1450 B.C. and Egyptian control of the area of Canaan lasted some four hundred years, so Egypt satisfies the criteria of one of the fallen kingdoms.

Sixth Empire

The sixth empire that ruled over the area of the Middle East was the Roman Empire. At the time John was given the vision, approximately 100 A.D., Rome was at the height of its power.

Seventh Empire

The seventh empire to control the area of the Middle East was the Arab-Muslim Empire. It is the final empire—the one which had not yet come at the time the angel spoke to John concerning his vision.

The angel's words to John rule out Western Europe as the revived Roman Empire and the fulfillment of the final kingdom (the beast) since the angel tells John that this king "is not yet come." Again, the Roman Empire had in fact already come and was at the height of its power. Additionally, the angel directly addresses the identity and the ancestry of the End-Times beast power:

And the beast that was, and is not, even he is the eighth, and is of the seven, and goeth into perdition.[4]

From Daniel, we learn that the beast on which the woman rides is actually a composite of all the empires—past, present, and future, including the seventh empire (the Muslim Empire). The image described by Daniel was broken down into body parts with each part representing a different empire—Babylon, Medo-Persia, Greece, Rome, and an empire represented by "iron mixed with miry clay."

Scripture does not contradict itself. In fact, all prophetic passages fit together perfectly just like the pieces of a puzzle. What we need to do is examine *all* the pieces: Daniel chapters 2, 7, 8, 9, and 11; Revelation 17; and all other passages that include any reference to the role of this End-Time entity. Before we begin this task, we have to address the following issues.

DANIEL 7 AND THE QUESTION OF THE FOURTH EMPIRE

Daniel 7:3-7 tells us that four empires/kingdoms will come up from the sea.

> And four great beasts came up from the sea, each different from the other. The first was like a lion, and had eagle's wings. I watched till its wings were plucked off; and it was lifted up from the earth and made to stand on two feet like a man, and a man's heart was given to it. And suddenly another beast, a second, like a bear. It was raised up on one side, and had three ribs in its mouth between its teeth. And they said thus to it: "Arise, devour much flesh!" After this I looked, and there was another, like a leopard, which had on its back four wings of a bird. The beast also had four heads, and dominion was given to it. After this I saw in the night visions, and behold, a fourth beast, dreadful and terrible, exceedingly strong. It had huge iron teeth; it was devouring, breaking in pieces, and trampling the residue with its feet. It was different from all the beasts that were before it, and it had ten horns.

A popular interpretation of this passage identifies the Roman Empire, with Rome as capital, as the fourth beast. For this to be true, the End-Times empire must be a continuation of the Roman Empire and must include the same boundaries. While a revived Roman Empire is feasible, it is important to examine this theory in light of Scripture.

This interpretation of Daniel 2—the Roman Empire as the fourth beast—can be correct only if it correlates with Revelation 17.

> Then the iron [Rome], the clay, the bronze [Greece], the silver [Persia] and the gold [Babylon] were crushed all at the same time and became like chaff from the summer threshing floors; and the wind carried them away so that not a trace of them was found. But the stone that struck the statue became a great mountain and filled the whole earth.[5]

Recognizing dual fulfillment, the immediate, short-term fulfillment in Daniel 2 is that all the kingdoms described have already ended. The

345

future, long-term fulfillment will be made manifest when Messiah (the stone) strikes the revived kingdoms and establishes His kingdom, which will cover the whole earth.

DANIEL 7 –HISTORY OR FUTURE

Daniel 7 includes this dual fulfillment. We see the fulfillment in the past demise of the four kingdoms, which is actually a "type" for the fulfillment to come. Sir Robert Anderson, a leading scholar of prophecy, stated "Verse 7 indicates that the rise of all these kingdoms was future," and he goes on

> In the history of Babylonia there is nothing to correspond with the predicted course of the first Beast, for it is scarcely legitimate to suppose that the vision was a prophecy of the career of Nebuchadnezzar.

> Neither is there in the history of Persia anything answering to the bear-like beast with that precision and fullness which prophecy demands. The language of the English version suggests a reference to Persia and Media but the true rendering appears to be; "It made for itself one dominion," instead of "It raised up itself on one side."

> While the symbolism of the sixth verse seems at first sight to point to the Grecian Empire, it will appear upon a closer examination that at its advent the leopard had four wings and four heads. This was its primary and normal condition, and it was in this condition that dominion was given to it. This surely is very different from what Daniel 8:8 describes and what the history of Alexander's Empire realized, viz., the rise of a single power, which in its decadence continued to exist in a divided state.

Anderson comes to the following conclusion:

> Each of the three first empires of the second chapter (Babylon, Persia, and Greece) was in turn destroyed by its successor; but the kingdoms of the seventh chapter all continued together upon the scene, though the dominion,

was with the fourth (Daniel 7:12). The verse seems to imply that the four beasts came up together, and at all events there is nothing to suggest a series of empires, each destroying its predecessor, though the symbolism of the vision was (in contrast with that of chap. 2) admirably adapted to represent this. Compare the language of the next vision. (Daniel 8:3-6)[6]

Concerning the Roman Empire, Anderson writes:

While the fourth beast is unquestionably Rome, the language of the seventh and twenty-third verses leaves no doubt that it is the Roman Empire in its revived and future phase. Without endorsing the views of Maitland, Browne, etc., it must be owned that there was nothing in the history of ancient Rome to correspond with the main characteristic of this beast unless the symbolism used is to be very loosely interpreted. To "devour the earth," "tread it down and break it in pieces," is fairly descriptive of other empires, but Ancient Rome was precisely the one power which added government to conquest, and instead of treading down and breaking in pieces the nations it subdued, sought rather to mould them to its own civilization and polity. All this—and more might be added—suggests that the entire vision of the seventh chapter may have a future reference.[7]

Anderson believes that Daniel 7 is speaking *only* of the End-Times empires that exist simultaneously. *Amazingly, he even stated that the Middle East would be the primary area of conflict.*

Now, Daniel 2 expressly names the Mediterranean ("the Great Sea") as the scene of the conflict between the four beasts. But there is no doubt that Egypt, Turkey, and Greece will be numbered among the ten kingdoms; and is it not improbable in the extreme that these nations will ever accept the leadership of a man who is to appear as the champion and patron of the Latin Church? A striking solution of this difficulty will probably be found in the definite prediction, that while the ten kingdoms will ulti-

347

mately own his suzerainty, three of the ten will be brought into subjection by force of arms. (Daniel 8:3-6)[8]

In Daniel 11:40, Egypt and Turkey (or whatever power will then possess Asia Minor) are expressly mentioned by their prophetic titles as separate kingdoms at this very time. Anderson, a respected Bible commentator, also has doubts regarding the Europe theory.

> To the scheme here indicated the objection may naturally be raised: Is it possible that the most powerful nations of the world, England, Germany, and Russia, are to have no part in the great drama of the last days? But it must be remembered, first, that the relative importance of the great powers may be different at the time when these events shall be fulfilled, and secondly, that difficulties of this kind may depend entirely on the silence of Scripture, or, in other words, on our own ignorance. I feel bound to notice, however, that doubts which have been raised in my mind regarding the soundness of the received interpretation of the seventh chapter of Daniel point to a more satisfactory answer to the difficulties in question.[9]

> It has been confidently urged by some that as the ten kingdoms were symbolized by the ten toes of Nebuchadnezzar's image – five on either foot – five of these kingdoms must be developed in the East, and five in the West. The argument is plausible, and possibly just; but its chief force depends upon forgetting that in the prophet's view the Levant and not the Adriatic, Jerusalem and not Rome, is the centre of the world.[10]

Anderson, finds problems with the revived "European" empire theory. The seven empires listed are those identified by Daniel, and the eighth empire is the End-Time beast. The future End-Times empire also has seven "horns," and we know from Daniel 7:8 that three of the ten horns are plucked from the root. The Antichrist will come from the seventh horn—the Seleucid portion of the Grecian Empire. However, all these empires and their kings originate from Babylon; they all come from the same system.

1	Egyptian Empire	1 horn
2	Babylonian Empire	1 horn
3	Assyrian Empire	1 horn
4	Persian Empire	1 horn
5	Greek Empire	4 horns
6	Roman Empire	1 horn
7	Ottoman Empire	1 horn

$$\text{10 horns}$$

The seven empires that have come and gone had 10 horns. The 11th horn is the little horn of Daniel 7:8, the revived 7th empire. The End-Times empire is of the seven previous empires

Daniel's image (chapter 2), is a representation of the revived confederacy of End-Times. The proof is that all the kingdoms represented by the image are destroyed at the same time—by the stone that was cut out without hands, that is, Messiah. The stone first strikes the feet, "then was the iron, the clay, the brass, the silver, and the gold, broken to pieces together." as we see in Daniel 2:35a. The stone then becomes a great mountain (or kingdom) that fills the whole earth.

In the same chapter, the image's head of gold represents the Babylonian Empire; the breast and arms of silver signify the Medo-Persian Empires; the belly and thighs of brass are the Grecian Empire; and the Roman Empire is represented by legs of iron.

The present-day Muslim nations that fall within this defined area comprised the major part of the Muslim Ottoman Empire, which also took in the area of the ancient Greek Empire, the eastern part of the Roman Empire, and most of the Western Roman Empire (North Africa). Because successive empires ruled the land, the areas are superimposed over one another. The beast is the Islamic Ottoman Empire that replaced the Roman Empire following its defeat of the Eastern Roman Empire. The Ottoman Empire is the wounded beast, and the world will marvel that it is "healed" and regains power.

The borders of the "beast" empire will resemble the borders of the ancient empires of Babylon, Assyria, Persia, Greece, and Rome. Although their borders overlapped at one time, Scripture shows that the kingdom of the Antichrist will occupy predominantly the area that was the ancient Grecian Empire. Once the borders of the beast empire are defined, Europe is disqualified from being the beast; that is, the Grecian Empire took in the eastern portion of the Roman Empire and not any part of Europe, except modern day Greece.

Daniel 8 depicts a vision of a ram with two horns that is attacked by a male-goat with one large horn. The goat grew very strong, but his large horn was broken and four notable horns came up in its place. From these four horns, a little horn grew exceedingly great toward the south—and the land of Israel. The ram is the Medo-Persian Empire, the two horns representing the two influences of the Medes and the Persians. The goat is the succeeding empire, that is, the Grecian Empire led by Alexander the Great who defeated the Medo-Persians. When Alexander died, his kingdom was divided into four areas, each under the rule of one of four generals. Antiochus Epiphanies, one of the four generals, ruled over the Syrian area; he pre-figures the little horn who is the Antichrist. By observing the "type" of the Antichrist, Antiochus Epiphanies, we learn that the actual Antichrist will arise from a kingdom that resembles the Greek Empire and not the Roman Empire. Notice that the area of the Greek Empire covers the whole Middle East and extends eastward; it does not extend into Europe. (See Figure 1, next page.)

It's interesting that almost every nation that is part of the Islamic Empire outlined in the map above is also mentioned in Scripture as participating in the End-Time prophecy.

And he said, "Look, I am making known to you what shall happen in the latter time of the indignation; for at the appointed time the end shall be.[11]

Daniel indicates that this is a *future* prophecy by using the phrases "the appointed time," "latter time," and "the latter time of the indignation." Daniel shows what will happen to his people in the latter days, that is, at the end of time. Further, in chapter 2, Daniel tells King Nebuchadnezzar that "the Great God has shown the king what will take place in the future. The dream is true and the interpretation is

Figure 1. Compare the Islamic Empire with the Greek Empire.

trustworthy." We see that this image depicts specific empires to be revived at a future time.

Daniel 7 outlines a confederacy formed from revived empires of the past and defines the area that will come under the control of this End-Time empire. "The four great beasts are four kingdoms that will rise from the earth."

IS THE EUROPEAN UNION THE REVIVED ROMAN EMPIRE?

There are arguments that assign the Roman Catholic Church and European nations a part in the attack on Israel as well as the judgments against those attackers. One current theory is that the Antichrist will come out of the European Union and will be part of the Roman Catholic Church. The theory is not specific as to which region of Europe is involved; some believe it is Italy while others point to Germany and France as likely candidates.

The C.I.S. Republics, which came into being following the fall of Communism, were part of the Roman Empire. Therefore, wouldn't the C.I.S. nations be required to join the European Union? To date, the C.I.S. nations have not.

The image found in Daniel has ten toes. As of January 1, 1995—when Austria, Finland, and Sweden joined the European Union—there were fifteen member nations, making Europe an unlikely candidate for Daniel's vision. So, for this interpretation of Europe to fit Daniel's image, we'd have to eliminate ten nations from the West and add five new nations from the East. Fairly heavy duty re-construction.

There are more basic problems, however. This theory would require five nations on each leg; but, in this case, we have fifteen toes on the western leg and no toes on the eastern one. Additionally, the Roman Empire was divided into western and eastern empires by a north-south line; the five Islamic states (Libya, Tunisia, Morocco, Mauritania, and Algeria) that were part of the Western Roman Empire are absent from the revived Roman Empire of this theory. This alone is a major problem, since Daniel 7:24 tell us that these nations will come from the fourth beast (the Roman Empire): "The ten horns *out of this kingdom* [the fourth]."

Finally, Turkey (the Eastern Roman Empire), which was refused entry into the EU, is now looking to the East for support. How can Turkey possibly fit the requirements of this theory, considering it was the seat of the Eastern Roman Empire and also the seat or throne of Satan (Revelation 2:12-13; Pergamos is in Turkey)? In order to join the EU, Turkey would have to resolve a number of human rights issues going back hundreds of years, and that seems highly unlikely.

Some people suggest that the Antichrist will come from the United States; in fact, they even point to the president of the U.S. as a possible candidate for the Antichrist, currently, President Bush, because he has been supporting the Road Map for Peace between Israel and the Palestinians.

It is remarkable that both America and Russia are offered as possible fulfillments of the Daniel prophecy without any support from the Biblical text. Why? Because of the sound of the names? For instance, "Assyria" is interpreted as "Russia." This is merely conjecture with no support from the text and depends on a completely allegorical interpretation of Scripture. It's a dangerous approach and it's resulted in a good deal of erroneous speculation, such as replacing the word "Israel" with the word "Church:" Replacement Theology.

REVELATION 13 CONFIRMS THE GREEK PART OF THE ROMAN EMPIRE

The End Time confederacy of nations must be a combination of ancient empires in terms of geography. In Daniel 7, the three ancient empires are referred to as a "lion" (Babylon) in verse 7, a "bear" (Persia) in verse 5, and a "leopard" (Greece) in verse 6. The fourth beast of Revelation 13:2 is a composite of these three empires—leopard (Greece), bear (Medo-Persia or Iran), and a lion (Babylonian).

> And the beast which I saw was like unto a leopard, and
> his feet were as the feet of a bear, and his mouth as the
> mouth of a lion.[12]

How is the last-days beast empire a composite of these three ancient empires? Today, the regions represented by all three empires are occupied by Muslim nations. Additionally, all three empires were located in the Middle East and at one time were included in the territories of the Greek Empire.

Anderson commented on this composite beast:

> As the vision of the second chapter [of Daniel] specifies
> the four empires which were successively to rule the
> world, and as the seventh chapter also enumerates four
> "kingdoms," and expressly identifies the fourth of these

with the fourth—kingdom of the earlier vision, the inference appears legitimate that the scope of both visions is the same throughout. And this conclusion is apparently confirmed by some of the details afforded of the kingdoms typified by the lion, the bear, and the leopard. So strong indeed is the prima facie case in support of this view that I have not felt at liberty to depart from it in the foregoing pages. At the same time I am constrained to own that this case is less complete than it appears to be, and that grave difficulties arise in connection with it; and the following observations are put forward tentatively to promote inquiry in the matter:

1st. Daniel 2 and 7 are both in the Chaldee portion of the Book, and are therefore bracketed together, and separated from what follows. This strengthens the presumption, therefore, which would obtain in any case, that the later vision is not a repetition of the earlier one. Repetition is very rare in Scripture. **2nd.** The date of the vision of the seventh chapter was the first year of Belshazzar, and therefore only some two or three years before the fall of the Babylonian empire. How then could the rise of that empire be the subject of the prophecy? Verse 17 appears definite that the rise of all these kingdoms was future.[13]

The last-days beast of Revelation 13 is identical to the fourth beast described in Daniel 7. Many interpreters of prophecy consider the fourth beast of Daniel 7 to be the ten Common Market nations of Europe that will be united under the authority of the Antichrist. This theory fell apart when the membership of the Common Market was increased to fifteen nations and out of the fifteen, all but one are in the West. On May 1, 2004, the EU expanded to 25 nations, adding ten nations from the Soviet Block.

THE QUESTION OF WHETHER ROME ACTUALLY FELL

Arguments that Rome never fell

1. The Roman Empire never ceased to exist.

2. The Roman Empire was not destroyed or conquered by another power; it fell from within.

3. Before the internal collapse of the Roman Empire, it stretched from Great Britain to Europe.

4. The New World Order is actually the Old World Order—the sixth kingdom, the "kingdom that is" at the time John recorded his Revelation. So, five kingdoms have fallen, one "is," and the seventh kingdom is the revived Roman Empire.

Response

The Western Roman Empire ended in 410 A.D. when Barbarians attacked the city of Rome. At that time, Zeno maintained the Roman imperial throne in the safety of Constantinople (modern-day Istanbul, Turkey), one thousand miles east of Rome. Edward Gibbons, one of the world's most renowned historians, described the final days of the empire and the end of Roman rule with the killing of the last holy Roman emperor by the Turks. In 1453 A.D., Turkish Muslims invaded and captured Constantinople to avenge the military Christian Crusades. From 1096 A.D. to 1212 A.D., Christian Crusaders fought to retake control of Jerusalem and the Holy Land. The Crusaders objected to Muslim dominance and control of these lands following the fall of the Western half of the Roman Empire. In his famous work, The Decline and Fall of the Roman Empire, Gibbons argues that Rome did indeed fall.

Further, the Roman world was not centered in the Italian peninsula. The Roman Empire was founded on the Hellenistic culture of the eastern Mediterranean. Daniel's prophecy is not referring to the Roman power that overcame Greece and conquered much of the pagan world. Unlike Greece, the Roman legions did not leave their mark on the lands of Nebuchadnezzar's first kingdom. However, Greek influence even affected the language of Holy Scripture containing the "good news." The New Testament Scriptures were written in Greek and not in Latin. Language, however, was not the only Greek influence on the customs and traditions of the East.

Hellenistic culture originated in the region of the Hellespont, in the eastern Balkans on the Sea of Marmara. Constantinople, which is situated on coastline, remained the imperial fortress city of the Christianized Roman world for a thousand years. Rome moved eastward, not westward. This fact is fundamental to an accurate understanding of End-Times prophecy.

At its peak, the Ottoman Empire extended from Venice and the borders of Germany to Persia, from Poland to the north of Africa, from Egypt to Morocco, and even took in the Land of Israel. The Turkish conquest of Constantinople marked the end of the imperial rule of Rome—its scepter broken forever. The sixth emperor of Rome was finally put to death one thousand years later than the date accepted by most Western historians and students of prophecy—and put to death by a different ruler than generally believed. In fact, he was put to death under the rule that had centuries earlier conquered the Promised Land. The end of the Islamic Turkish Empire and the decline of Muhammadism were necessary to make way for the Zionist Movement and Israel's rebirth in 1947. The Islamic Empire ruled the East until 1918 when the Ottoman Empire fell to the British Empire.

The beast suffered a wound so that the Jews could return to the land as prophesied. The only rulership in history that fulfills the prophecy of the seventh king is the Islamic Caliphate, which began with the Hashemite Dynasty and ended with the Ottoman Empire. The *Encyclopedia Britannica* records the following about the Ottoman Turks: The Ottoman Empire, one of the most powerful states in the world during the 15th and 16th centuries, spanned more than 600 years and ended only in 1922, when it was replaced by the Turkish Republic and various successor states in southeastern Europe and the Middle East. At its height it included most of southeastern Europe to the gates of Vienna, including modern Hungary, Serbia, Bosnia, Romania, Greece, and Ukraine; Iraq, Syria, Israel, and Egypt; North Africa as far west as Algeria; and most of the Arabian Peninsula.[14] The Turks also ruled what is today Georgia, Armenia, Azerbaijan, the Crimea, regions north of the Black Sea, and part of Iran.

This "seventh king" held control of the Promised Land until the last year of World War I. Further, the Temple Mount is still controlled by the Hashemites. The Hashemite kingdom of Jordan is ruled by King Abdullah who is a descendant of Muhammad. Still, "an eighth" king must emerge from the seven past kingdoms. It is clear that the eighth king will be Islamic. Could the British Empire be the eighth kingdom?

If we learn the identity of the seventh kingdom, we should be able to identify the eighth.

"And the beast that was and is not, is himself also an eighth, and is of the seven; and he goeth into perdition." [15]

This is the only passage that identifies a ruler based on his predecessors. Scripture tells us that the eighth kingdom is of, or from, the seven; and the seventh has been clearly identified as the Islamic Ottoman Empire. In effect, the seventh king defines important factors of the eighth. The Caliphate is the authority over all Islam, and we hear the call for the Caliphate throughout the Islamic world. Muslims are killing non-Muslims all over the globe based on national and Shari'a law. In Islamism, there is no compliance with "there is no compulsion in religion." (Surah 2:256) Compelling infidels to convert is what Islamism does; the alternative is death. It is clearly Satan's aim to turn us against God and away from eternal life. What empire, other than the Islamic Ottoman Empire (the seventh kingdom), demonstrates so many characteristics of a false religious system *and* has its roots in Babylon?

Chapter Sixteen
ISLAM AND END-TIMES

The End-Time battle prophesied in the Bible is a religious, not a political, war. The major political threats of our time, Communism, Nazism and Fascism, have been replaced by Islamic fundamentalism. It is this militant-religious jihad movement that should be the focus of our End-Time prophecy study. Prophetic passages do show the European nations, such as Spain and Rome, engaged in the struggle against the Antichrist, and they are mentioned over a dozen times in Scripture, but never within the context of End-Time judgments. *Every nation that incurs the wrath of God's End-Time judgments in Scripture is today an Islamic nation.*

There is debate about Ezekiel 38, since it refers to Ethiopia, a non-Muslim nation. However, the Hebrew word "Cush," which is rendered "Ethiopia" in modern English translations of the Bible, is actually modern-day Sudan.

Today, not a single Islamic nation has a democratic form of government, although the United States is at this moment attempting to create a democracy in Iraq. The Islamic governments are good actors. If they anger a Western nation, they flirt with democracy or pretend to some "moderate" system of rule. This pacifies the critics, buys the Islamic governments some time, and brings in financial support from the West, usually the United States, because we want to shore up any move toward democracy, or at least, something less than a dictatorship.

When the criticism abates, or the funding stops, so does the experiment in democracy.

The world fails to understand the danger in these experiments. The West, and particularly America, has a failed history of supporting "rebels" or "freedom fighters" who then remove their masks and rule as vicious dictators. Our financial aid is often seed money for the next terrorist regime. In his effort to combat Communism, President Jimmy Carter funded Operation Cyclone with $500 million; the result was the spread of Islamism in Central Asia. An additional $4 billion went for training for Jihad in Pakistan and for establishing the Taliban movement in Afghanistan.

Satan and the Islamic Nations Cast into the Pit

Revelation 19 parallels much of Ezekiel regarding the casting of the Antichrist and the "beast" into the pit (hell).

> And the beast was taken, and with him the false prophet that wrought miracles before him, with which he deceived them that had received the mark of the beast, and them that worshiped his image. These both were cast alive into a lake of fire burning with brimstone.[1]

Much of Ezekiel refers to the death of the Antichrist and the binding of Satan, along with a multitude of Islamic nations that are cast into the pit of hell. Many Christian scholars attempted to interpret the writings of John regarding the beast of End-Times, but have not treated Scripture as seamless. That failure to make the connection between the Prophets of the Old Testament and the book of Revelation results in incorrect conclusions.

The key to correctly interpreting John's Revelation is found in the book of Ezekiel, including the names of Satan and the peoples deceived by him:

Compare the passage from Revelation 19:20 just cited, with Ezekiel 28:8, which prophecies Satan's being cast into the pit.

> They shall bring thee [Satan] down to the pit, and thou shalt die the deaths of [them that are] slain in the midst of the seas. In the midst of the seas [the nations], shall the Antichrist be killed and thrown to the pit.

In Ezekiel 31:15-18, the Antichrist is finally thrown into hell.

> Thus saith the Lord GOD; in the day when he went down to the grave I caused mourning: I covered the deep for him, and I restrained the floods thereof, and the great waters were stayed: and I caused Lebanon to mourn for him, and all the trees of the field fainted for him. I made the nations to shake at the sound of his fall, when I cast him down to hell with them that descend into the pit: and

all the trees of Eden, the choice and best of Lebanon, all that drink water, shall be comforted in the nether parts of the earth. They also went down into hell with him unto [them that be] slain with the sword; and [they that were] his arm, [that] dwelt under his shadow in the midst of the heathen. To whom art thou thus like in glory and in greatness among the trees of Eden? Yet shalt thou be brought down with the trees of Eden unto the depths of the earth: thou shalt lie in the midst of the uncircumcised with [them that be] slain by the sword. This [is] Pharaoh and all his multitude, saith the Lord GOD.

This passage from Ezekiel echoes Revelation 19:20, which tells of the great disappointment of the many nations which are also cast into hell with Satan. [Also, see Ezekiel 32:22–23.]

"Asshur [is] there and all her company: his graves [are] about him: all of them slain, fallen by the sword: Whose graves are set in the sides of the Pit, and her company is round about her grave; all of them slain, fallen by the sword, which caused terror in the land of the living."

Asshur, which is Assyria, encompasses at least the regions of modern day Syria and Iraq; these nations are cast into hell with the Antichrist. Again, all the nations referenced here are Muslim nations. Now, Muslims are circumcised and Ezekiel refers to the people who are slain by the sword as "uncircumcised." So, if Muslims are circumcised, how can Islam be driven by the power of Satan?

Let's look at the use of the word *circumcision*. In Ezekiel 44:7, God is angry because foreigners who are "uncircumcised in the heart and uncircumcised in the flesh" are profaning His sanctuary. This and many other passages reveal that there are *two* aspects to circumcision—circumcision of the heart (*arel leb*) and circumcision of the flesh (*arel basar*). In the passage in Ezekiel 32, only the word *arel* is used, so it is impossible to distinguish between the two circumcisions.

We know that circumcision is the mark of God's covenant with Abraham and Isaac [Genesis 17:19]. Because all male members of the household were circumcised [Genesis 17:12–13], Ishmael was therefore circumcised—even though the covenant was not made with him.

Before the coming of Messiah, circumcision was recognized as a covenant between God and the descendants of Abraham and his seed, Isaac. Those who did not worship the one true God were identified as such in Scripture as "uncircumcised"; in Ezekiel 36:6, God also refers to the nations (the nations surrounding Israel) as heathen. Circumcision of the flesh is symbolic of the circumcision of the heart revealed in the New Covenant, the New Testament of Christian Scripture. Circumcision of the heart occurs when one comes to faith in Messiah and becomes sanctified by the Holy Spirit. As we see in Jeremiah 4:4, circumcision of the flesh does not save the soul.

"Circumcise yourselves to Jehovah and take away the foreskins of your heart, ye men of Judah and inhabitants of Jerusalem."

Circumcision of the heart was made possible through the death and resurrection of the Messiah, that is, the atonement of our sins through Messiah's blood. The apostle Paul teaches that God desires the circumcision of the heart; Gentiles who have had their hearts circumcised do not need to be circumcised in the flesh. The term "uncircumcised" to the Jews meant "unbeliever."

Ezekiel 33 and 34 explain that God sends the heathen, uncircumcised nations as punishment, and gathers Israel for "forgiveness." Ezekiel 35:10 concerns God's judgment of Edom and the Arabs,

"Because thou hast said, these two nations and these two countries shall be mine, and we will possess it; whereas the LORD was there."

Today Israel is divided into two peoples and two nations— Israel and Palestine. The land originally assigned by God to Israel covers far more territory than present day Israel. In fact, the boundaries assigned by God extend to the Euphrates. The Arab nations, however, have always claimed that the land belongs to them. Both history and prophecy tell us that the Arab nations will take further action on this claim. In Ezekiel 36:6, God refers to the nations that would overtake Israel as "heathen."

"Thus saith the Lord GOD; Behold, I have spoken in my jealousy and in my fury, because ye have borne the shame of the heathen."

Islam, which unequivocally denies the fundamental tenets of Judaism and Christianity, is clearly the heathen religion and therefore cannot be the truth. Islam does not believe in the one true God, despite Muslim protests to the contrary. Muslims claim that Islam is the final or ultimate religion because the Quran is the final revelation of God, and because the Quran comes after the Torah, the Zabur (Psalms), and the Gospels. The following list identifies the regions listed in Scripture with the nations' modern names. Because boundaries have changed over time, there is some overlap.

Elam (Iran)

Elam encompasses the region of modern day Iran and perhaps regions of Afghanistan. Scripture states that Elam, along with the Antichrist, goes down to the pit.

As we see in Ezekiel 32:34,

> "There [is] Elam and all her multitude round about her grave, all of them slain, fallen by the sword, which are gone down uncircumcised into the nether parts of the earth, which caused their terror in the land of the living; yet have they borne their shame with them that go down to the pit." Meshech, Tubal, and all her multitude (Turkish nations and C.I.S. south of Russia)

The prophecies of Ezekiel also cover the region of modern day Turkey, Turkmenistan, Uzbekistan, Gergezstan, Tajikistan and Azerbaijan (C.I.S. south of Russia).

> There [is] Meshech, Tubal, and all her multitude: her graves [are] round about him: all of them uncircumcised, slain by the sword, though they caused their terror in the land of the living. And they shall not lie with the mighty [that are] fallen of the uncircumcised, which are gone down to hell with their weapons of war: and they have laid their swords under their heads, but their iniquities shall be upon their bones, though [they were] the terror of the mighty in the land of the living.[2]

Edom (Jordan)

Edom is comprised of parts of Jordan—an Arab, Islamic land.

"There [is] Edom, her kings, and all her princes, which with their might are laid by [them that were] slain by the sword: they shall lie with the uncircumcised, and with them that go down to the pit."[3]

Sidon (Syria and Lebanon)

Sidon is the region of present-day Syria and Lebanon; all the "princes of the North" refers to Turkey and her allies.

"There [be] the princes of the north, all of them, and all the Sidonians, which are gone down with the slain; with their terror they are ashamed of their might; and they lie uncircumcised with [them that be] slain by the sword, and bear their shame with them that go down to the pit."[4]

Ethiopia and Libya

"Ethiopia, and Libya, and Lydia, and all the mingled people, and Chub, and the men of the land that is in league, shall fall with them by the sword."[5] *[Persia, Lud (Turkey), Phut (Lybia, Algeria, Tunisia, Maurit, and Morocco]*

"They of Persia and of Lud and of Phut were in thine army, thy men of war: they hanged the shield and helmet in thee; they set forth thy comeliness."[6]

Indeed, Phut (North Africa) includes the Moors, soldiers of Islam who captured Spain and occupied it for hundreds of years. Lud (Turkey) takes in the Ottoman Empire and the Janissaries, and the military might of Islam, which were instrumental in the Ottoman Empire's spread of Islam. *Dedan, Arabia, Kedar, Haran, Canneh, Eden, Sheba, Asshur.*

The following verses cover Dedan, Arabia, and all the princes of Kedar, Haran, and Canneh, Eden (Yemen), and the merchants of Sheba, Asshur. The remainder of Ezekiel 27, verses 28-35, speaks of these very nations in the End-Times, along with Satan's final defeat. The merchants of Tyre, in Ezekiel 27, match the people of the nations of Gog and Magog and their hordes in Ezekiel 38.

Ezekiel 26 describes the destruction of Tyre, and chapter 27 outlines a long-term, End-of-Days prediction that includes the nations that traded with ancient Tyre. The merchants of Tyre symbolize both the nations of the world that are deceived into buying and selling Satan's lies and future world deception.

In Ezekiel, God curses the nations that traded with Tyre. Again, it is a long-term prophecy for the mystery, Babylon the Great. The people who traded with Tyre are, for the most part, Muslim nations. We see in Ezekiel 27:3a: "And say unto Tyrus, O thou that art situate at the entry of the sea." This is a literal reference to the Tyre of that day and an allegorical reference to a future Tyre, the mystery, Babylon the Great, referred to in Revelation. Note that Saudi Arabia is called "The Arabic Island" and sits on many seas—the Indian Ocean, the Persian Gulf, the Red Sea, and the Mediterranean.

"Thy borders [are] in the midst of the seas, thy builders have perfected thy beauty." [7]

Islam is the religion of the harlot "that sitteth upon many waters" (remember, in Scripture "waters" is frequently used as a symbol for nations or peoples) as we see in Revelation 17:1, and in Revelation 17:3, the woman that sits on the "scarlet-colored beast." Each year millions of Muslims, representing every tribe and nation and tongue, gather in Mecca to worship Allah in the Kaaba. In the end, these nations will be Islam's men of war.

There might appear to be a contradiction in the interpretation of the King of Tyre as a figurative term for Islam when Saudi Arabia, the country from which Islam originated, is actually trading with Tyre. However, Saudi Arabia, as the chief propagator of Islam, is indeed trading with Tyre—the false religious system that deals in the buying and selling of lies. Today's movement toward Islamic imperialism emanates from Saudi Arabia, and the Islamic nations we see today are actually the fruit of that movement. Saudi Arabia, part of the Islamic kingdom, is trading with Tyre/Islam.

"The merchants among the people shall hiss at thee; thou shalt be a terror, and never [shalt be] any more." [8]

The merchants weep over the destruction of ancient Tyre, just as they will weep over future Tyre, the Harlot City. There is an interesting similarity in the merchandise of the Tyre in Ezekiel 27 and the merchandise of Babylon in Revelation 18:

"Son of man, say unto the prince of Tyrus, thus saith the Lord God: Because thine heart [is] lifted up, and thou hast said, I [am] a God, I sit [in] the seat of God, in the midst of the seas; yet thou [art] a man, and not God, though thou set thine heart as the heart of God." [9]

The prince of Tyre is actually one of the titles used for Satan. The Antichrist will sit in the Temple of God in Jerusalem.

"Behold, therefore I will bring strangers upon thee, the terrible of the nations: and they shall draw their swords against the beauty of thy wisdom, and they shall defile thy brightness." [10]

This passage contradicts the popular theory concerning a one-world government. God will raise up several nations to attack the Antichrist. "Brightness" in this passage is a reference to Satan who is depicted as a star, *Hilal ben Shachar* (Isaiah 14:12) and as an angel of light (II Corinthians 11:14).

"Wilt thou yet say before him that slayeth thee, I [am] God? But thou [shalt be] a man, and no God, in the hand of him that slayeth thee." [11]

Just as in Isaiah 14, this angel is referred to as a man, none other than the Antichrist himself. This conclusion is supported by the following passage.

"Now we beseech you, brethren, by the coming of our Lord Jesus Christ, and [by] our gathering together unto him, That ye be not soon shaken in mind, or be troubled, neither by spirit, nor by word, nor by letter as from us, as that the day of Christ is at hand. Let no man deceive you by any means: for [that day shall not come], except there come a falling away first, and that man of sin be revealed, the son of perdition; Who opposeth and exalteth himself above all that is called God, or that is worshiped; so that he as God sitteth in the temple of God, showing himself that he is God. [12]

In addition, "Son of man, take up a lamentation upon the king of Tyrus, and say unto him, Thus saith the Lord God; Thou sealest up the sum, full of wisdom, and perfect in beauty. Thou hast been in Eden the garden of God." [13]

When has the King of Tyre been in the garden of God? In the Garden of Eden, there were Adam and Eve, who were cast out for their rebellion, and Satan, who deceived them. This leaves no room for doubt as to the identity of the "King of Babylon," the "Prince of Tyre" and "Pharaoh of Egypt."

> "Thou [art] the anointed cherub that covereth; and I have set thee [so]: thou wast upon the holy mountain of God; thou hast walked up and down in the midst of the stones of fire." [14]

The anointed cherub is a rebellious angel, none other than the devil himself.

> "By the multitude of thy merchandise they have filled the midst of thee with violence, and thou hast sinned: therefore I will cast thee as profane out of the mountain of God: and I will destroy thee, O covering cherub, from the midst of the stones of fire." [15]

What merchandise is Satan selling? The father of lies is peddling a false religion that promotes violence—"they have filled the midst of thee with violence."

> "Thine heart was lifted up because of thy beauty, thou hast corrupted thy wisdom by reason of thy brightness: I will cast thee to the ground, I will lay thee before kings, that they may behold thee." [16]

Satan appears as an angel of light, thus the "brightness." Here he is bound for the kings of the world to look at, exactly as described in Isaiah 14:16:

> "They that see thee shall narrowly look upon thee, [and] consider thee, [saying, is] this the man that made the earth to tremble, that did shake kingdoms."

This "anointed cherub" has many titles, including "the Assyrian," and he will be cast into hell as foretold in Isaiah 14:6: "Yet thou shalt be brought down to hell, to the sides of the pit" which also gives us the reason for this punishment:

"He who smote the people in wrath with a continual stroke, he that ruled the nations in anger, is persecuted, [and] none hindereth." The remainder of the passages tell us which nations he ruled; this list of nations is in fact the means for identifying the End-Time confederacy."

"And there shall be no more a pricking brier unto the house of Israel, nor [any] grieving thorn of all [that are] round about them, that despised them; and they shall know that I [am] the Lord GOD." [17]

The nations troubling Israel are the nations that the Antichrist ruled in anger. This theme is repeated in other verses in the Bible. For instance, Zechariah 12:2 refers to the nations "round about" Israel. All the nations surrounding Israel today are Muslim nations and certainly fit the description of a "pricking brier." These nations, in fact, have been a thorn in Israel's flesh for decades. Now we can rule out any theory that the European Union, America, or any other Western nations fall under this judgment.

> "Thus saith the Lord GOD; When I shall have gathered the house of Israel from the people among whom they are scattered, and shall be sanctified in them in the sight of the heathen, then shall they dwell in their land that I have given to my servant Jacob. And they shall dwell safely therein, and shall build houses, and plant vineyards; yea, they shall dwell with confidence, when I have executed judgments upon all those that despise them round about them; and they shall know that I [am] the LORD their God." [18]

Verses 25-26 refer to the gathering of Israel as a nation. This does not refer to ancient Tyre or Sidon, as these nations had already been destroyed. Further, Israel produces an abundance of fruit to satisfy the needs of many countries: wheat, barley, grapes, figs, pomegranates, olives, dates, and of course Jaffa oranges.

THE FALLING AWAY MUST COME TO PASS

Perhaps what we in the West should fear most is not the establishment of an Antichrist government, but a falling away. In our understanding of prophecy, have we substituted the Antichrist's governmental system for the falling away described in II Thessalonians 2:3?

All Christian cultures in the East that fell away were taken over by Islam. Today, Muslims are immigrating to Western nations by the hundreds of thousands. Al-Ghazzali, one of the most respected theologians of Islam stated:

"Muslims could live under non-Muslim rule as long as they do not forget that they are Allah's missionaries and, if needed, His soldiers." [19]

A MUSLIM ANTICHRIST?

Several factors suggest that both the Antichrist and the revived beast empire will very likely be Muslim:

1. The Antichrist Will Change Times and Laws; Wounding of the Beast

Islam invoked Shari'a law and changed the calendar system from AD to AH, based on the Muslim calendar of Hijra. Islam is the beast that was wounded and later healed. At one time a prominent force in the world, Islam lost influence and power (was wounded) but is now on the healed and on the rise. But because Islamists have been so successful at playing "underdog" to a liberal media, and because of the "politically correct" Western governments, the world ignores what is standing in front of its collective face and calls Islam a "peaceful" religion. We refuse to acknowledge the profound hate that Islamists feel toward the infidels, which is every non-Muslim nation.

We saw a true picture of how the Islamists work with the train massacres in Spain in 2004, yet we continue to claim narrowly that the terrorists are the problem, when, in truth, it is Islam itself. This is how Nazism rose to power.

"He will speak against the Most High and oppress the saints and try to change set times and the laws." [20]

"Times" is an obvious reference to the calendar; "laws" refers to the system of governance Islam adopted with the Hijra calendar, marking Muhammad's journey from Mecca to Medina. Islam holds that Muhammad is the last of a long line of prophets, and the Quran was revealed to him through the angel Gabriel by order of Allah. The Hijra, in fact, marks the beginning of Islam's ascendance as a world religion.

What the politicians and the liberal media tell us about changes in governance in the Middle East is wrong. Consider what happened in Afghanistan. Since the defeat of the Taliban, much of the world believes that Afghanistan operates under Western democratic law. That is not true. The new "democratic" government adopted Islamic law, Shari'a, only now it is enforced covertly. In Pakistan, which we perceive to be a secular state, the North West Frontier province has adopted Shari'a law, and the imams are working to establish Shari'a law for the entire nation. And each day we read of the bombings and shootings in Iraq, stemming partly from factional differences, and because the strict Muslims want the American troops out so that Shari'a law can be enforced.

> "Fight those who believe not in Allah nor the Last Day, nor hold that forbidden which hath been forbidden by Allah and His Messenger, nor acknowledge the Religion of Truth, from among the People of the Book, until they pay the Jizya with willing submission, and feel themselves subdued." [21]

"Yes, the time is coming that whoever kills you will think that he offers God service." [22]

Muslims believe they are offering service to Allah by killing infidels; and they believe both Christians and Jews are infidels. Christians insult Allah by accepting the deity of Jesus, who to Muslims, was only a mere man and a messenger of God. Further, the Jews are "occupying" the land of Israel, which Muslims believe belongs to them. Therefore, they are commanded to fight and kill in jihad to receive greater rewards in paradise. The Quran does contain verses that speak of peace, but Surah 9:29, known as the verses of the sword, abrogates any preceding verses of peace.

As mentioned earlier, Muslim ideology makes provision for a false treaty or *hudna* to be used during a time of weakness. You create the illusion of a peace treaty with your enemy because you know you are too weak to win the battle. However, when you regain power, the treaty can be broken and that resurgence of strength is the signal for war. The precedent was set by the *Hudabiya*, a treaty that Muhammad signed with the Quraish tribe, promising to avoid war for ten years.

However, it was a *hudna*. Two years later, when Muhammad's forces were strong, he declared war on the Quraish.

Yasser Arafat used this very same hudna. At the same time he pretended to "negotiate" peace treaties with Israel, he addressed the Palestinians, citing Muhammad's famous Hudabiya treaty. President Musharraf of Pakistan has taken a similar tack in signing on with the United States to fight the global war on terror. These are merely clever ploys used to deceive the unsuspecting West.

Shari'a law is not limited to Muslim nations. The Arbitration Act of 1991 includes plans for launching an Islamic Institute of Civil Justice in Ontario, Canada, to enforce Shari'a law. In this situation, Shari'a applies only to those who consent to arbitration proceedings. Enforcement is limited to civil matters; criminal law cannot be enforced through this arbitration process, and the arbitrator must act in accordance with the Canadian Penal Code. However, the Canadian Council of Muslim Women is concerned that women may be "persuaded" to agree to Shari'a arbitration simply because they are Muslim.

Turkey is an important marker for fulfillment of End-Times. Prophecy regarding the Antichrist, (that is Antichrist the individual, as opposed to the Beast or Empire), tells us that he shall change times and laws. Kemal Ataturk, who governed Turkey after the defeat of the Ottoman Empire, objected strongly to Islamic imperialism and reacted accordingly. He forbid the practice of veiling and changed the calendar from Islamic to Georgian. He also implemented oral and written language reforms, changing from Persian script (similar to Arabic) to the European alphabet. Today, the West believes Turkey is a secular state, but, in truth, it is increasing its affiliation with the Islamic faith and a number of political parties are lobbying for greater Islamic influence. Turkey will change the times and laws back to Shari'a when the lawless one shows up.

Those who expect the power of the Beast to arise from the European community should take a closer look at European culture and the laws that reflect that culture. As opposed to Islamic violence, in Europe, even spanking children is considered abuse. This is not the culture that would produce the Beast.

2. Islam Persecutes the Saints and Institutes Beheading as a Form of Punishment

Revelation 20:4 says "Then I saw the souls of those who had been beheaded for their witness to Jesus and for the word of God, who had not worshiped the Beast or his image, and had not received his mark on their foreheads or on their hands."

Who besides Muslims sees the killing of Jews and Christians as a religious obligation, as doing a service to God? Around the world, Muslims blow up embassies and other Western and Israeli targets in the name of Allah. Although the Roman Catholic Church, burdened with its own violent past, might be seen as the possible fulfillment of the harlot, the kingdom of the Antichrist practices beheading its enemies. Only in Islam is beheading a continuing practice.

Modern revisionist historians revere Babur (1483–1530), founder of the Mughal dynasty, as a paragon of Muslim tolerance. Yet in his autobiography, *Baburnama*, concerning infidel prisoners of a jihad campaign he says, "Those who were brought in alive [having surrendered] were ordered beheaded, after which a tower of skulls was erected in the camp." [23]

> The beheading of criminals with a sword or axe was common practice among ancient civilizations for thousands of years. This practice was widely used in Europe, Asia, and Africa—in both Muslim and non-Muslim nations—until the very early twentieth century. Only recently has the entire civilized world abandoned the practice of beheading. Again, this barbarism is present only in the Muslim world—including Saudi Arabia, Qatar, Yemen, Iran, and until recently, Talibani Afghanistan. Recently, Jihadis in Algeria, Nigeria, Kashmir, Chechnya, and the Muslim-dominated southern Philippines carried out beheadings. Iranian mullahs cut off the heads of some political figures. The Beirut CIA station chief, William Buckley, was kidnapped by Hezbollah and sent to Iran, where he was beheaded in 1986.

Mamoun Fandy is a columnist for two daily newspapers, *Asharq al-Awsat* in London and *al-Ahram* in Cairo. Fandy expressed his anger in a Washington Post essay titled "Where's the Arab Media's Sense of Outrage?"

> As I scanned Arab satellite channels and Arabic newspapers, I found a lot of reporting on the brutal attacks by the terrorists, but very little condemnation and a widespread willingness to run the stomach-turning video and photos (beheadings) again and again. Showing videotapes of people being shot, beheaded or held hostage with a curved sword aimed at their neck is largely new terrain for the Arab media. As a media critic whose focus is the Arab world, I have watched perhaps a dozen Arab channels and read countless newspapers in recent weeks. I found that few Arab commentators and journalists noted either that major shift or its significance. In particular, the Kim and Johnson beheadings were reported as if they were quite ordinary. Al-Jazeera (Jihad News) is the famous Arab network that calls every Arab suicide bomber a *shaheed*, or martyr. Islamic radicals have killed writers in Algeria, Egypt and elsewhere whose work challenged the logic of martyrdom and "random jihad," or killing foreigners in the name of Islam. However, the lack of condemnation of the beheadings, despite their barbarism, is a direct result of a broad and dangerous trend in Arab media and in Arab culture broadly. The Arab world today swims in a sea of linguistic violence that justifies terrorism, making it seem acceptable—especially to the young. The same method is used in Bangladesh where Jamati Islami killed opponents according to Shari'a law—beheading and cutting off hands and feet.

The Saudis, founders and protectors of Islam, support the practice of beheading as punishment (Qisas), claiming it is sanctioned by Islamic tradition. State-ordered beheadings are performed in courtyards outside crowded mosques in major cities after weekly Friday prayer services. Centuries earlier, Muhammad ordered eight hundred

Jewish prisoners from Banu Quraiza to be separated from their wives and children, beheaded, and their bodies thrown into a trench. Their wives and families were sold into captivity. This was the first Muhammadan massacre.

According to Adrian Fortescue in *The Lesser Eastern Churches*:

> In 1389, a great procession of Copts who had accepted Muhammad under fear of death, marched through Cairo. Repenting of their apostasy, they now wished to atone for it by the inevitable consequence of returning to Christianity. So as they marched, they announced that they believed in Christ and renounced Muhammad. They were seized and all the men were beheaded in an open square before the women. But this did not terrify the women; so they, too, were all martyred.

And on it went. In 1896 alone, an estimated 200,000 Armenians died. During World War I, Armenia became the battleground for the Russian and Turkish armies. As the war continued, Turkish atrocities against Armenian Christians increased. As reports of those atrocities continued, the United States government finally sent a formal note of protest to Turkey on February 17, 1916. But the massacres continued, and privations and famine added to the numbered dead, estimated to total 800,000 Armenians during the war period. Constantine Koukides, a refugee from Pontius, recalled:

> I was five or six years old in 1922, and I still remember the songs of Akrita and the mourning of the Greek women who carried baskets full of severed heads down from the mountains. I will never forget the woman who suddenly realized that one of the heads in the basket she carried was that of her son.[24]

In <u>Greek Fire</u>, Nicholas Cage details the destruction of Smyrna in September 1922 with the massacre of nearly 300,000 inhabitants. The death toll resulting from Islamic hudna can be staggering. Cage reports that English, American, Italian and French battleships anchored in the harbor repelled fleeing victims who swam out to them for help.

All Islamic nations have persecuted and killed Christians, and the killing—and beheadings—continue today. Yet there is not a single Roman Catholic state today, or any other Catholic entity, that would support beheading. The Catholic Church clearly does not fit the profile of the harlot of End-Time prophecy.

Author Andrew G. Bostom comments on the Islamic practice of beheading:

> Reactions to the grotesque jihadist decapitation of yet another "infidel Jew," Mr. Berg, make clear that our intelligentsia are either dangerously uninformed, or simply unwilling to come to terms with this ugly reality: *such murders are consistent with sacred jihad practices, as well as Islamic attitudes towards all non-Muslim infidels, in particular, Jews,* which date back to the 7th century, and the Prophet Muhammad's own example...

> It is also important to note that no other modern movement, legal system or nation condones beheading as a form of punishment. The Shari'a law, however, requires it for many specified offenses. According to Muhammad's sacralized biography by Ibn Ishaq, Muhammad himself sanctioned the massacre of the Qurayza, a vanquished Jewish tribe. He appointed an "arbiter" who soon rendered this concise verdict: the men were to be put to death, the women and children sold into slavery, the spoils to be divided among the Muslims. Muhammad ratified this judgment stating that it was a decree of God pronounced from above the Steven Heavens. Thus some 600 to 900 men from the Qurayza were led on Muhammad's order to the Market of Medina. Trenches were dug and the men were beheaded, and their decapitated corpses buried in the trenches while Muhammad watched in attendance. Women and children were sold into slavery, a number of them being distributed as gifts among Muhammad's companions, and Muhammad chose one of the Qurayza women (Rayhana) for himself. The Qurayza's property and other possessions (including weapons) were also divided up as

additional "booty" among the Muslims, to support further jihad campaigns.[25]

The classical Muslim jurist, al-Mawardi of Baghdad, was a seminal and prolific scholar who lived during the so-called "Golden Age" of the Abbasid-Baghdadian Caliphate. He wrote the following passage regarding the treatment of infidel prisoners of jihad campaigns, based on accepted interpretations of the Quran and Sunna,

> As for the captives, the amir [ruler] has the choice of taking the most beneficial action of four possibilities: the first to put them to death by cutting their necks; the second, to enslave them and apply the laws of slavery regarding their sale and manumission; the third, to ransom them in exchange for goods or prisoners; and fourth, to show favor to them and pardon them. Allah, may he be exalted, says, "When you encounter those [infidels] who deny [the Truth, Islam] then strike [their] necks.[26]

According to well-known translator, Dr. Asadullah Yate at the University of Cambridge, all four classical schools of Islamic jurisprudence throughout the Muslim empire advocated these rules. Beheadings were common for hundreds of years along the Iberian Peninsula. In 711 or 712, when Arab Muslims first invaded Iberian Toledo, Christians submitted to Muslim rule. In 713, however, when Christians revolted, Muslim reprisal was severe. As jihad roared on, all the well-known Christians of Toledo had their throats slit.

Most alarming though, are the recent beheadings throughout the world, including Christians in Indonesia, the Philippines, and Nigeria, as well as Hindu priests and "unveiled" Hindu women in Kashmir. Recently, the terrorists used videotapes of kidnapped victims to blackmail the West; if their demands were not met, their victims were beheaded and these pictures became part of the evening news. Wall Street Journal reporter, Daniel Pearl, was beheaded simply because he was Jewish. As Andrew Bostom states,

"...such gruesome acts are in fact sanctioned by core Islamic sacred texts, and classical Muslim jurisprudence. Empty claims that jihad decapitations are somehow "alien to true Islam," however well intentioned, undermine serious efforts to reform and desacralize Islamic doctrine. This process requires frank discussion, both between non-Muslims and Muslims, and within the Muslim community." [27]

Islamic beheading is in fact common. Consider Chechnya, Kosovo, Bosnia, and the Philippines. One such gruesome episode was recorded on film when twenty-six Serbian prisoners of war were beheaded.

Ali Ben Abi Taleb, *Muhammad's nephew*, claimed that to behead a person is an honor:

> Our flowers are the sword and the dagger
> Narcissus and myrtle are naught.
> Our drink is our blood of our foemen;
> Our goblet his skull, when we've fought. [24]

With a philosophic foundation like this, we shouldn't be surprised that members of Hamas say, "We will knock on the gates of heaven with the skulls of Jews." Just as in Nazi Germany, displays of anti-Semitism, such as posters showing the skulls of Jews, are part of everyday life in the Palestinian territories.

Islamism is not confined to the Palestinian territories. Islamic extremists came to power in Bangladesh in October 2001, with the goal of making it a pure Islamic country. Since then, thousands of homes have been looted; hundreds of thousands of non-Muslim girls and women from the ages of seven to seventy have been abducted and raped. In East Timor, Indonesia, ex-President Suharto had 200,000 East Timorese murdered out of a population of 600,000. Now there are over 64,000 madrassas, fundamentalist Islamic religious schools in Bangladesh.

Alija Izetbegovic, the former president of Bosnia who is hailed as a hero, stated in his "Islamic Declaration" (*Islamska deklaracija*) that "there can be no peace or coexistence between the Islamic faith and non-Islamic societies and political institutions. Islam clearly excludes the right and possibility of activity of any strange ideology on its own turf." Izetbegovic's declaration is similar to *Mein Kampf* in its broad agenda for "the implementation of Islam in all fields of individuals' personal lives, in family and in society, by renewal of the Islamic religious thought and creating a uniform Muslim community from Morocco to Indonesia."

3. Islam denies Christ's Diety and the Trinity

The following passages could not be more clear:

> "Who is a liar, but he that denieth that Jesus is the Christ? He is Antichrist that denieth the Father and the Son." [28]

> Beloved, believe not every spirit, but try the spirits whether they are of God: because many false prophets are gone out into the world. Hereby know ye the Spirit of God: Every spirit that confesseth that Jesus Christ is come in the flesh is of God: And every spirit that confesseth not that Jesus Christ is come in the flesh is not of God: and this is that of antichrist, whereof ye have heard that it should come; and even now already is it in the world. [29]

The doctrine of the Holy Trinity is a one of the major tenets of the Catholic faith. Catholics also believe that Jesus is the incarnation of God. These tenets clearly disqualify Catholicism as a candidate for fulfilling prophecies of the antichrist or the whore of Babylon. Conversely, look at Islam's position on the Holy Trinity. In addition, Islam denies that God came in the flesh; this is, in fact, its main argument with Christianity.

> "For many deceivers are entered into the world, who confess not that Jesus Christ is come in the flesh. This is a deceiver and an antichrist." [30]

Islam claims that the Quran is the final revelation of the Almighty—taking precedence over Torah, the Psalms, and the Gospels. This claim alone attacks the basic tenets of Biblical Judaism and Christianity.

4. Islam Denies Rights to Women

The Antichrist will have no regard for women's rights. Women will have no voice in his empire, just as they do not in Islam.

"Neither shall he regard the gods of his fathers nor the desire of women." [31]

ISLAM HONORS A GOD OF WAR

"...nor [shall he] regard any god; for he shall magnify himself above all. He will exalt himself above all gods." [32]

The Antichrist is Satan personified and he is the god of war—jihad.

"But in his estate shall he honor the God of forces: and a god whom his fathers knew not shall he honor with gold, and silver, and with precious stones, and pleasant things." [33]

Interestingly, all Muslims are required to honor Allah once a year by fulfilling one of the five pillars of Islam called *Zakat*, the requirement that each Muslim give a percentage of his wealth from money, gold, silver, and any other resources.

5. All the Prophets predicted a showdown with the nations that are today all Muslim

"Blow ye the trumpet in Zion, and sound an alarm in my holy mountain: let all the inhabitants of the land tremble: for the day of the LORD cometh, for it is nigh at hand." [34]

The day of the Lord speaks of the return of the Lord Jesus Christ, the Messiah:

"A day of darkness and of gloominess, a day of clouds and of thick darkness, as the morning spread upon the mountains: a great people and a strong; there hath not been ever the like, neither shall be any more after it, even to the years of many generations." [35]

"The earth shall quake before them; the heavens shall tremble: the sun and the moon shall be dark, and the stars shall withdraw their shining." [36]

This passage is clearly referring to the day of the Lord, and we can find confirmation of these events in Ezekiel 38, Isaiah 29, and Revelation 20:8.

"And the LORD shall utter his voice before his army: for his camp is very great: for he is strong that executeth his word: for the day of the LORD is great and very terrible; and who can abide it?"[36]

In this passage, Messiah comes in person to lead the defense of Jerusalem, confirming that believers will engage in a physical battle for Jerusalem.

"Therefore also now, saith the LORD, turn ye even to me with all your heart, and with fasting, and with weeping, and with mourning."[37]

Mourning for the Son of Man is also prophesied in chapters 12 and 14 of Zechariah—for the Son of Man who was pierced.

> Blow the trumpet in Zion, sanctify a fast, call a solemn assembly: Gather the people, sanctify the congregation, assemble the elders, gather the children, and those that suck the breasts: let the bridegroom go forth of his chamber, and the bride out of her closet.[38]

He (the bridegroom) and the bride (the believers in Messiah), prepare for war leading up to the Marriage Supper of The Lamb. That is, believers in Messiah will participate in the Battle for Jerusalem prior to the Marriage Supper of the Lamb.

> Let the priests, the ministers of the LORD, weep between the porch and the altar, and let them say, Spare thy people, O LORD, and give not thine heritage to reproach, that the heathen should rule over them: wherefore should they say among the people, Where is their God? Then will the LORD be jealous for his land, and pity his people.[40]

The conflict in the Middle East has spawned numerous international summits. Those summits, as well as the existence of the United Nations and the World Court, make it appear that international law is absolute and that consensus prevails. However, the fact is that most members of the international community implicitly or explicitly oppose the very existence of Israel as a nation. The claim is that Israel is illegally occupying the land. As I have explained earlier, that is merely an excuse, a political cover for the real issue: hatred of the faith. Land is a factor, but ultimately the conflict is about God.

If Israel has no right to the land, why does the God of the Bible, the God of Israel, chastise Israel time and time again but later always calls her back with loving kindness? It is because of His faithfulness to her ancestors. On the other hand, Allah, the god of Islam, wants Israel driven into the sea. The Lord is jealous for His land and His people, a people He set apart to be holy unto Himself.

Consider the millions who died in the Iran–Iraq war; this conflict had nothing to do with land. The mass murders occurring in Sudan today, where the Arab Muslim regime is massacring black Christian citizens, has nothing to do with land. And land was never an issue with the hundreds murdered in Algeria, with Saddam Hussein's attack on Kuwait, or with Syrian leader Hafez El-Assad's killing of tens of thousands of his own people. The reality is that the doctrines and practice of Islam produce massacres.

Let's set the record straight on another myth: the rise of terrorism has nothing to do with poverty and despair, as claimed by New York Times columnist Thomas Friedman. After all, the poorest regions of the world by far are Africa and India. Yet, how many terrorist and suicide bombers do we have coming out of those regions? The same is true of Muslim Pakistan, which at one time was part of India.

We can't exterminate the pestilence of terrorism easily. We have to root out the source of terrorism and to cut off its funding. And we must close the militant mosques, the point of origin for terrorism.

In February 2004, representatives from over forty terrorist organizations assembled in Tehran for a ten-day summit designated the "Ten Days of Dawn." Hamas, Hezbollah, Islamic Jihad, and allies of Al-Qaeda attended the summit. Among the topics discussed was the development of a new strategy to drive America out of the Middle East, the destruction of Israel, and the installation of fundamentalist Islamic governments in all Arab nations. The purpose is clear—the *destruction of Israel.*[41]

In 1948, approximately 540,000 "Palestinians" left Israel *at the insistence of the surrounding Arab nations.* The failed plan was to whisk the Arab residents to safety, then the Arab alliance would storm in and annihilate the Jews and the Palestinian Arabs would return and take full possession of the land. Then they called it a "refugee" problem. Compare the 540,000 "Palestinian refugees" with the 850,000 Jews who were expelled or fled from their homes in Arab lands. Israel, a tiny nation, has absorbed these emigrants, who left behind approximately $1 billion worth of property. Also, consider that most of the "Palestinian refugees" who left Israel were actually migrants rather than people who had lived in the land for thousands of years—unlike the Jews who have had a presence in the land throughout the last three thousand years.

> But I will remove far off from you the northern army, and will drive him into a land barren and desolate, with his face toward the east sea, and his hinder part toward the utmost sea, and his stink shall come up, and his ill savour shall come up, because he hath done great things.[42]

The "northern army" of Joel 2:20 parallels Ezekiel 38, including the "death and stink."

"The sun shall be turned into darkness, and the moon into blood, before the great and terrible day of the LORD comes. And it shall come to pass, that whosoever shall call on the name of the LORD shall be delivered: for in mount Zion and in Jerusalem shall be deliverance, as the LORD hath said, and in the remnant whom the LORD shall call."[43]

The prophecy of Micah 5:1-6, that Messiah will fight "the Assyrian" and that Israel shall waste the land of Assyria with the sword, concurs with passages from Isaiah 14 and Ezekiel 38, as well as Joel:

> "And it shall come to pass in that day, that I will call my servant Eliakim the son of Hilkiah: And I will clothe him with thy robe, and strengthen him with thy girdle, and I will commit thy government into his hand: and he shall be a father to the inhabitants of Jerusalem, and to the house of Judah. And the key of the house of David will I lay upon his shoulder; so he shall open, and none shall shut; and he shall shut, and none shall open. And I

will fasten him [as] a nail in a sure place; and he shall be for a glorious throne to his father's house."[44]

This passage echoes the theme of Isaiah 9:6 that the "government shall be upon His shoulders." Eliakim, the son of Hilkiah, is actually a "type" for Messiah. In the above passage, God commits "the government into his hand" and lays "the key of David" "upon his shoulder; so he shall open, and none shall shut; and he shall shut and none shall open." Compare this with the following passage from Revelation 3:7:

"...These things saith he that is holy, he that is true, he that hath the key of David, he that openeth, and no man shutteth; and shutteth, and no man openeth."

The Messiah, protector of Jerusalem, will deliver Israel from the Assyrian.

6. Isaiah prophecies the destruction of nations that are today Muslims

The burden of the desert of the sea

As whirlwinds in the south pass through; [so] it cometh from the desert, from a terrible land. A grievous vision is declared unto me; the treacherous dealer dealeth treacherously, and the spoiler spoileth. Go up, O Elam: besiege, O Media; all the sighing thereof have I made to cease. Therefore are my loins filled with pain: pangs have taken hold upon me, as the pangs of a woman that travaileth: I was bowed down at the hearing [of it]; I was dismayed at the seeing [of it]. My heart panted, fearfulness affrighted me: the night of my pleasure hath he turned into fear unto me. Prepare the table, watch in the watchtower, eat, drink: arise, ye princes, [and] anoint the shield. For thus hath the Lord said unto me, Go, set a watchman, let him declare what he seeth. And he saw a chariot [with] a couple of horsemen, a chariot of asses, [and] a chariot of camels; and he hearkened diligently with much heed: And he cried, A lion: My lord, I stand continually upon the watchtower in the daytime, and I am set in my ward whole nights: And, behold, here cometh a chariot of men, [with] a couple of horsemen. And he answered and said, Babylon is fallen, is fallen;

and all the graven images of her gods he hath broken unto the ground. O my threshing, and the corn of my floor: that which I have heard of the LORD of hosts, the God of Israel, have I declared unto you.[45]

Burden of Dumah (Arabia)

"He calleth to me out of Seir, Watchman, what of the night? Watchman, what of the night? The watchman said, 'The morning cometh, and also the night: if ye will enquire, enquire ye: return, come.'" [46]

Burden against Arabia

In the forest in Arabia shall ye lodge, O ye traveling companies of Dedanim. The inhabitants of the land of Tema brought water to him that was thirsty, they prevented with their bread him that fled. For they fled from the swords, from the drawn sword, and from the bent bow, and from the grievousness of war. For thus hath the Lord said unto me, Within a year, according to the years of a hireling, and all the glory of Kedar shall fail: And the residue of the number of archers, the mighty men of the children of Kedar, shall be diminished: for the LORD God of Israel hath spoken [it].[47]

This prophecy concerning Kedar, Tema, Dedan and Dumah is directed at Arabia—that is, concerning the curses on Arabia, "burden of the desert of the sea" (Isaiah 21:1). Dumah is in Saudi Arabia near Yathrib (Medina), and today is known as "Dawmat el-Jandal." Dumah, one of the sons of Ishmael, is also associated with Edom and Seir in Isaiah 21:11. Kedar, another of Ishmael's sons, is the line from which Muhammad descended. Could Mecca be the "glory of Kedar?"

Dumah is generally identified by historians with the Addyrian Adummatu people. Esarhaddon related how, in his attempt to subdue the Arabs, his father, Sennacherib, struck against their capital, Adummatu, which he called the stronghold of the Arabs. Sennacherib captured their king, Haza'il, who was called King of the Arabs. In one inscription of Ashurbanipal, Kaza'il is referred to as King of the Kedarites. From a geographical standpoint, Adummatu is often associated with the medieval Arabic Dumat el-Jandal, which was in ancient times a very important and strategic junction on the major trade route between Syria, Babylon, Najd and the Hijaz area. Dumat el Jandal is at the Southeastern end of Al Jawf, which is a desert basin, and often denotes the entire lower region of Wadi as Sirhan, the famous depression situated halfway between Syria and Mesopotamia. This area has water, and was a stop over for caravan traders travelling from Tayma, to Syria or Babylonia. This strategic location effectively made Dumah the entrance to north Arabia. This oasis was the center of rule for many north Arabian kings and queens, as related in Assyrian records.[48] By these and other references, we can conclude that Dumah stands for Arabia.

All the locations mentioned in the above passages from Isaiah 21 are in Arabia, the desert surrounded by many seas. Saudi Arabia, in fact, is sometimes referred to as the "Arab Island." These references agree with passages in Jeremiah and Revelation regarding the harlot city. The names used in these passages make it clear that the reference is not to ancient Babylon where the cities are Nineveh, Ur, Babel, Erech, Accad, Sumer, Assur, Calneh, Mari, Karana, Ellpi, Eridu, Kish, and Tikrit. There are many theories concerning Babylon: Babylon is the United States of America or the Vatican, or even that ancient Babylonia is punishing Arabia. However, none of these theories is supported by the text.

7. Obadiah confirms the destruction of nations that today are Muslim

Obadiah 1:4 is a prophecy concerning Petra in the land of Edom; however, it is a prophecy with a long-term fulfillment.

> "Though thou exalt thyself as the eagle, and though thou
> set thy nest among the stars, thence will I bring thee
> down, saith the LORD."

In prophecy, "star" refers to an angel, or a fallen angel, specifically Satan in this passage. As we know from Scripture, Satan took pride in his beauty and exalted himself as God, rebelling against the hosts of heaven. When he was cast down from heaven (a fallen angel), he took one third of the angels with him. This passage from Obadiah refers to the height of his pride—"nest among the stars [angels]"—and to his destruction: "Thence I will bring thee [the Antichrist] down."

"If thieves came to thee, if robbers by night, (how art thou cut off!) would they not have stolen till they had enough? If the grape gatherers came to thee, would they not leave some grapes?" [49]

Those under the power of the Antichrist are driven by greed: "How are the things of Esau searched out! How are his hidden things sought up!" [50]

Esau, like Tyre, represents Islam. This passage from Obadiah reveals an underlying evil. Esau rebelled against his father and married women who were Ishmaelites, ancestors of the Arabs and the line from which Muhammad descended. The God of Israel declared that He "hated Esau" [51]

> "All the men of thy confederacy have brought thee even to the border: the men that were at peace with thee have deceived thee and prevailed against thee; they that eat thy bread have laid a wound under thee: there is none understanding in him." [52]

Could the confederacy referred to here actually be the End-Time confederacy?

> Shall I not in that day, saith the LORD, even destroy the wise men out of Edom, and understanding out of the mount of Esau? And thy mighty men, O Teman, shall be dismayed, to the end that every one of the mount of Esau may be cut off by slaughter. For thy violence against thy brother Jacob, shame shall cover thee, and thou shalt be cut off forever. [53]

This prophecy speaks to the future. Jacob is Israel, and there will be judgment against Esau for the violence committed against Israel. The "mount of Esau" refers to an empire. Today, the Islamic empire is committing violence against Israel. There may be "Palestinian" sympathizers among the Western nations, but they do not incite violence against Israel or live solely to wipe Israel from the face of the earth. The Jews have suffered terribly throughout history at the hand of many nations, but we do not see organized violence against them today, other than from Islam and the Arabs. Islam is the perpetrator of anti-Semitism today.

Historically, many groups, such as those that conducted the Spanish Inquisition, had Jewish blood on their hands because of jealousy of Jewish affluence and success. What sets Islam apart is that Islam despises *the Jewish religion itself,* and that hatred incites Muslims to lay claim to the Land of Israel. It's not just a land grab; it is direct defiance and opposition to God's eternal covenant with Abraham, Isaac and Jacob.

"In the day that thou stoodest on the other side, in the day that the strangers carried away captive his forces, and foreigners entered into his gates, and cast lots upon Jerusalem, even thou wast as one of them."[54]

Today, all the Muslim nations are casting lots, claiming, "Jerusalem is ours." Muslims claim Jerusalem as the third holiest site of Islam—after Mecca and Medina.

As we see in Obadiah 1:15, "For the day of the LORD is near upon all the heathen: as thou hast done, it shall be done unto thee: thy reward shall return upon thine own head." Again, the word *heathen* is used in this passage, as it is in Ezekiel. God hates these people for what they do to Israel. The "Day of the Lord" is no doubt Armageddon. This could not have been fulfilled in the past.

"For as ye have drunk upon my holy mountain, so shall all the heathen drink continually, yea, they shall drink, and they shall swallow down, and they shall be as though they had not been."[55]

The "holy mountain" is the Temple Mount in Jerusalem; Psalm 2:6b, "upon my holy hill of Zion." Muslims today stand on God's holy mountain: the Al-Aqsa Mosque, or "Dome of the Rock," is built on the Jewish Temple Mount.

The following passage from the Quran underscores the hatred incited by the sacred text of Islam.

"Fight those who believe not in Allah nor the Last Day, nor hold that forbidden which hath been forbidden by Allah and His Messenger, nor acknowledge the Religion of Truth, from among the People of the Book, until they pay the Jizya with willing submission, and feel themselves subdued."[56]

However, the *degree* of violence cannot be appreciated in this English translation by Yusuf Ali. "Fight" is his English translation for the Arabic word *katil*, but it actually means "*kill*." And people living in Muslim countries must pay a tax for being infidels. These conditions apply only to the "People of the Book," Jews and Christians— that is, those who have received revelation but do not believe in Allah. There is no mention of pagans, Hindu, Buddhists, atheists, or mystics. Allah quite clearly has a problem only with Jews and Christians. Are these the only religious groups that worship the one true God? I have heard it said that Satan is not interested in the unbelievers; they are already lost in darkness. Satan is after the believers, the true worshippers of God because they are the only threat to his kingdom.

Tyre, Magog, Mount Seir, Teman, Babylon, Mystery, Edom, Dummah and others, when mentioned in the context of End-Time prophecy, all refer to the same thing: the Islamic world. In each prophecy, when we look at the geographic locations of the names, we find the same thing—the Islamic world. Europe, the European Union, and the Roman Catholic Church do not fit the description of the prophetic text.

"But upon mount Zion shall be deliverance, and there shall be holiness; and the house of Jacob shall possess their possessions."[57] This passage is referring to both deliverance from Islamic occupation and the redemption of Israel when the Messiah returns.

"And the house of Jacob shall be a fire, and the house of Joseph a flame, and the house of Esau for stubble, and they shall kindle in them, and devour them; and there shall not be any remaining of the house of Esau; for the LORD hath spoken it."[58] This prophecy is repeated in Psalm 83:13—"as stubble before the wind."

"And saviours shall come up on mount Zion to judge the mount of Esau; and the kingdom shall be the LORD'S."[59] The "saviours" in Obadiah 1:21 are the believers who will judge the nations with the Messiah.

8. David confirms a battle with nations that are today Muslim

This important passage from the Psalms is seldom included in discussions of Israel and the struggle with her enemies. The Arab allies gather to destroy Israel at her birth: "They have said, 'Come, and let us cut them off from being a nation, That the name of Israel may be remembered no more.'" [60]

President Nasser of Egypt was at least forthcoming when he declared, "Our basic goal is the destruction of Israel." Azaam Pasha, Secretary General of the Arab League announced, "This will be a war of extermination and momentous massacre which will be spoken of like the Mongolian massacres and Crusades."

The "confederacy" of Obadiah 1:7 is repeated in this passage: "For they have consulted together with one consent: they are confederate against thee." [61]

Psalm 83 describes these nations as:

Edom, Moab, Ammon, children of Lot—Currently Jordan and the Jordanian people (children of Lot).

Gebal—Current location is in Lebanon, 25 miles north of Beirut (according to the *Unger Bible Dictionary*).

The inhabitants of Tyre—currently the people of Lebanon. The reference to "the people of Tyre," rather than simply "Tyre," is likely because Tyre would have been destroyed as prophesied in Ezekiel 26. However, there are inhabitants still living in what is called Lebanon today.

Philistia—Gaza, Ekron, Ashdod, Ashkelon, and Gath. Gaza is now part of the Palestinian state.

Ishmaelites and Hagarites—currently the Arabs.

Assyria—Iraq and Syria.

Amalek—Jordanians southwest of the Dead Sea (Genesis 14:7), modern-day Lebanon.

This prophecy identifies the enemies of Israel by referring to the name of the place or country, unless the people moved or assimilated into other nations. When a place name does not accurately identify them, then the name of the people or their ancestry is used.

We witnessed partial fulfillment of this Scripture in the 1948 Arab-Israeli War and the 1967 Six Day War. In these wars, Israel triumphed, echoing Israel's first birth when Joshua triumphed on the seventh day of a six-day battle.

THE EVIDENCE:

Psalm 83:5: "For they have consulted together with one consent, they form a confederacy against you [Israel]." The only time these nations and peoples have formed an alliance, or "confederacy," was to fight Israel, culminating in what is known as the Arab-Israeli War.

Psalm 83:16 predicts the end of this alliance: "Fill their faces with shame, That they may seek Your name, O Lord."

Psalm 83:4: "They have said, Come, and let us cut them off from being a nation, That the name of Israel may be remembered no more."

"They" and "us" refer to the confederacy of nations that speak with one voice—that is the Arab outcry to throw the Jews into the Mediterranean Sea. In Biblical terminology, "to cut off" is to destroy. The purpose of the confederacy in Psalm 83—"to cut them off from being a nation, that the name of Israel may be remembered no more"—is the same purpose so fervently embraced by the Arab nations today: prevent the rebirth of Israel.

Psalm 83:8: "Assyria [Iraq] also is joined with them; they have helped the children of Lot." The "Children of Lot" is the nation of Jordan, which requested Iraq's help in the 1948 Arab-Israeli War.

It is important to emphasize that God's purpose in dealing with the nations of this confederacy (to "make them afraid" and to "fill their faces with shame) is that they will seek the name of the Lord (verse 16). Their defeat was not born out of revenge or hatred; it is an appeal to these nations to reconcile with God and recognize His authority and will—"that men may know that thou, whose name alone is Jehovah, art the Most High over all the earth" (verse 18). Menachem Begin's prayer on his first visit to the Western Wall following its liberation in 1967: "God of our Fathers, Abraham, Isaac and Jacob, Lord of Hosts, be Thou our help. Our enemies encompassed us about, yea they encompassed us about and arose to destroy us as a people. Yet has their counsel been destroyed and their schemes will not be accomplished."

###

When I was a young boy in Jericho, the American Consul sent representatives from Jerusalem when they heard that a major war was about to erupt. They started evacuating all Americans in the area; and because my mother was an American, they came to rescue her. My father, however, refused the offer to leave because he loved his country.

The Six Day War began, and the Jews captured old Jerusalem and the rest of Palestine. The Israeli victory was a great disappointment to Arabs and Muslims worldwide. I remember many things about the war—the thunder of the bombs and clatter of machine guns that continued for six days and nights.

As the Arab people ran in fear from the Israelis and crossed the Jordan River, many of their fellow citizens and neighbors in Jericho began looting the stores and houses. The Israeli soldiers announced that everyone should post a white flag on their gate. Israel won the war in six days, and on the seventh day, Rabbi Goren blew the ram's horn on the Wailing Wall in Jerusalem, declaring victory.

Many see this war as a parallel to Joshua at Jericho, when Joshua and the Israelites marched around the walls of Jericho for six days. On the seventh day, they marched around the city seven times. On the seventh day, the priests blew the trumpets and the people shouted with one voice, the walls tumbled, and the Israelites took the city.

The Arabs have lost every war they waged against Israel, exactly as the Bible prophesied in the Scriptures I have cited. Yet after all these losses, we still hoped for that one victory, which we believed was all that was necessary to destroy Israel. Many Muslims in the land claim that Israel is God's punishment for allowing bad government to rule the Islamic world. This belief is what fuels the attempts by majority Muslim populations to topple ruling governments. Consider the words of Syrian President Hafez Assad: "The Arabs are willing to lose several wars to come with Israel. All they need to do is defeat Israel once." The God of Israel has promised, "they shall not be pulled up." The Arab and Muslim worlds continue to try, but God has promised they will fail.

Psalm 83:18 declares,

"That men may know that You, whose name alone is Jehovah, art the Most High over all the earth."

God's promises never fail; He fulfills them to the letter. Arabs feel that the God of the Bible is biased toward the Jews, but the Lord desires that the Arab people turn to Him (the one true God). We should not ignore the many verses that declare punishments against Israel. After the Jews refused to accept Christ's sacrifice, the final offering for sin, the Temple was destroyed and the great "Diaspora" began; the Jews were scattered into all the earth, separated from their homeland and far from Jerusalem. God allowed them to be killed and tormented more than any other people in the world. There is no other people in history who have tasted the agony of war and pain more than the Jews have; they are the true refugees of the world.

9. Psalm 74 and the destruction of Jewish holy places

Psalm 74:1 also refers to the Muslim people. "O God, why hast thou cast us off for ever? Why doth thine anger smoke against the sheep of thy pasture?"

Israel has been cast off for its sins and the Jews believe God has neglected them. In Psalm 74:2 we hear their plea, "Remember thy congregation, which thou hast purchased of old; the rod of thine inheritance, which thou hast redeemed; this mount Zion, wherein thou hast dwelt."

God has ordained Israel to proclaim the truth to the nations, as Psalm 74:3 says, "Lift up thy feet unto the perpetual desolations; even all that the enemy hath done wickedly in the sanctuary." Who has done wickedly in God's sanctuary but the present occupiers—the Islamic crowds who daily pollute the sanctuary with their abominations.

One of the most egregious examples is the construction (or rather, destruction) project undertaken by the Waqf, the Muslim religious authority that controls the Temple Mount. The purpose of the project is to create a second entrance to the al-Marawani Mosque, which is located under the southeastern quadrant of the Mount—an area popularly, although mistakenly, known as Solomon's stables.

The huge underground mosque attracts thousands of worshippers, so there is no question that a second entryway is important for safety reasons. However, the Waqf's decision to haul material from the area and dump it in the dead of night in the nearby Kidron Valley has come under attack as irresponsible destruction of an important archaeological site. Israeli archaeologists called for a professional, controlled excavation to no avail. Now the only remaining option is for personnel from the Israel Antiquities Authority (IAA) to sift through the dump in the Kidron Valley in the hopes of gaining some raw data, but unfortunately, without context.

They dig up precious Jewish artifacts and destroy them to prevent the Jews from claiming the site of their temple; they do this because they worship a God who is not the God of Israel, the one true God. Under the direction of the Muslim authorities, bulldozers cart away huge mounds of earth from underneath the Temple Mount in Jerusalem, one of the most revered and sacred sites in the world. Israeli archaeologists are outraged, claiming that the Muslim authorities are damaging the inside of the Mount's eastern retaining wall and destroying priceless historical data in the process.

The Muslims have also attacked synagogues in Israel and throughout the world, including Turkey and Tunisia. Roman Catholics do not burn synagogues or attack Jewish shrines nor do Jews ever destroy churches or mosques. Yet Muslims have gone so far as to desecrate the tombs of Abraham, Sarah, Rachel and Joseph.

"Thine enemies roar in the midst of thy congregations; they set up their ensigns for signs." [62]

The sound of the enemy roar can be heard as Muslims, from their position on the Temple Mount, throw stones at the Jews below as they congregate to pray at the Western Wall. Compare Psalm 74:4 with the following account reported by TruthNews.net. July 30, 2001.

> Israeli police stormed the Temple Mount in Jerusalem's walled Old City on Sunday to quell a riot by Muslims. The clashes began after Muslims rioters began throwing stones at Jews praying below them at the adjoining Western Wall. Israeli police rushed onto the Temple Mount, site of the Jewish Temples in Biblical times, and

fired stun grenades at Muslim rioters. The clash took place in the most sensitive area in the Israeli-Arab conflict. The Temple Mount is the site of the holy temples in Biblical times, and is regarded as the most sacred place in the Jewish world. Since the Muslim conquest of Jerusalem in the 7th century A.D., the area has also been home to the Dome of the Rock and Al-Aqsa mosque. Muslims claim the site as the third holiest site in Islam, after Mecca and Medina in Saudi Arabia.

Fifteen police officers and 20 Palestinians were injured in the clashes, which continued intermittently throughout the afternoon.[63]

10. As police approach to stop the riot, Palestinians throw shoes at them

Psalm 74:5 refers to the man or men who cut down trees to build God's holy sanctuary with axes and hammers.

"A man was famous according as he had lifted up axes upon the thick trees."

And we are told in Psalm 74:6:

"But now they break down the carved work thereof at once."

This reference to breaking down the carved works (verse 6) is fulfilled not only by the destruction accomplished by the Waqf, but also by the destruction of Joseph's Tomb in Shechem (present-day Nablus). Palestinians relentlessly hammered at the tomb with pick axes and hammers (see accompanying photo).

Muslim mobs burned and destroyed Joseph's tomb, then danced in celebration. Over sixteen synagogues were desecrated on the West Bank, literally *all the* synagogues in Judea.

"They said in their hearts, Let us destroy them together: they have burned up all the synagogues of God in the land."[64] What else could fulfill these Scriptures more precisely than these acts of violence and desecration in these holy places?

"They have cast fire into thy sanctuary, they have defiled by casting down the dwelling place of thy name to the ground."[65]

Muslim mob destroying Joseph's Tomb. They later rebuilt it as a Mosque. [JCS Int'l copyright 1999-2002]

Muslims hate the Jews. As they commit violent acts against the Jews, they deny the God of Israel His place to be worshiped. With their voices and with ensigns, they proclaim that only Allah is god; they are against the one true God.

"We see not our signs: there is no more any prophet: neither is there among us any that knoweth how long."[66]

Today Jews are perplexed as never before as to how long this violence can continue. Synagogues are burned, just as prophesied in this Scripture. Psalm 74:14 leaves no doubt that this violence against the Jews (God's chosen people) will continue until the end of the Tribulation as described in the following verses from Psalm 74:

"Thou brakest the heads of leviathan in pieces, [and] gavest him [to be] meat to the people inhabiting the wilderness." [67]

The seven-headed beast of Revelation is destroyed.

Remember this, [that] the enemy hath reproached, O LORD, and [that] the foolish people have blasphemed thy name. O deliver not the soul of thy turtledove unto the multitude [of the wicked]: forget not the congregation of thy poor forever. Have respect unto the covenant: for the dark places of the earth are full of the habitations of cruelty. O let not the oppressed return ashamed: let the poor and needy praise thy name. Arise, O God, plead thine own cause: remember how the foolish man reproacheth thee daily. Forget not the voice of thine enemies: the tumult of those that rise up against thee increaseth continually." [68]

This passage agrees with Joel 3 and Matthew 25—the core of this issue is the oppression of Israel. God will arise, *Kumma Elohim,* to respond to the cruelty of the multitude, the Muslim multitude, for killing the Jewish people and for destroying His holy places. They conspire together with other Islamic nations to destroy the Jews. They plan first to destroy the Saturday people (the Jews) and then the Sunday people (the Christians). *Kumma Elohim* is the Hebrew for Arise O God. This is a desperate appeal to God to arise from His throne and come to the earth to fight the enemies of Israel. In this verse, we see that the destroyers of God's holy places are the blasphemers of God. Compare this passage with Revelation, which states that the title or name of this system is blasphemous. It is clear that God, who upholds His Word, will not allow these things to continue; he will judge those who come against His chosen people Israel.

The following excerpt is from a sermon delivered over live Palestinian TV:

"Wherever you are, kill the Jews, the Americans, who are like them, and those who stand by them. They are all in one accord against the Muslims."

"It is forbidden to befriend Israelis in any way. Don't love them or enter into agreement with them, don't help them or sign accords with them. Anyone who does this is one of them." This is the word of Allah for which various Surahs are cited, such as Surah 9:5.

So when the sacred months have passed away, then slay the idolaters wherever you find them, and take them captives and besiege them and lie in wait for them in every ambush, then if they repent and keep up prayer and pay the poor-rate, leave their way free to them; surely Allah is Forgiving, Merciful."[69]

11. Islamic teaching concerning Jews and Christians

The sermon sends the same message as the following passage from Surah 9:29, which refers to Jews and Christians.

"Fight those who believe not in Allah nor the Last Day, nor hold that forbidden which hath been forbidden by Allah and His Messenger, nor acknowledge the Religion of Truth, from among the People of the Book, until they pay the Jizya with willing submission, and feel themselves subdued." If you do not believe in Allah and Muhammad, his messenger to mankind, then you must be killed. The Ayatollah Khomeini of Iran said that one of his goals is the eradication Israel. In 1998, Osama bin Laden echoed that goal, urging Jihad against Americans and Jews. He claimed that it is the obligation of all Muslims to kill the infidels in Muslim lands and to drive out those whom he considers are plundering Muslim resources (oil, gas and minerals.)

On June 8, 2001, Sheikh Ibrahim Madhi used a "sermon" to issue the following warning over Palestinian television:

"Allah is willing for the unjust state of Israel to be erased. The unjust state, the United States will be erased. The unjust state, Britain, will be erased."

In fact, Muslims are waiting for the Mahdi, who they believe will bring peace and he is to come before Jesus returns.

> ...There will come forth a man from my nation who will talk according to my Sunnah. God will send upon him rain from heaven, and the earth will sprout forth for him its blessing. The earth will be filled through him with equity and justice, as it has been filled with injustice and crime. He will direct the affairs of this nation for seven years, and he will settle in Jerusalem.

In light of Biblical prophecy, the Quranic prophecy of seven years is remarkable. In fact, there is a great deal in the description of the Mahdi of Islam to indicate that he is actually the greatest of all deceivers—Gog, also known as the Antichrist!

"And he shall make a firm covenant with many for one week [seven years]: and in the midst of the week he shall cause the sacrifice and the oblation to cease."[70]

In Daniel's prophecy, one day represents one year, and a week represents seven years. In Daniel, the person referred to will make a covenant or treaty with Israel; that is, he will come peacefully, but in the remainder of this verse, we see that he violates the treaty:

" ...and for the overspreading of abominations he shall make [it] desolate, even until the consummation, and that determined shall be poured upon the desolate and on the 'wing of abominations' shall come one that maketh desolate; and even unto the full end, and that determined, shall wrath be poured out upon the desolate."

Chapter Seventeen
The Final Showdown:
Christ vs. the Assyrian

MICAH 5—SHOWDOWN: CHRIST VS. THE ASSYRIAN

Most Christians refer to Micah 5 simply as the prophecy of the place of Jesus. However, Micah also sums up His First and Second Coming to defeat the Antichrist.

"Now gather thyself in troops, O daughter of troops: he hath laid siege against us: they shall smite the judge of Israel with a rod upon the cheek." [1]

In Christian theology, here Messiah is struck in accordance with Isaiah 53.

"But thou, Bethlehem Ephratah, though thou be little among the thousands of Judah, yet out of thee shall he come forth unto me that is to be ruler in Israel; whose goings forth have been from of old, from everlasting." [2]

This tells us His birthplace. Next, Israel is wandering, persecuted through the ages.

"...until the time that she which travaileth hath brought forth: then the remnant of his brethren shall return unto the children of Israel." [3]

"She" is Israel, and after she gives birth to the new, current Israel, and the remnant of Israel return back to the land,

"And he shall stand and feed in the strength of the LORD, in the majesty of the name of the LORD his God; and they shall abide: for now shall he be great unto the ends of the earth." [9]

Messiah will establish His kingdom and His power will be great unto the ends of the earth.

"And this man shall be the peace, when the *Assyrian* shall come into our land: and when he shall tread in our palaces..." [5]

The Assyrian (Antichrist) will attack Israel. Messiah will be the one to establish our true peace.

> ...then shall we raise against him *seven shepherds*, and *eight principal men*. And they shall waste the land of Assyria with the sword, and the land of Nimrod in the entrances thereof: thus shall He deliver us from the *Assyrian*, when He cometh into our land, and when He treadeth within our borders.[6]

God will raise seven shepherds and eight principled men from the world, and these leaders will destroy the Antichrist. This is a prophecy concerning the Messiah or Christ's advent upon this Earth to the holy hill, Mount Zion. The "Assyrian" here is clearly another title of the Antichrist.

WHO ARE THE SEVEN SHEPHERDS?

Who are these seven shepherds that will destroy the Assyrian? Why does the Bible have *seven* on the side of Christ fighting *seven* on the side of Antichrist? Remember in Daniel 7:8, *three* are plucked out of the *ten*. This leaves Antichrist with seven. It is plausible that seven nations will stand on the side of Christ and Israel in the end. Could it be seven Western nations? Could America be on this list of righteous defenders?

ISAIAH—SHOWDOWN: CHRIST VS. THE ASSYRIAN

In Isaiah 31:4, the text emphases *Assyria* and that *"The Lord will come down to fight for Mount Zion"* and in verse 8, because of His coming, we see that *"Assyria shall fall by a sword not of man."* Jesus clearly never fought battles against Assyria in His First Coming, therefore, this must refer to Christ's Second Advent.

> Woe to Assyria, the rod of my anger! And my fury is the staff in their hand. I will send him against an ungodly nation, and against the people of my wrath. I will command him to plunder, and to strip off spoil and to trample them like the mud in the streets...And it shall be in that day, the remnant of Israel...shall not

any more lean on him who struck him. But they will truly lean on Yahweh, the Holy One of Israel. The remnant shall return, the remnant of Jacob, to the mighty God...And a shoot [David] goes out from the stump of Jesse, and a Branch [Messiah] will bear fruit out of his roots...and he shall strike the earth with the rod of his mouth...*and the wolf shall live with the lamb...*[7]

This passage is clearly referring to the future End-Times of Assyria, when the *wolf will lay with the lamb*. Verse 17 shows that this destruction is carried out by Israel:

"And the light of Israel shall be for a fire, and his Holy One for a flame: and it shall burn and devour his thorns and his briers in one day."[8]

When in the past did Israel destroy Assyria? And in one day? The millennial restoration of Israel is a direct result of the same defeat of this End-Times empire with several names—"Mystery Babylon," "Assyria," "Tyre," "Mount of Esau," "Edom," "Mount Sinai," and "Gog and Magog."

As we have learned, the Antichrist has many guises and many titles: "King of Babylon," "the Assyrian," (Babylon was a part of the Assyrian empire), "King of Tyre," "Prince of Tyre," and "cedar of Lebanon," to name a few.

If the Antichrist's predecessor, "the little horn," was Antiochus Epiphanies from Syria, then indeed he was an Assyrian. If one argues that Turkey is the "seat of Satan" (Antichrist), then how does Turkey fit with his being Assyrian?

The Assyrian homeland encompasses what was once the core of the Assyrian Empire, which included modern eastern Turkey, Syria, Lebanon, Palestine, Israel, western Iran, Kuwait, and Egypt.

Finally, we must address Islam, which started in Babylon with worship of the Moon-god. Today, people in their vanity ascribe greatness to something other than the true God, an idol called the Black Stone. And sacrificing for Allah during the Haj in Mecca is really idolatrous worship. First Corinthians 10:10-21 puts it bluntly:

"…what say I then? That the idol is any thing, or that which is offered in sacrifice to idols is any thing? But I say that the things which the Gentiles sacrifice, they sacrifice to devils, and not to God: and I would not that ye should have fellowship with devils. Ye cannot drink the cup of the Lord, and the cup of devils: ye cannot be partakers of the Lord's Table, and of the table of devils."

#

Now it is our time to choose whether to dine at the table of the devils or at the table of the Lord.

Sources

Chapter One: Confession of a Terrorist

1. Bat Ye'or, Islam and Dhimmitude, p. 153.
2. Sheik Muhammad Ibrahim Al-Madhi, Friday Sermon on PA TV: "We Must Educate our Children on the Love of Jihad," special dispatch #240, Memri.org. Jul. 11, 2001, via online Israel's War Against Terror.
3. Abu Hamaid al-Ghazali, FrontPagemag.com, conversation with Kamal Nawash, Walid Shoebat and Professsor Khaleel Mohammed, Asst. Prof. Dept. Relig. Studies at San Diego state Univ., Aug. 13, 2004.
4. Ibid.
5. Khalid Abou el Fadl, quoted in The Link online re: "Define Jihad Please", by gharbala, April 7, 2003.
6. Al-Mawardi, The Laws of Islamic Governance, trans. by Dr. Asadullah Yate, (London, Ta-Ha Publishers Ltd., 1996), p. 192, as quoted in the Jerusalem Post Forum online article, "The Sacred Muslim Practice of Beheading," May 13, 2004.
7. Hanaqi Fiqh, "The True Meaning of Jihad in Islam," from Prophet of Peace online.
8. Haj Amin al-Husseini, the Grand Nazi Mufti of Jerusalem, Israel Forum Bulletin v3.0.3.
9. Jarid al-Kidwa, PLO TV, June, 1997, reported in Ha'aretz, 7-6, 1997.
10. Israeli daily, Ha'aretz, al-Kidwa, "Are Today's Jews Really Ancient Israel?" Omega Letter online, Jack Kinsella, Sept. 19, 2003.
11. Al-Bushra website, an Arab Christian view.
12. Chapman, Rev. Colin, Whose Promised Land? (Lion Publishing), p. 240.
13. Lewis, Bernard, Semites & Anti-Semites, (New York: WW Norton & Co., 1986), p. 81.
14. Lewis, Bernard. The Pro-Islamic Jews, p. 401.
15. Saifur Rahman al-Mubarakpuri, "AR-Raheeq Al-Makhtum," FaithFreedom.org, see Bukhari, Vol. 5, Book 59, #443.
16. Sunan Abu Daud, Book 38, #4390.

17. Lucy Dawidowicz, The War Against the Jews, Anti-Jewish Legislation, p. 72.
18. Ibid., p. 75.
19. Ibid., p. 84.
20. Middle Eastern Studies, 1971, p. 232.
21. Narrated Abu Burda. Volume 9, Book 84, Number 58.
22. Narrated Anas Bin Malik, Hadith Sahih Bukhari Vol. 1 # 387
23. Faqeeh Al-Muluk, "Omar bin Al-Khattab, Islam's second Caliph after Muhammad the Prophet of Islam", reference, volume 2, pages 124-136, the Omar Covenant.
24. Lady Magnus, Outlines of Jewish History, Life Under The Kaliphs, second ed. p.125.
25. Ibid., p. 126.
26. G. E. von Grunebaum, quoted from Bat Ye'or, p.61.
27. Associated Press.
28. Carl Savich, Serbianna, The Bosnian Conflict: Origins and History, Bosnia-Herzegovina Under Ottoman Rule—463-1878, July 13, 2003.
29. Faqeeh Al-Muluk, Omar Charter, vol. 2, pages 124-136.
30. Sahih Al-Bukhari, 9:57.
31. Ibid., 9:50.
32. Malik, Book 43, #43.15.8b.
33. Al-Bukhari, 4:392.
34. Narrated by a Muslim, 2167.
35. Leonard J. Davis, and M. Decter, Myths and Facts—a Concise Record of the Arab-Israeli Conflict, Washington DC: Near East Report, 1982, p. 199.
36. Anis Mansour, 1973.
37. From the Simon Wiesenthal Center website: http://motlc.wiesenthal.org
38. The American Christian Palestine Committee, Arab War Effort, p.3.
39. Arab Higher Committee, submitted to the United Nations, May 1947.
40. Ibid.
41. Rep. Michael McNulty, Newsday, November 1, 1987.

42. Arabic translation of the introduction to Adolf Hitler's Mein Kampf, distributed by Al-Shurouq, a Ramallah-based book distributor, in East Jerusalem and territories controlled by the Palestinian Authority.

43. American Jewish Yearbook, 1983, New York.

44. Bat Ye'or, The Decline of Eastern Christianity Under Islam.

45. Ibid.

46. Serge Trifkovic, FrontPageMagazine.com, November 15, 2002.

47. Ibid.

48. Ibn Ishaq, page 752.

49. Al-Kindy, p. 47.

50. Journal of the Royal Asiatic Society of Great Britain and Ireland, 1976, Uyun al-athar, I, 16-7.

51. Na'aeem Bek, The Armenian Atrocities, page 43.

52. Frank S. DeHass, History, vol. V, p.393.

53. Maimonides, Epistle Concerning Apostasy, 1160 AD, Historical Society of Jews from Egypt.

54. Friday prayer sermon by PA Mufti Ikrima Sabri broadcast on the official PA radio station the Voice of Palestine, July 11, 1997.

55. Jacob Saphir, "Eben Sappir," i. 67a, (Lyck, 1866), p. 52.

56. Garsten Niebuhr, Reisebeschreibungen, vol. 1, p.422, translation by Robert Herson.

57. Norman Stillman, The Jews of Arab Lands in Modern Times.

58. Associated Press, November 26, 29, 1956, New York World Telegram.

59. Judith Miller and Dr. Laurie Mylroie, Saddam Hussein and the Crisis in the Gulf, p. 34.

60. New York Times, February 18, 1973.

61. Ibid.

Chapter Two: Confession — Our Nazi Education

1. Narrated by Abu Huraira. vol. 1, book 2, no. 25.

2. Transmitted by Sheikh Khalil in Mukhtasar Al-Khalil.

3. Fiqh Imam Shirazi in Al-Muhazab Fil Fiqh Al-Shaafi.

4. Fiqh Imam Ibn Qudama Al-Maqdisi.

5. Studies in Theology: Tradition and Morals, Palestinian text-book, Grade 11, 2001 pp. 291-92.
6. Sahih Muslim, 5203.
7. Andrew G. Bostom, Jihad Watch, June 30, 2004, "Textbook Jihad in Egypt," quoting "Commentary on the Surahs of Muhammad, Al-Fath, Al-Hujurat and Qaf," Grade 11, 2002 p. 9.
8. Ibid.
9. E. W. Lane, Modern Egyptians, p. 575.
10. Andrew G. Bostom, article re: Goitein, S.D. commentary, January 1949, "Cross-Currents in Arab National Feeling," p. 161, June 30, 2004.
11. Antoine Fattal, Let Statut Legal de Musulmans en Pays' d'Islam, (Beirut, 1958), pp. 369, 372.
12. Jerusalem Post, March 22, 1996.
13. Jerusalem Post, Feb. 1996.
14. Washington Post, May 2, 1995.
15. Jerusalem Post, Feb. 18 & Feb. 19, 1994.
16. Yasser Arafat, Jerusalem Post, April 1, 1990.
17. Al-Hayat Al-Jadeeda, December 8, 1997.
18. Palestinian paper, Al-Ayyam, October 29, 1997.
19. "Al-Aqsa Surrounded by Conspiracies," Al-Hayat Al-Jadeeda, October 26, 1997.
20. The Palestinian daily, Al-Quds, October 15, 1997.
21. Abdel Hamid al-Qudsi, PA Deputy Minister of Supplies, speech to Chamber of Commerce in Tulkarem, Itim news agency, July 9, 1997.
22. Abdel Hamid al-Qudsi, PA Deputy Minister of Supplies, newspaper interview, Yediot Aharonot, June 25, 1997.
23. Saleh Abdulal, Director of the Inspection Department of the PA Ministry of Supplies, Al-Hayat Al-Jadeeda, May 26, 1997.
24. Abdel-Razek Al-Majeeda, Commander of the Palestinian General Security Service in Gaza, Al-Hayat Al-Jadeeda, May 15, 1997.
25. PA Information Ministry press release, March 29, 1997.
26. Nabil Ramlawi, Palestinian representative to United Nations Commission on Human Rights in Geneva, Jerusalem Post, March 17, 1997.

27. PA Information Ministry Press Release, December 10, 1997.
28. Article in the official PA newspaper, Al-Hayat Al-Jadeeda, December 9, 1997.
29. Interview with Islamic author Safi Naz Kassam, Al-Hayat Al-Jadeeda, September 1, 1997.
30. Suleiman Roumi, member of the PA Legislative Council, Al-Hayat Al-Jadeeda, August 10, 1997.
31. Article in the Palestinian daily, Al-Ayyam, July 18, 1997.
32. Ahmed al-Awadeh, Palestinian researcher, Al-Hayat Al-Jadeeda, September 1, 1997.
33. Interview with Palestinian National Council member Ahmad Sidqi al-Dajani, Al-Hayat Al-Jadeeda, October 20, 1997.
34. Yihya Yakhlaf, Al-Ayyam, PA Under-Secretary for Culture, August 7, 1997.
35. Hasan Al-Kashef, Director-General of the PA Information Ministry, Al-Hayat Al-Jadeeda, July 7, 1997.
36. Ha'aretz, 15 June 1997.
37. Nabil Ramlawi, Palestinian U.N. representative, United Nations Commission on Human Rights in Geneva, Jerusalem Post, March 17, 1997.
38. Fuad Abu Hijla, October 31, 1997.
39. Al-Hayat Al-Jadeeda, August 5, 1997.
40. Ibid. July 27, 1997.
41. "The Banks and Shylock," Al-Hayat Al-Jadeeda, editor Hafez al- Barghouti, November 5, 1997.
42. Othman Abu Gharbiya, PA Chairman Yasser Arafat's Adviser on National Political Guidance, in an interview with the official PA radio station, the Voice of Palestine, March 15, 1997.
43. "The Legend of Jewish Superiority," Palestinian daily, Al-Quds, November 11, 1997.
44. Excerpts from a position paper issued by Yasser Arafat's Fatah faction of the PLO, Al- Hayat Al-Jadeeda, October 18, 1997.
45. Al-Hayat Al-Jadeeda, August 6, 1997.
46. Yasser Arafat, Jerusalem Report, Dec. 26, 1996.
47. Ha'aretz, October 9, 1996.
48. Yasser Arafat, Ma'ariv, October 11, 1996.
49. Sheikh Ismail Jamal, PLO Director of the Islamic Wakf in Jericho, Chicago Jewish Sentinel, May 18, 1995.

50. Jerusalem Post, February 22, 1995.
51. Al-Hayat Al-Jadeeda, November 30, 1997.
52. Khaled Abu Tuama, correspondent for the weekly Jerusalem newspaper, Yerushalayim, November 5, 1999.
53. Ha'aretz, November 3, 1999.
54. Friday prayer sermon by PA Mufti Ikrima Sabri from the Temple Mount (Al-Aqsa Mosque), Voice of Palestine, July 11, 1997.
55. PA Mufti Ikrama Sabri, Al-Bilad, July 31, 1997.
56. PA Mufti Ikrama Sabri, The New York Times, May 18, 1997.
57. Sheikh Hamid Al-Bitawi, chairman of the Palestine Religious Scholars Association and head of the PA's Shari'a Court of Appeals in Nablus, Al-Hayat Al-Jadeeda, July 27, 1997.
58. An excerpt from the weekly Friday prayer sermon at Al-Aqsa Mosque, Voice of Palestine, October 24, 1997.
59. Al-Hayat Al-Jadeeda, editor Hafez al- Barghouti, November 18, 1997.
60. Voice of Palestine, program about the media, December 3, 1997.
61. From a communiqué issued by Yasser Arafat's Fatah faction of the PLO, Al-Hayat Al-Jadeeda, November 4, 1997.
62. Al-Quds, November 1, 1997.
63. Hafez al-Barghouti, editorial, Al-Hayat Al- Jadeeda, October 30, 1997.
64. Al-Hayat Al-Jadeeda, October 29, 1997.
65. Hafez al-Barghouti, ed., Al-Hayat Al-Jadeeda, October 14, 1997.
66. Al-Hayat Al-Jadeeda, August 11, 1997.
67. Hasan Al-Kashef, Director-General of the PA Information Ministry, quoted in Al-Hayat Al-Jadeeda, July 7, 1997.
68. Voice of Palestine, June 24, 1997.
69. Poem read on the Voice of Palestine, May 22, 1997, as part of a series of Songs of the Homeland. The poem was previously read during the September 1996 riots.
70. Assad Abdel Rahman, PA Minister for Refugee Affairs, Al-Hayat Al-Jadeeda, December 6, 1997.
71. Al-Hayat Al-Jadeeda, December 8, 1997.

72. Abdel Jawad Saleh, PA Agriculture Minister, Al-Hayat Al-Jadeeda, November 6, 1997.

73. Al-Hayat Al-Jadeedah, September 3, 1997.

74. Ibid., Aug. 17, 1997.

75. PA Information Ministry press release, April 22, 1997.

76. PA Information Ministry press release, December 10, 1997.

77. Al-Quds, November 17, 1997.

78. Brig. Gen. Khaled Al-Musmar, Deputy Head of the PA's Indoctrination Directorate, Falastin Al-Yaum, August 21, 1997.

79. Freih Abu Middein, PA Justice Minister, Yediot Aharonot, April 13, 1997.

80. Nahid Munir Al-Rayyis, a member of the PA's Legislative Council, Al-Quds, October 15, 1997.

81. PA Police Chief Ghazi Jabali, in reaction to the arrest warrant issued against him by Israel for his involvement in terrorist attacks, Ma'ariv, September 12, 1997.

82. Jerusalem Post, Jan. 26, 1995.

83. Cultural affairs program broadcast on Voice of Palestine, August 25, 1997.

84. Al-Wahidi, Abir, female Fatah terrorist released in February 1997, in an interview on Voice of Palestine, February 13, 1997.

85. The Washington Post, December 2, 1998.

86. Tayseer Qaba, deputy chairman of the PLO's Palestine National Council, An-Nahar, September 19, 1995, p. 16.

87. Palestine Broadcasting Corporation, August 6, 1995.

88. Yasser Arafat, in a speech given on August 6, 1995 at a party to celebrate the birth of his daughter, reported in Ha'aretz, September 6, 1995, the Jerusalem Post, September 7, 1995.

89. Suleiman Adwan, PLO police officer and member of the "Al Quds" Brigade, in Jenin, Davar Rishon, November 20, 1995, p. 2.

90. Yasser Arafat, PLO Chairman, Voice of Palestine, November 11, 1995.

91. An-Nahar, April 11, 1995; Al Quds, April 14, 1995.

92. Col. Jibril Rajoub, chief of the PA's Preventive Security Service, interview with Al-Jazeera TV, May 27, 1998.

93. Russian newspaper Novoya Vremy, May 25, 1997.

94. An-Nahar, March 9, 1996.

95. Jerusalem Post, July 25, 1995.
96. Al Hayat, April 17, 1995.
97. United Press International, September 12, 1996.
98. An-Nahar, April 11, 1995; Al Quds, April 14, 1995.
99. Reuters, Oct. 28, 1994.
100. United Press International, Oct. 28, 1994.
101. New York Times, January 8, 1996; Peace Watch, June 1996
    Report, p.15; Jerusalem Post, Dec. 17, 1996.
102. New York Times, July 2, 1994
103. Jewish Telegraphic Agency, April 6, 1998.
104. Ma'ariv, March 28, 1997
105. ZOA press release, October 8, 1998

Chapter Three: Distorting Biblical Text

1. Joel 3:4.
2. Exodus 33:1-3.
3. Num 21:2-3 4. Israel in Prophecy.
5. Matt. 10:23.
6. Matt. 2:20-21.
7. Romans 11:1-2.
8. Jer. 31:35.
9. Jarid al-Kidwa, Palestinian Arab historian, PLO TV.
10. Nathan Ausubel, Pictorial History of the Jewish People, 1953.
11. Vasilii V. Grigoriev, "O dvoystvennosti verkhovnoy vlasti u
    khazarov," (1835), reprinted in his 1876 compilation book
    Rossiya i Aziya, p. 66.
12. Genesis 17:7-8.
13. Genesis 26:3-4.
14. Genesis 35:12.
15. Psalm 105:7-11.
16. Jeremiah 30:2-3.
17. Isaiah 41:8, 9.
19. Jer. 31:35.
20. Gen 22:18.

21. Ezek. 37:21.
23. Matthew 2:6.
24. Matt 15:24.
25. Matt 23:37-39.
26. Jer. 3:17.
27. Rev. 20:1-5.
28. Luke 21:24.
29. Psalm 53:6.
30. John 4:22.
31. Psalm 102:13-22.
32. Joel 3:2.
33. Isaiah 41:22.
34. Zech 13:6-14:4
35. Zech 14:1-4
36. Zech. 14:3
37. Amos 9:14, 1
38. Ezekiel 36:21-26.
39. Khaled al-Azm's memoirs, (Beirut 1973), part 1, pp. 386-387.
40. Harry C. Stebbens, London Evening Standard, January 10, 1969.
41. Ash Sha'ab, editorial, January 30 1948, Haifa.
42. Msgr. George Hakim, Greek Catholic Bishop, Sada al Janub, May 5, 1948, Beirut, as quoted in London Times, August, 1948.
43. The Economist, October 2, 1948, London.
44. Falastin, editorial, February 19, 1949, Amman.
45. Near East Arabic Broadcasting Station, April 3 1949, Cyprus.
46. Kenneth Bilby, New Star in the Near East, pp. 30-31, (New York, 1950).
47. Iraqi Prime Minister Nuri Said, as quoted by Nimr el Hawari, former Commander of the Palestine Arab Youth Organization, 'Sir Am Nakbah' The Secret Behind the Disaster, 1952, Nazareth.
48. Edward Atiyah, Secretary of the Arab League Office in London, as quoted in The Arabs, (London, 1955), p. 183.
49. Emil Ghoury, Secretary of the Arab Higher Committee, quoted in the Daily Telegraph, September 6, 1948, Beirut.

50. Habib Issa, in the daily US-published Lebanese newspaper, Al Hoda, June 8, 1951, New York.
51. A refugee, quoted in the Jordanian daily newspaper Ad Difaa, September 6, 1954.

Chapter Four: Israel and the Land Controversy

1. Isaiah 62:1-2 & 6.
2. Deuteronomy 11:12.
3. Mark Twain, Harper's Magazine, 1899.
4. Al-Kidwa, Palestinian historian on Palestine TV.
5. Frank DeHass, History, p. 258. John of Wuzburg list from Reinhold Rohricht edition, pp. 41, 69.
6. Ernst Frankenstine, Justice for My People, (London, Nicholson and Watson, 1943), p. 127.
7. D. G. Hogarth, "Arabs and Turks."
8. Rev. Colin Chapman, Whose Promised Land? p. 224.
9. Frank S. DeHass, History, p.337, citing The Palestine Exploration Fund, Quarterly statement, 1925, p. 197.
10. Thomas Shaw, Travels and Observations, (London 1767), p. 331.
11. J. S. Buckingham, Travels in Palestine, p. 146.
12. Mark Twain, Innocents Abroad, p. 349.
13. DeHaas, Report of Commerce of Jerusalem, 1863, F.O. 195/808, May, 1864.
14. Turkish Census 1844; Calendar of Palestine 1895; British Census 1962; Israel Central Bureau; Jerusalem Municipality Report.
15. De Haas, History, p. 407.
16. Carl Herman Voss, The Palestine Problem Today, Israel and its Neighbors, Boston, 1953, p. 13.
17. Frankenstine, ibid, p. 127.
18. Walter Laqueur, speech on Nasser and the Jews, pp. 175-185.

Chapter Five: Israel—Blamed No Matter What

1. New York Daily News, Feb. 28, 1994, p.6.
2. Human Rights Watch, New York, February 12, 1995.
3. Daniel McGowan, Hobart and William Smith Colleges, New York. McGowan, press release, March 22, 1998.
4. Ibid. March 25, 1998.

Chapter Six: The Church—Replacement Theology

1. Ewald Plass, editor, What Luther Says, 1:36, (St. Louis: Concordia Publishing House, 1959)
2. Martin Luther, Jesus Christ Was Born a Jew, 1523.
3. James Parkes, The Conflict of the Church and Synagogue: a Study in the Origins of Anti-Semites, (New York: Hermon Press, 1974).
4. Joel 3.
5. Jerusalem Post, June 24, 1997.
6. Ha'aretz, Jan. 7, 1997.
7. Aharon Domb, the Secretary General of the Council of Jewish Communities in Judea, Samaria and Gaza, June-December 1996.
8. Zechariah 12:2.
9. Zechariah 12:6.
10. Frederick Schweitzer, a History of the Jews Since the First Century AD, p. 295.
11. Elgin S. Moyer, The Wycliffe Biographical Dictionary of the Church, p. 73.
12. Peter Jurieu, Approaching Deliverance of the Church, 1687.
13. Napoleon Bonaparte's Appeal to the Jews, encamped at Mount Tabor before his defeat at Acre, 1798.
14. Isaiah 11:11
15. Amos 9:14, 15.
16. Jeremiah 3:17.
17. Psalm 2:6.
18. Jeremiah 31:10-1.
19. Isaiah 60.
20. Romans 11:26.
21. Isaiah 14:1, 2.

22. Isaiah 49:22-26.
23. Rev. Malcolm Hedding, Ex. Dir. Int. Christian Embassy Jerusalem, at the 4th Int. Christian Congress on Biblical Zionism, February, 2001.
24. Isaiah 57:14.
25. Romans 2:28, 29.
26. Romans: 2:29.
27. Rom 11:25-26.
28. Isaiah 2:2-3.
29. Zechariah 14:16-21.
30. Galatians 3:1.
31. Galatians 2:12.
32. Galatians 6:12-13.
33. Galatians 4:11.
34. Galatians 6:16.
35. Galatians 1:11-13.
36. Galatians 2:11-13.
37. Romans 9:6-8.
38. 2 Peter 1:20.
39. 2 Pet 1:21.
40. Genesis 15:18-21.
41. Ezekiel 11:17.
42. Zechariah 8:8.
43. Jeremiah 12:14-15.
44. Jeremiah 16:14-15.
45. Jeremiah 31:8-10.
46. Jeremiah 31:8.
47. Jeremiah 46:28.
48. Ezekiel 26:3-14.
49. Alec Field, The Destruction of Tyre, Commentary on Revelation, apocalipsis.org
50. Loeb Classical Library: Quintius Curtius IV, 2. 18-19.
51. Nina Jidejian, An Amazing Prophecy – Tyre as quoted in AbrahamicFaith online.
52. Ibid.
53. Ibid.
54. Matthew 24:2.
55. Romans 11:1-2.

56. Jeremiah 16:14-15.
57. Jeremiah 31:36.
58. Hosea 11:8, 9.
59. Psalm 147:19, 20.
60. Psalm 94:14.
61. Romans 11:1.
62. Ephesians 2:12, 19.
63. Galatians 3:17, 18.
64. Jeremiah 31:10-12.
65. Zechariah 2:8.
66. Zechariah 2:10.
67. Zephaniah 3:9.
68. Isaiah 27:6.
69. Joel 2:23.
70. Revelation 11:1-2.
71. Labib Qubti, Al-Bushra.
72. Al-Bushra, 7th issue, Aug 1996.
73. Al-Bushra, What is the Truth.
74. Muhammad the Prophet of Islam, narrated by Abu Hurraira.
75. John Samaha, Al-Bushra.
76. Cardinal William Keeler, Al-Bushra.
77. Ibid.
78. Daud Kuttab's Page, Sept. 30, 1999.
80. Interview with Emil Salayta, April 9, 1997.
81. Labib Qubti, Al-Bushra.

Chapter Seven—Gog and Magog War

1. Matt 23:39.
2. Ezekiel 38:19-20.
3. Ezekiel 39:7.
4. Revelation 20:7
5. Daniel 11:36.
6. Deut 6:4.
7. Deut 6:4.
8. Strong's Concordance.
9. Herodotus IV.11.
10. Herodotus I. 14.

11. Ibid.
12. Genesis 10:2, 1:5.
13. Archibald Sayce, Races of the Old Testament, 1891.
14. Donald F. Logan, The Vikings in History, (Totowa, NJ 1994), p. 186.
15. Herodotus. ibid.
16. Grant Jeffrey, Final Warning, p. 123.
17. C. Marvin Pate, and Calvin B. Haines, Jr., Doomsday Delusions: What's Wrong With Predictions About the End of the World, (Downer Grove, IL, InterVarsity Press, 1995), pp. 62-63.
18. Edwin M Yamauchi, Foes from the Northern Frontier: Invading Hordes from the Russian Steppes, (Grand Rapids, MI Baker Book House, 1982).

Chapter Eight: Marriage Supper

1. Cor. 15:51-55.
2. Joel 2:1.
3. Joel 2:8.
4. Joel 2:9-11.
5. Daniel 7:9-10.
6. Joel 2:17.
7. Joel 2:11.
8. Joel 2:3.
9. Joel 2:32.
10. Revelation 19:14-16.
11. Revelation 6:9-11.
12. Isaiah 63:1-6.
13. Amos 1.11-12.
14. Isaiah 1:18.
15. 2 Sam 1:24.
16. Luke 19:44.
17. Hosea 4:6.
18. 2 Pet 2:5.
19. 1 Thes. 4:17.
20. Thes. 4:16.
21. Zechariah 1:14

22. Zechariah 1:15.
23. Zechariah 1:16.
24. Zechariah 14:3.
25. Zechariah 14:12.
26. Zechariah 14:14.
27. Micah 4:2.
28. Zechariah 2:10.
29. Psalm 9:13-14.
30. Zechariah 2:11
31. Zechariah 2:12.
32. Chronicles 6:6.
33. 2 Chronicles 7:16.
34. 2 Chronicles 33:7.

Chapter Nine: Turkey and the End-Times

1. Serge Trifkovic, Islam, the Sword of the Prophet, p. 203.
2. Zechariah 9:13.
3. Ionian. Encyclopædia Britannica Premium Service. July 2, 2004, www.britannica.com.
4. Zechariah 9:14-16.
5. Ibid. 9.
6. John Hooper, "Islam on Probation," The Guardian, August 7, 1996.
7. Ibid.
8. Stanley Cohen, Professor of Criminology, Hebrew University, Jerusalem, Law and Social Inquiry, vol. 20, no. 1, winter, 1995, pp. 7, 50.
9. Ezekiel 38:13.
10. Jonah 1:3.
11. Josephus, Antiquities of the Jews, 6.1.127.
12. James Hastings, Tarsus, Vol. 4 p.686, A Dictionary of the Bible, (Peabody, Mass. Hendrickson Publications, 1898, 1988 reprint.)
13. Charles F. Pfeiffer, Karatepe, The Biblical World, A Dictionary of Biblical Archaeology. (Nashville, Tennessee, Broadman Press, 1966), cf. p. 336.

14. Madeleine S. Miller, Tarsus, The New Harper's Bible Dictionary, (New York, Harper & Row, 1973), p. 727.
15. Henry Hodges, Technology in the Ancient World, (Baltimore, Maryland, Penguin Books, 1971), p.108.
16. William Harms, "Aslihan Yener and the Bronze Age Source of Tin Found in Turkey," Biblical Archaeology Review, vol. 20, no. 3, May-June, 1994, p.16-17.
17. Isaiah 23:1-2.
18. Isaiah 60:9
19. Isaiah 60:6-7.
20. Isaiah 66:19.
21. Ezekiel 29:10.
22. Revelation 16:12.
23. Isaiah 49:12.
24. Daniel 7, the fourth beast—Rome.
25. Ezekiel 44:1-3.
26. Daniel 8:17.
27. Daniel 8:10.
28. Luke 10:18.
29. Daniel 11:2-4.
30. Matt. 24:15.
31. J.G. MacQueen, The Hittites and Their Contemporaries—Asia Minor, (Boulder, Colorado, Westview Press, 1975), p. 78.
32. Daniel 11:40-45.

Chapter Ten: The Crescent Connection

1. Ezekiel 38:2, 38:3, 38:14, 38:16, 38:18, 39:1, 39:11, Revelation 20:8.
2. Isaiah 10:5, 10:24, 14:25, 19:23, 23:13, 30:31, 31:8, Ezekiel 31:3, Micah 5:5, 6.
3. 1 John 2:22, 2 John 1:17.
4. John 17:12, 2 Thessalonians 2:3.
5. Isaiah 14:12.
6. Expositor's Bible Commentary, Isaiah 14, General Editor Frank Gaebelein, Zondervan.
7. Ibn Warraq. Why I am not a Muslim.
8. Finn Rasmussen, Early Letter Names.
9. Quran, Surah: 97.

10. Ten Days of Dawn, The Terrorism Research Center, February 1, 1979, Khomeini Returns From Exile Called the Beginning of the Ten Days of Dawn, commemorating the ten days of unrest which ended with Khomeini taking power on February 11 (the Day of Victory.

11. Yousuf Islam, Islamiway.Spyw.com, Jihad Songs.

12. Isaiah 14:19-20.

13. Isaiah 14:24-27.

14. Isaiah 14:16.

15. Isaiah 14:22-23.

16. Josephus, 226, 1987 ed., p 440.

17. Yadin Yigal, Hazor, (New York: Random House, 1975), (London: Oxford, 1972), (Jerusalem: Magnes, 1958).

18. The Hastings' Encyclopedia of Religion and Ethics, volume I, p.326.

19. Abdul Rahman al-Wahabi, Yawmul-Ghadhab hal-Bada'a be-Intifadat Rajab? The Day of Wrath, it will start with the Month of Rajab Uprising.

20. Rev 9:11.

21. Rev 9:12-15.

22. Rev 9:2.

23. Rev 9:3-4.

24. Rev 9: 5-6.

25. Rev 9:11.

26. Rev 9:16-17.

27. Rev 9:19.

28. Jeremiah 50:9.

29. Rev 9:18.

30. Revelation 17:15.

31. Ibn Warraq, Why I am not a Muslim, The Origins of Islam, Margoliouth (3) in MW vol. 20, p. 241.

32. Acts 19:35.

33. 2 Thes. 2:9.

34. Rev 13:13-14.

35. Psalm 83:14-15.

36. Psalm 97:3.

37. Psalm 104:4.

38. Psalm 105:32.

39. Psalm 106:18.
40. Gen 19:24.

Chapter Eleven: Mystery Babylon

1. Lev. 14:4, 6, 49–52; Num. 19:6.
2. Ex. 28:4–8, 15, 33, 39:1–8, 24, 29.
3. Narrated Mu'adh ibn Jabal: Translation of Sunan Abu-Dawud, Battles, Kitab Al-Malahim, Book 37, Number 4281.
4. Jeremiah 49:34-395.
5. Isaiah 34:8-10.
6. Revelation 18:11.
7. Jeremiah 51:9.
8. Isaiah 47:15.
9. Revelation 18:7.
10. Isaiah 47:10.
11. Isaiah 47:10.
12. Revelation 18:9.
13. Revelation 18:11.
14. Michael Theodoulou, "Saudi Bomb Attacks Have Whiff of Illicit Alcohol Trade," special to the Christian Science Monitor, May 10, 2001.
15. Revelation 18:11.
16. Revelation 18:19.
17. Narrated Mu'adh ibn Jabal: Translation of Sunan Abu-Dawud, Battles, Kitab Al-Malahim, Book 37, Number 4281.
18. Ibid. 428.
19. Ernest L. Martin, Ph.D., "Mystery Babylon the Great," online, 1974, edited by David Sielaff, September 2003. Quote from Muhammed Abdul Majiid Siddiiqiiwww.everymuslim.com.
20. Ibid.
21. Revelation 17:18.
22. Revelation 11:8.
23. Genesis 10:12.
24. Joshua 10:2.
25. Obadiah 1:8.
26. Ezekiel 35:15.
27. Habakkuk 3:3.

28. Isaiah 34:6.
29. Isaiah 34:8.

Chapter Twelve: The One-World Government

1. Zechariah 12:3
2. Daniel 8:5
3. I Kings 10:24
4. Zechariah 12:3
5. Daniel 3:29
6. II Kings 17:29
7. Zechariah 12:3
8. Zechariah 12:9
9. Zechariah 14:16
10. Zechariah 9:13
11. Jeremiah 50:41
12. Jeremiah 50:9
13. Psalm 79:12
14. Psalm 80:6
15. Jeremiah 12:14
16. Zola Levitt, Foreshadows of Wrath (part 3), Levitt Letter online, May 1999: Volume21, Number 5.

Chapter Thirteen: The Antichrist, The Beast, and the Mark

1. Rev. 13:1.
2. Rev. 13:3.
3. Rev. 12:3.
4. Rev. 19:20.
5. Dan. 7:17.
6. Rev. Chap. 4, 5, and 6.
7. Rev. 5:6.
8. Isaiah 45:23.
9. Rev. 13:16–18.
10. Rev. 14:11.
11. Rev. 17:5.
12. Rev. 19:13.
13. Rev. 19:16

14. Rev. 13:1.
15. I John 2:22.
16. Quran, Surah Maryam 19:88–93.
17. Rev. 13:18
18. Rev. 17:15.
19. Rev. 13:16–18.
20. Rev. 13:15.
21. Rev. 13:1.
22. Rev. 13:2.
23. Rev. 13:3.
24. Rev. 13:4.
25. Rev. 13:5–6.
26. Rev. 13:7.
28. Rev. 13:9–10.
29. Rev. 13:10.
30. Rev. 13:11.
31. Rev. 13:12.
32. Rev. 13:13–14.
33. Rev. 13:15.
34. Hosea 3:4.

Chapter Fourteen: How to Interpret End Time Prophecy

1. Habakkuk 2:2.
2. II Peter 1:20.
3. Acts 17:11.
4. The Aeneid, VI, p. 785.
5. Revelation 17:9.
6. Ezekiel 34:6.
7. Jeremiah 51:15.
8. Daniel 2:35.
9. Isaiah 11:9.
10. Revelation 17:15
11. Isaiah 64:1–3
12. Isaiah 42:15.
13. Isaiah 43:2.
14. Ezekiel 29:4.
15. Ezekiel 29:5.

16. Ezekiel 30:12
17. Daniel 7:14.
18. Psalm 72:8.
19. Revelation 17:18.
20. Jeremiah 22:6.
21. Ezekiel 31:3–4.
22. Revelation 8:7.
23. Obadiah 1:4
24. Daniel 8:10.
25. Daniel 8:25.

Chapter Fifteen: The Revived Roman Empire

1. Revelation 17:3.
2. Revelation 17:9.
3. Revelation 17:10.
4. Revelation 17:11.
5. Daniel 2:35.
6. Sir Robert Anderson, The Coming Prince, Appendix II, Miscellaneous: Who and When, Tregelles, p. 34.
7. Ibid.
8. Ibid.
10. Ibid.
11. Ibid.
12. Daniel 8:19.
13. Revelation 13:2.
14. Anderson. ibid.
15. Revelation 17:11.

Chapter Sixteen: Islam and the End-Times

1. Revelation 19:19.
2. Ezekiel 32:26-27.
3. Ezekiel 32:26–29.
4. Ezekiel 32:30.
5. Ezekiel 30:5
6. Ezekiel 27:10.
7. Ezekiel 27:4.

8. Ezekiel 27:36.
9. Ezekiel 28-2.
10. Ezekiel 28:7
11. Ezekiel 28:9.
12. II Thessalonians 2:3–4.
13. Ezekiel 28:12–13.
14. Ezekiel 28:14.
15. Ezekiel 28:16
16. Ezekiel 28:17.
17. Ezekiel 28:24.
18. Ezekiel 28:25-26.
19. Al-Ghazzali.
20. Daniel 7:25.
21. Surah 9:29.
22. John 16:2
23. Wheeler M. Thackston, trans. and ed. The Baburnama: Memoirs of Babur, Prince and Emperor, (Oxford University Press, 1966), p. 188.
24. S. and S. Trifkovic, Sword of the Prophet: History, Theology, Impact on the World, (Regina Orthodox Press, 2002), chap. 3, p. 87.
25. Andrew G. Bostom, The Sacred Muslim Practice of Beheading.
26. Dr. Asadullah Yate, trans., Quran Surah 47, verse 4, Abu'l-Hasan al- Mawardi, al-Ahkam as- Sultaniyyah, The Laws of Islamic Governance, (London, Ta-Ha Publishers Ltd., 1996), p. 192.
27. Bostom. Ibid.
28. I John 2:22.
29. I John 4:1–3.
30. II John 1:7.
31. Ibid.
32. Daniel 11:36.
33. Daniel 11:38.
34. Joel 2:1.
35. Joel 2:2.
36. Joel 2:10.
37. Joel 2:11.
38. Joel 2:12.

39. Joel 2:15–16
40. Joel 2:17–18.
41. World Net Daily, posted February 7, 2004.
42. Joel 2:20
43. Joel 2:31–32
44. Isaiah 22:20–23.
45. Isaiah 21:1–10.
46. Isaiah 21:11–12
47. Isaiah 21:13–17
48. "The 12 Tribes of Ishmael," Nabataea.net.
49. Obadiah 1:5.
50. Obadiah 1:6.
51. Malachi 1:3.
52. Obadiah 1:7.
53. Obadiah 1:8–10.
54. Obadiah 1:11.
55. Obadiah 1:16.
56. Surah 9.29.
57. Obadiah 1:17
58. Obadiah 1:18
59. Obadiah 1:21.
60. Psalm 83:4.
61. Psalm 83:5
62. Psalm 74:4 .
63. TruthNews.net July 30, 2001.
64. Psalm 74:8-9
65. Psalm 74:7.
66. Psalm 74:8–9.
67. Psalm 74:14.
68. Psalm 74:18-23.
69. Surah 9:5.
70. Daniel 9:27.

Chapter 17

1. Micah 5:1
2. Micah 5:2
3. Micah 5:3

4. Micah 5:4
5. Micah 5:4
6. Micah 5:5
7. Isaiah 10:5, 6, 20, 21; 11:1, 4.
8. Isaiah 10:17

Notes

Notes

Notes

Notes

Notes

Notes